尾田栄一郎

I'm going to tell you the weird song I used to sing with my friends. Please sing it for any of your friends that are crying.

"Don't cry, don't cry, I'll give you a sweet potato, my little tart. Never mind, that's gonna make you fart."

-Eiichiro Oda, 2007

Eiichiro Oda began his manga career at the age of 17, when his one-shot cowboy manga **Wanted!** won second place in the coveted Tezuka manga awards. Oda went on to work as an assistant to some of the biggest manga artists in the industry, including Nobuhiro Watsuki, before winning the Hop Step Award for new artists. His pirate manga **One Piece**, which debuted in Weekly Shonen Jump in 1997, quickly became one of the most popular manga in Japan.

D1041320

ONE PIECE VOL. 46
WATER SEVEN PART 15 &
THRILLER BARK PART 1

SHONEN JUMP Manga Edition

STORY AND ART BY EIICHIRO ODA

English Adaptation/Jason Thompson
Translation/Labaaman, HC Language Solutions, Inc.
Touch-up Art & Lettering/Primary Graphix
Design/Sean Lee
Supervising Editor/Yuki Murashige
Editor/Alexis Kirsch

Printed in the U.S.A.

Published by VIZ Media, LLC
P.O. Box 77010
San Francisco, CA 94107

10 9 8 7 6 5
First printing, May 2010
Fifth printing, August 2016

www.viz.com

PARENTAL ADVISORY
ONE PIECE is rated T for Teen and is recommended for ages 13 and up. This volume contains fantasy violence and tobacco usage.
ratings.viz.com

THE WORLD'S MOST POPULAR MANGA
www.shonenjump.com

Vol. 46

ADVENTURE ON GHOST ISLAND

STORY AND ART BY
EIICHIRO ODA

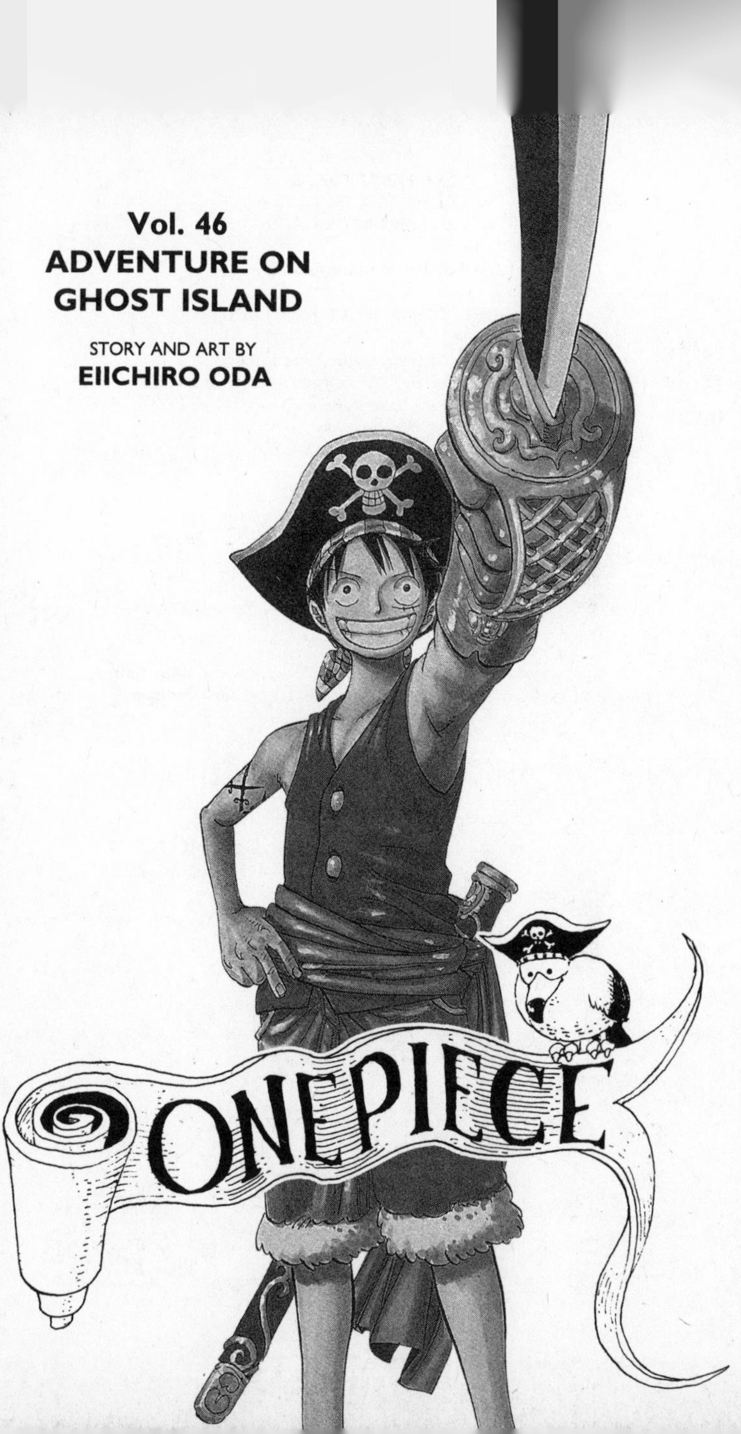
ONEPIECE

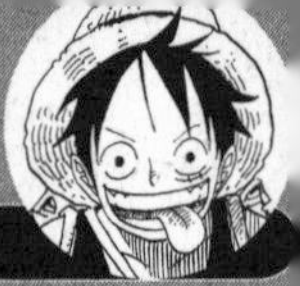

Boundlessly optimistic and able to stretch like rubber, he is determined to become King of the Pirates.

Monkey D. Luffy

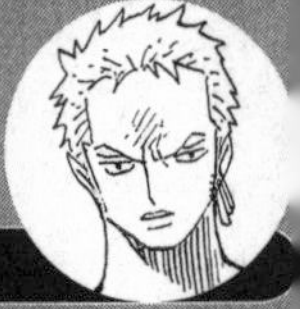

A former bounty hunter and master of the "three-sword" style. He aspires to be the world's greatest swordsman.

Roronoa Zolo

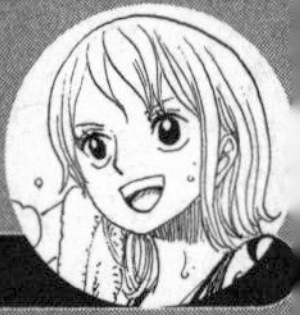

A thief who specializes in robbing pirates. Nami hates pirates, but Luffy convinced her to be his navigator.

Nami

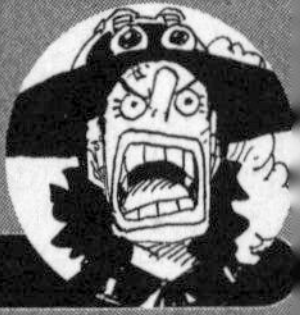

A village boy with a talent for telling tall tales. His father, Yasopp, is a member of Shanks's crew.

Usopp

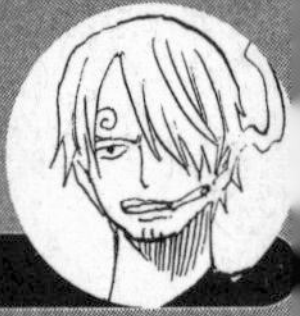

The bighearted cook (and ladies' man) whose dream is to find the legendary sea, the "All Blue."

Sanji

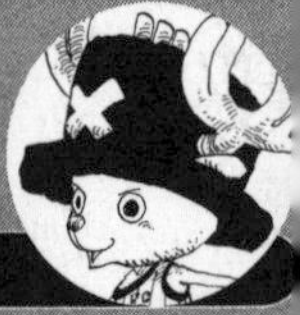

A blue-nosed man-reindeer and the ship's doctor.

Tony Tony Chopper

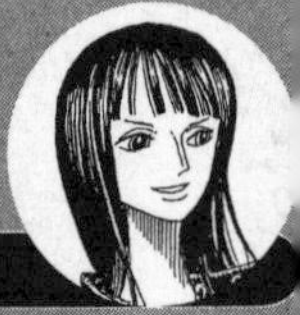

A mysterious woman in search of the Ponegliff on which true history is recorded.

Nico Robin

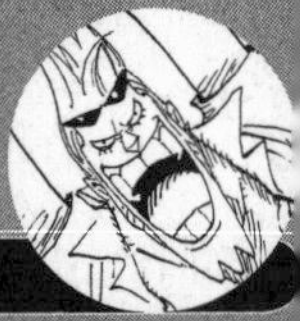

A softhearted cyborg and talented shipwright.

Franky

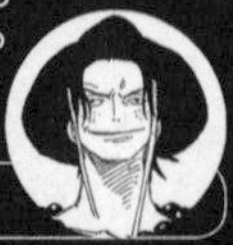

Luffy's brother, he is the leader of the Second Division of the Whitebeard pirates. Whitebeard ordered him to hunt down Blackbeard, who was guilty of killing a fellow crewmate.

Portgaz D. Ace

THE STORY OF ONE PIECE

Volume 46

Monkey D. Luffy started out as just a kid with a dream—to become the greatest pirate in history! Stirred by the tales of pirate "Red-Haired" Shanks, Luffy vowed to become a pirate himself. That was before the enchanted Devil Fruit gave Luffy the power to stretch like rubber, at the cost of being unable to swim—a serious handicap for an aspiring sea dog. Undeterred, Luffy set out to sea and recruited some crewmates—master swordsman Zolo; treasure-hunting thief Nami; lying sharpshooter Usopp; the high-kicking chef Sanji; Chopper, the walkin' talkin' reindeer doctor; and the mysterious archaeologist Robin.

After many adventures, Luffy and his crew travel to Water Seven, the city of shipwrights. Their goal: to find a shipwright to join their crew and to get a new ship, since their old ship, the *Merry Go,* is badly damaged. Things go wrong when Robin is captured by the secret government organization CP9, which wants to use her archaeological knowledge to decipher the blueprints for the ancient super weapon Pluton. In a fierce battle, Luffy and his crew invade the government base of Enies Lobby, defeat CP9 and save Robin. But in the process, the *Merry Go* is completely destroyed, and the heroes bid farewell to their trusted ship as it sinks to the bottom of the sea. Returning to Water Seven, the heroes receive a new ship, the *Thousand Sunny,* a gift from the master shipwright Franky. Since Franky is also wanted by the government for his involvement in the raid on Enies Lobby, Luffy convinces him to join his pirate crew, and together they set sail for their next destination, Fish-Man Island.

Meanwhile, on a faraway island, another battle between pirates has just begun. Portgaz D. Ace, Luffy's big brother, has tracked down his former crewmate Blackbeard, who is wanted for murdering a member of their crew. But as the fight goes on, Blackbeard reveals his true, dark power…

Blackbeard Pirates

After pillaging the Drum Kingdom, they now seek to join the Seven Warlords of the Sea.

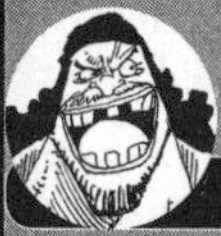

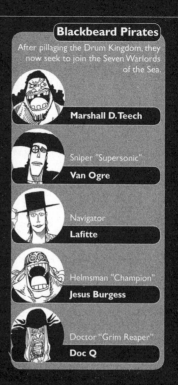

Marshall D. Teech

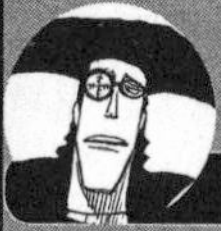

Sniper "Supersonic"

Van Ogre

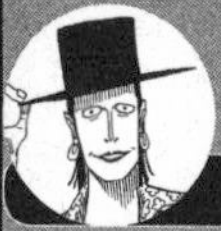

Navigator

Lafitte

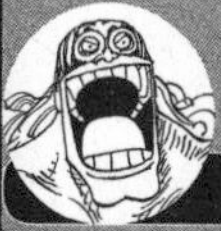

Helmsman "Champion"

Jesus Burgess

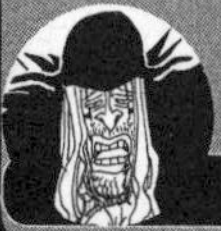

Doctor "Grim Reaper"

Doc Q

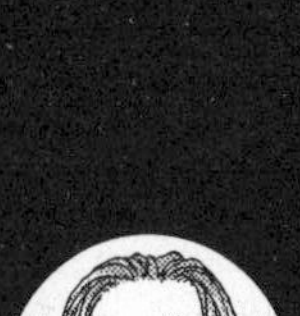

A pirate that Luffy idolizes. Shanks gave Luffy his trademark straw hat.

"Red-Haired" Shanks

THRILLER BARK

ONE PIECE

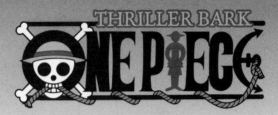

Vol. 46

Adventure on Ghost Island

CONTENTS

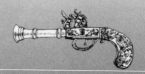

Chapter 441:

DUEL ON BANARO ISLAND

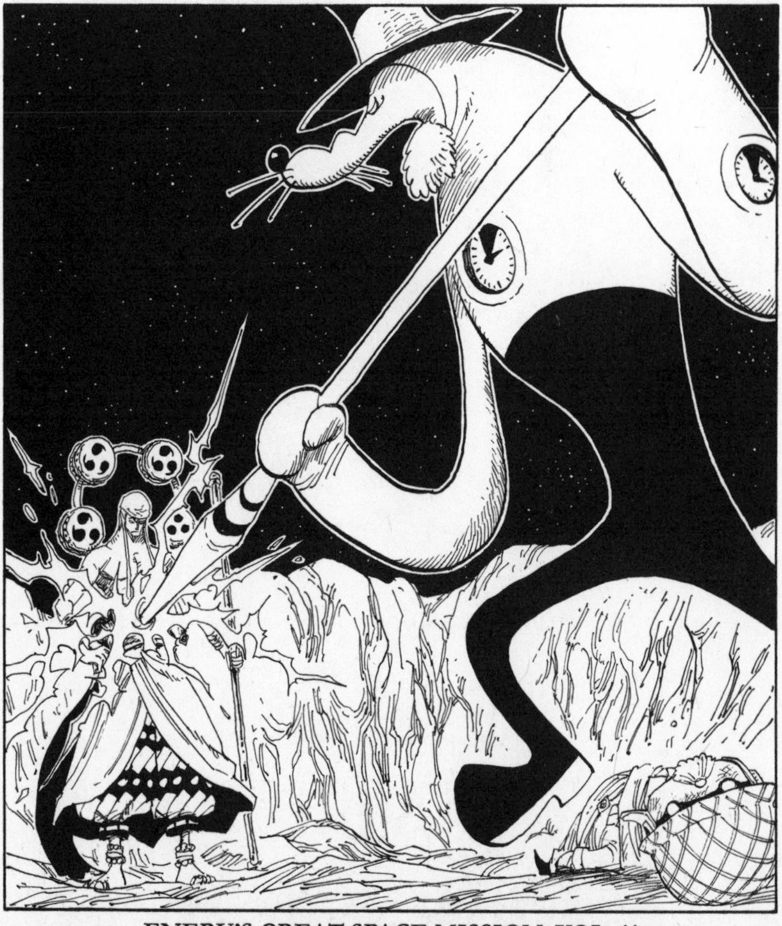

ENERU'S GREAT SPACE MISSION, VOL. 11:
"THE MERCILESS SPACE PIRATE"

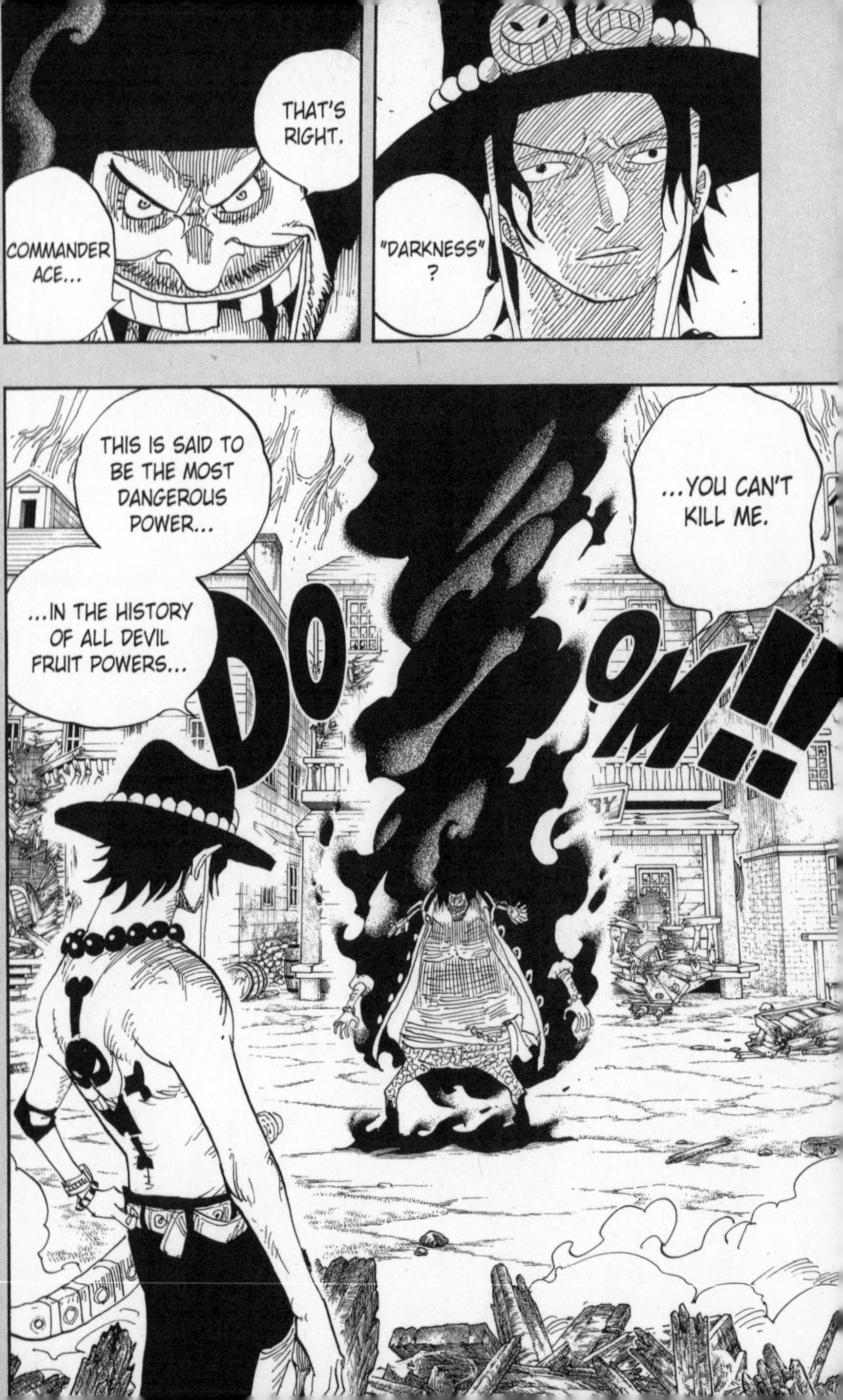
"DARKNESS" ?
THAT'S RIGHT.
COMMANDER ACE...
...YOU CAN'T KILL ME.
DOOM!!
THIS IS SAID TO BE THE MOST DANGEROUS POWER...
...IN THE HISTORY OF ALL DEVIL FRUIT POWERS...

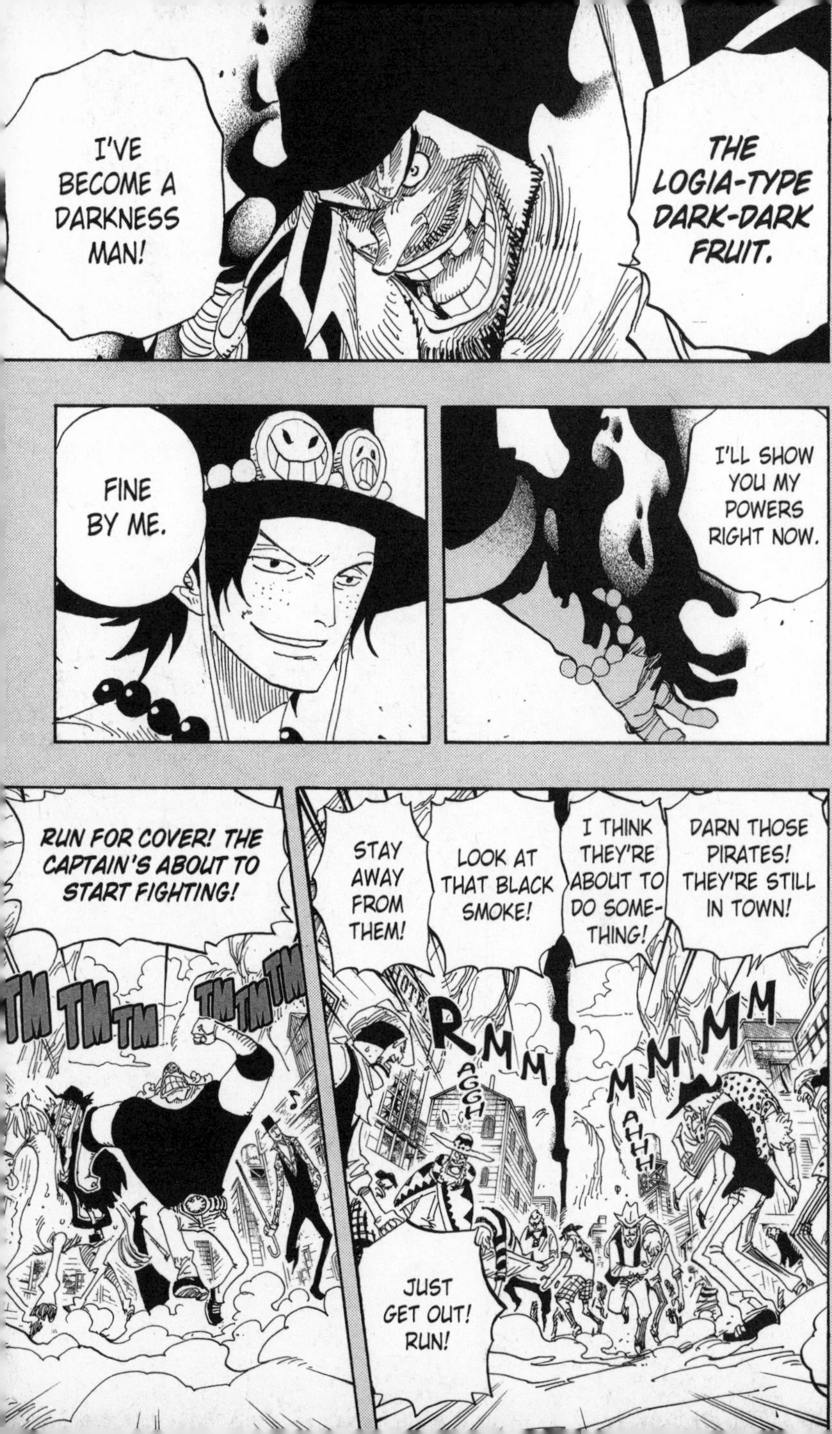
THE LOGIA-TYPE DARK-DARK FRUIT.
I'VE BECOME A DARKNESS MAN!
I'LL SHOW YOU MY POWERS RIGHT NOW.
FINE BY ME.
DARN THOSE PIRATES! THEY'RE STILL IN TOWN!
I THINK THEY'RE ABOUT TO DO SOME-THING!
LOOK AT THAT BLACK SMOKE!
STAY AWAY FROM THEM!
RMMM
MMMMM
AGGH
AHHH
JUST GET OUT! RUN!
RUN FOR COVER! THE CAPTAIN'S ABOUT TO START FIGHTING!
TM TM TM
TM TM TM

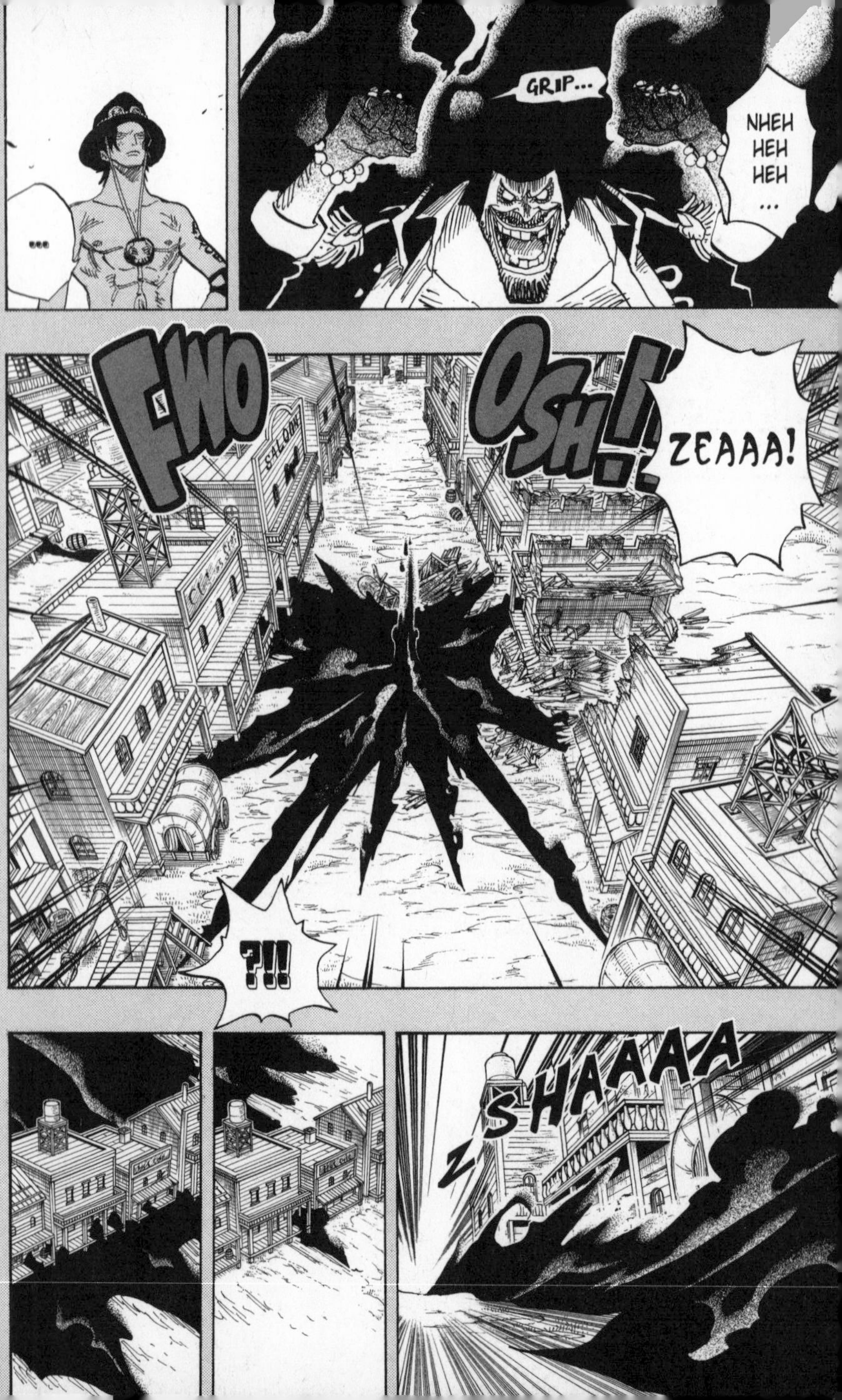
GRIP...
NHEH HEH HEH ...
...
FWOOSH!!
ZEAAA!
?!!
ZSHAAAA

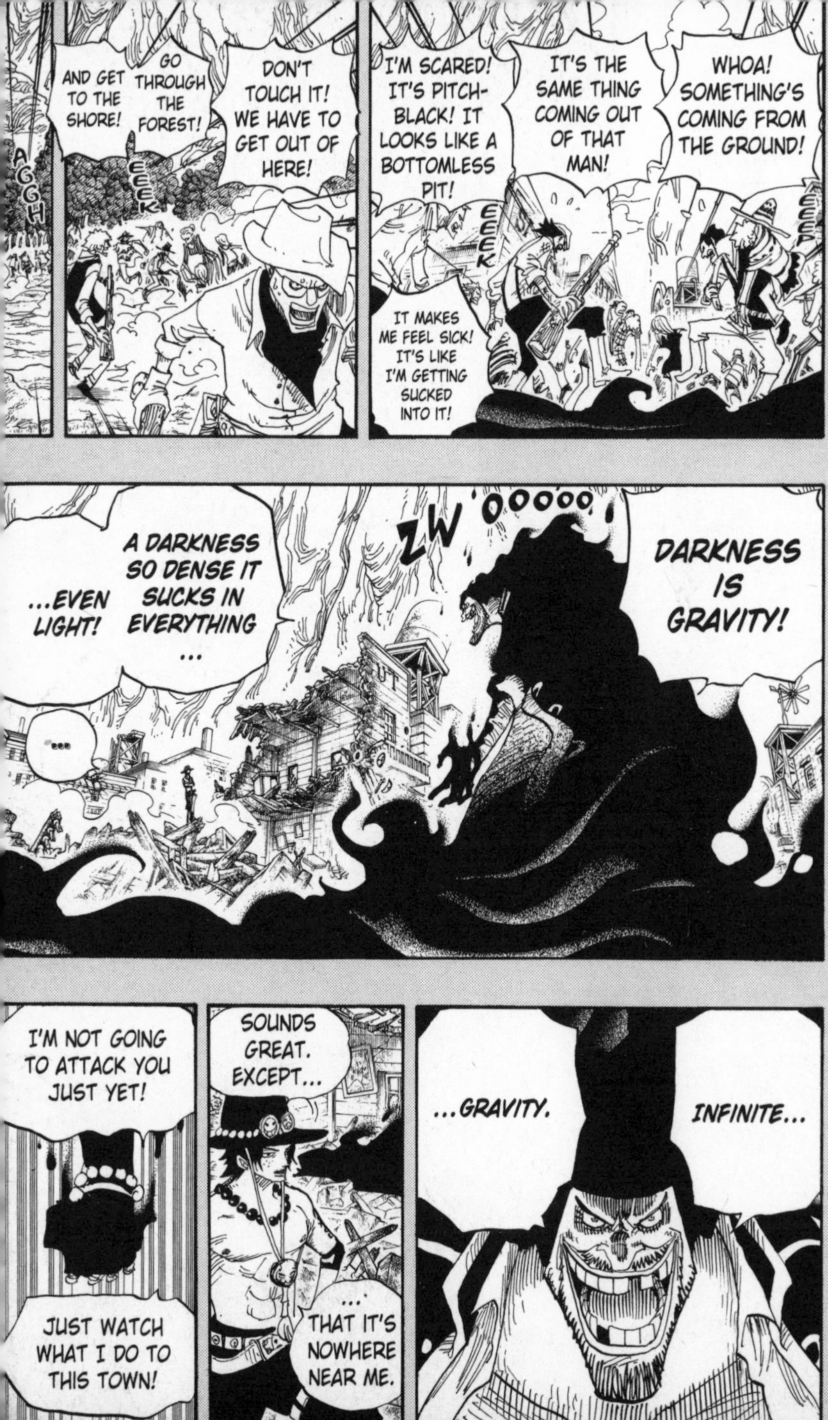
WHOA! SOMETHING'S COMING FROM THE GROUND!
EEEP
IT'S THE SAME THING COMING OUT OF THAT MAN!
I'M SCARED! IT'S PITCH-BLACK! IT LOOKS LIKE A BOTTOMLESS PIT!
EEEEK
IT MAKES ME FEEL SICK! IT'S LIKE I'M GETTING SUCKED INTO IT!
DON'T TOUCH IT! WE HAVE TO GET OUT OF HERE!
GO THROUGH THE FOREST!
AND GET TO THE SHORE!
EEEK
AGGH
DARKNESS IS GRAVITY!
ZWOOOOO
A DARKNESS SO DENSE IT SUCKS IN EVERYTHING...
...EVEN LIGHT!
...
INFINITE...
...GRAVITY.
SOUNDS GREAT. EXCEPT...
...THAT IT'S NOWHERE NEAR ME.
I'M NOT GOING TO ATTACK YOU JUST YET!
JUST WATCH WHAT I DO TO THIS TOWN!

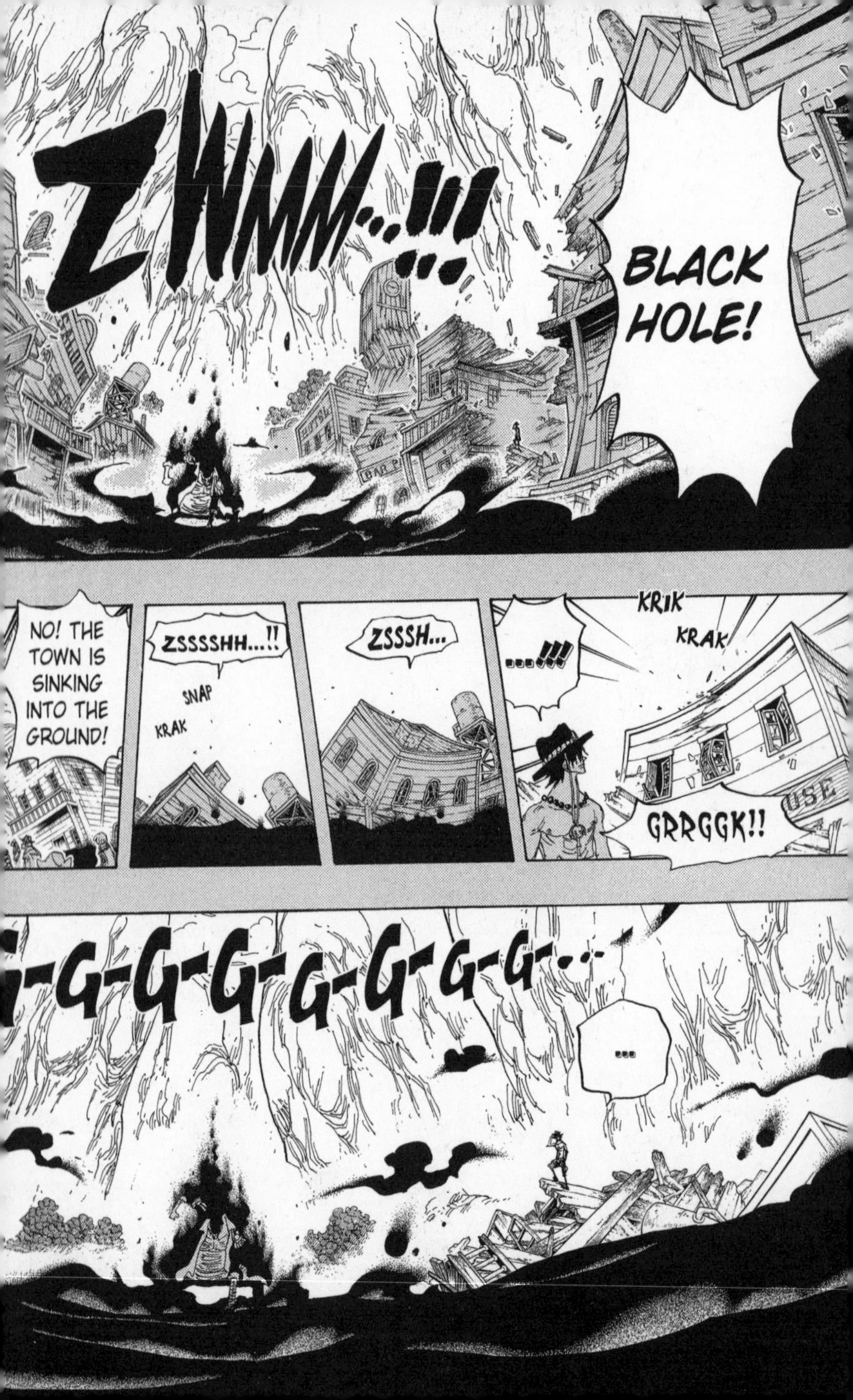
BLACK HOLE!
ZWMM...!!!
KRIK
KRAK
...!!!
GRRGGK!!
USE
ZSSSH...
ZSSSSHH...!!
SNAP
KRAK
NO! THE TOWN IS SINKING INTO THE GROUND!
...
G-G-G-G-G-G-G-G...

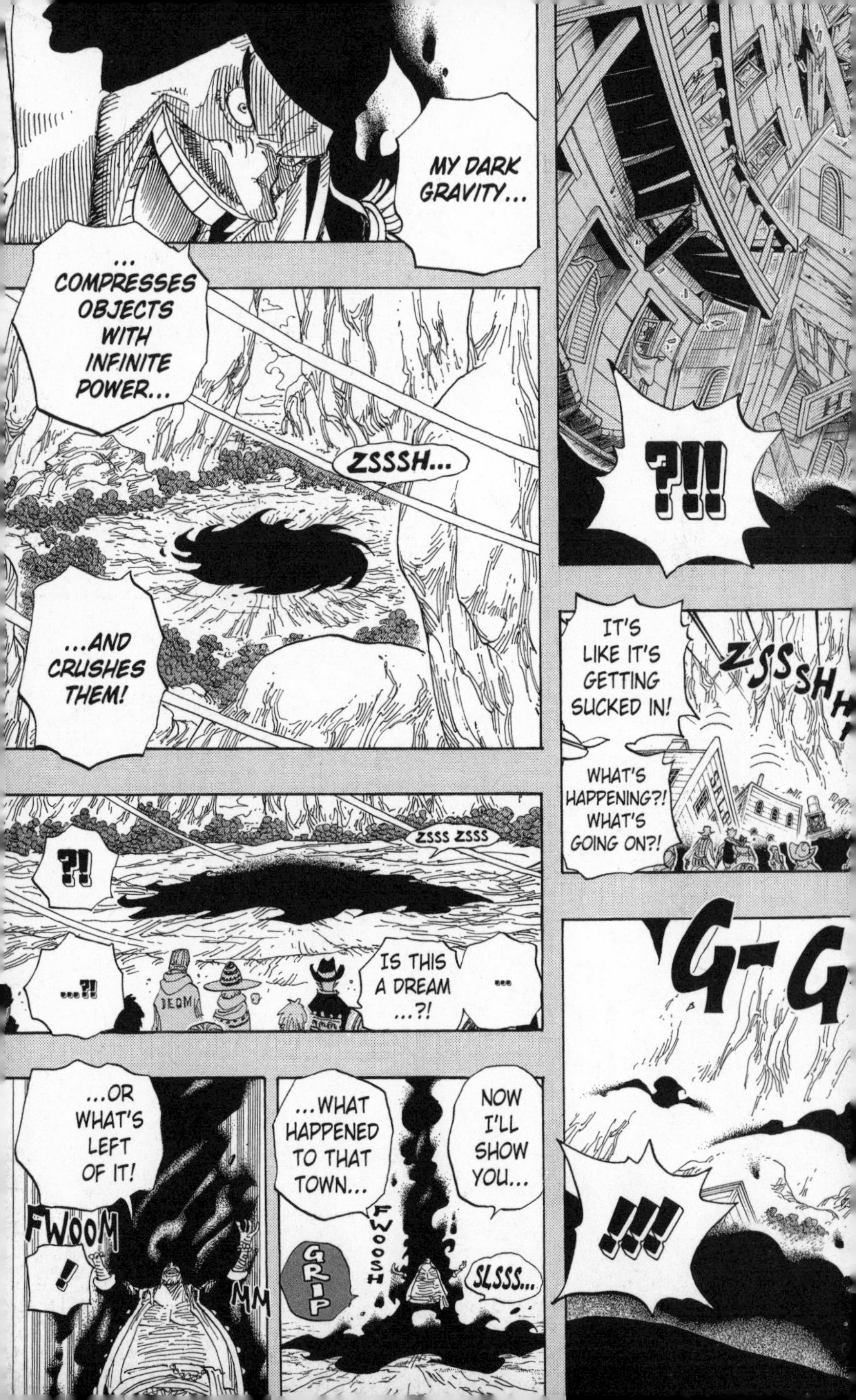
NOW I'LL SHOW YOU...
...WHAT HAPPENED TO THAT TOWN...
FWOOSH
GRIP
SLSSS...
...OR WHAT'S LEFT OF IT!
FWOOM
!
MM
MY DARK GRAVITY...
...COMPRESSES OBJECTS WITH INFINITE POWER...
ZSSSH...
...AND CRUSHES THEM!
ZSSS ZSSS
?!
IS THIS A DREAM ...?!
...
...?!
?!!
IT'S LIKE IT'S GETTING SUCKED IN!
ZSSSHH
WHAT'S HAPPENING?! WHAT'S GOING ON?!
G-G
!!!

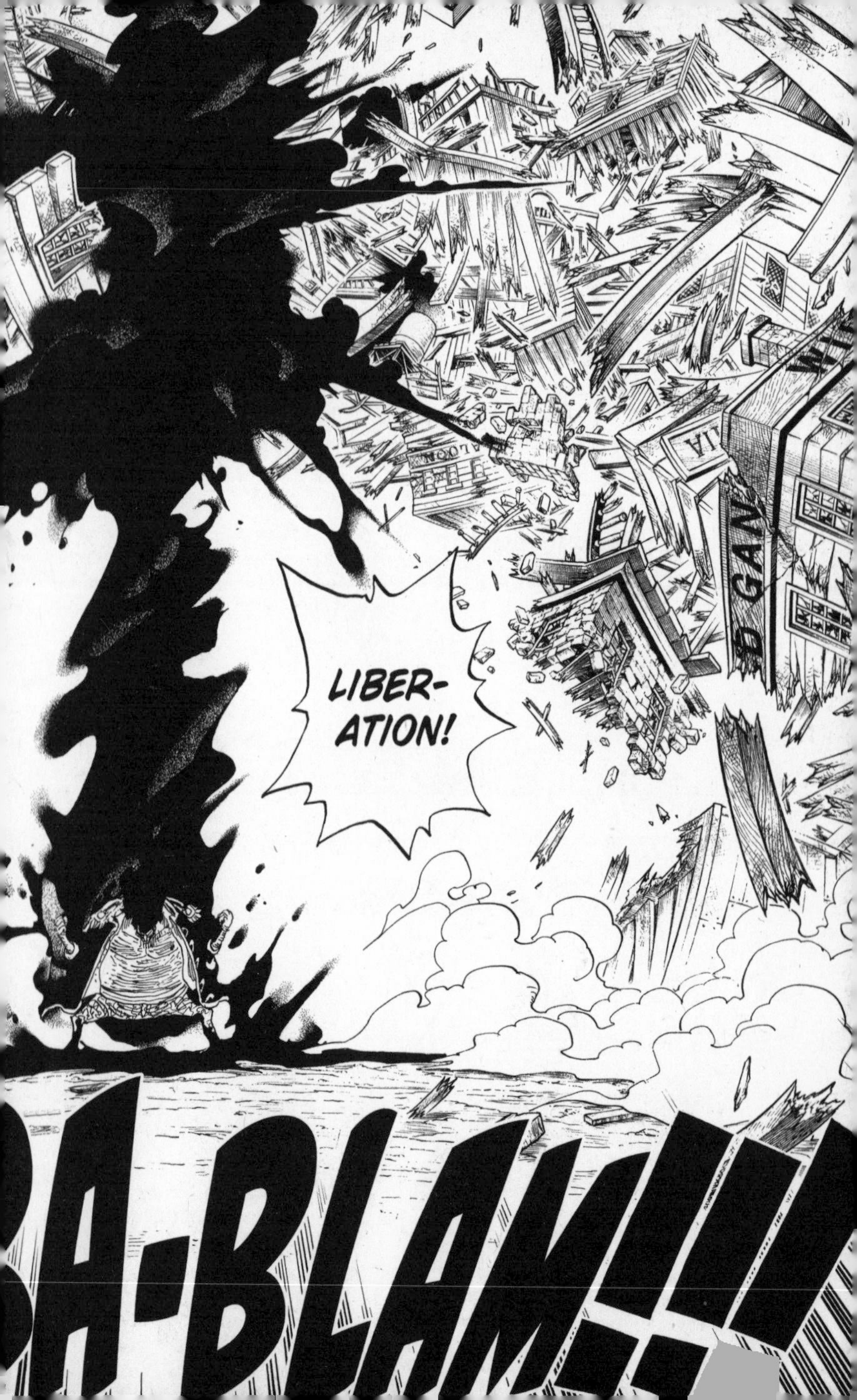
LIBER-
ATION!
A-BLAM!!

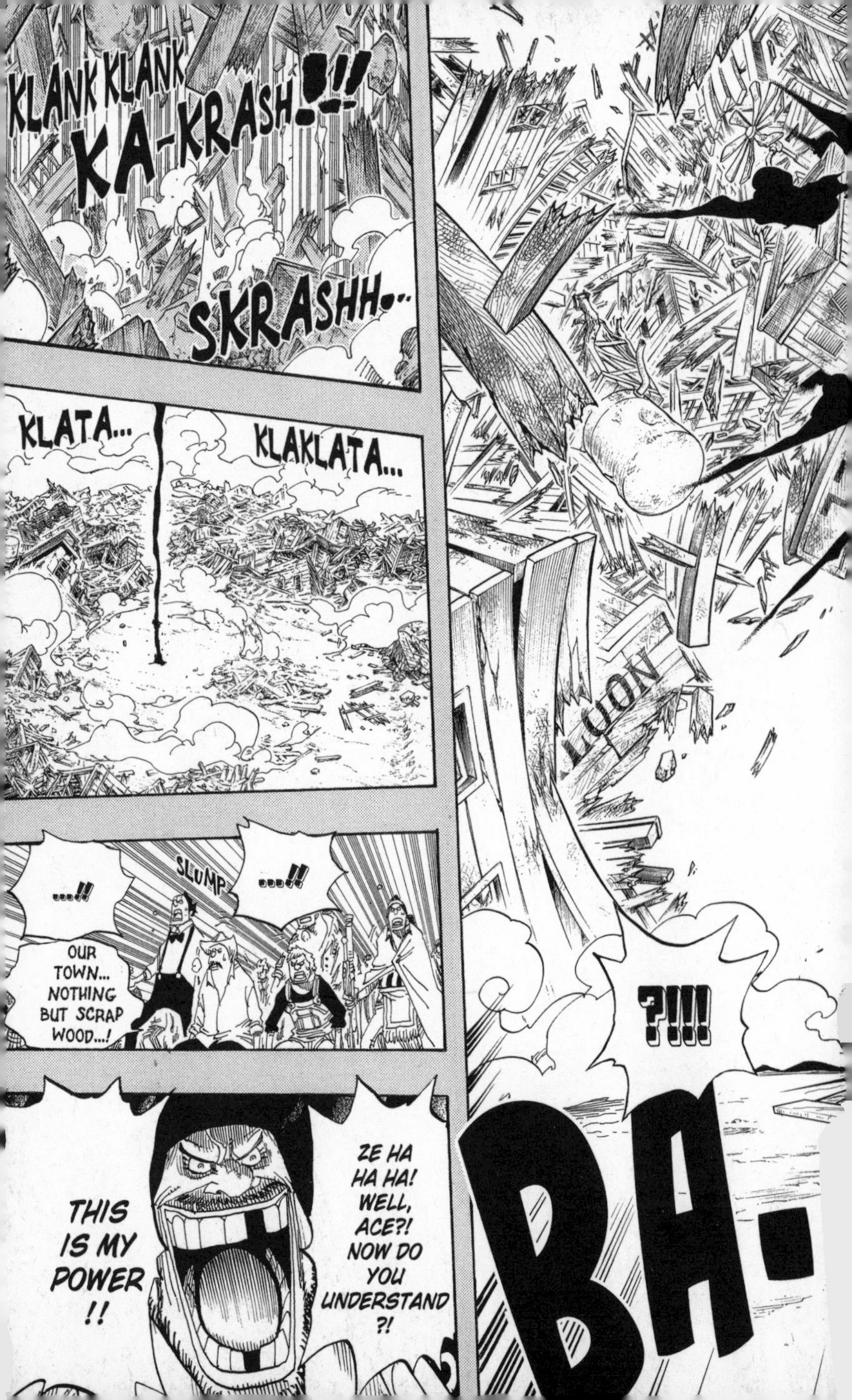
LOON
?!!!
BA-
KLANK KLANK
KA-KRASH!!
SKRASHH...
KLAKLATA...
KLATA...
...!!
SLUMP
...!!
OUR TOWN... NOTHING BUT SCRAP WOOD...!
ZE HA HA HA! WELL, ACE?! NOW DO YOU UNDERSTAND?!
THIS IS MY POWER!!

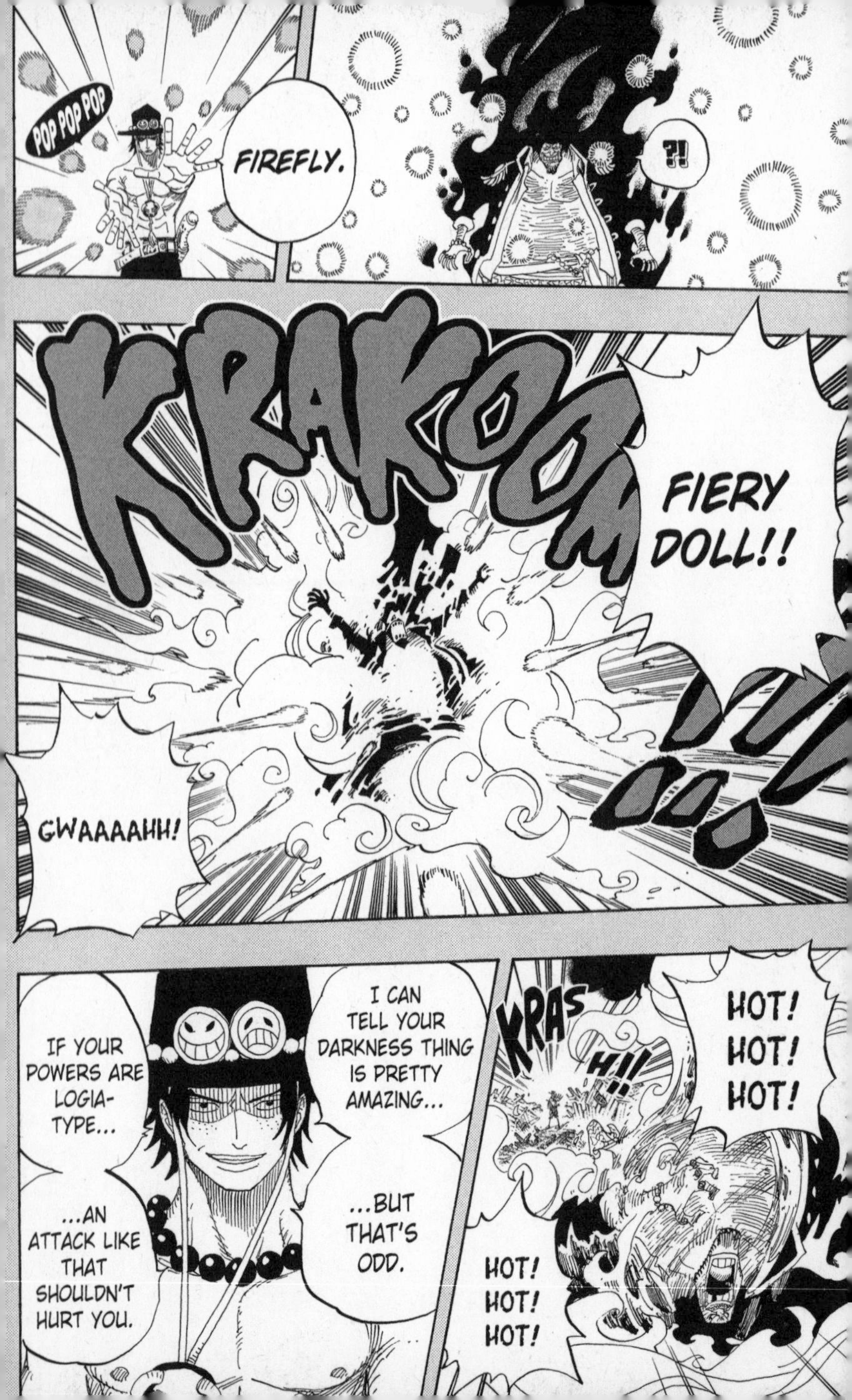
?!
FIREFLY.
POP POP POP
KRAKOOM
FIERY DOLL!!
GWAAAAHH!
HOT! HOT! HOT!
KRASH!!
HOT! HOT! HOT!
I CAN TELL YOUR DARKNESS THING IS PRETTY AMAZING...
IF YOUR POWERS ARE LOGIA-TYPE...
...BUT THAT'S ODD.
...AN ATTACK LIKE THAT SHOULDN'T HURT YOU.

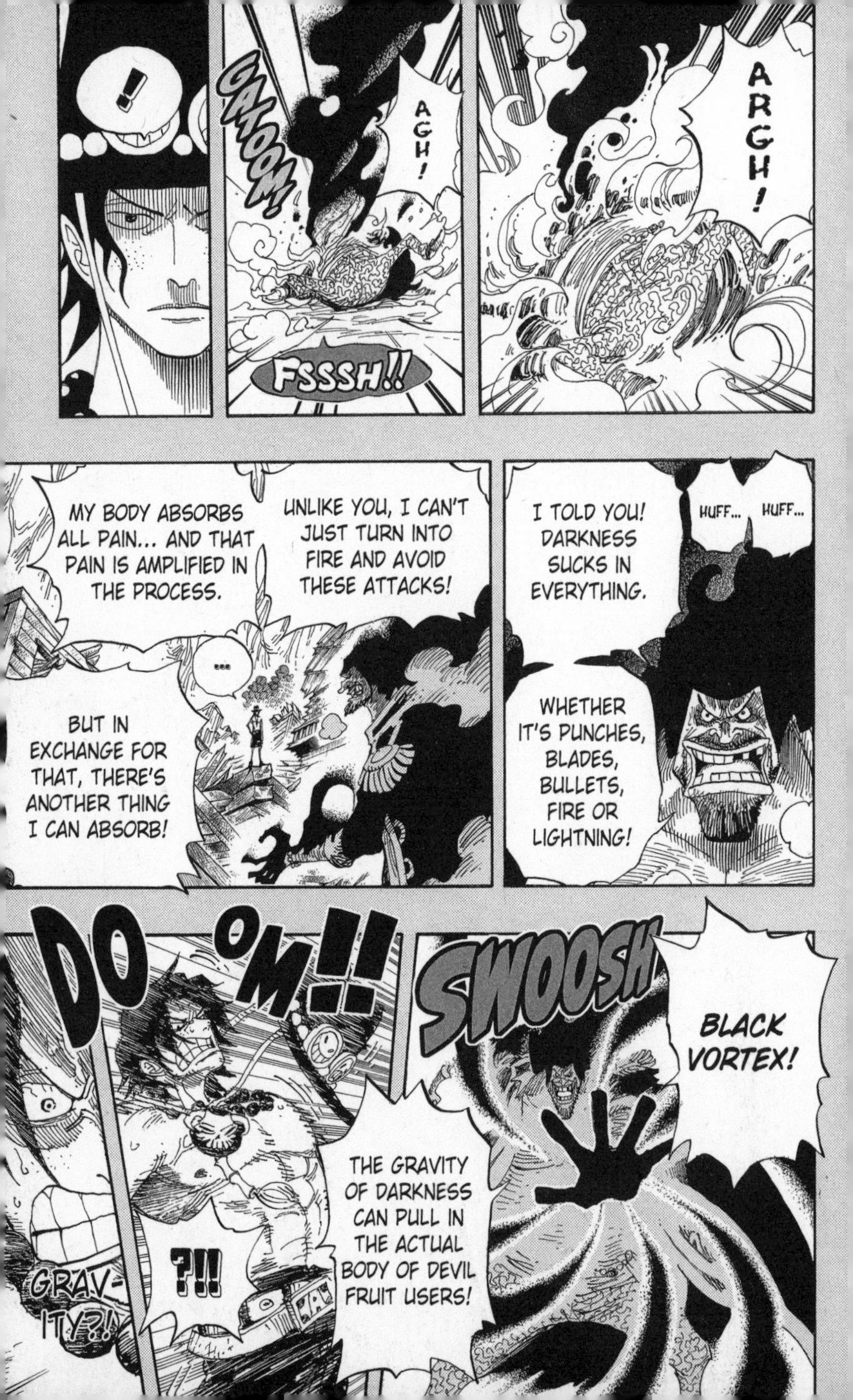
ARGH!
GAKOOM!
AGH!
FSSSH!!
!
HUFF... HUFF...
I TOLD YOU! DARKNESS SUCKS IN EVERYTHING.
WHETHER IT'S PUNCHES, BLADES, BULLETS, FIRE OR LIGHTNING!
UNLIKE YOU, I CAN'T JUST TURN INTO FIRE AND AVOID THESE ATTACKS!
MY BODY ABSORBS ALL PAIN... AND THAT PAIN IS AMPLIFIED IN THE PROCESS.
...
BUT IN EXCHANGE FOR THAT, THERE'S ANOTHER THING I CAN ABSORB!
SWOOSH
BLACK VORTEX!
THE GRAVITY OF DARKNESS CAN PULL IN THE ACTUAL BODY OF DEVIL FRUIT USERS!
DOOM!!
?!!
GRAV-ITY?!

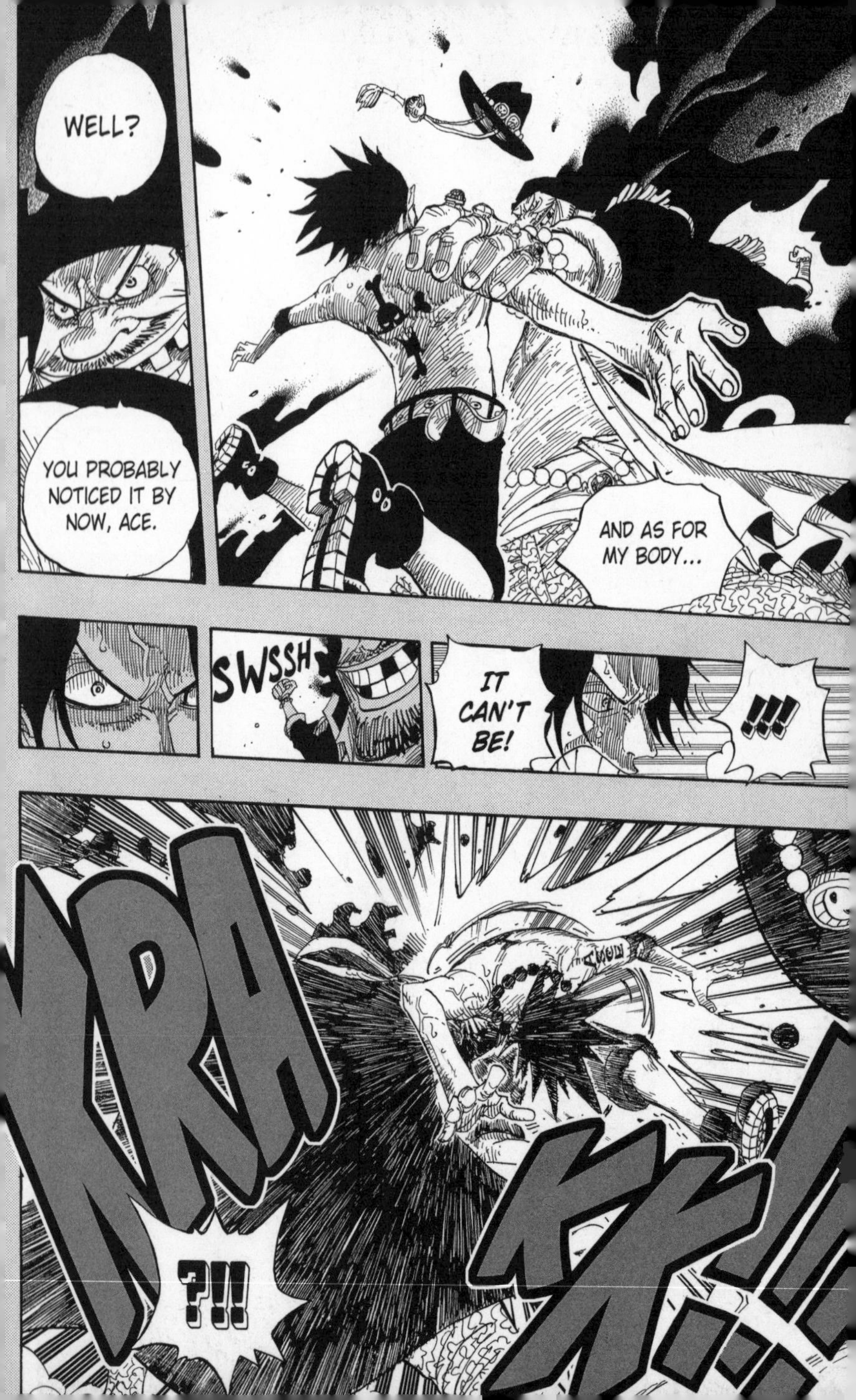
AND AS FOR MY BODY...
WELL?
YOU PROBABLY NOTICED IT BY NOW, ACE.
!!!
IT CAN'T BE!
SWSSH
?!!

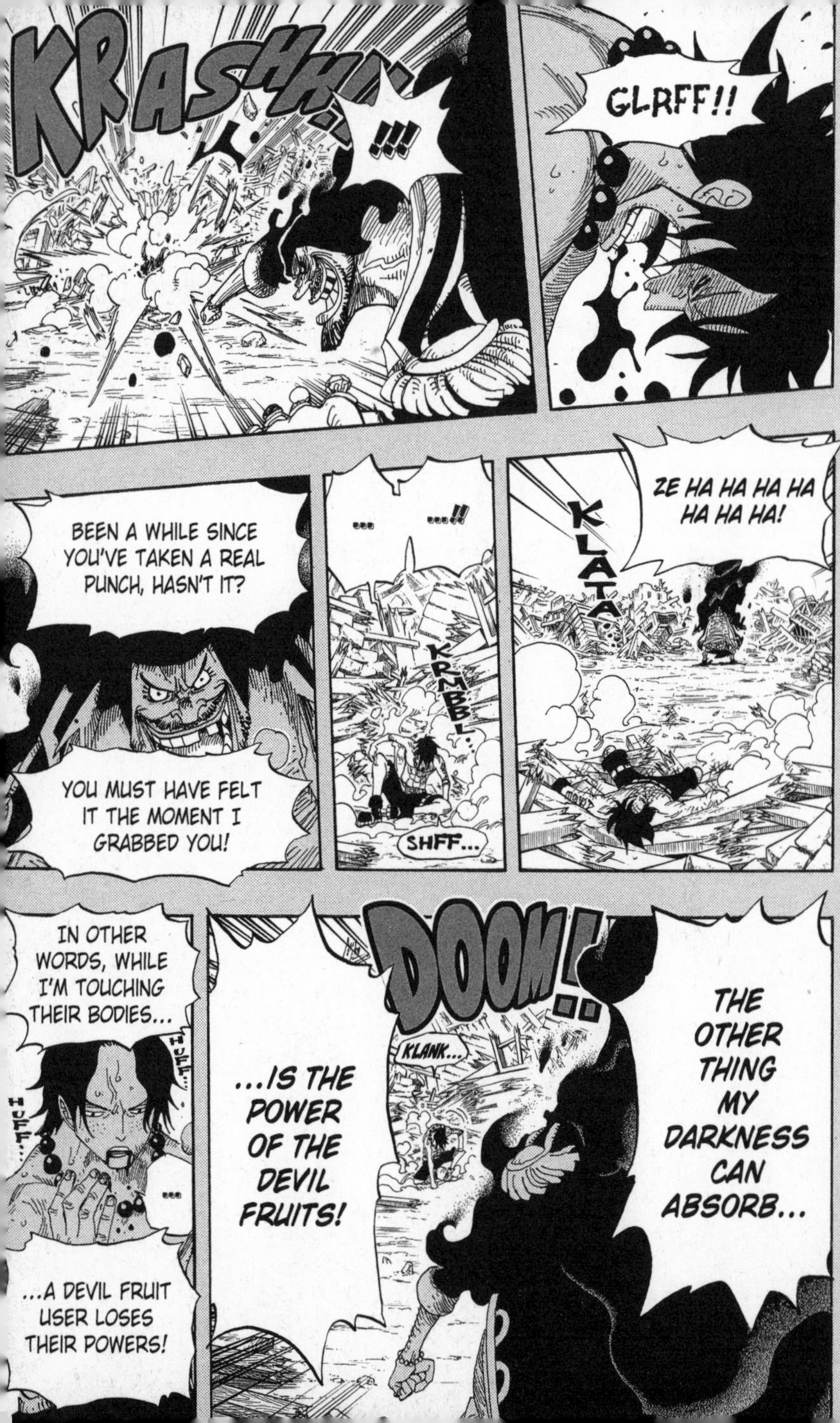
GLRFF!!
KRASHH
ZE HA HA HA HA HA HA HA!
KLATA...
...
...!!
KRMBBL...
SHFF...
BEEN A WHILE SINCE YOU'VE TAKEN A REAL PUNCH, HASN'T IT?
YOU MUST HAVE FELT IT THE MOMENT I GRABBED YOU!
THE OTHER THING MY DARKNESS CAN ABSORB...
DOOM!!
KLANK...
...IS THE POWER OF THE DEVIL FRUITS!
IN OTHER WORDS, WHILE I'M TOUCHING THEIR BODIES...
HUFF...
HUFF...
...
...A DEVIL FRUIT USER LOSES THEIR POWERS!

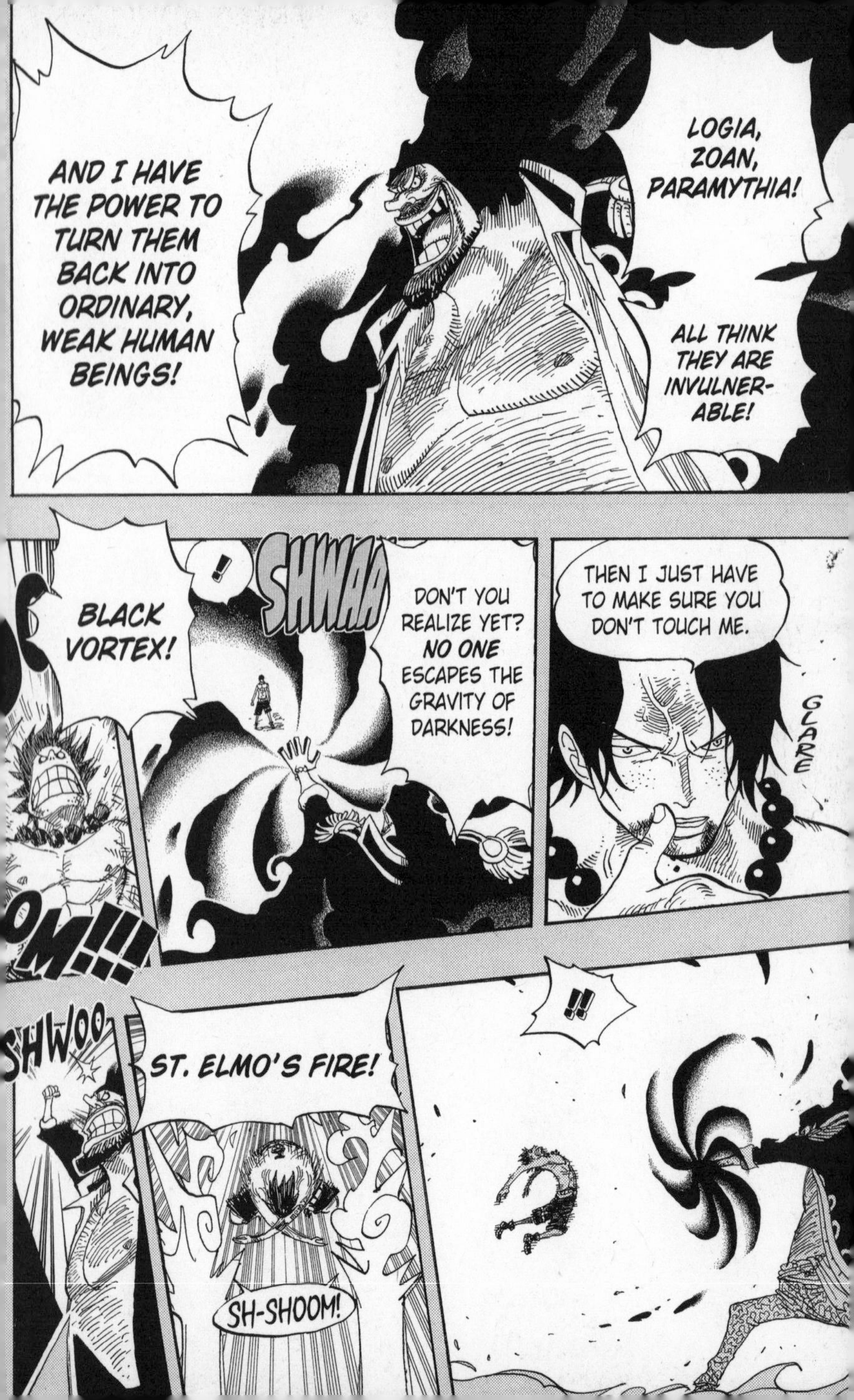
LOGIA, ZOAN, PARAMYTHIA!
ALL THINK THEY ARE INVULNER-ABLE!
AND I HAVE THE POWER TO TURN THEM BACK INTO ORDINARY, WEAK HUMAN BEINGS!
THEN I JUST HAVE TO MAKE SURE YOU DON'T TOUCH ME.
GLARE
SHWAA
DON'T YOU REALIZE YET? NO ONE ESCAPES THE GRAVITY OF DARKNESS!
!
BLACK VORTEX!
OM!!!
!!
ST. ELMO'S FIRE!
SHWOO
SH-SHOOM!

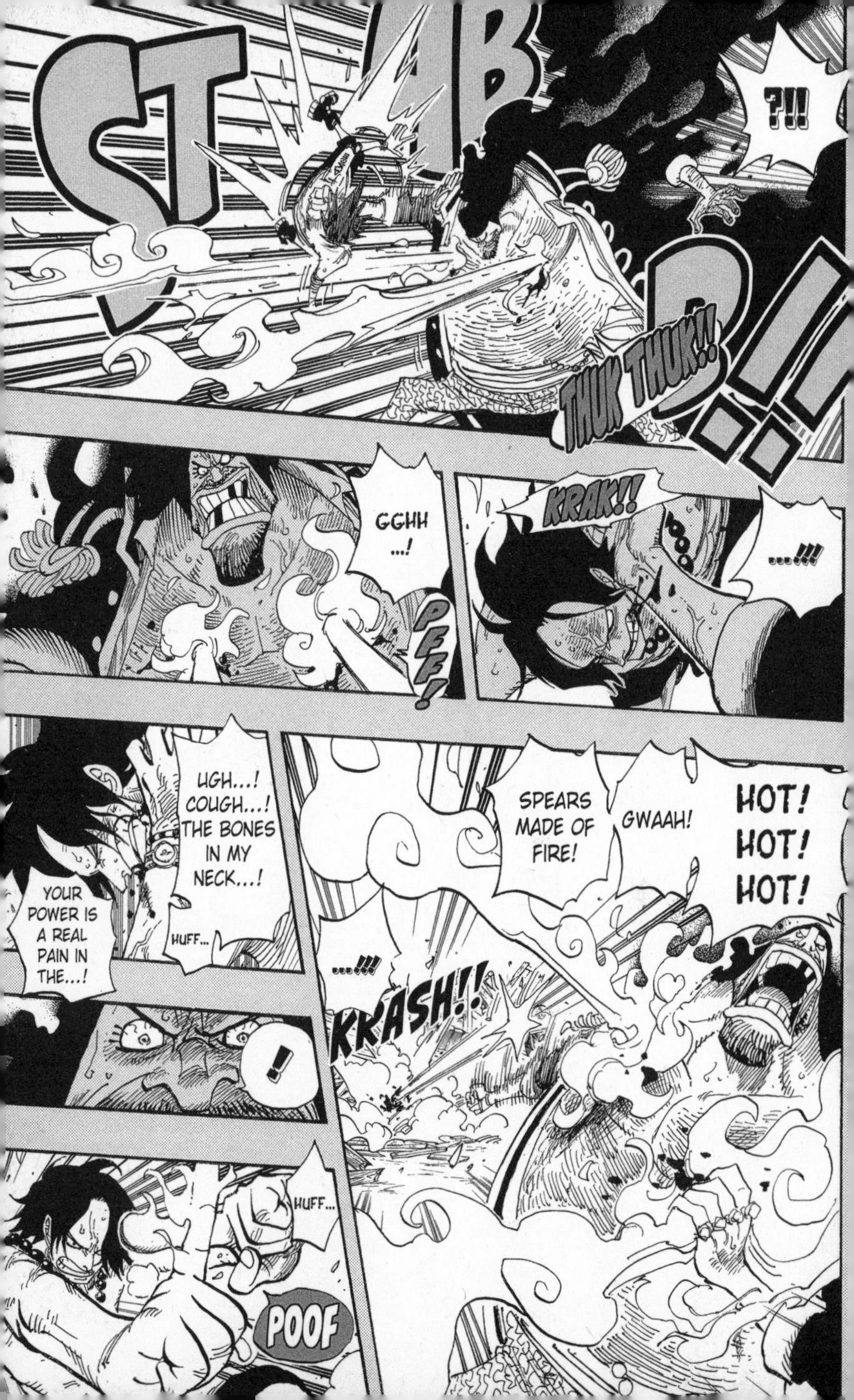
STAB
?!!
THUK THUK!!
...!!!
KRAK!!
GGHH ...!
PFF!
HOT! HOT! HOT!
GWAAH!
SPEARS MADE OF FIRE!
...!!!
KRASH!!
UGH...! COUGH...! THE BONES IN MY NECK...!
HUFF...
YOUR POWER IS A REAL PAIN IN THE...!
!
HUFF...
POOF

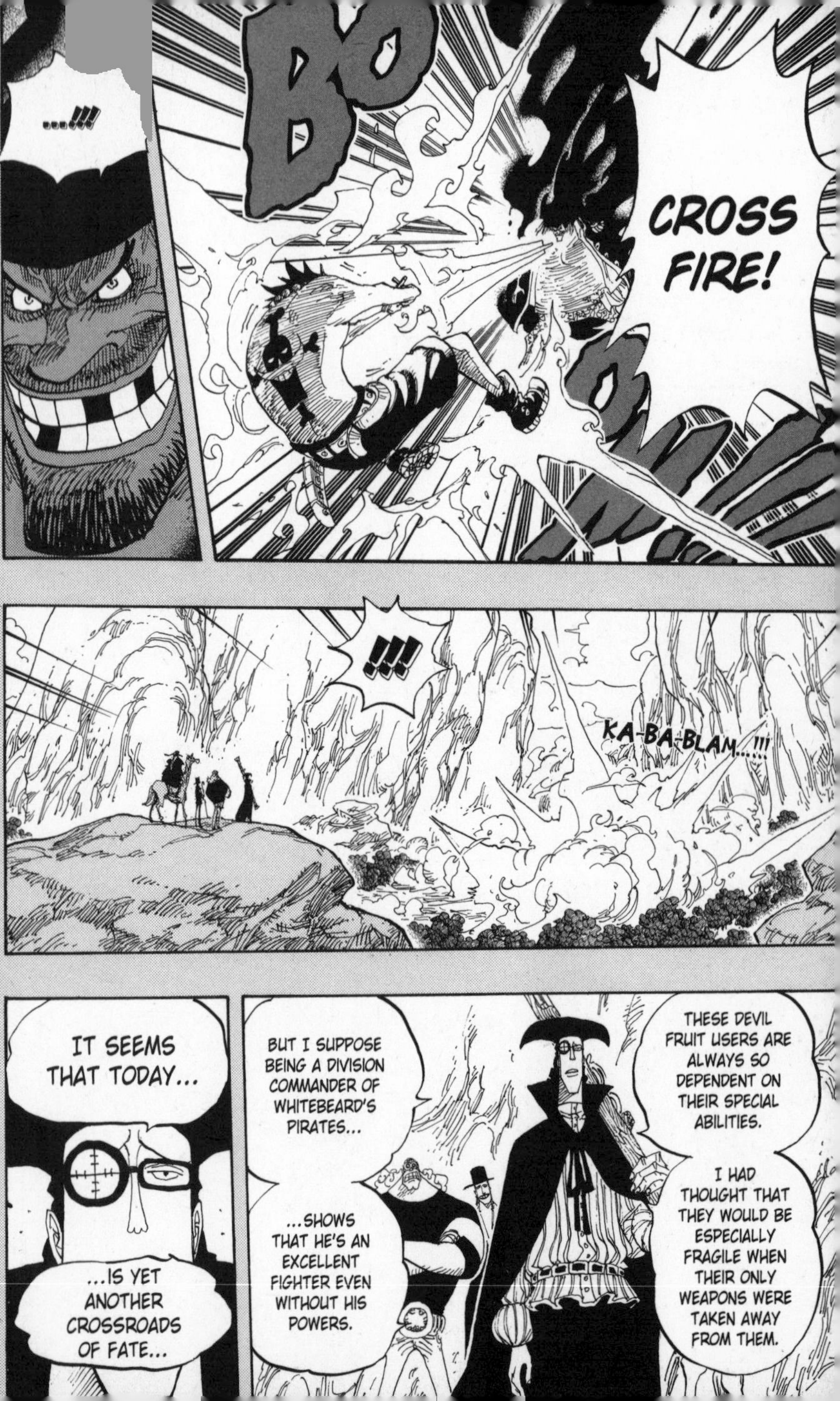
CROSS FIRE!
...!!!
!!!
KA-BA-BLAM...!!!
THESE DEVIL FRUIT USERS ARE ALWAYS SO DEPENDENT ON THEIR SPECIAL ABILITIES.
I HAD THOUGHT THAT THEY WOULD BE ESPECIALLY FRAGILE WHEN THEIR ONLY WEAPONS WERE TAKEN AWAY FROM THEM.
BUT I SUPPOSE BEING A DIVISION COMMANDER OF WHITEBEARD'S PIRATES...
...SHOWS THAT HE'S AN EXCELLENT FIGHTER EVEN WITHOUT HIS POWERS.
IT SEEMS THAT TODAY...
...IS YET ANOTHER CROSSROADS OF FATE...

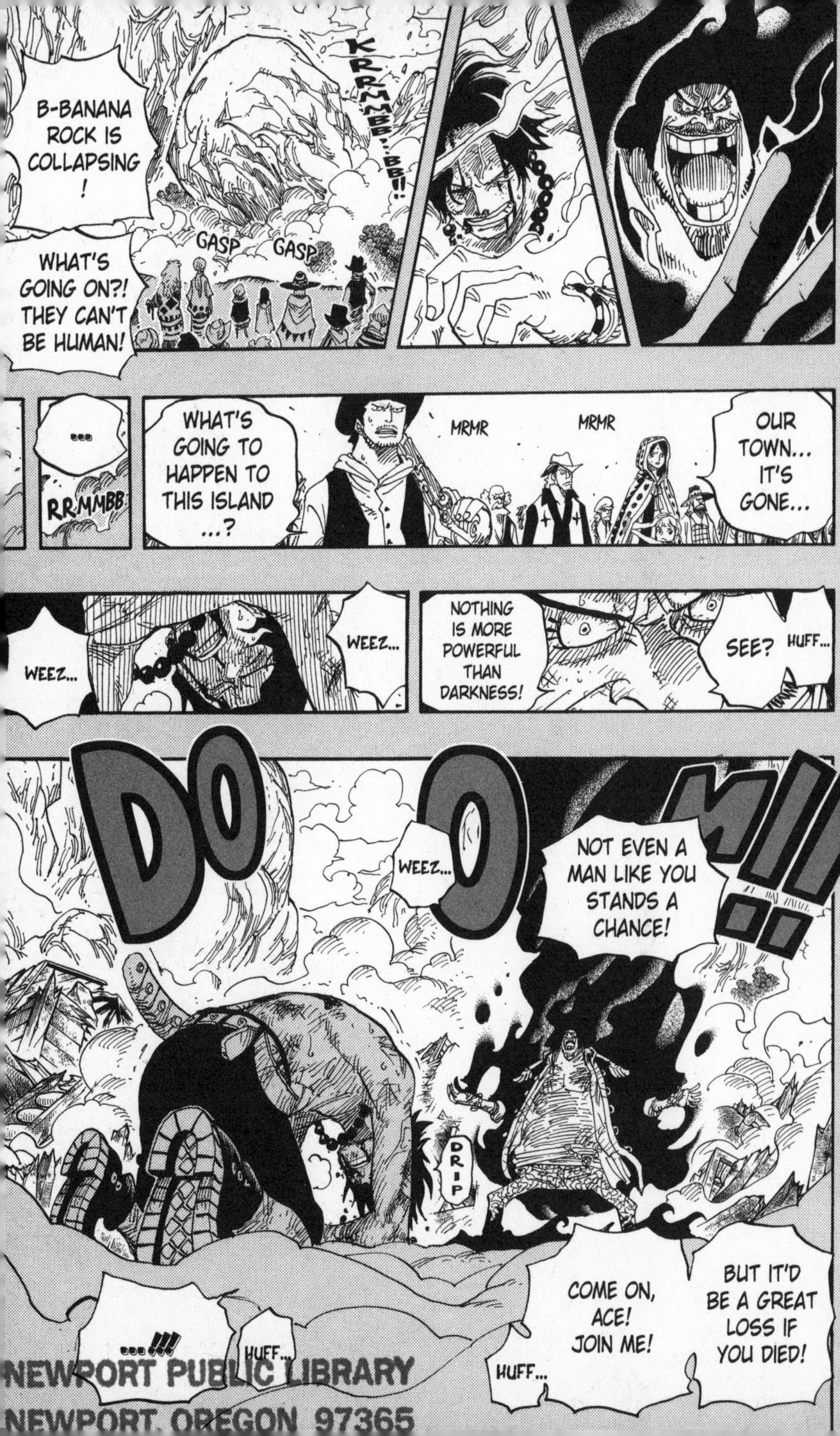
KRRMMBB...BB!!
B-BANANA ROCK IS COLLAPSING!
GASP
GASP
WHAT'S GOING ON?! THEY CAN'T BE HUMAN!
OUR TOWN... IT'S GONE...
MRMR
MRMR
WHAT'S GOING TO HAPPEN TO THIS ISLAND...?
...
RR MMBB
HUFF...
SEE?
NOTHING IS MORE POWERFUL THAN DARKNESS!
WEEZ...
WEEZ...
DOOM!!
NOT EVEN A MAN LIKE YOU STANDS A CHANCE!
WEEZ...
DRIP
BUT IT'D BE A GREAT LOSS IF YOU DIED!
COME ON, ACE! JOIN ME!
HUFF...
HUFF...
...!!!

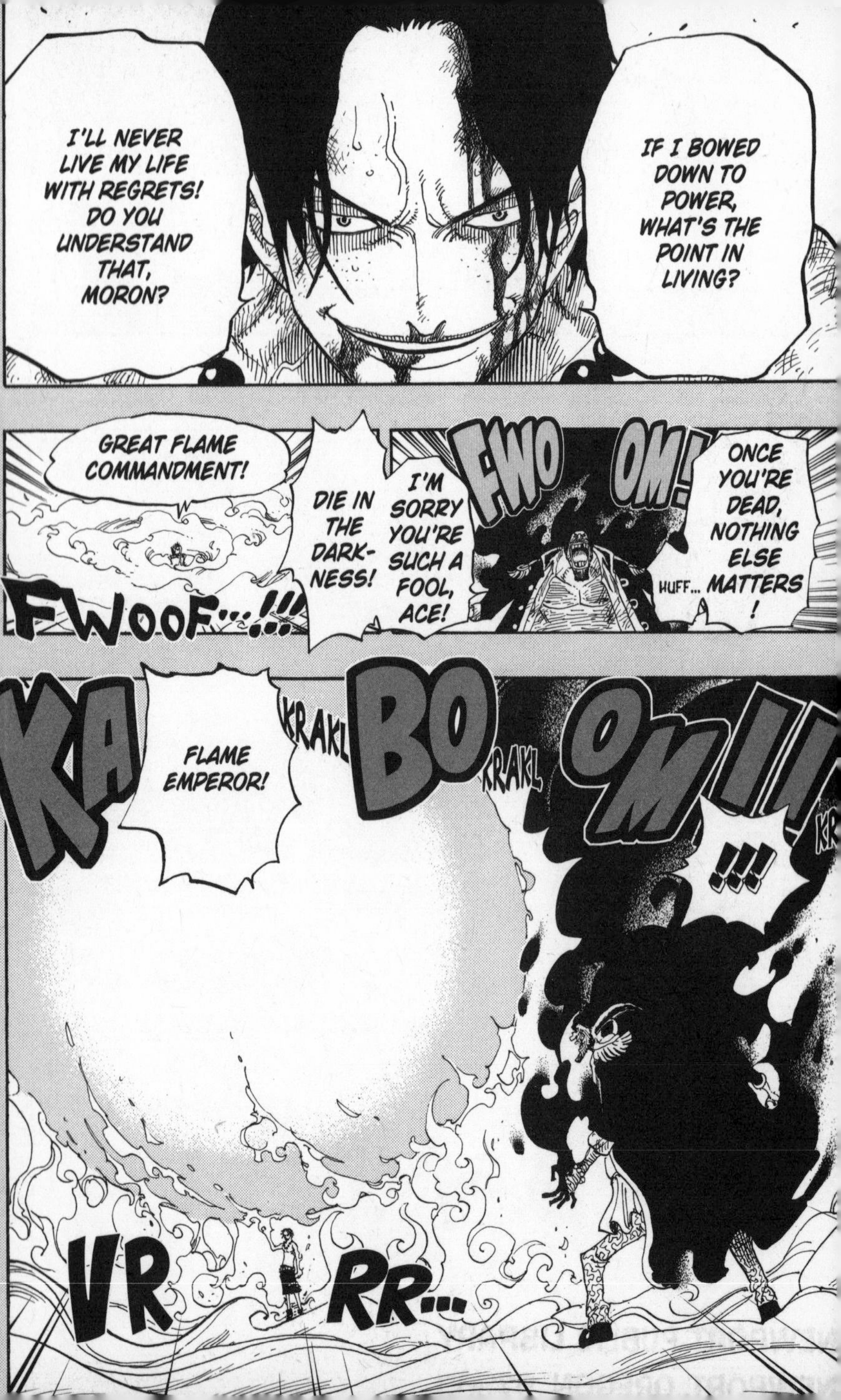

IF I BOWED DOWN TO POWER, WHAT'S THE POINT IN LIVING?
I'LL NEVER LIVE MY LIFE WITH REGRETS! DO YOU UNDERSTAND THAT, MORON?
ONCE YOU'RE DEAD, NOTHING ELSE MATTERS!
FWOOM!
HUFF...
I'M SORRY YOU'RE SUCH A FOOL, ACE!
DIE IN THE DARKNESS!
GREAT FLAME COMMANDMENT!
FWOOF...!!!
KR
KRAKL
KRAKL
KABOOM!!!
FLAME EMPEROR!
VRRR...

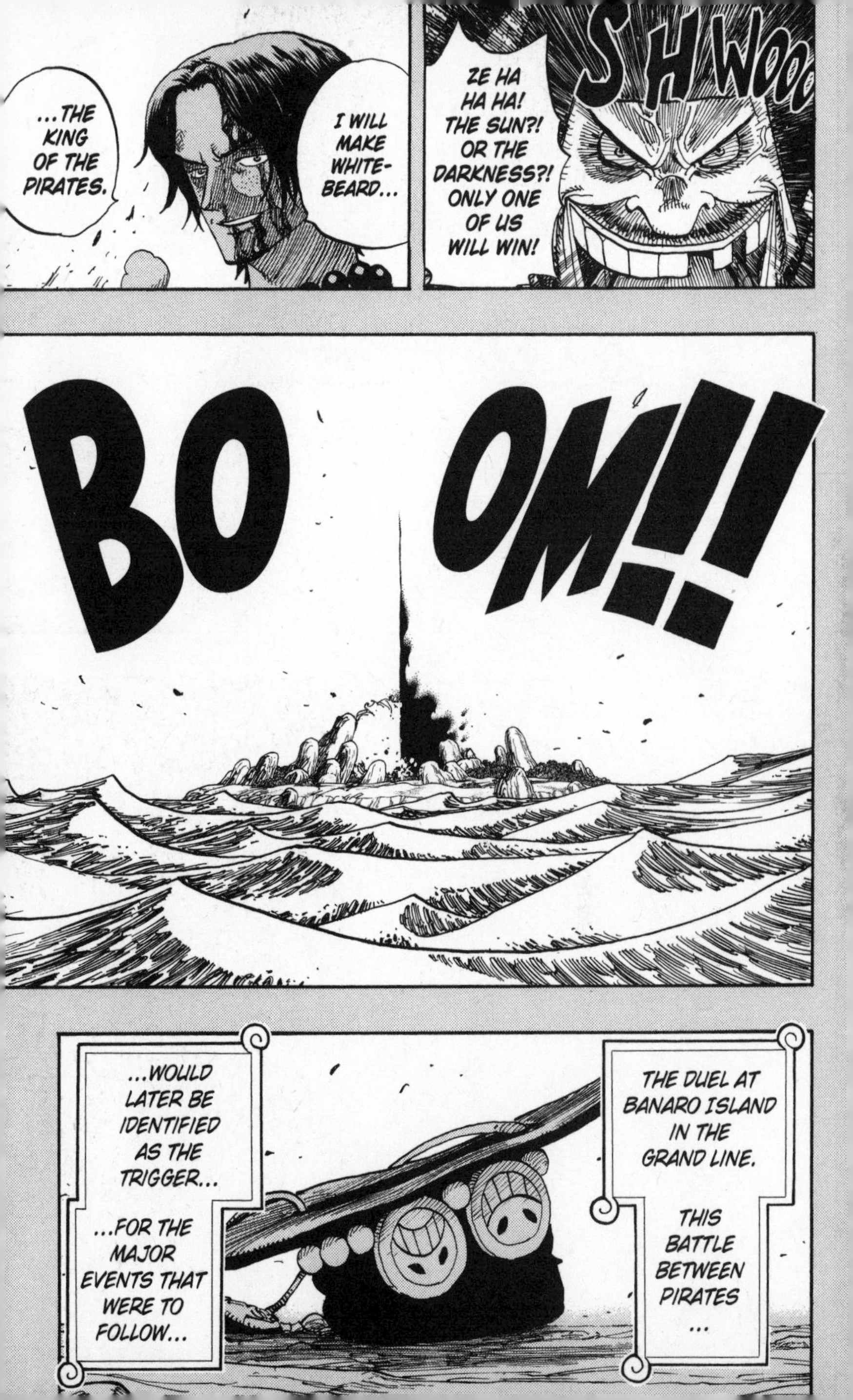
SHWOO
ZE HA HA HA! THE SUN?! OR THE DARKNESS?! ONLY ONE OF US WILL WIN!
I WILL MAKE WHITE-BEARD...
...THE KING OF THE PIRATES.
BOOM!!
THE DUEL AT BANARO ISLAND IN THE GRAND LINE.
THIS BATTLE BETWEEN PIRATES ...
...WOULD LATER BE IDENTIFIED AS THE TRIGGER...
...FOR THE MAJOR EVENTS THAT WERE TO FOLLOW...

QUESTION CORNER SPECIAL! COMPLETE DIAGRAM!
THE THOUSAND SUNNY!

Oda: Hi, everyone! I got tons of Question Corner letters from readers wanting to know what's inside Sunny! That's why I'm going to take a break from the Question Corner and show you exactly what Sunny is like! All 18 pages of it! Enjoy!

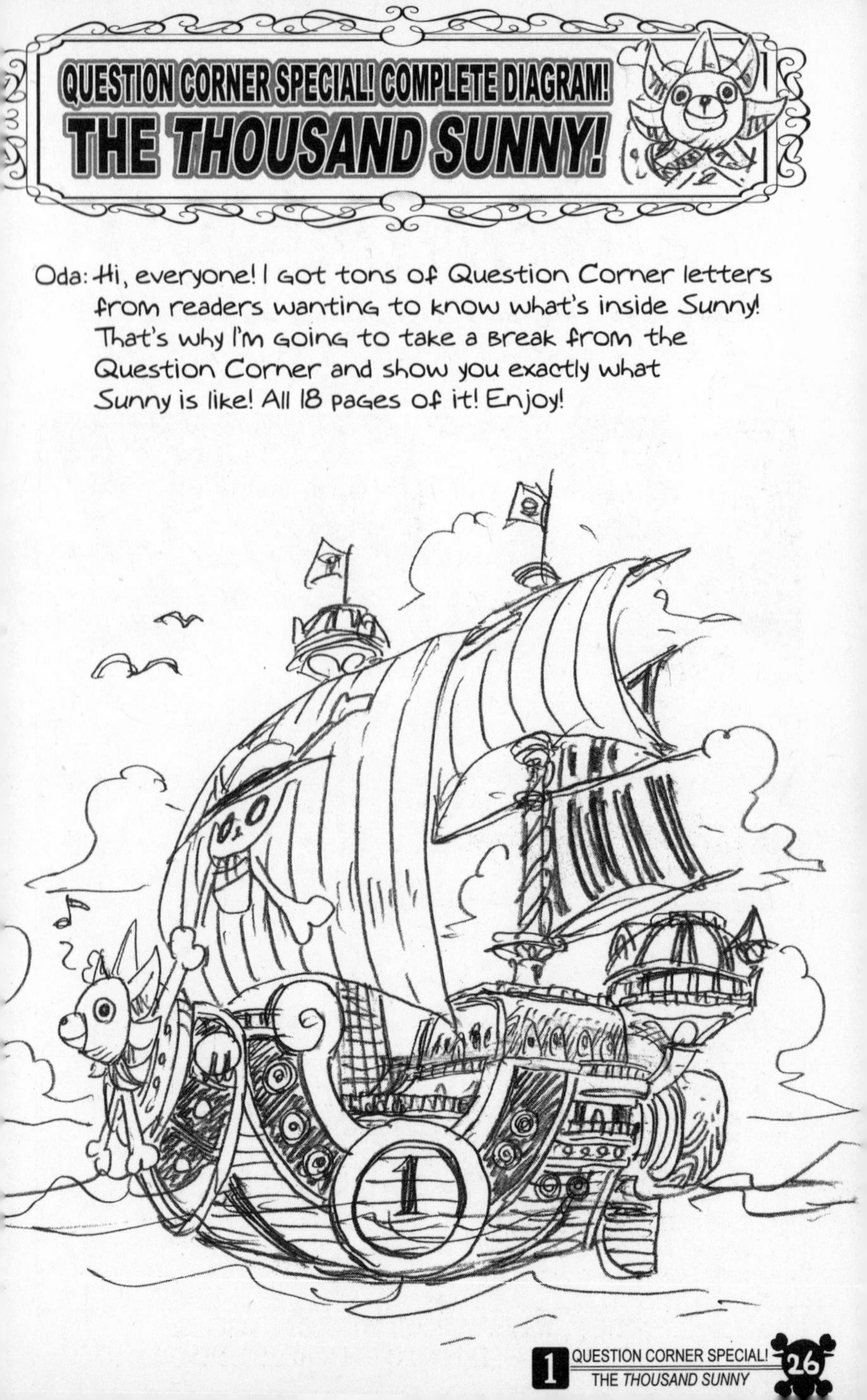

Chapter 442:
ADVENTURE IN THE DEMONIC SEA

ENERU'S GREAT SPACE MISSION, VOL. 12:
"DIVINE PUNISHMENT TO THE BLASPHEMER"

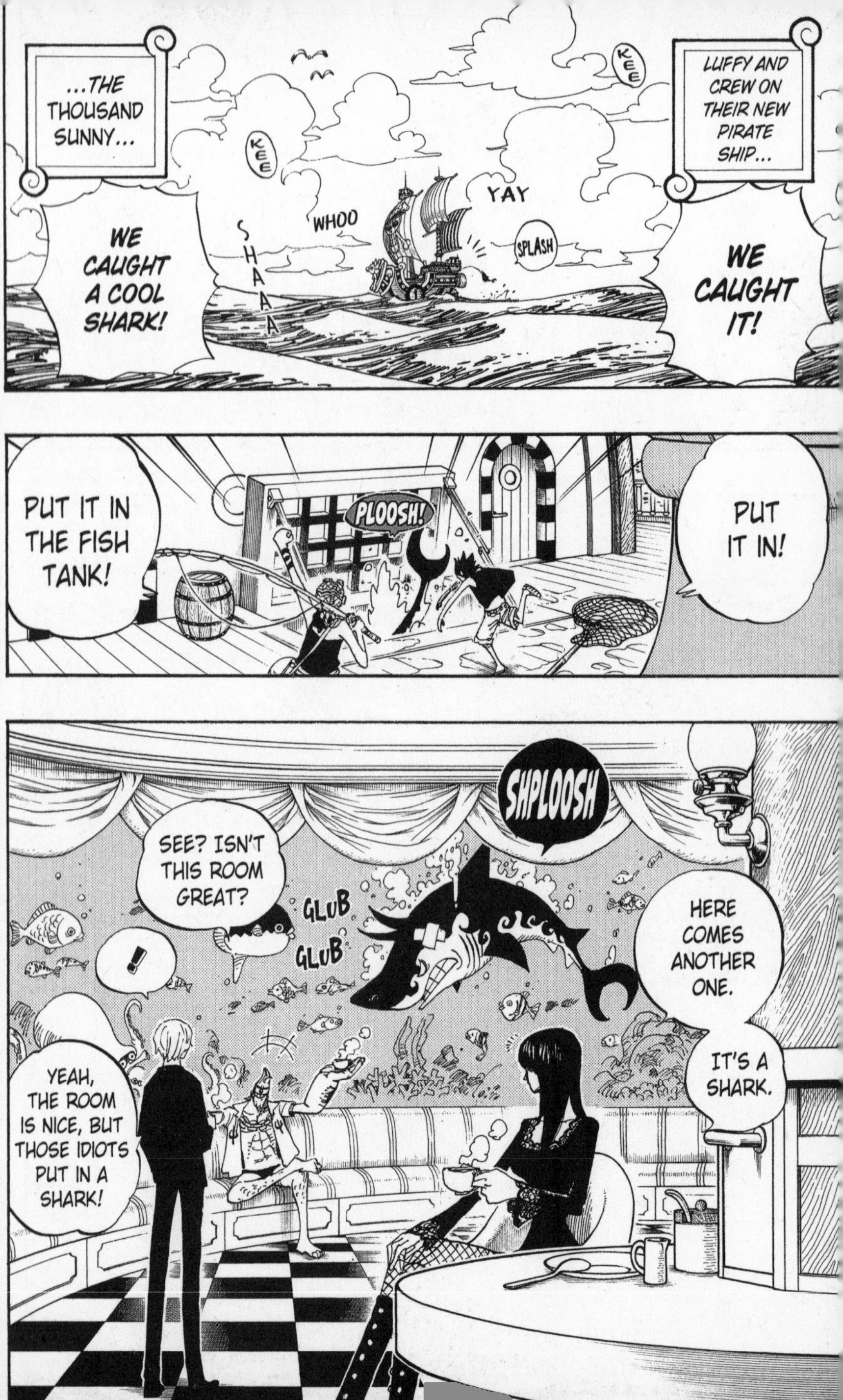
LUFFY AND CREW ON THEIR NEW PIRATE SHIP...
KEE
WE CAUGHT IT!
SPLASH
YAY
WHOO
KEE
SHAAAA
...THE THOUSAND SUNNY...
WE CAUGHT A COOL SHARK!
PUT IT IN!
PLOOSH!
PUT IT IN THE FISH TANK!
SHPLOOSH
HERE COMES ANOTHER ONE.
IT'S A SHARK.
SEE? ISN'T THIS ROOM GREAT?
GLUB
GLUB
!
YEAH, THE ROOM IS NICE, BUT THOSE IDIOTS PUT IN A SHARK!

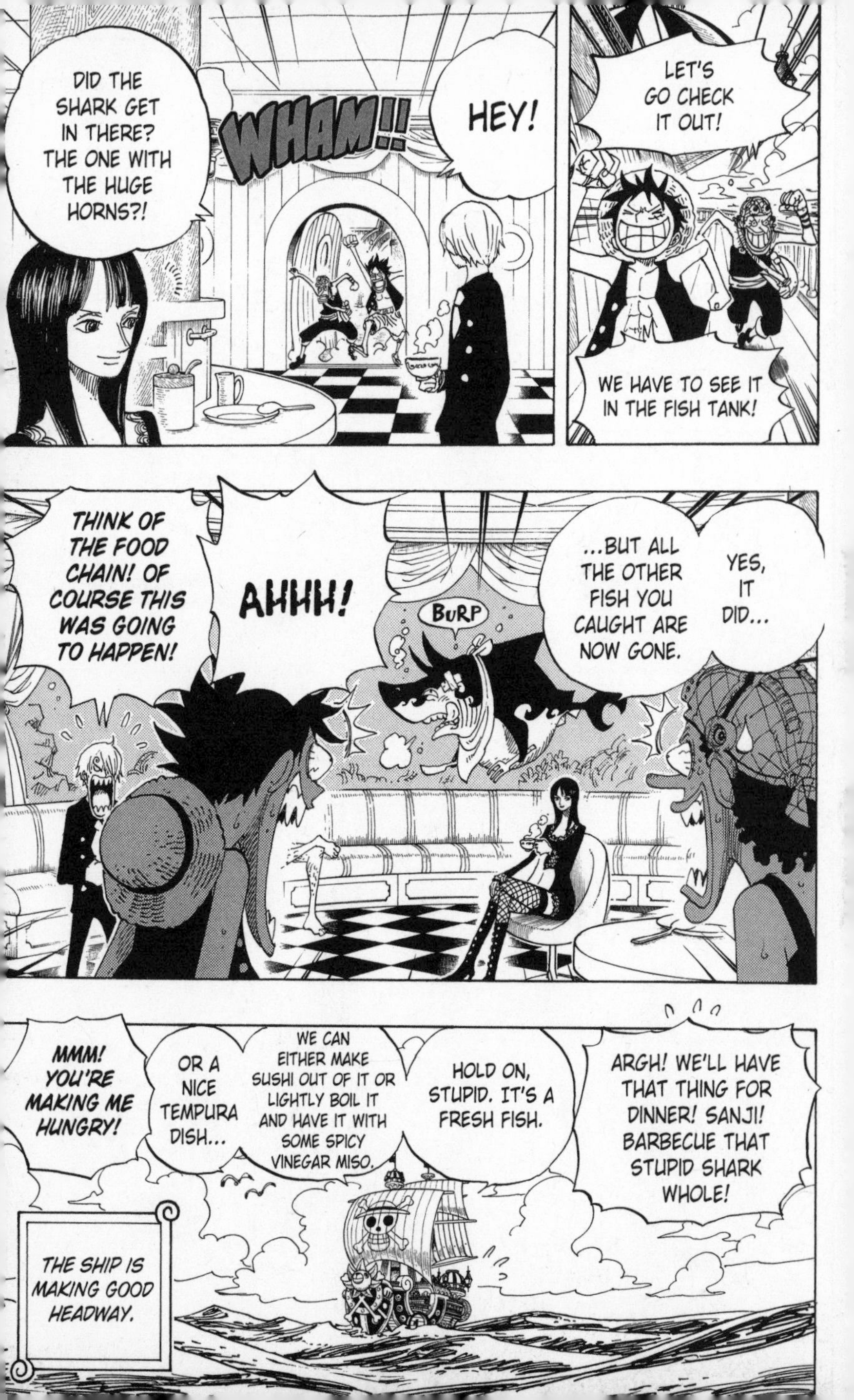
LET'S GO CHECK IT OUT!
WE HAVE TO SEE IT IN THE FISH TANK!
HEY!
WHAM!!
DID THE SHARK GET IN THERE? THE ONE WITH THE HUGE HORNS?!
YES, IT DID...
...BUT ALL THE OTHER FISH YOU CAUGHT ARE NOW GONE.
BURP
AHHH!
THINK OF THE FOOD CHAIN! OF COURSE THIS WAS GOING TO HAPPEN!
ARGH! WE'LL HAVE THAT THING FOR DINNER! SANJI! BARBECUE THAT STUPID SHARK WHOLE!
HOLD ON, STUPID. IT'S A FRESH FISH.
WE CAN EITHER MAKE SUSHI OUT OF IT OR LIGHTLY BOIL IT AND HAVE IT WITH SOME SPICY VINEGAR MISO.
OR A NICE TEMPURA DISH...
MMM! YOU'RE MAKING ME HUNGRY!
THE SHIP IS MAKING GOOD HEADWAY.

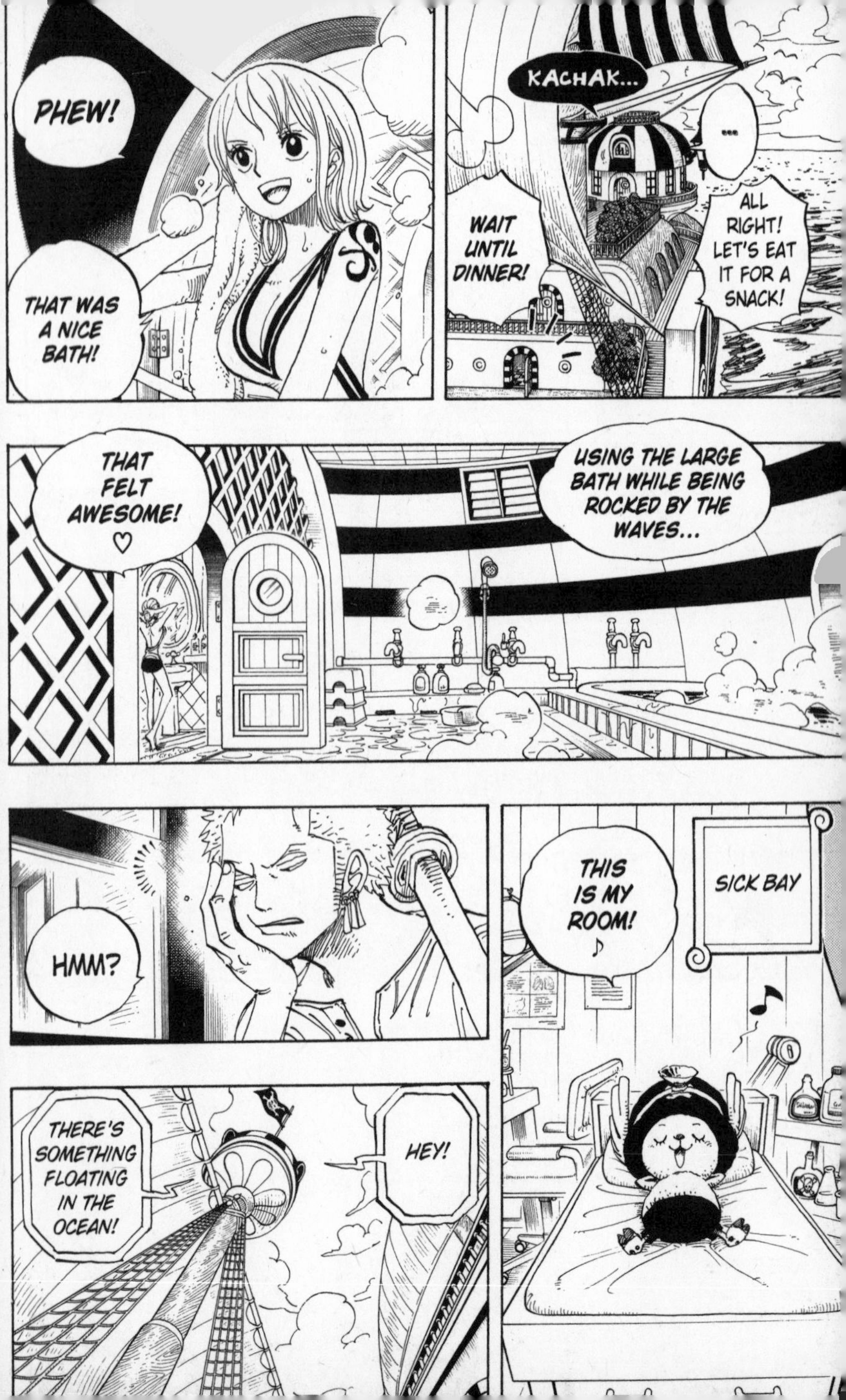
KACHAK...
...
ALL RIGHT! LET'S EAT IT FOR A SNACK!
WAIT UNTIL DINNER!
PHEW!
THAT WAS A NICE BATH!
USING THE LARGE BATH WHILE BEING ROCKED BY THE WAVES...
THAT FELT AWESOME! ♡
SICK BAY
THIS IS MY ROOM! ♪
HMM?
HEY!
THERE'S SOMETHING FLOATING IN THE OCEAN!

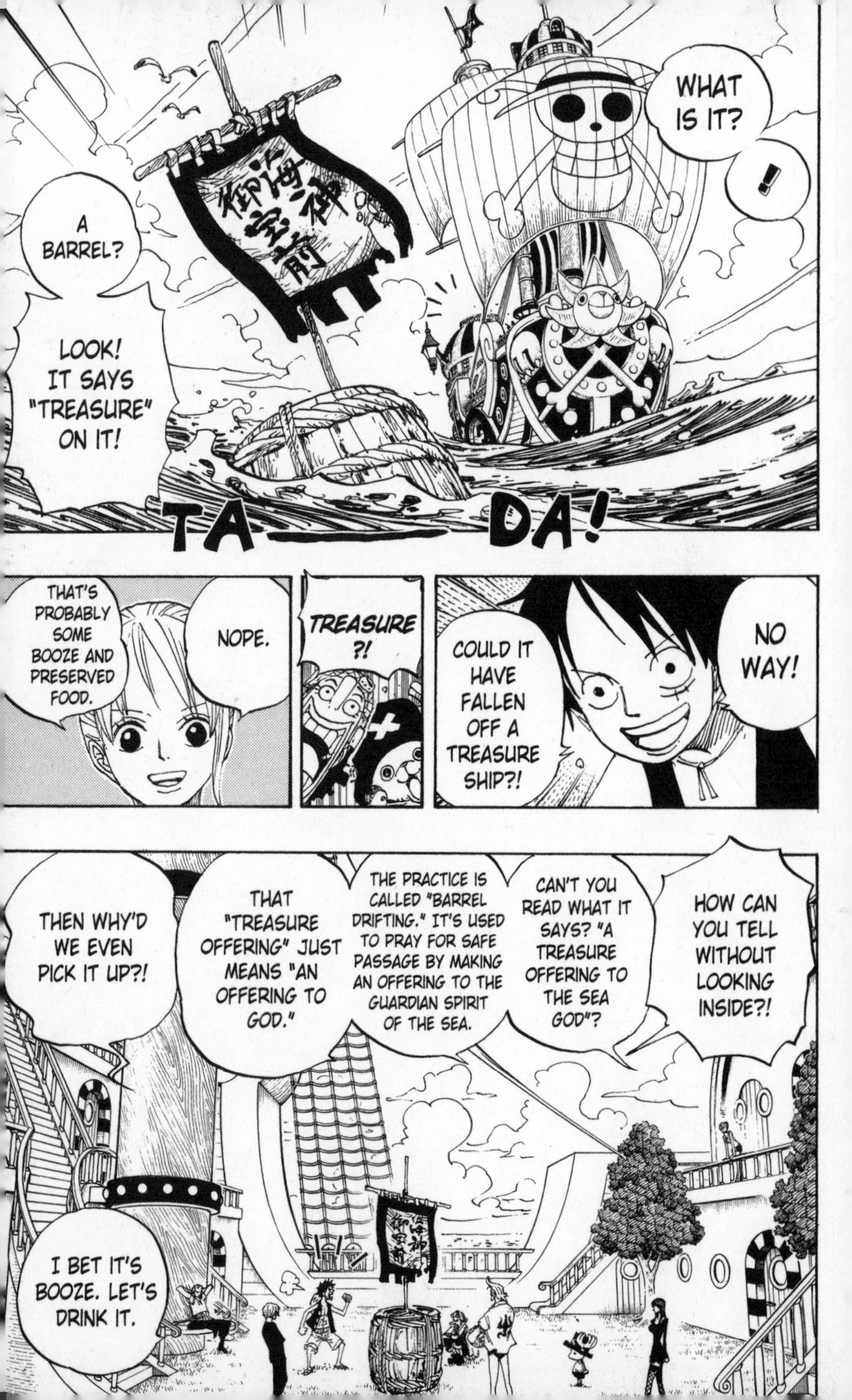
WHAT IS IT?
!
A BARREL?
LOOK! IT SAYS "TREASURE" ON IT!
TA—DA!
NO WAY!
COULD IT HAVE FALLEN OFF A TREASURE SHIP?!
TREASURE ?!
NOPE.
THAT'S PROBABLY SOME BOOZE AND PRESERVED FOOD.
HOW CAN YOU TELL WITHOUT LOOKING INSIDE?!
CAN'T YOU READ WHAT IT SAYS? "A TREASURE OFFERING TO THE SEA GOD"?
THE PRACTICE IS CALLED "BARREL DRIFTING." IT'S USED TO PRAY FOR SAFE PASSAGE BY MAKING AN OFFERING TO THE GUARDIAN SPIRIT OF THE SEA.
THAT "TREASURE OFFERING" JUST MEANS "AN OFFERING TO GOD."
THEN WHY'D WE EVEN PICK IT UP?!
I BET IT'S BOOZE. LET'S DRINK IT.

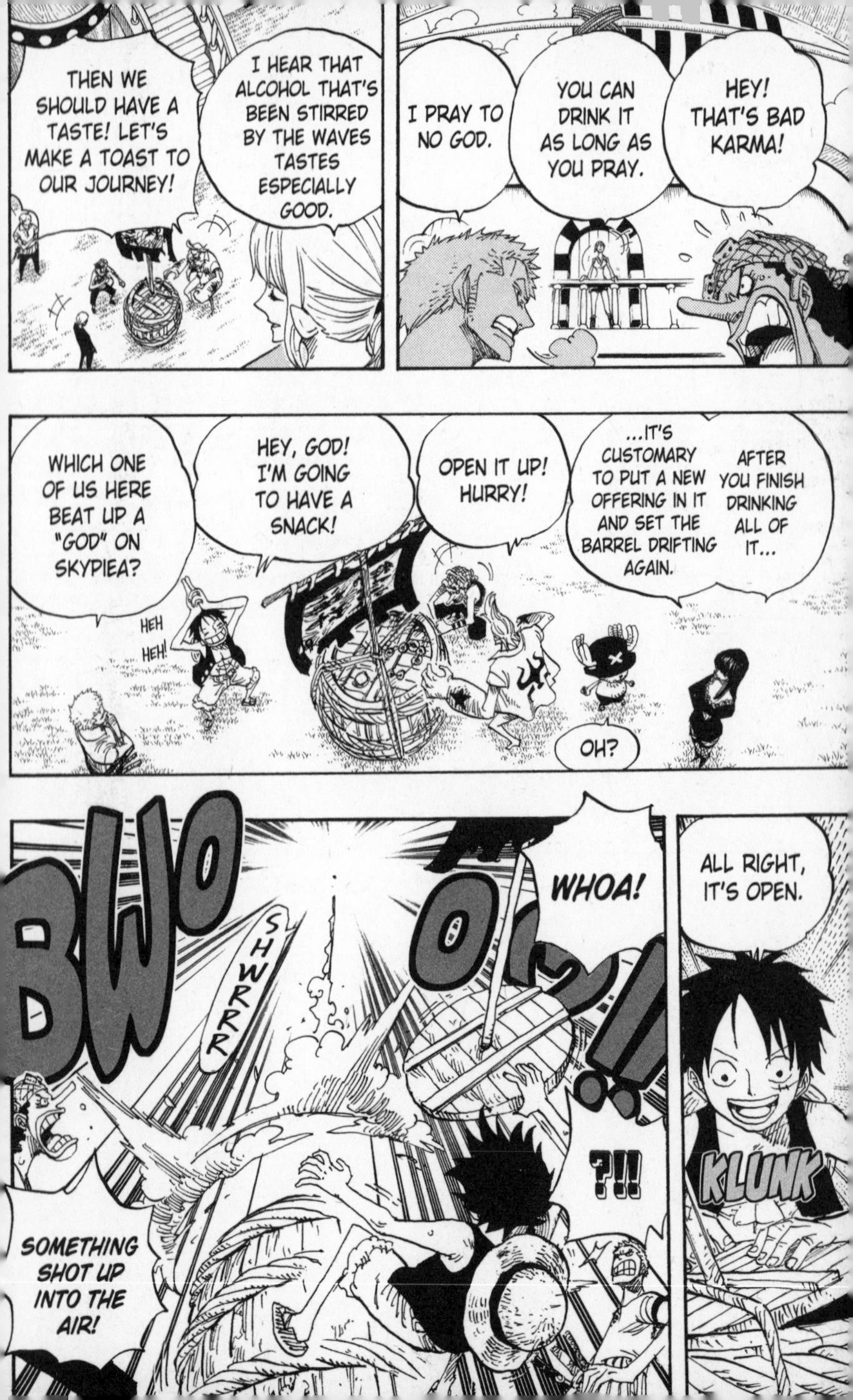
HEY! THAT'S BAD KARMA!
YOU CAN DRINK IT AS LONG AS YOU PRAY.
I PRAY TO NO GOD.
I HEAR THAT ALCOHOL THAT'S BEEN STIRRED BY THE WAVES TASTES ESPECIALLY GOOD.
THEN WE SHOULD HAVE A TASTE! LET'S MAKE A TOAST TO OUR JOURNEY!
AFTER YOU FINISH DRINKING ALL OF IT...
...IT'S CUSTOMARY TO PUT A NEW OFFERING IN IT AND SET THE BARREL DRIFTING AGAIN.
OPEN IT UP! HURRY!
HEY, GOD! I'M GOING TO HAVE A SNACK!
WHICH ONE OF US HERE BEAT UP A "GOD" ON SKYPIEA?
OH?
HEH HEH!
ALL RIGHT, IT'S OPEN.
KLUNK
WHOA!
?!!
SHWRRR
BWO
SOMETHING SHOT UP INTO THE AIR!

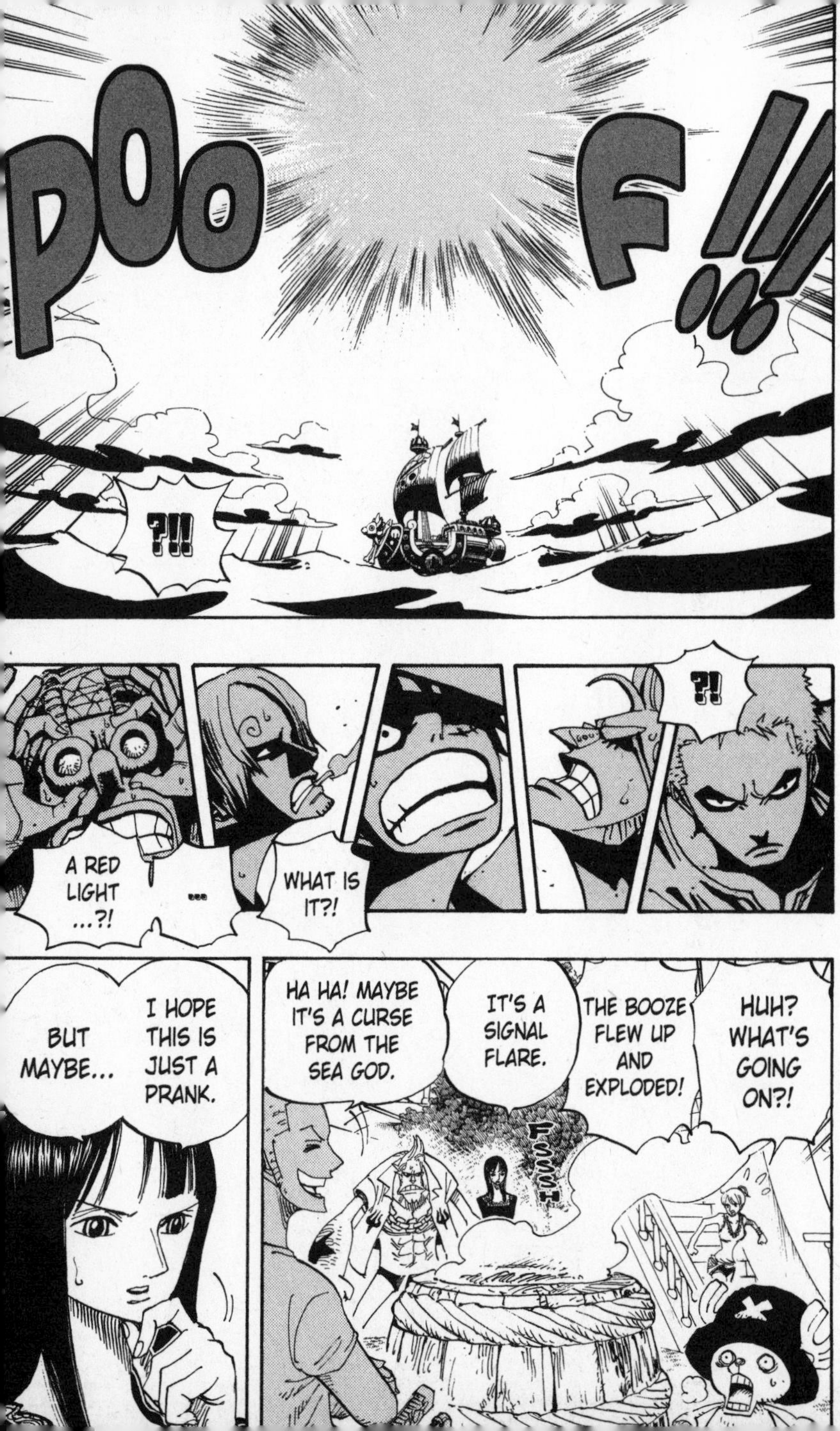
POOOF!!
?!!
?!
WHAT IS IT?!
...
A RED LIGHT ...?!
HUH? WHAT'S GOING ON?!
THE BOOZE FLEW UP AND EXPLODED!
IT'S A SIGNAL FLARE.
HA HA! MAYBE IT'S A CURSE FROM THE SEA GOD.
FSSSH
I HOPE THIS IS JUST A PRANK.
BUT MAYBE...

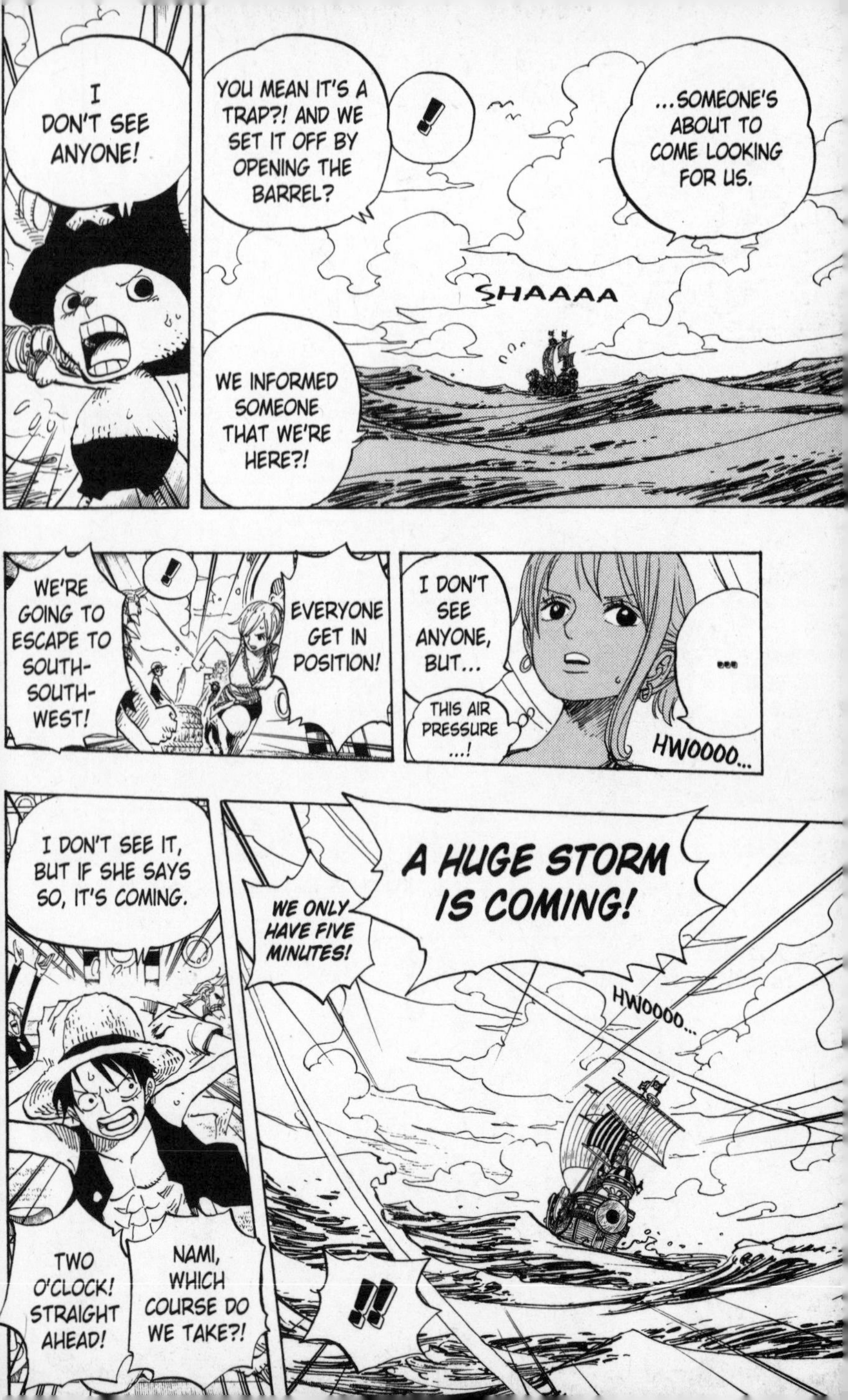
...SOMEONE'S ABOUT TO COME LOOKING FOR US.
!
YOU MEAN IT'S A TRAP?! AND WE SET IT OFF BY OPENING THE BARREL?
SHAAAA
WE INFORMED SOMEONE THAT WE'RE HERE?!
I DON'T SEE ANYONE!
...
I DON'T SEE ANYONE, BUT...
THIS AIR PRESSURE ...!
HWOOOO...
EVERYONE GET IN POSITION!
!
WE'RE GOING TO ESCAPE TO SOUTH-SOUTH-WEST!
A HUGE STORM IS COMING!
WE ONLY HAVE FIVE MINUTES!
HWOOOO...
!!
I DON'T SEE IT, BUT IF SHE SAYS SO, IT'S COMING.
NAMI, WHICH COURSE DO WE TAKE?!
TWO O'CLOCK! STRAIGHT AHEAD!

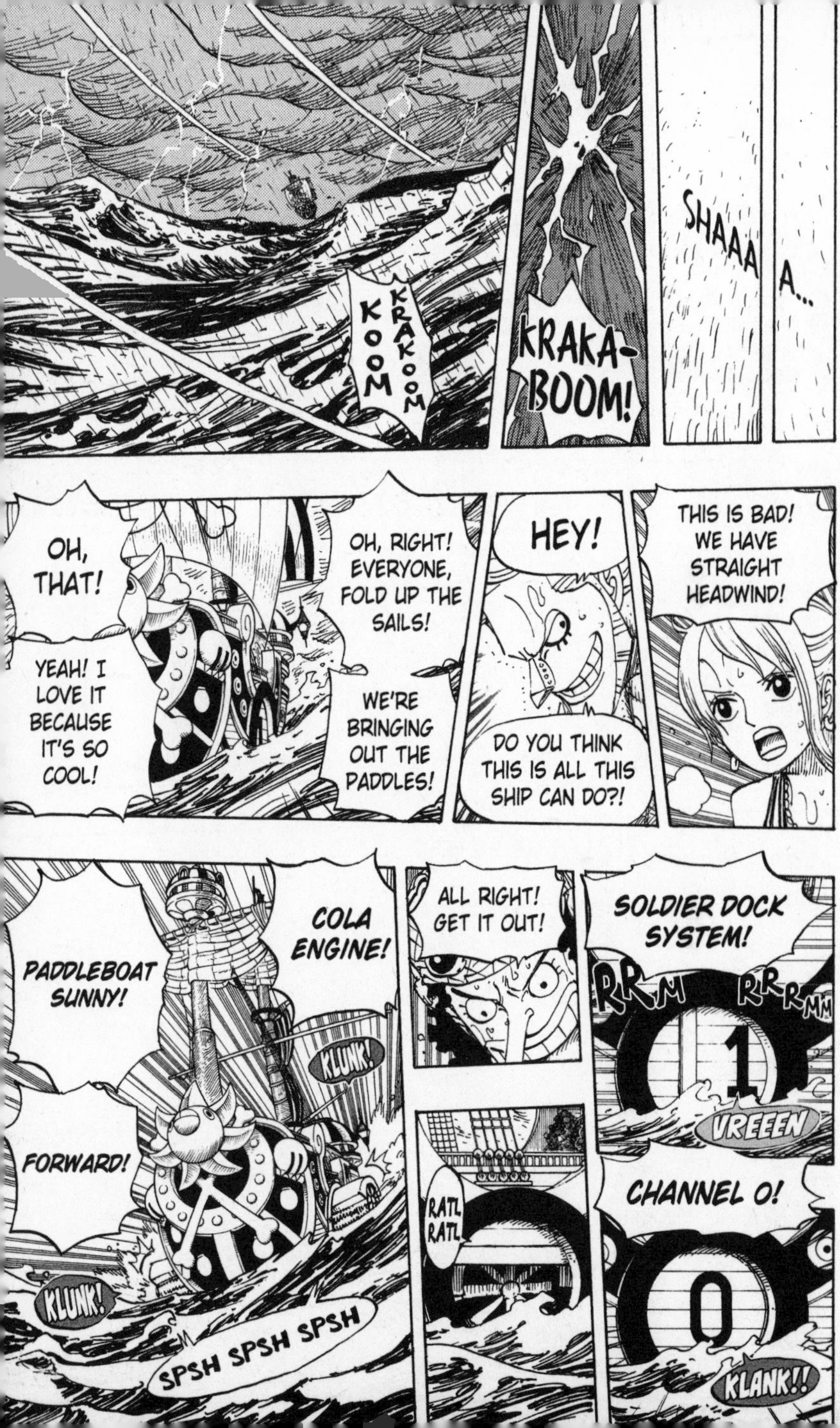
SHAAAA...
KRAKA-BOOM!
KRAKOOM
KOOM
THIS IS BAD! WE HAVE STRAIGHT HEADWIND!
HEY!
DO YOU THINK THIS IS ALL THIS SHIP CAN DO?!
OH, RIGHT! EVERYONE, FOLD UP THE SAILS!
WE'RE BRINGING OUT THE PADDLES!
OH, THAT!
YEAH! I LOVE IT BECAUSE IT'S SO COOL!
SOLDIER DOCK SYSTEM!
RRM
RRRMM
1
VREEEN
CHANNEL O!
0
KLANK!!
ALL RIGHT! GET IT OUT!
RATL RATL
COLA ENGINE!
PADDLEBOAT SUNNY!
KLUNK!
FORWARD!
KLUNK!
SPSH SPSH SPSH

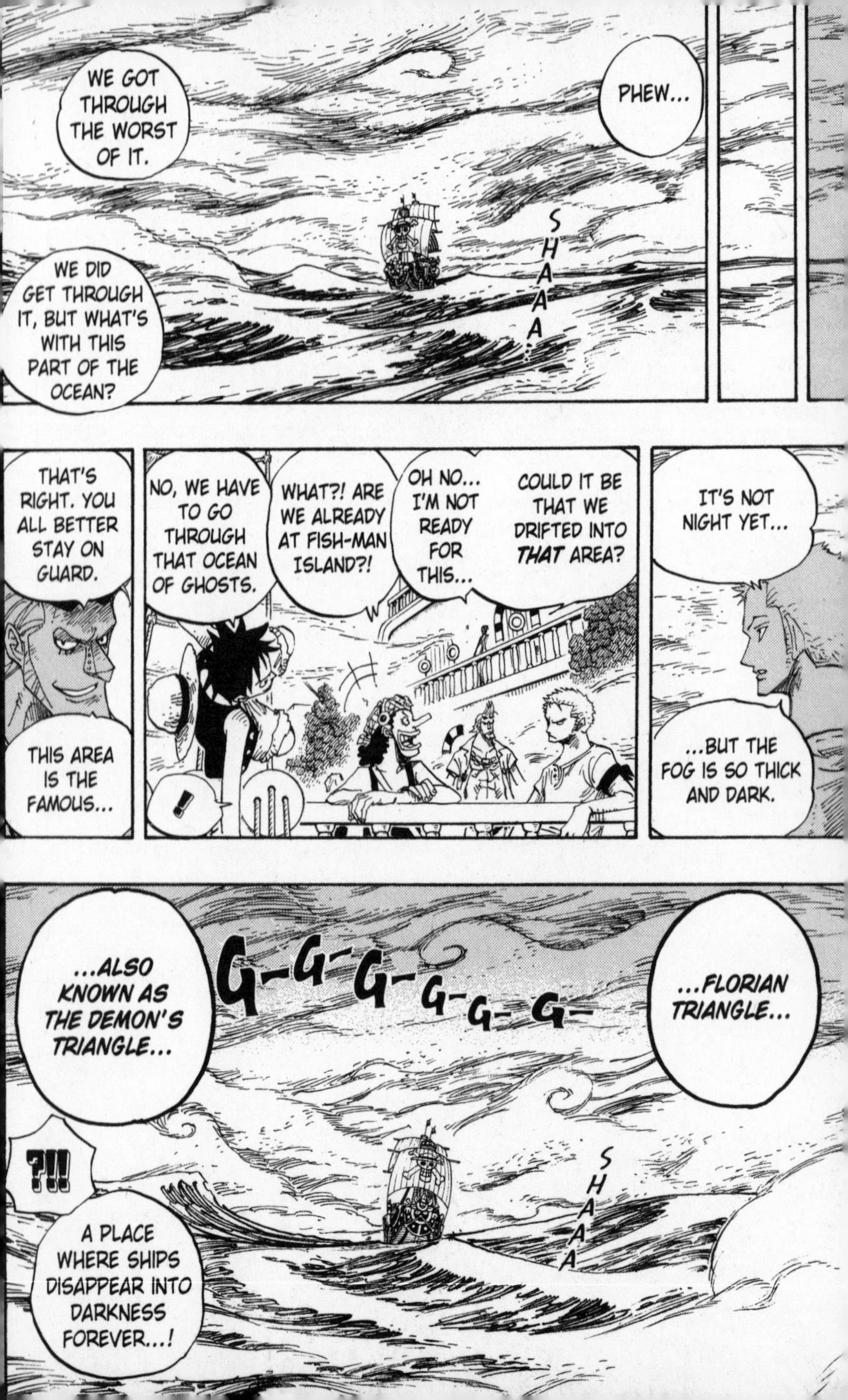
PHEW...
WE GOT THROUGH THE WORST OF IT.
SHAAAA...
WE DID GET THROUGH IT, BUT WHAT'S WITH THIS PART OF THE OCEAN?
IT'S NOT NIGHT YET...
...BUT THE FOG IS SO THICK AND DARK.
COULD IT BE THAT WE DRIFTED INTO *THAT* AREA?
OH NO... I'M NOT READY FOR THIS...
WHAT?! ARE WE ALREADY AT FISH-MAN ISLAND?!
NO, WE HAVE TO GO THROUGH THAT OCEAN OF GHOSTS.
!
THAT'S RIGHT. YOU ALL BETTER STAY ON GUARD.
THIS AREA IS THE FAMOUS...
...FLORIAN TRIANGLE...
G-G-G-G-G-G-
...ALSO KNOWN AS THE DEMON'S TRIANGLE...
SHAAAA
?!!
A PLACE WHERE SHIPS DISAPPEAR INTO DARKNESS FOREVER...!

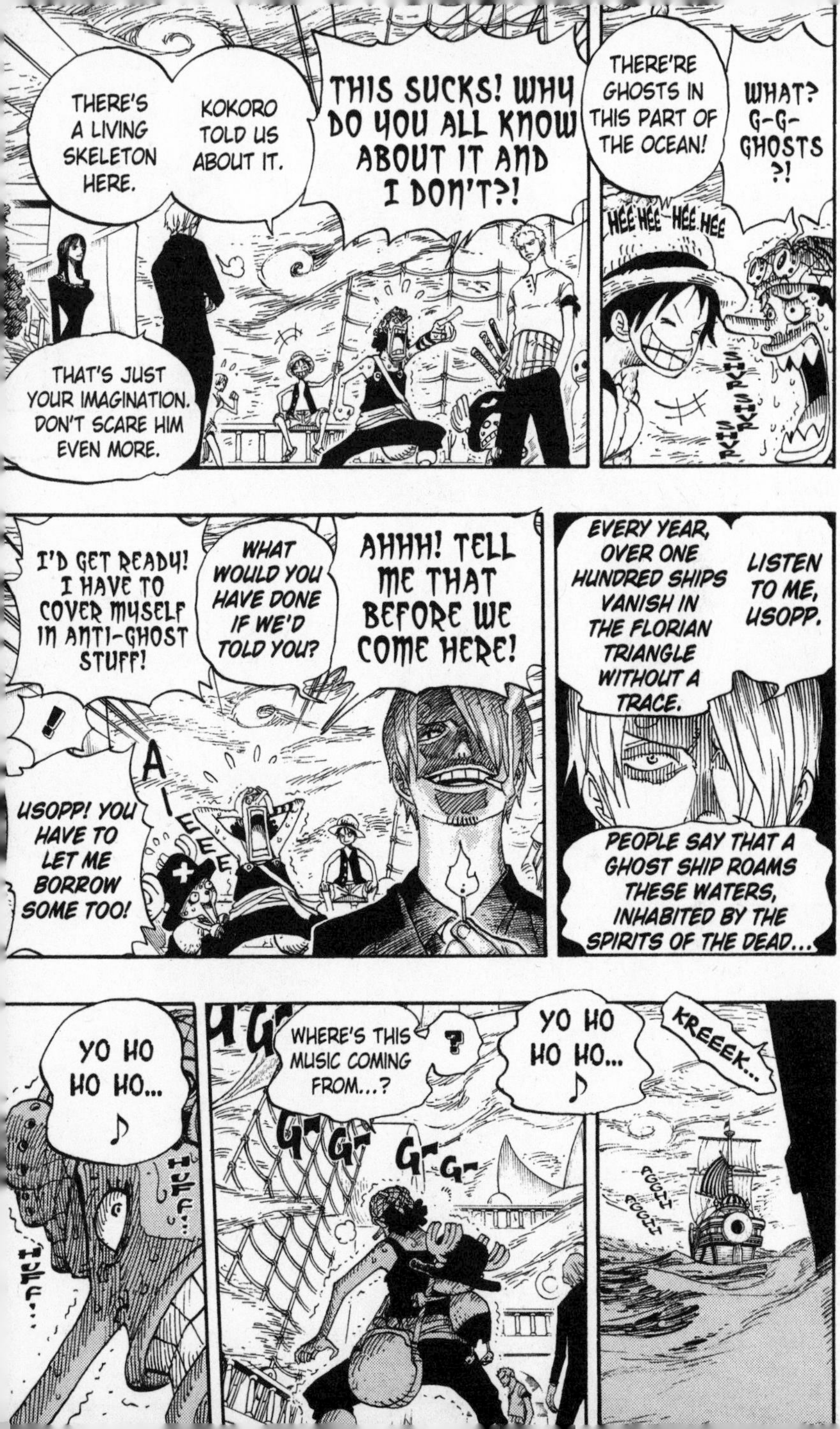
THERE'RE GHOSTS IN THIS PART OF THE OCEAN!
WHAT? G-G-GHOSTS ?!
HEE HEE HEE HEE
SHIVR SHIVR SHIVR
THIS SUCKS! WHY DO YOU ALL KNOW ABOUT IT AND I DON'T?!
KOKORO TOLD US ABOUT IT.
THERE'S A LIVING SKELETON HERE.
THAT'S JUST YOUR IMAGINATION. DON'T SCARE HIM EVEN MORE.
LISTEN TO ME, USOPP.
EVERY YEAR, OVER ONE HUNDRED SHIPS VANISH IN THE FLORIAN TRIANGLE WITHOUT A TRACE.
PEOPLE SAY THAT A GHOST SHIP ROAMS THESE WATERS, INHABITED BY THE SPIRITS OF THE DEAD...
AHHH! TELL ME THAT BEFORE WE COME HERE!
WHAT WOULD YOU HAVE DONE IF WE'D TOLD YOU?
I'D GET READY! I HAVE TO COVER MYSELF IN ANTI-GHOST STUFF!
!
AIEEEE
USOPP! YOU HAVE TO LET ME BORROW SOME TOO!
KREEEK...
AGGHH AGGHH
YO HO HO HO... ♪
?
WHERE'S THIS MUSIC COMING FROM...?
G-G-G-G-
YO HO HO HO... ♪
HUFF... HUFF...

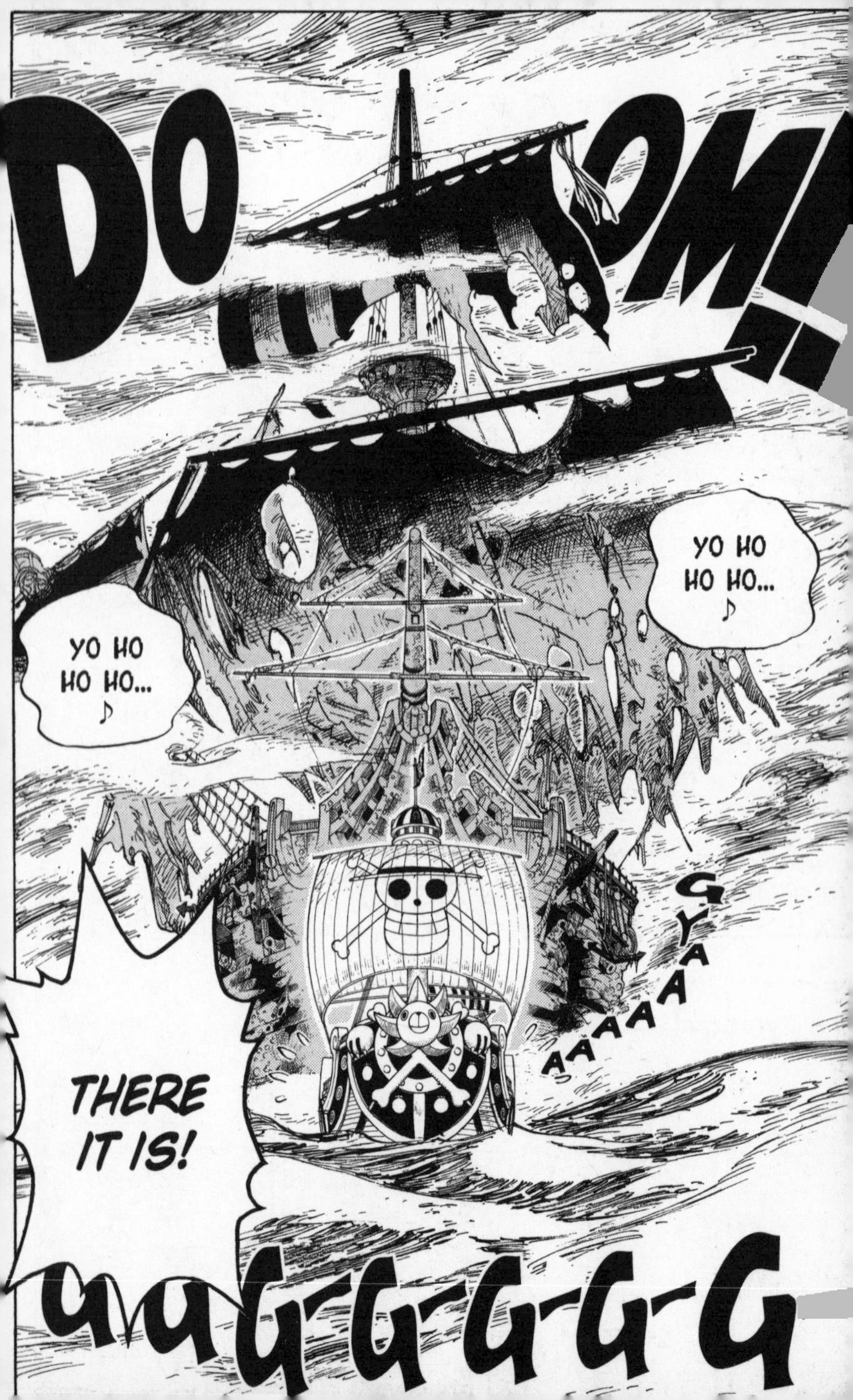
DO OM!!
YO HO HO HO... ♪
YO HO HO HO... ♪
GYAAAAAAA
THERE IT IS!
GGG-G-G-G-G

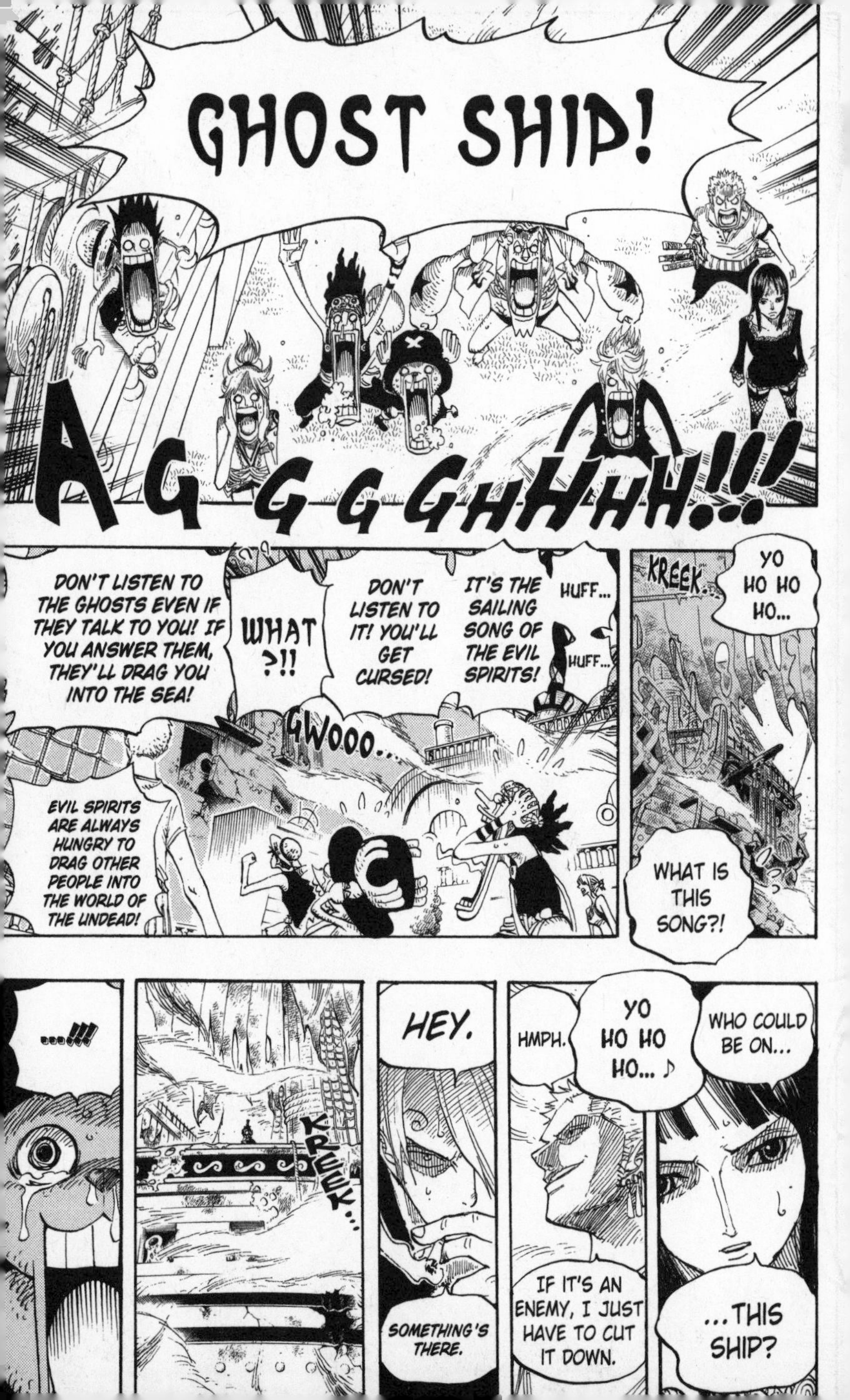
GHOST SHIP!
AGGGGHHHH!!!
KREEK...
YO HO HO HO...
WHAT IS THIS SONG?!
HUFF...
HUFF...
IT'S THE SAILING SONG OF THE EVIL SPIRITS!
DON'T LISTEN TO IT! YOU'LL GET CURSED!
WHAT ?!!
DON'T LISTEN TO THE GHOSTS EVEN IF THEY TALK TO YOU! IF YOU ANSWER THEM, THEY'LL DRAG YOU INTO THE SEA!
GWOOO...
EVIL SPIRITS ARE ALWAYS HUNGRY TO DRAG OTHER PEOPLE INTO THE WORLD OF THE UNDEAD!
WHO COULD BE ON...
...THIS SHIP?
YO HO HO HO... ♪
HMPH.
IF IT'S AN ENEMY, I JUST HAVE TO CUT IT DOWN.
HEY.
SOMETHING'S THERE.
KREEK...
...!!!

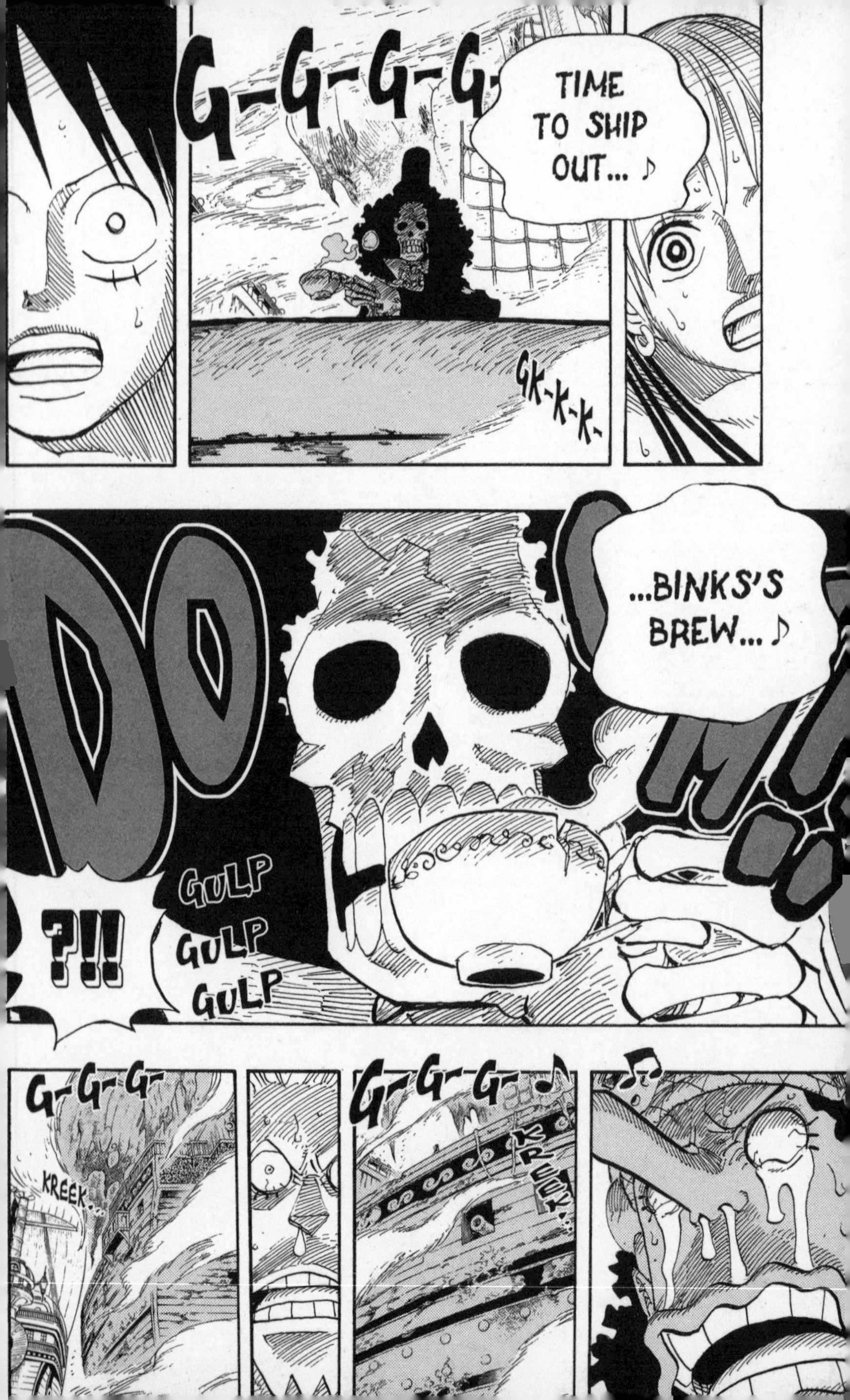
TIME TO SHIP OUT... ♪
G-G-G-G-
GK-K-K-
...BINKS'S BREW... ♪
DOOM
?!!
GULP GULP GULP
G-G-G- ♪
KREEK...
G-G-G-
KREEK...

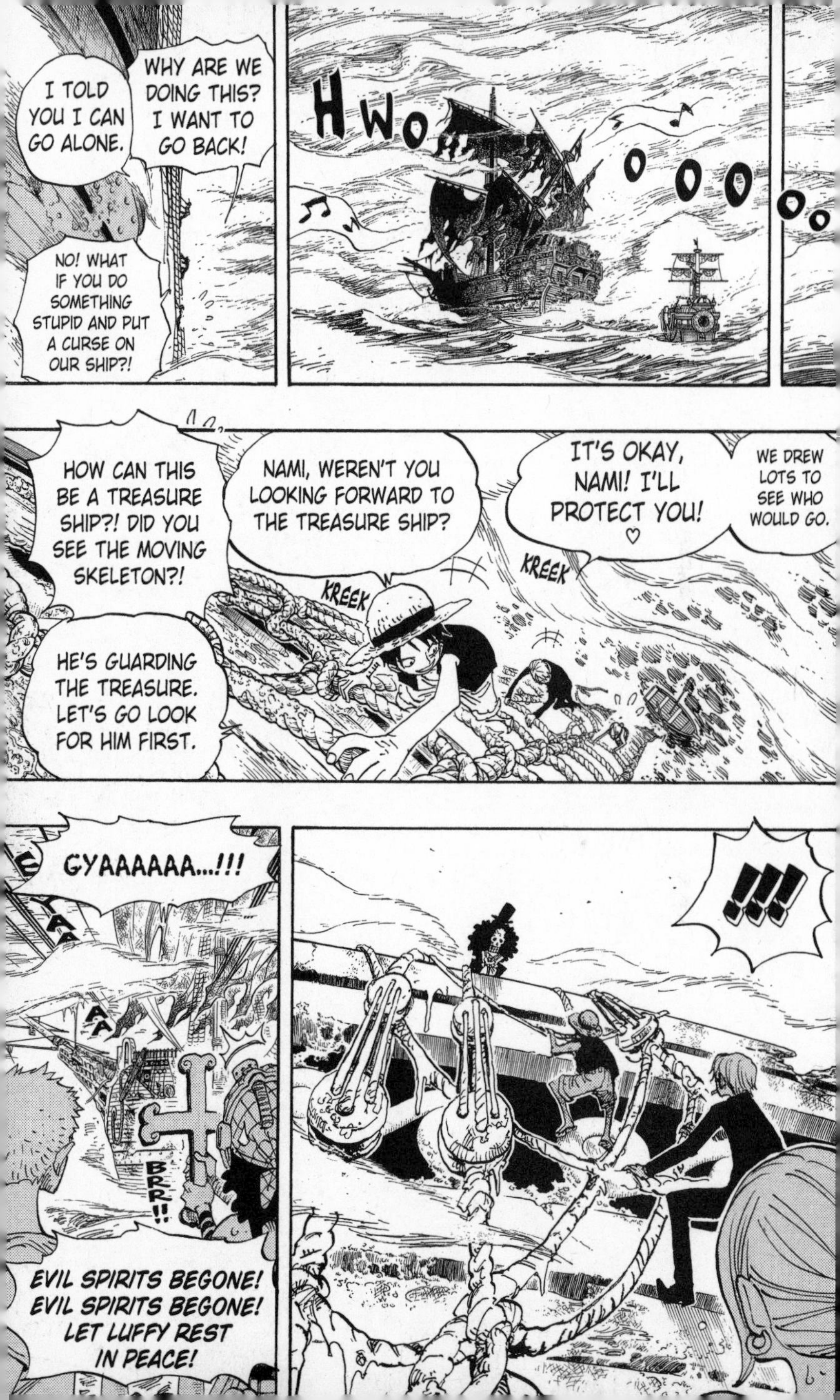
HWOOOOOO
WHY ARE WE DOING THIS? I WANT TO GO BACK!
I TOLD YOU I CAN GO ALONE.
NO! WHAT IF YOU DO SOMETHING STUPID AND PUT A CURSE ON OUR SHIP?!
WE DREW LOTS TO SEE WHO WOULD GO.
IT'S OKAY, NAMI! I'LL PROTECT YOU! ♡
KREEK
NAMI, WEREN'T YOU LOOKING FORWARD TO THE TREASURE SHIP?
KREEK
HOW CAN THIS BE A TREASURE SHIP?! DID YOU SEE THE MOVING SKELETON?!
HE'S GUARDING THE TREASURE. LET'S GO LOOK FOR HIM FIRST.
!!!
GYAAAAAA...!!!
BRR!!
EVIL SPIRITS BEGONE! EVIL SPIRITS BEGONE! LET LUFFY REST IN PEACE!

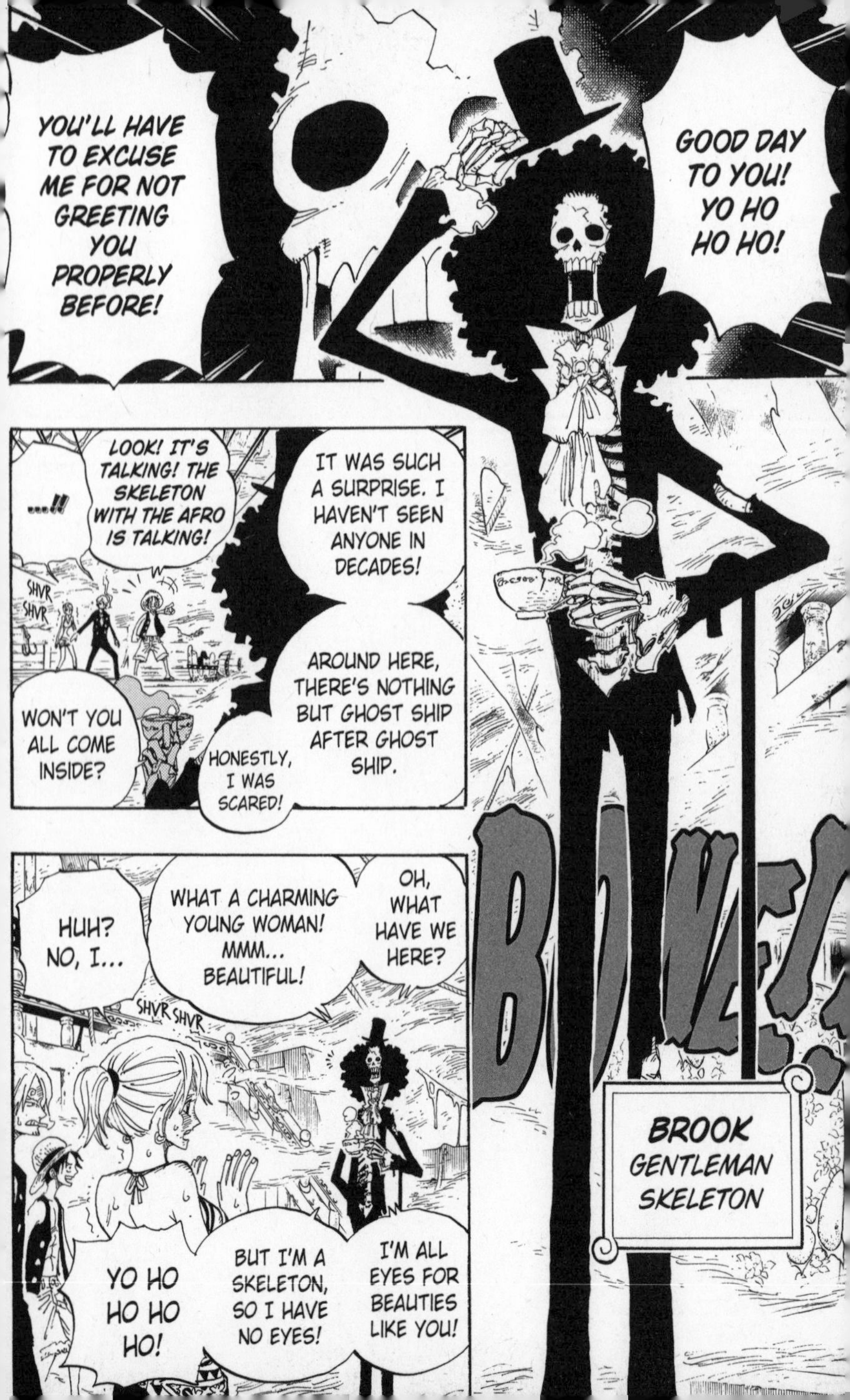

GOOD DAY TO YOU! YO HO HO HO!
YOU'LL HAVE TO EXCUSE ME FOR NOT GREETING YOU PROPERLY BEFORE!
BROOK
GENTLEMAN SKELETON
IT WAS SUCH A SURPRISE. I HAVEN'T SEEN ANYONE IN DECADES!
AROUND HERE, THERE'S NOTHING BUT GHOST SHIP AFTER GHOST SHIP.
HONESTLY, I WAS SCARED!
LOOK! IT'S TALKING! THE SKELETON WITH THE AFRO IS TALKING!
...!!
SHVR SHVR
WON'T YOU ALL COME INSIDE?
OH, WHAT HAVE WE HERE?
WHAT A CHARMING YOUNG WOMAN! MMM... BEAUTIFUL!
HUH? NO, I...
SHVR SHVR
I'M ALL EYES FOR BEAUTIES LIKE YOU!
BUT I'M A SKELETON, SO I HAVE NO EYES!
YO HO HO HO HO!

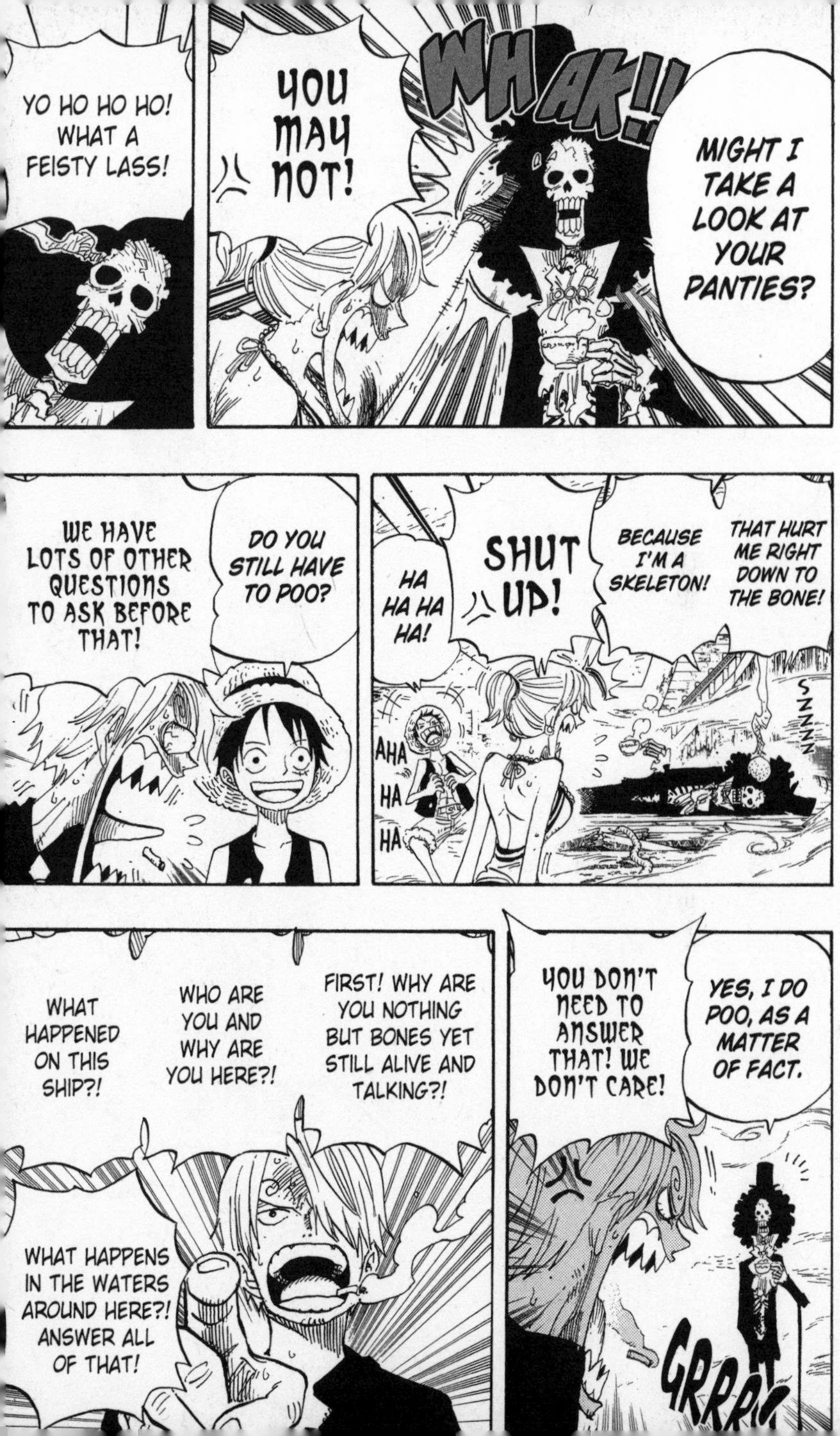
MIGHT I TAKE A LOOK AT YOUR PANTIES?
WHAK!!
YOU MAY NOT!
YO HO HO HO! WHAT A FEISTY LASS!
THAT HURT ME RIGHT DOWN TO THE BONE!
BECAUSE I'M A SKELETON!
SHUT UP!
HA HA HA HA!
SZZZZ
AHA HA HA
DO YOU STILL HAVE TO POO?
WE HAVE LOTS OF OTHER QUESTIONS TO ASK BEFORE THAT!
YES, I DO POO, AS A MATTER OF FACT.
YOU DON'T NEED TO ANSWER THAT! WE DON'T CARE!
GRRR
FIRST! WHY ARE YOU NOTHING BUT BONES YET STILL ALIVE AND TALKING?!
WHO ARE YOU AND WHY ARE YOU HERE?!
WHAT HAPPENED ON THIS SHIP?!
WHAT HAPPENS IN THE WATERS AROUND HERE?! ANSWER ALL OF THAT!

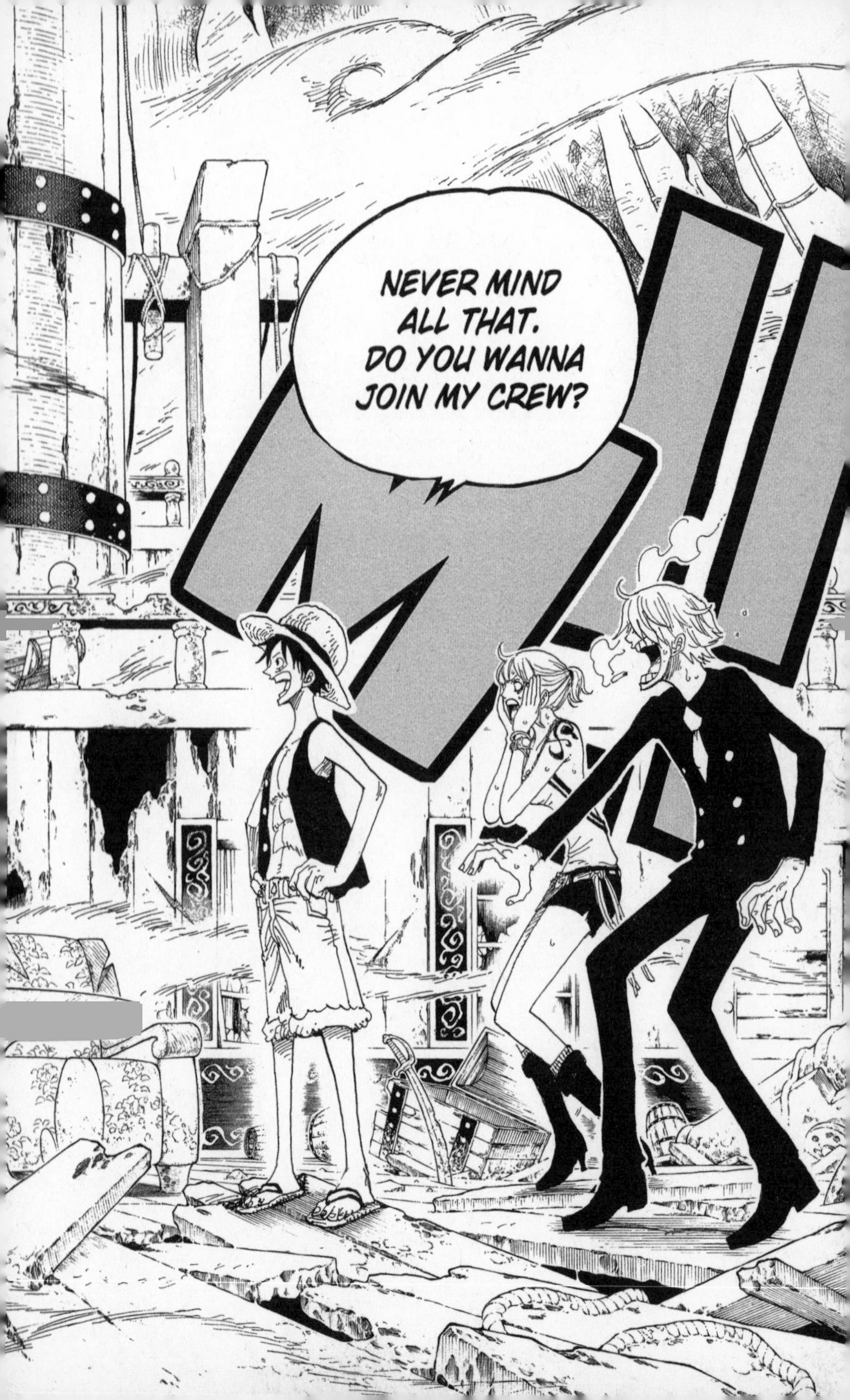
NEVER MIND ALL THAT. DO YOU WANNA JOIN MY CREW?

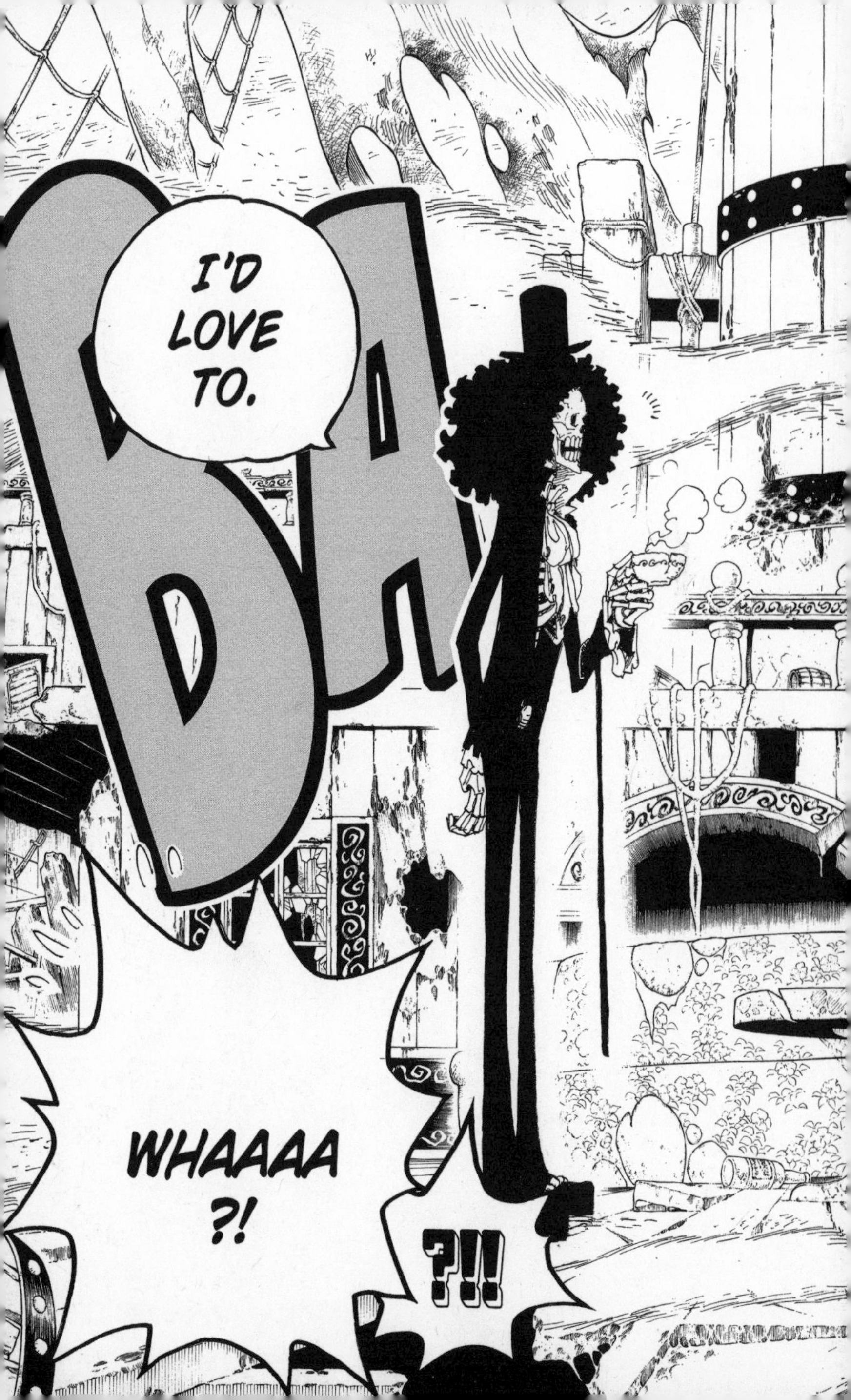
I'D LOVE TO.
BA
WHAAAA ?!
?!!

F3

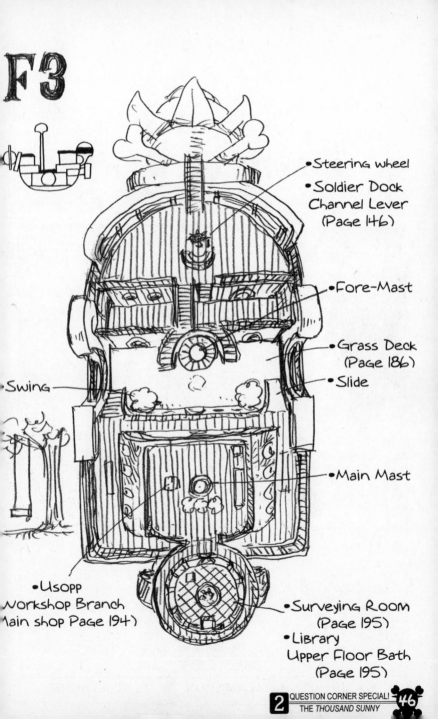

- Steering wheel
- Soldier Dock Channel Lever (Page 146)
- Fore-Mast
- Grass Deck (Page 186)
- Slide
- Swing
- Main Mast
- Usopp Workshop Branch Main shop Page 194)
- Surveying Room (Page 195)
- Library Upper Floor Bath (Page 195)

Chapter 443:
THRILLER BARK

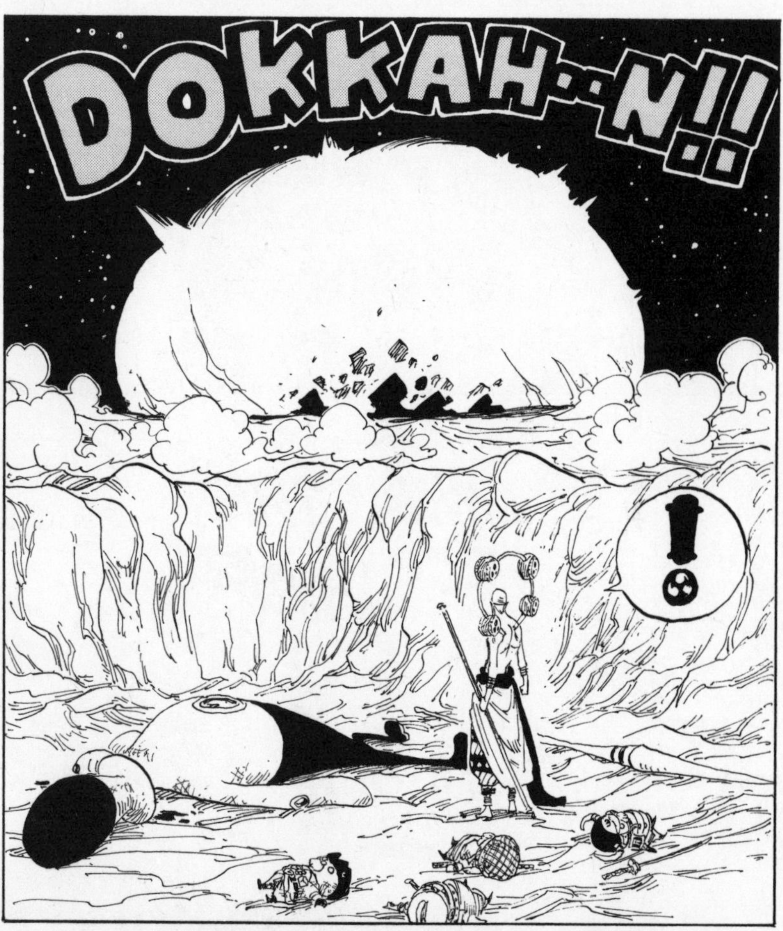
DOKKAH...N!!
!

ENERU'S GREAT SPACE MISSION, VOL. 13: "EXPLOSION"

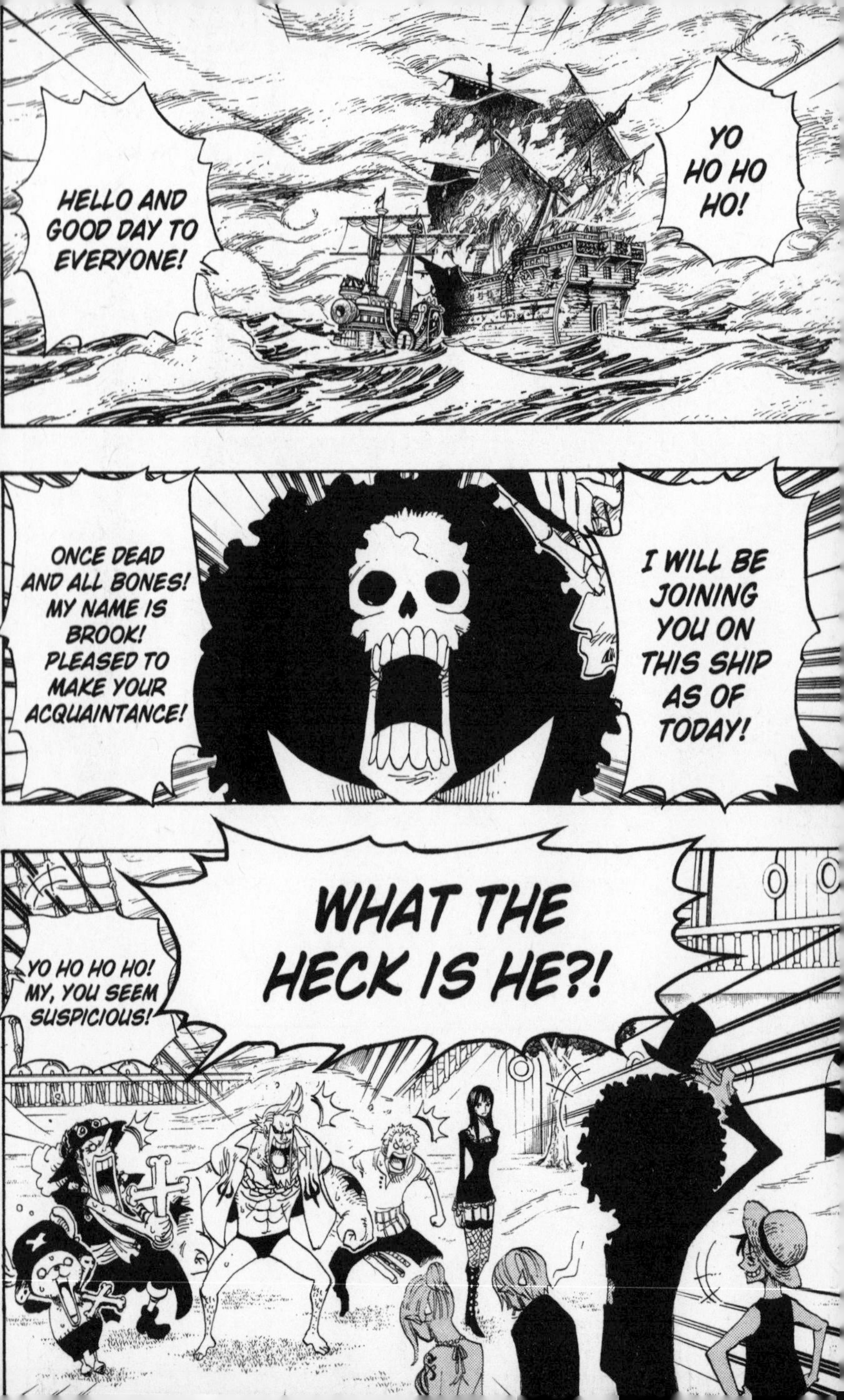
YO HO HO HO!
HELLO AND GOOD DAY TO EVERYONE!
I WILL BE JOINING YOU ON THIS SHIP AS OF TODAY!
ONCE DEAD AND ALL BONES! MY NAME IS BROOK! PLEASED TO MAKE YOUR ACQUAINTANCE!
WHAT THE HECK IS HE?!
YO HO HO HO! MY, YOU SEEM SUSPICIOUS!

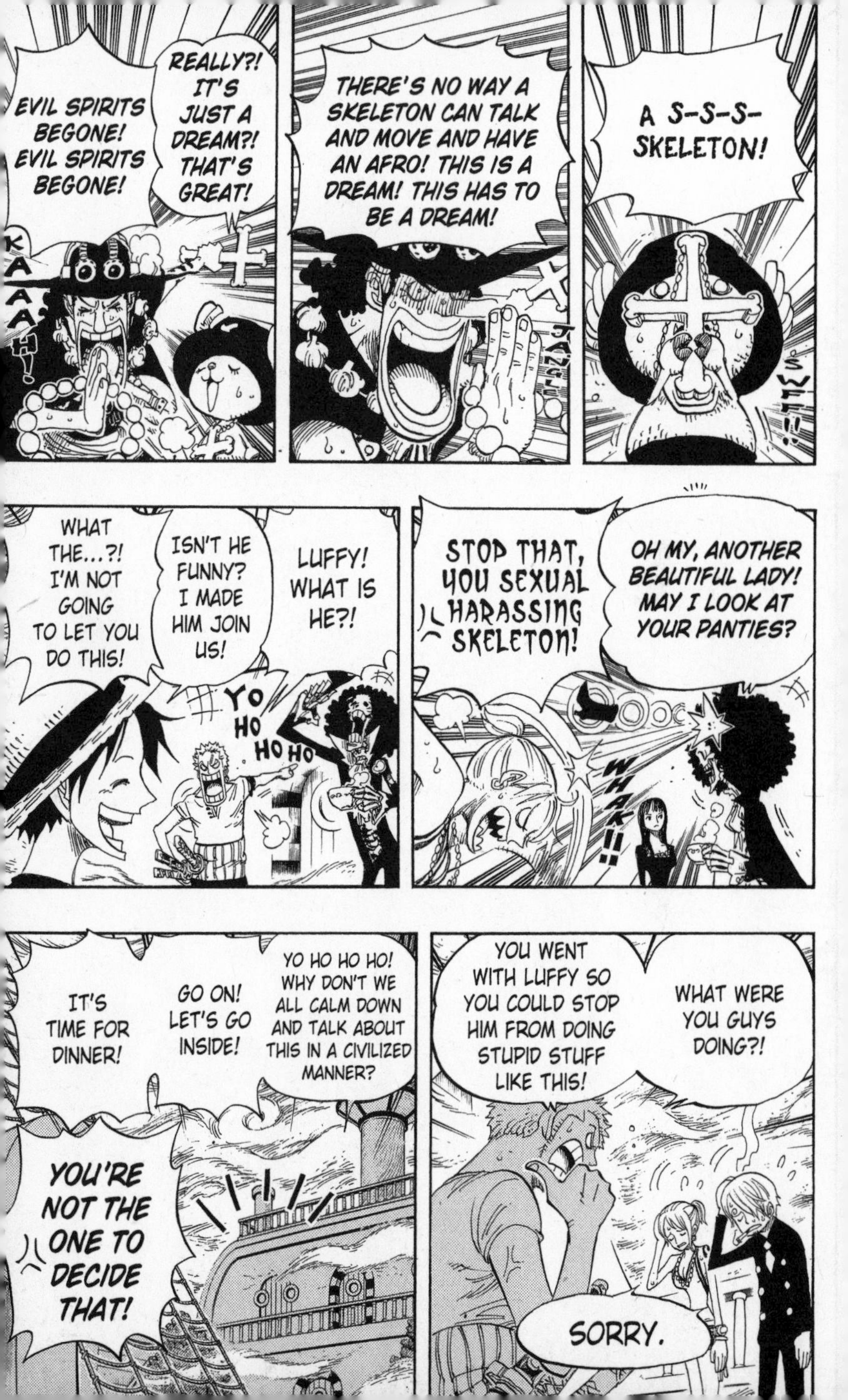
A S-S-S-SKELETON!
SWF!!
THERE'S NO WAY A SKELETON CAN TALK AND MOVE AND HAVE AN AFRO! THIS IS A DREAM! THIS HAS TO BE A DREAM!
JANGLE
REALLY?! IT'S JUST A DREAM?! THAT'S GREAT!
EVIL SPIRITS BEGONE! EVIL SPIRITS BEGONE!
KAAAAH!
OH MY, ANOTHER BEAUTIFUL LADY! MAY I LOOK AT YOUR PANTIES?
STOP THAT, YOU SEXUAL HARASSING SKELETON!
WHAK!!
LUFFY! WHAT IS HE?!
ISN'T HE FUNNY? I MADE HIM JOIN US!
WHAT THE...?! I'M NOT GOING TO LET YOU DO THIS!
YO HO HO HO
WHAT WERE YOU GUYS DOING?!
YOU WENT WITH LUFFY SO YOU COULD STOP HIM FROM DOING STUPID STUFF LIKE THIS!
SORRY.
YO HO HO HO! WHY DON'T WE ALL CALM DOWN AND TALK ABOUT THIS IN A CIVILIZED MANNER?
GO ON! LET'S GO INSIDE!
IT'S TIME FOR DINNER!
YOU'RE NOT THE ONE TO DECIDE THAT!

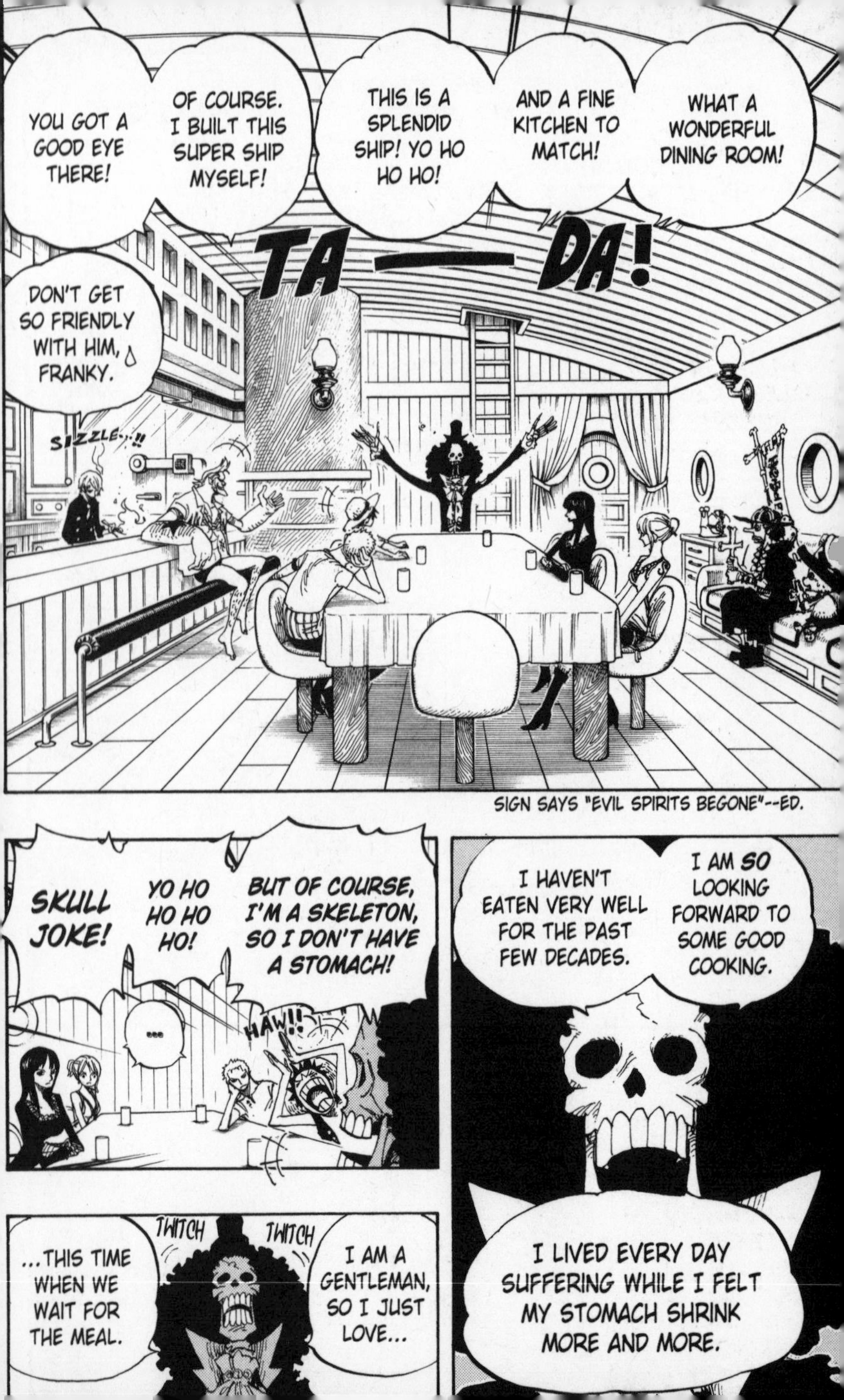
WHAT A WONDERFUL DINING ROOM!
AND A FINE KITCHEN TO MATCH!
THIS IS A SPLENDID SHIP! YO HO HO HO!
OF COURSE. I BUILT THIS SUPER SHIP MYSELF!
YOU GOT A GOOD EYE THERE!
TA—DA!
DON'T GET SO FRIENDLY WITH HIM, FRANKY.
SIZZLE...!!
SIGN SAYS "EVIL SPIRITS BEGONE"--ED.
I AM SO LOOKING FORWARD TO SOME GOOD COOKING.
I HAVEN'T EATEN VERY WELL FOR THE PAST FEW DECADES.
I LIVED EVERY DAY SUFFERING WHILE I FELT MY STOMACH SHRINK MORE AND MORE.
BUT OF COURSE, I'M A SKELETON, SO I DON'T HAVE A STOMACH!
YO HO HO HO HO!
SKULL JOKE!
HAW!!
...
I AM A GENTLEMAN, SO I JUST LOVE...
TWITCH
TWITCH
...THIS TIME WHEN WE WAIT FOR THE MEAL.

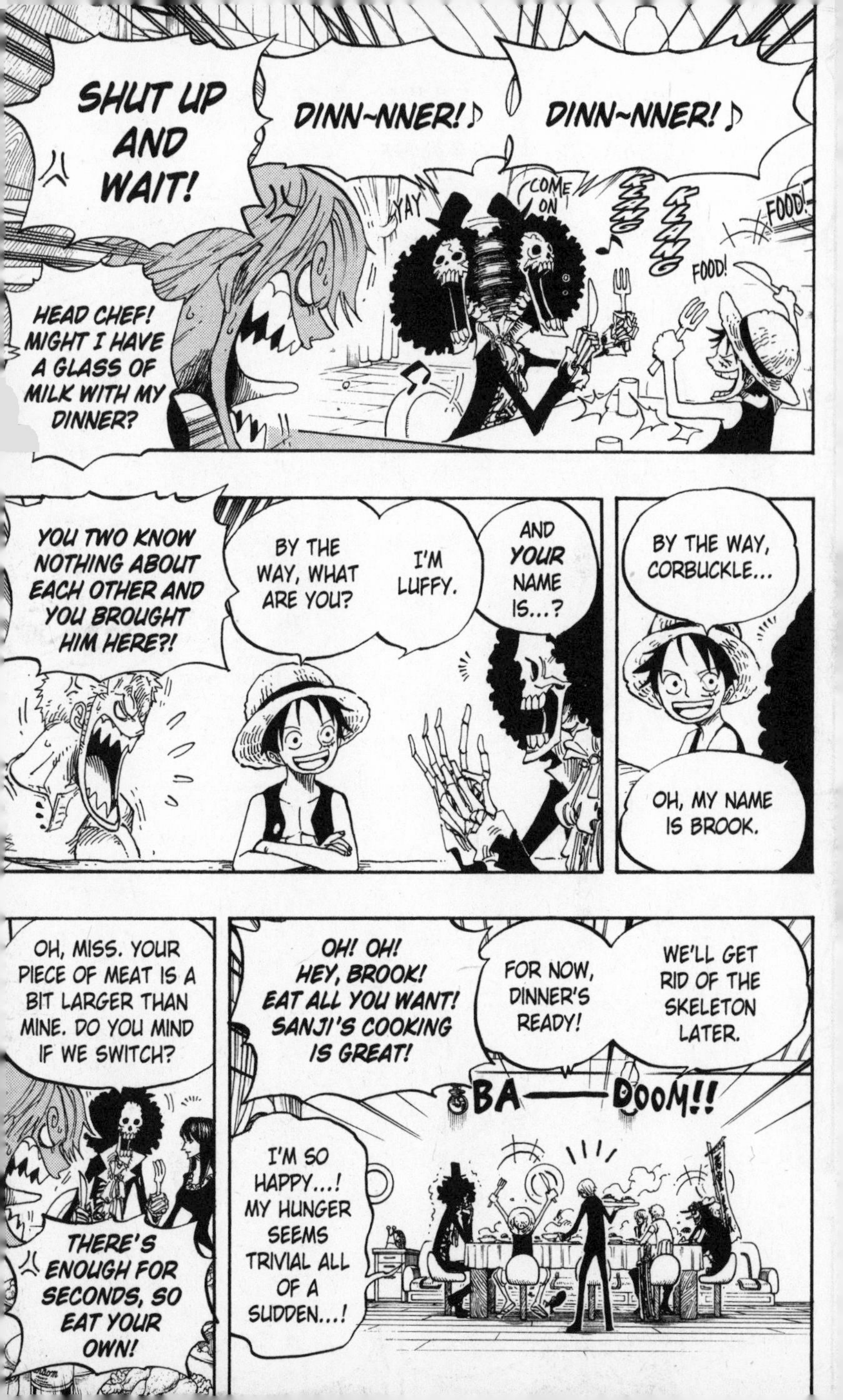
DINN~NNER!♪
DINN~NNER!♪
COME ON
KLANG
KLANG
FOOD!
FOOD!
YAY
SHUT UP AND WAIT!
HEAD CHEF! MIGHT I HAVE A GLASS OF MILK WITH MY DINNER?
BY THE WAY, CORBUCKLE...
OH, MY NAME IS BROOK.
AND YOUR NAME IS...?
I'M LUFFY.
BY THE WAY, WHAT ARE YOU?
YOU TWO KNOW NOTHING ABOUT EACH OTHER AND YOU BROUGHT HIM HERE?!
WE'LL GET RID OF THE SKELETON LATER.
FOR NOW, DINNER'S READY!
OH! OH! HEY, BROOK! EAT ALL YOU WANT! SANJI'S COOKING IS GREAT!
BA——DOOM!!
I'M SO HAPPY...! MY HUNGER SEEMS TRIVIAL ALL OF A SUDDEN...!
OH, MISS. YOUR PIECE OF MEAT IS A BIT LARGER THAN MINE. DO YOU MIND IF WE SWITCH?
THERE'S ENOUGH FOR SECONDS, SO EAT YOUR OWN!

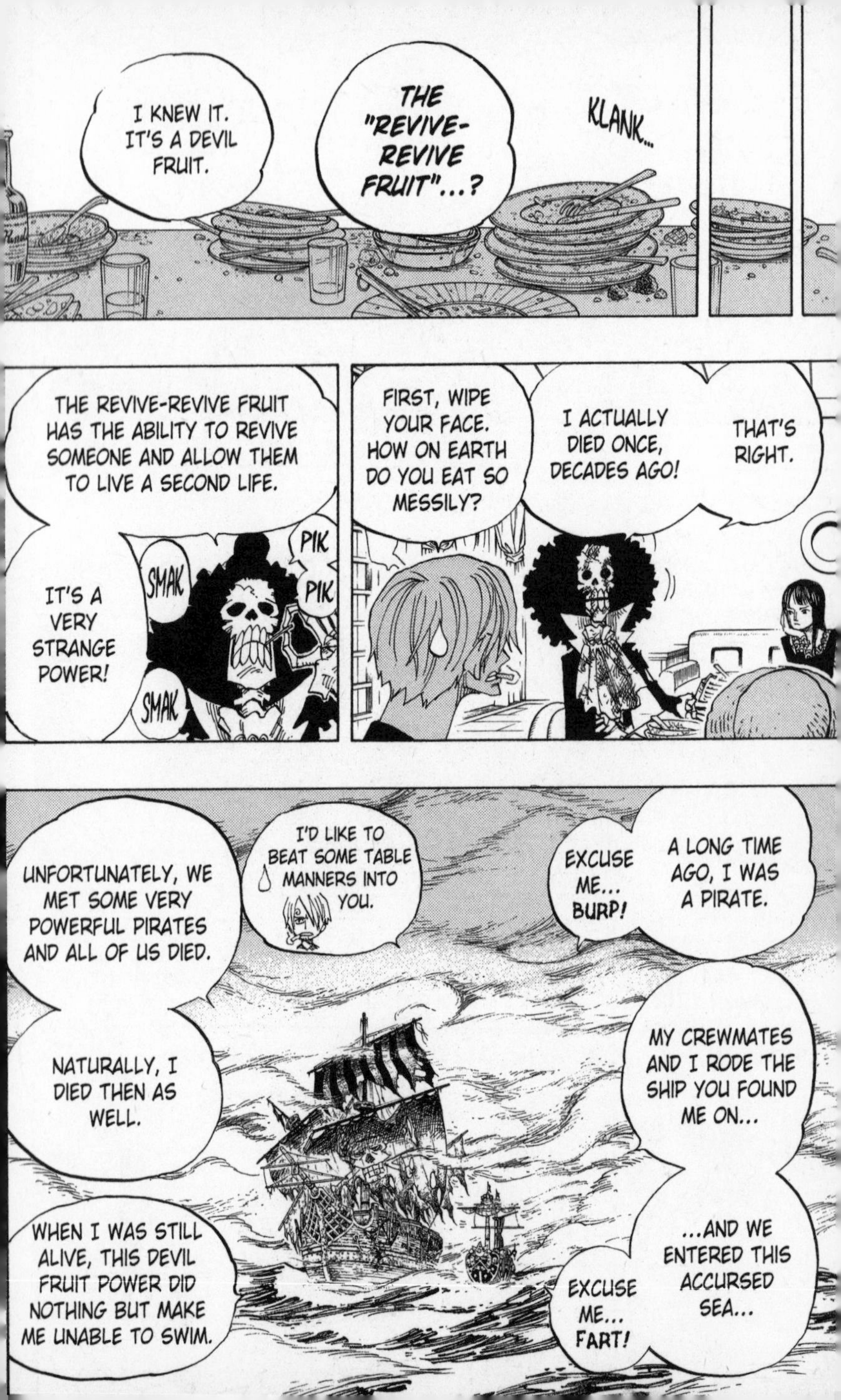
KLANK...
THE "REVIVE-REVIVE FRUIT"...?
I KNEW IT. IT'S A DEVIL FRUIT.
THAT'S RIGHT.
I ACTUALLY DIED ONCE, DECADES AGO!
FIRST, WIPE YOUR FACE. HOW ON EARTH DO YOU EAT SO MESSILY?
THE REVIVE-REVIVE FRUIT HAS THE ABILITY TO REVIVE SOMEONE AND ALLOW THEM TO LIVE A SECOND LIFE.
PIK
PIK
SMAK
IT'S A VERY STRANGE POWER!
SMAK
A LONG TIME AGO, I WAS A PIRATE.
EXCUSE ME... BURP!
I'D LIKE TO BEAT SOME TABLE MANNERS INTO YOU.
MY CREWMATES AND I RODE THE SHIP YOU FOUND ME ON...
...AND WE ENTERED THIS ACCURSED SEA...
EXCUSE ME... FART!
UNFORTUNATELY, WE MET SOME VERY POWERFUL PIRATES AND ALL OF US DIED.
NATURALLY, I DIED THEN AS WELL.
WHEN I WAS STILL ALIVE, THIS DEVIL FRUIT POWER DID NOTHING BUT MAKE ME UNABLE TO SWIM.

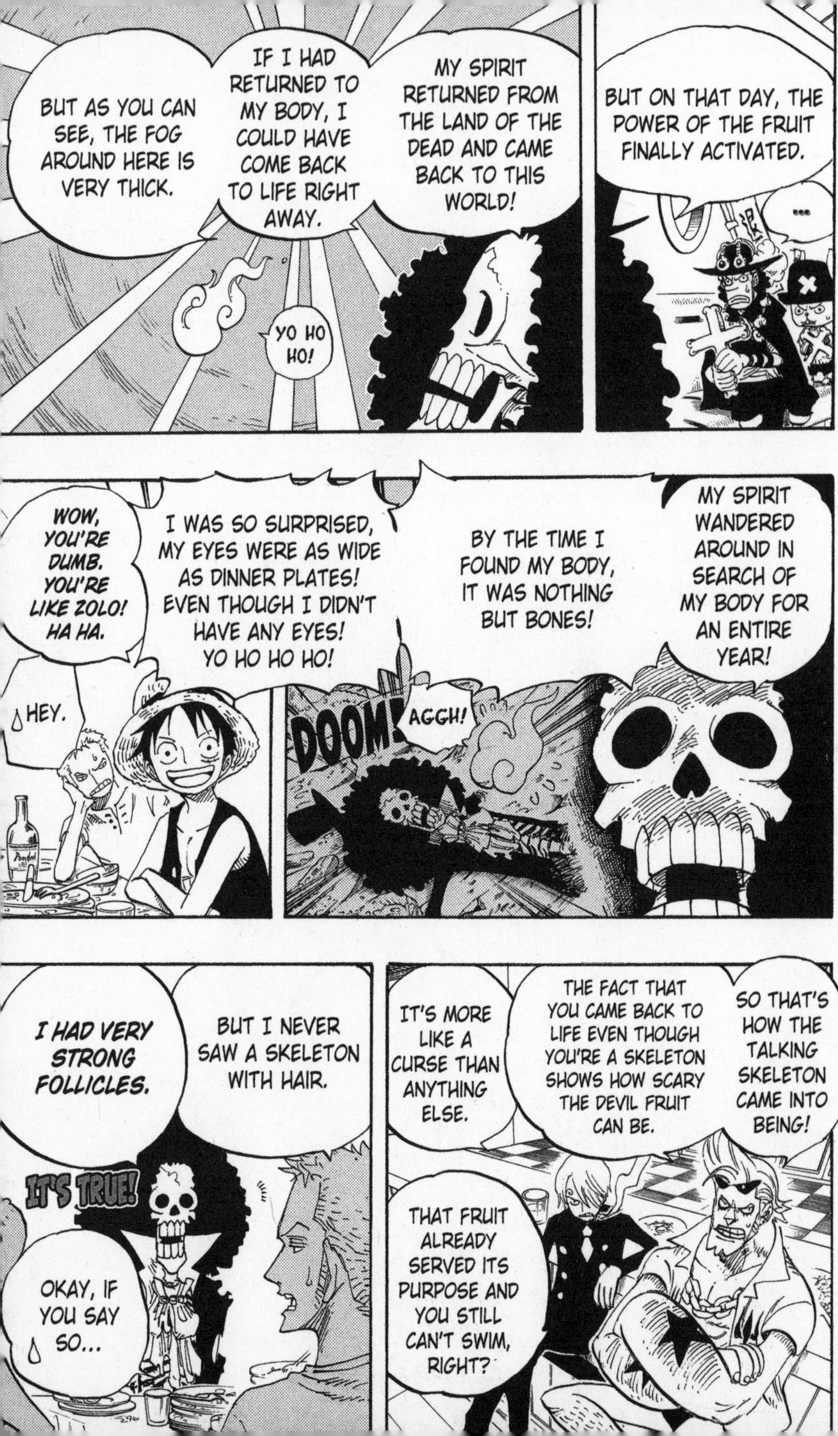
BUT ON THAT DAY, THE POWER OF THE FRUIT FINALLY ACTIVATED.
...
MY SPIRIT RETURNED FROM THE LAND OF THE DEAD AND CAME BACK TO THIS WORLD!
IF I HAD RETURNED TO MY BODY, I COULD HAVE COME BACK TO LIFE RIGHT AWAY.
BUT AS YOU CAN SEE, THE FOG AROUND HERE IS VERY THICK.
YO HO HO!
MY SPIRIT WANDERED AROUND IN SEARCH OF MY BODY FOR AN ENTIRE YEAR!
BY THE TIME I FOUND MY BODY, IT WAS NOTHING BUT BONES!
AGGH!
DOOM!
I WAS SO SURPRISED, MY EYES WERE AS WIDE AS DINNER PLATES! EVEN THOUGH I DIDN'T HAVE ANY EYES! YO HO HO HO!
WOW, YOU'RE DUMB. YOU'RE LIKE ZOLO! HA HA.
HEY.
SO THAT'S HOW THE TALKING SKELETON CAME INTO BEING!
THE FACT THAT YOU CAME BACK TO LIFE EVEN THOUGH YOU'RE A SKELETON SHOWS HOW SCARY THE DEVIL FRUIT CAN BE.
IT'S MORE LIKE A CURSE THAN ANYTHING ELSE.
THAT FRUIT ALREADY SERVED ITS PURPOSE AND YOU STILL CAN'T SWIM, RIGHT?
BUT I NEVER SAW A SKELETON WITH HAIR.
I HAD VERY STRONG FOLLICLES.
IT'S TRUE!
OKAY, IF YOU SAY SO...

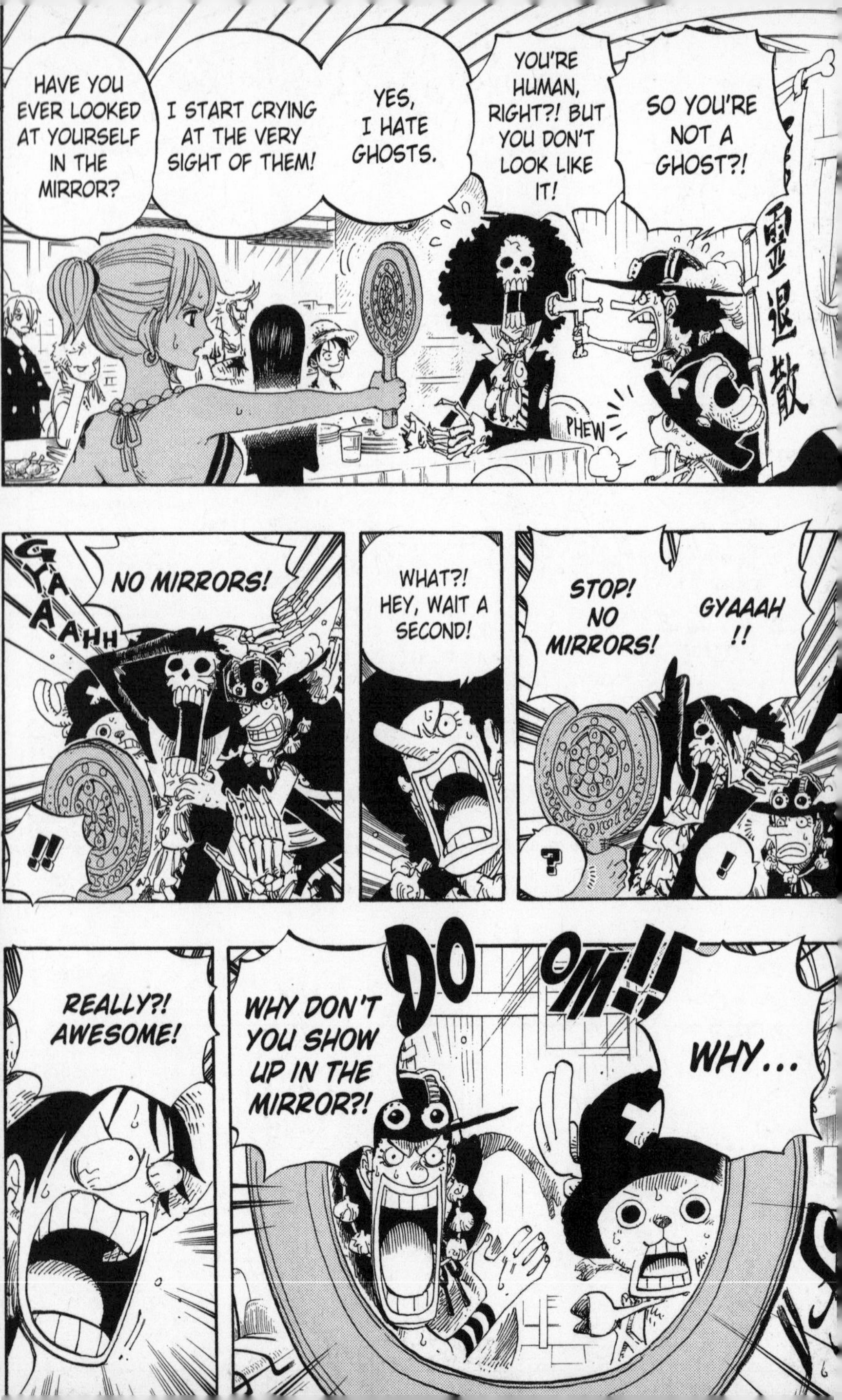
SO YOU'RE NOT A GHOST?!
霊退散
YOU'RE HUMAN, RIGHT?! BUT YOU DON'T LOOK LIKE IT!
YES, I HATE GHOSTS.
I START CRYING AT THE VERY SIGHT OF THEM!
HAVE YOU EVER LOOKED AT YOURSELF IN THE MIRROR?
PHEW
GYAAAH !!
STOP! NO MIRRORS!
!
?
WHAT?! HEY, WAIT A SECOND!
NO MIRRORS!
GYAAAHH
!!
WHY...
DOOM!!
WHY DON'T YOU SHOW UP IN THE MIRROR?!
REALLY?! AWESOME!

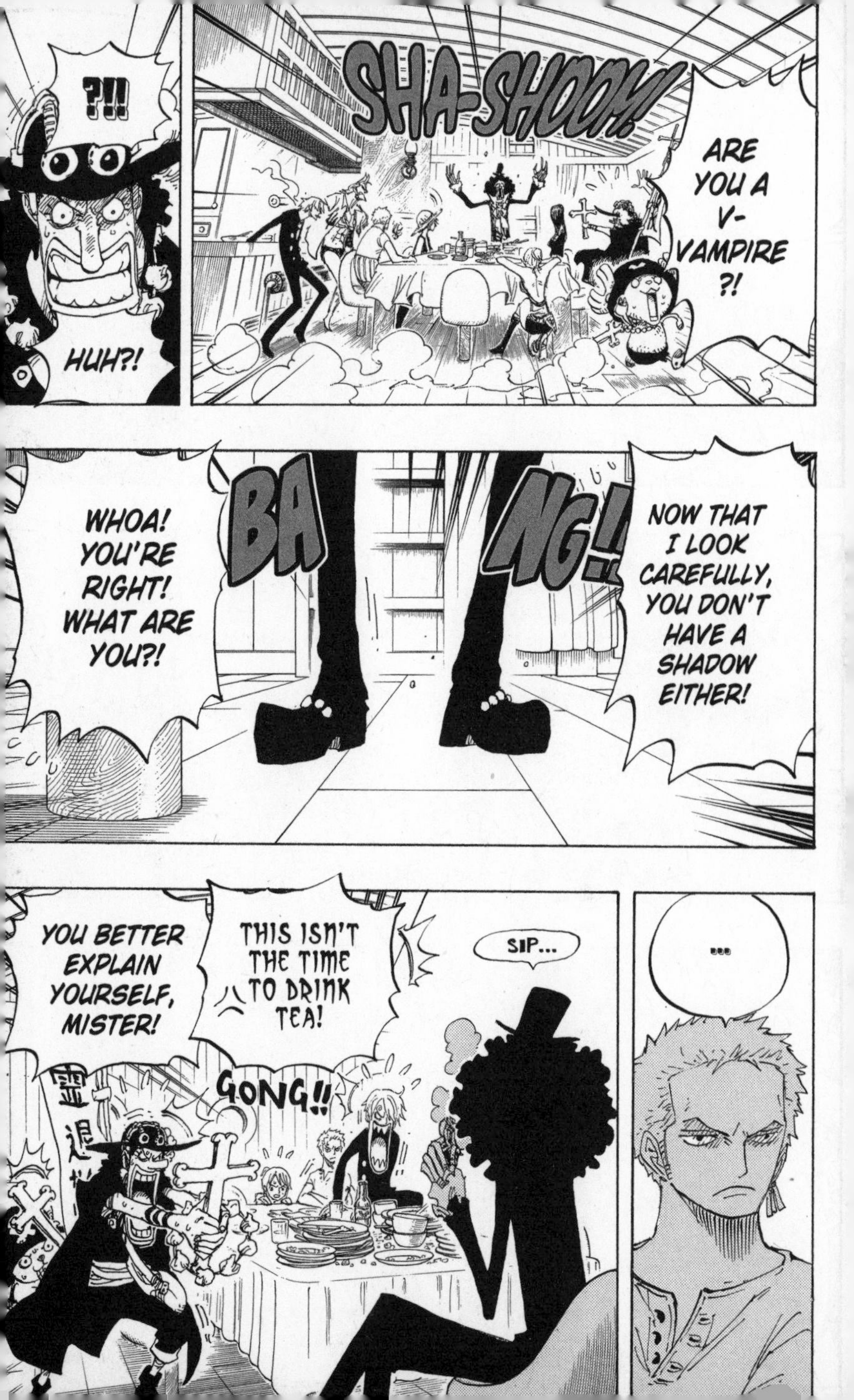
SHA-SHOOM!
ARE YOU A V-VAMPIRE?!
?!!
HUH?!
NOW THAT I LOOK CAREFULLY, YOU DON'T HAVE A SHADOW EITHER!
BANG!!
WHOA! YOU'RE RIGHT! WHAT ARE YOU?!
...
SIP...
THIS ISN'T THE TIME TO DRINK TEA!
YOU BETTER EXPLAIN YOURSELF, MISTER!
GONG!!

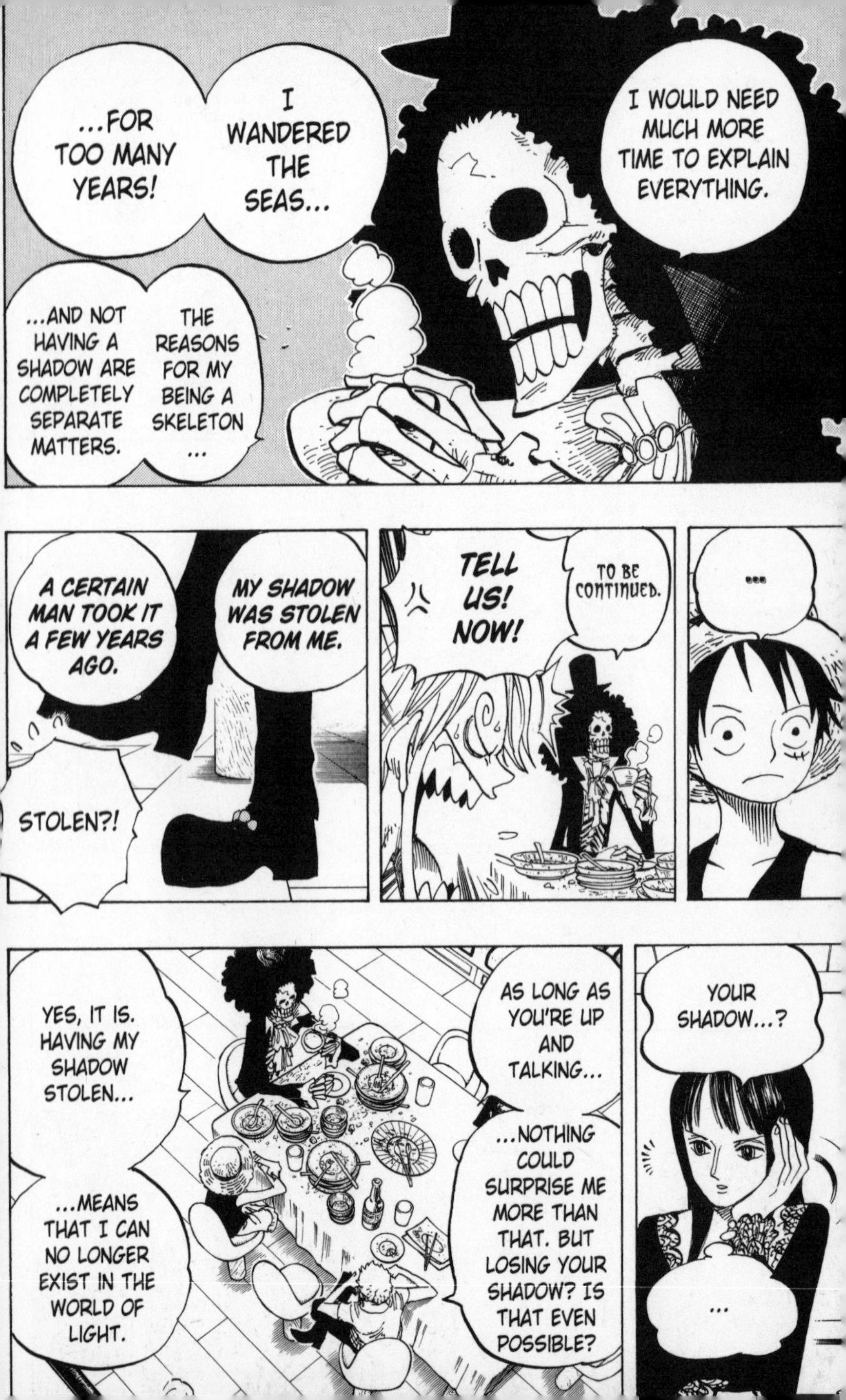

I WOULD NEED MUCH MORE TIME TO EXPLAIN EVERYTHING.
I WANDERED THE SEAS...
...FOR TOO MANY YEARS!
THE REASONS FOR MY BEING A SKELETON...
...AND NOT HAVING A SHADOW ARE COMPLETELY SEPARATE MATTERS.
...
TO BE CONTINUED.
TELL US! NOW!
MY SHADOW WAS STOLEN FROM ME.
A CERTAIN MAN TOOK IT A FEW YEARS AGO.
STOLEN?!
YOUR SHADOW...?
...
AS LONG AS YOU'RE UP AND TALKING...
...NOTHING COULD SURPRISE ME MORE THAN THAT. BUT LOSING YOUR SHADOW? IS THAT EVEN POSSIBLE?
YES, IT IS. HAVING MY SHADOW STOLEN...
...MEANS THAT I CAN NO LONGER EXIST IN THE WORLD OF LIGHT.

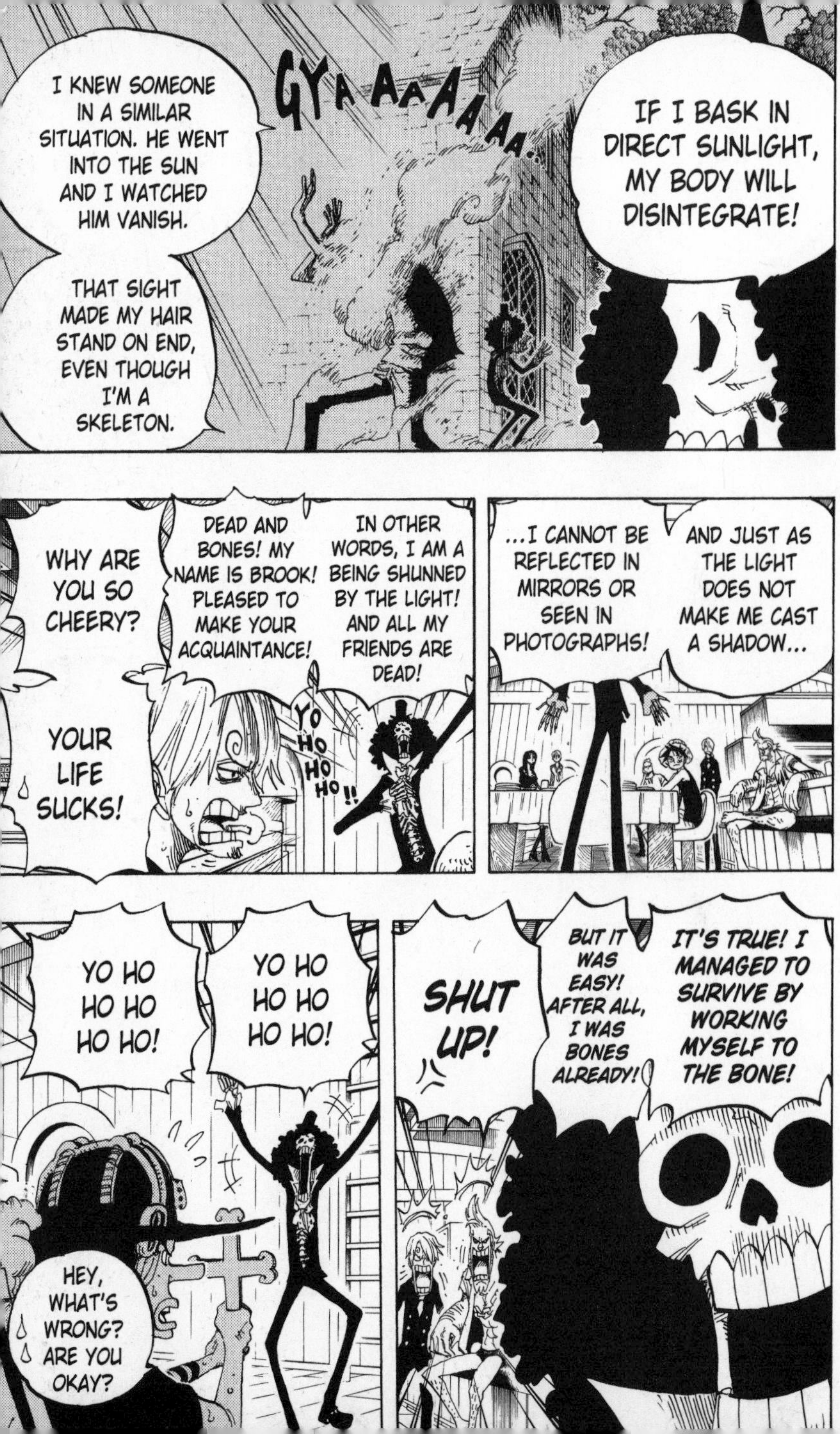
IF I BASK IN DIRECT SUNLIGHT, MY BODY WILL DISINTEGRATE!
GYAAAAAAA..
I KNEW SOMEONE IN A SIMILAR SITUATION. HE WENT INTO THE SUN AND I WATCHED HIM VANISH.
THAT SIGHT MADE MY HAIR STAND ON END, EVEN THOUGH I'M A SKELETON.
AND JUST AS THE LIGHT DOES NOT MAKE ME CAST A SHADOW...
...I CANNOT BE REFLECTED IN MIRRORS OR SEEN IN PHOTOGRAPHS!
IN OTHER WORDS, I AM A BEING SHUNNED BY THE LIGHT! AND ALL MY FRIENDS ARE DEAD!
DEAD AND BONES! MY NAME IS BROOK! PLEASED TO MAKE YOUR ACQUAINTANCE!
YO HO HO HO!!
WHY ARE YOU SO CHEERY?
YOUR LIFE SUCKS!
IT'S TRUE! I MANAGED TO SURVIVE BY WORKING MYSELF TO THE BONE!
BUT IT WAS EASY! AFTER ALL, I WAS BONES ALREADY!
SHUT UP!
YO HO HO HO HO HO!
YO HO HO HO HO HO!
HEY, WHAT'S WRONG? ARE YOU OKAY?

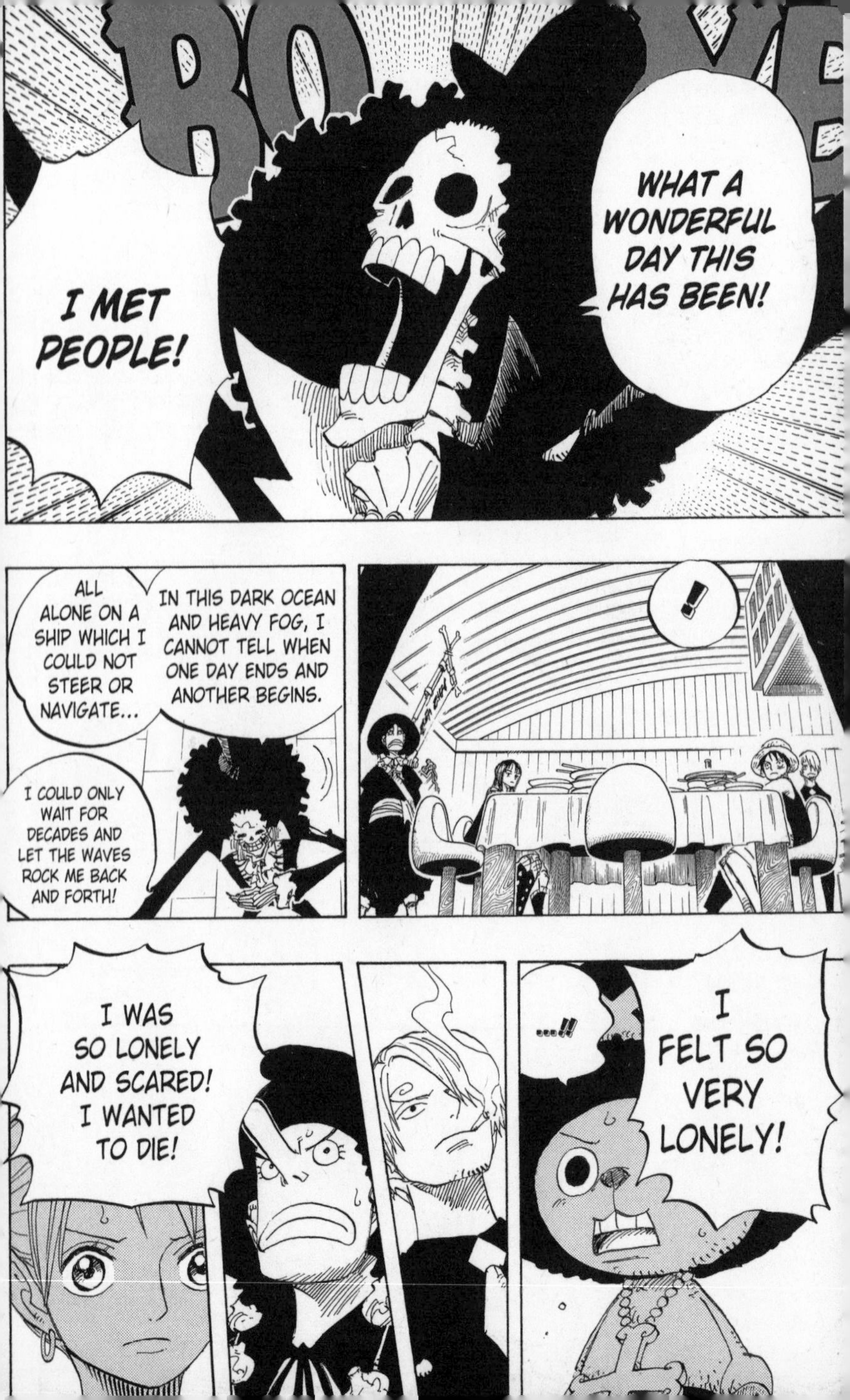
WHAT A WONDERFUL DAY THIS HAS BEEN!
I MET PEOPLE!
!
IN THIS DARK OCEAN AND HEAVY FOG, I CANNOT TELL WHEN ONE DAY ENDS AND ANOTHER BEGINS.
ALL ALONE ON A SHIP WHICH I COULD NOT STEER OR NAVIGATE...
I COULD ONLY WAIT FOR DECADES AND LET THE WAVES ROCK ME BACK AND FORTH!
I FELT SO VERY LONELY!
...!!
I WAS SO LONELY AND SCARED! I WANTED TO DIE!

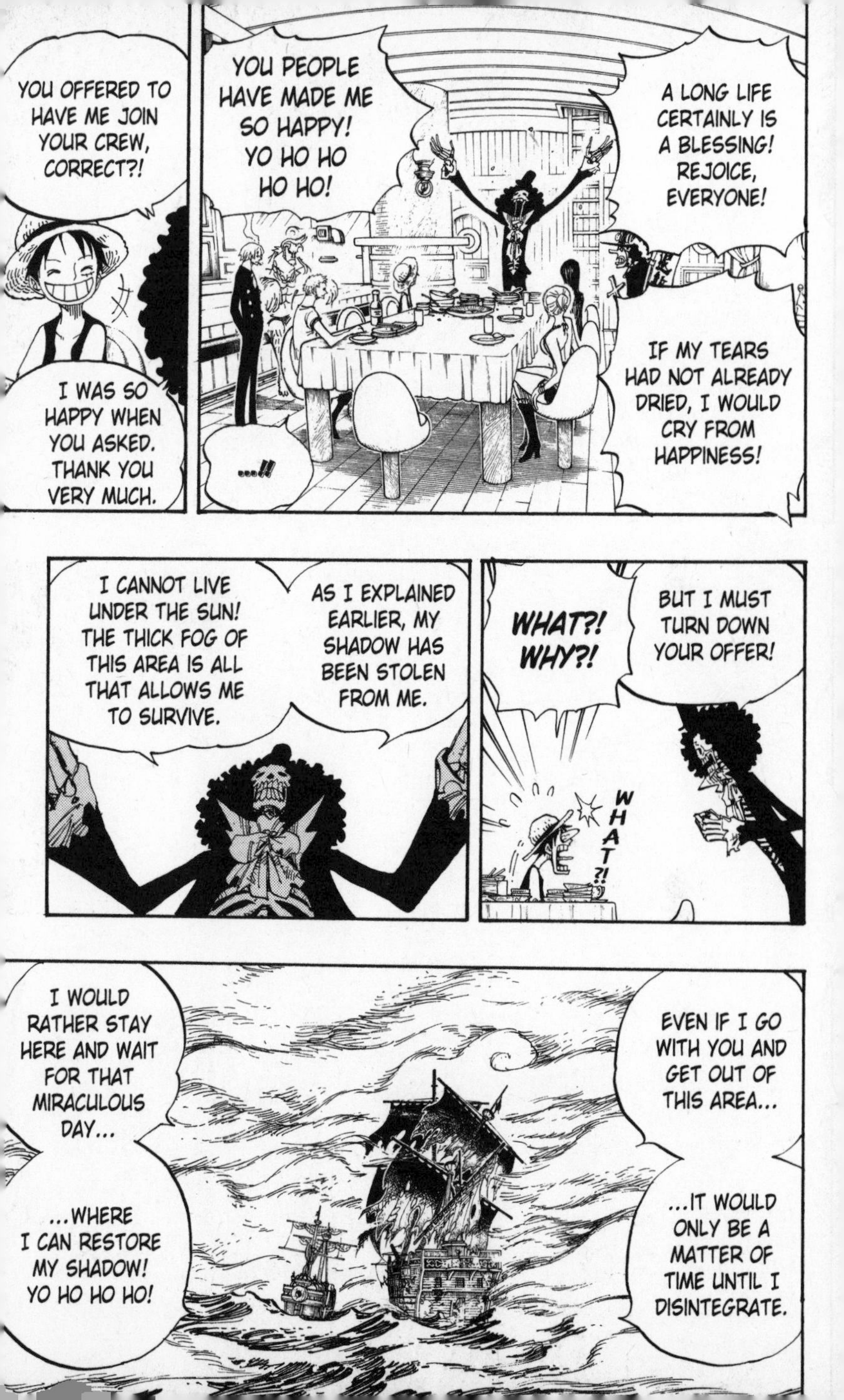
A LONG LIFE CERTAINLY IS A BLESSING! REJOICE, EVERYONE!
YOU PEOPLE HAVE MADE ME SO HAPPY! YO HO HO HO HO!
IF MY TEARS HAD NOT ALREADY DRIED, I WOULD CRY FROM HAPPINESS!
...!!
YOU OFFERED TO HAVE ME JOIN YOUR CREW, CORRECT?!
I WAS SO HAPPY WHEN YOU ASKED. THANK YOU VERY MUCH.
BUT I MUST TURN DOWN YOUR OFFER!
WHAT?! WHY?!
WHAT?!
AS I EXPLAINED EARLIER, MY SHADOW HAS BEEN STOLEN FROM ME.
I CANNOT LIVE UNDER THE SUN! THE THICK FOG OF THIS AREA IS ALL THAT ALLOWS ME TO SURVIVE.
EVEN IF I GO WITH YOU AND GET OUT OF THIS AREA...
...IT WOULD ONLY BE A MATTER OF TIME UNTIL I DISINTEGRATE.
I WOULD RATHER STAY HERE AND WAIT FOR THAT MIRACULOUS DAY...
...WHERE I CAN RESTORE MY SHADOW! YO HO HO HO!

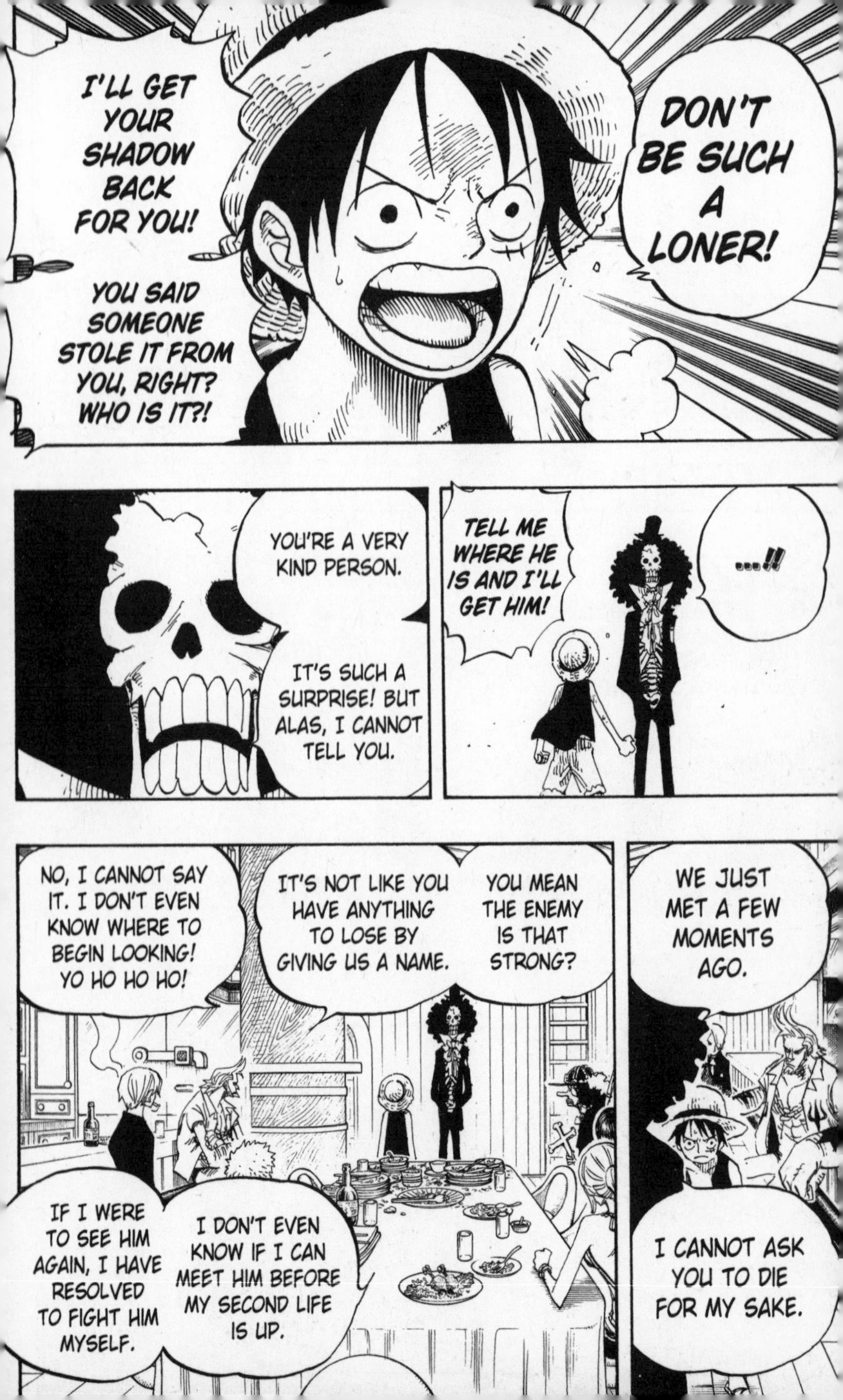
DON'T BE SUCH A LONER!
I'LL GET YOUR SHADOW BACK FOR YOU!
YOU SAID SOMEONE STOLE IT FROM YOU, RIGHT? WHO IS IT?!
...!!
TELL ME WHERE HE IS AND I'LL GET HIM!
YOU'RE A VERY KIND PERSON.
IT'S SUCH A SURPRISE! BUT ALAS, I CANNOT TELL YOU.
WE JUST MET A FEW MOMENTS AGO.
I CANNOT ASK YOU TO DIE FOR MY SAKE.
YOU MEAN THE ENEMY IS THAT STRONG?
IT'S NOT LIKE YOU HAVE ANYTHING TO LOSE BY GIVING US A NAME.
NO, I CANNOT SAY IT. I DON'T EVEN KNOW WHERE TO BEGIN LOOKING! YO HO HO HO!
I DON'T EVEN KNOW IF I CAN MEET HIM BEFORE MY SECOND LIFE IS UP.
IF I WERE TO SEE HIM AGAIN, I HAVE RESOLVED TO FIGHT HIM MYSELF.

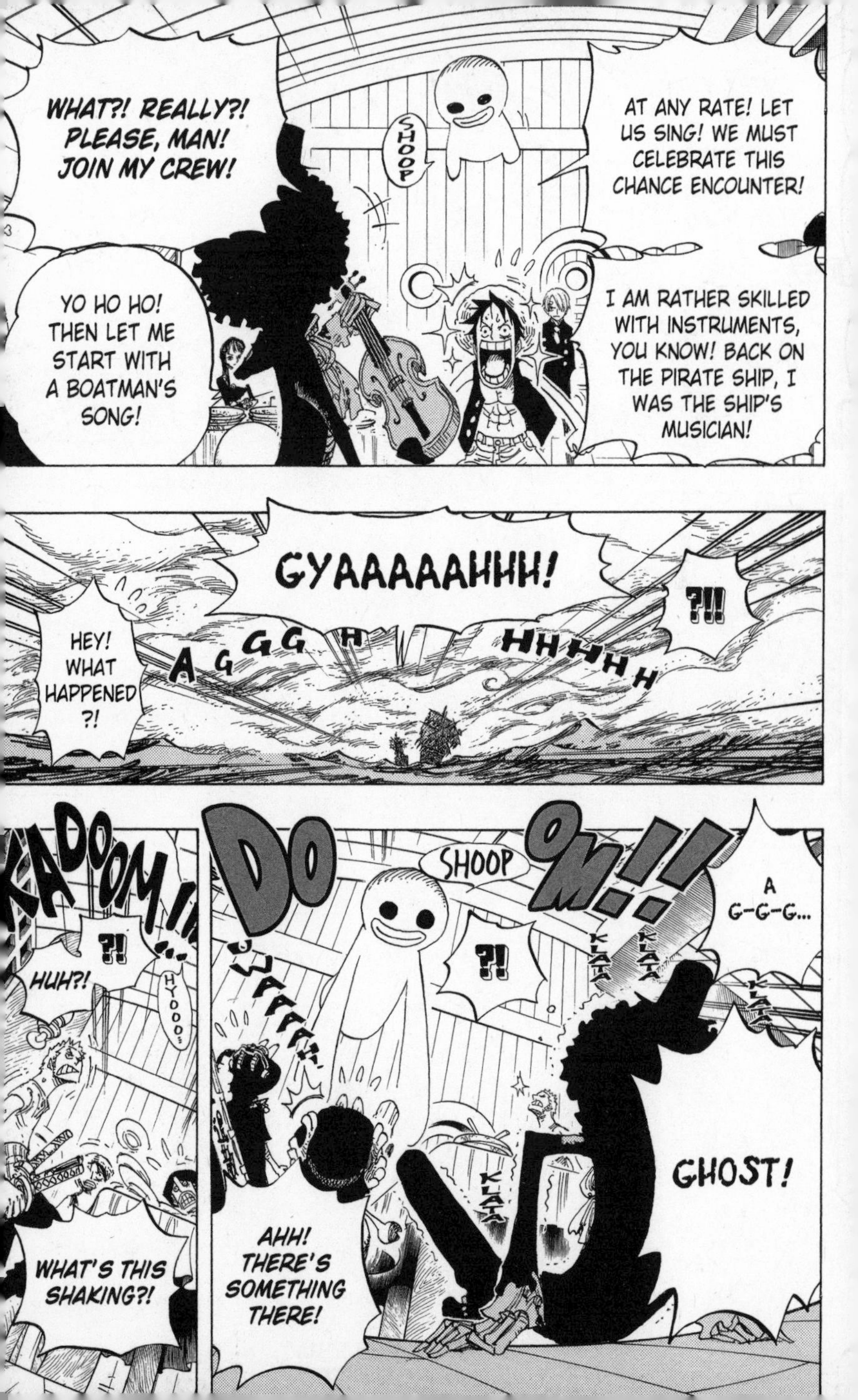
AT ANY RATE! LET US SING! WE MUST CELEBRATE THIS CHANCE ENCOUNTER!
SHOOP
I AM RATHER SKILLED WITH INSTRUMENTS, YOU KNOW! BACK ON THE PIRATE SHIP, I WAS THE SHIP'S MUSICIAN!
WHAT?! REALLY?! PLEASE, MAN! JOIN MY CREW!
YO HO HO! THEN LET ME START WITH A BOATMAN'S SONG!
GYAAAAAAHHH!
?!!
AGGGH HHHHHH
HEY! WHAT HAPPENED ?!
DOOM!!
SHOOP
A G-G-G...
?!
KLATA KLATA KLATA
GHOST!
KLATA
AHH! THERE'S SOMETHING THERE!
KADOOM!!
?!
HUH?!
HYOOOO
WHAT'S THIS SHAKING?!

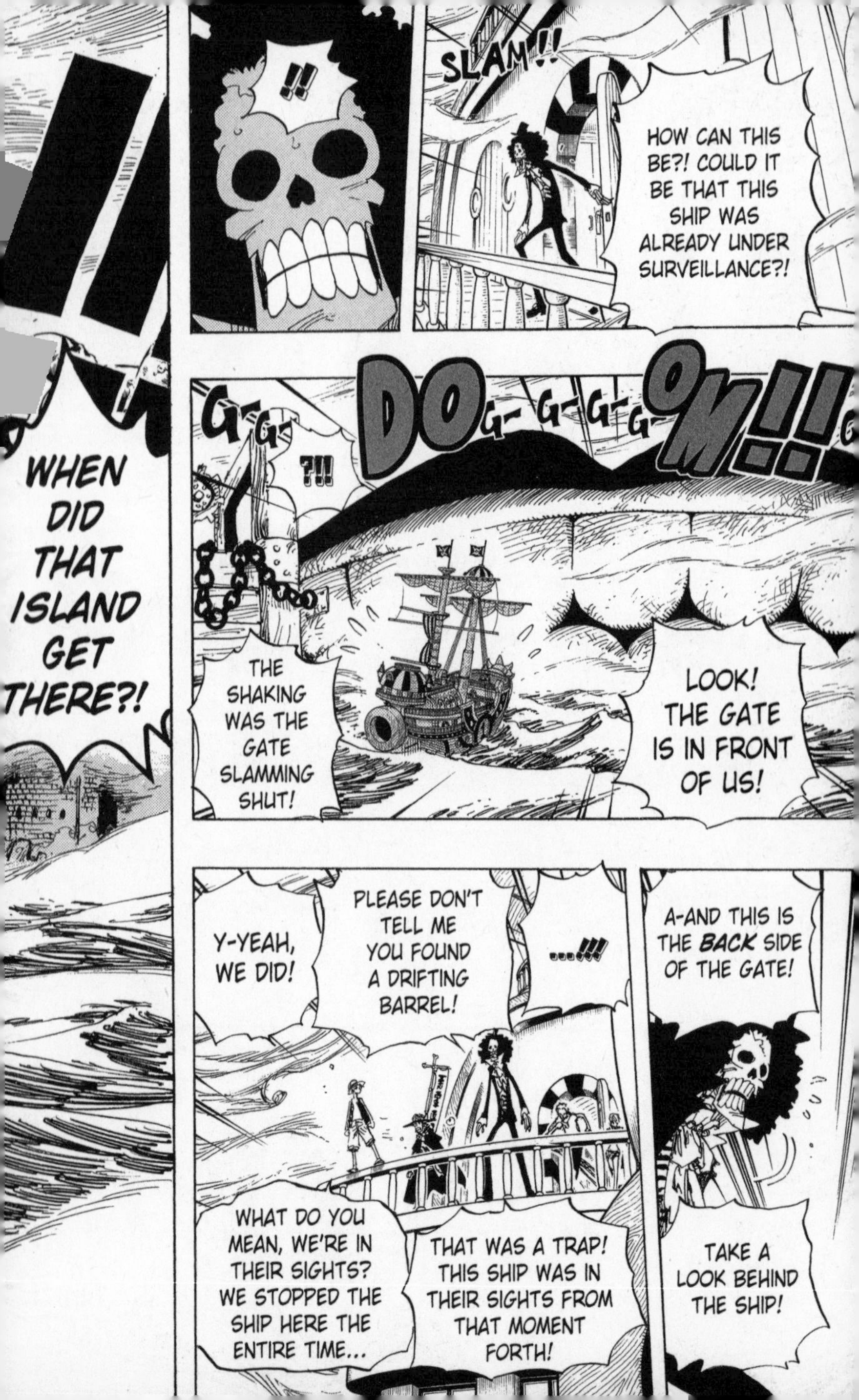
SLAM!!
HOW CAN THIS BE?! COULD IT BE THAT THIS SHIP WAS ALREADY UNDER SURVEILLANCE?!
!!
DOGGGGGOM!!!
?!!
LOOK! THE GATE IS IN FRONT OF US!
THE SHAKING WAS THE GATE SLAMMING SHUT!
A-AND THIS IS THE BACK SIDE OF THE GATE!
TAKE A LOOK BEHIND THE SHIP!
...!!!
PLEASE DON'T TELL ME YOU FOUND A DRIFTING BARREL!
Y-YEAH, WE DID!
THAT WAS A TRAP! THIS SHIP WAS IN THEIR SIGHTS FROM THAT MOMENT FORTH!
WHAT DO YOU MEAN, WE'RE IN THEIR SIGHTS? WE STOPPED THE SHIP HERE THE ENTIRE TIME...
WHEN DID THAT ISLAND GET THERE?!

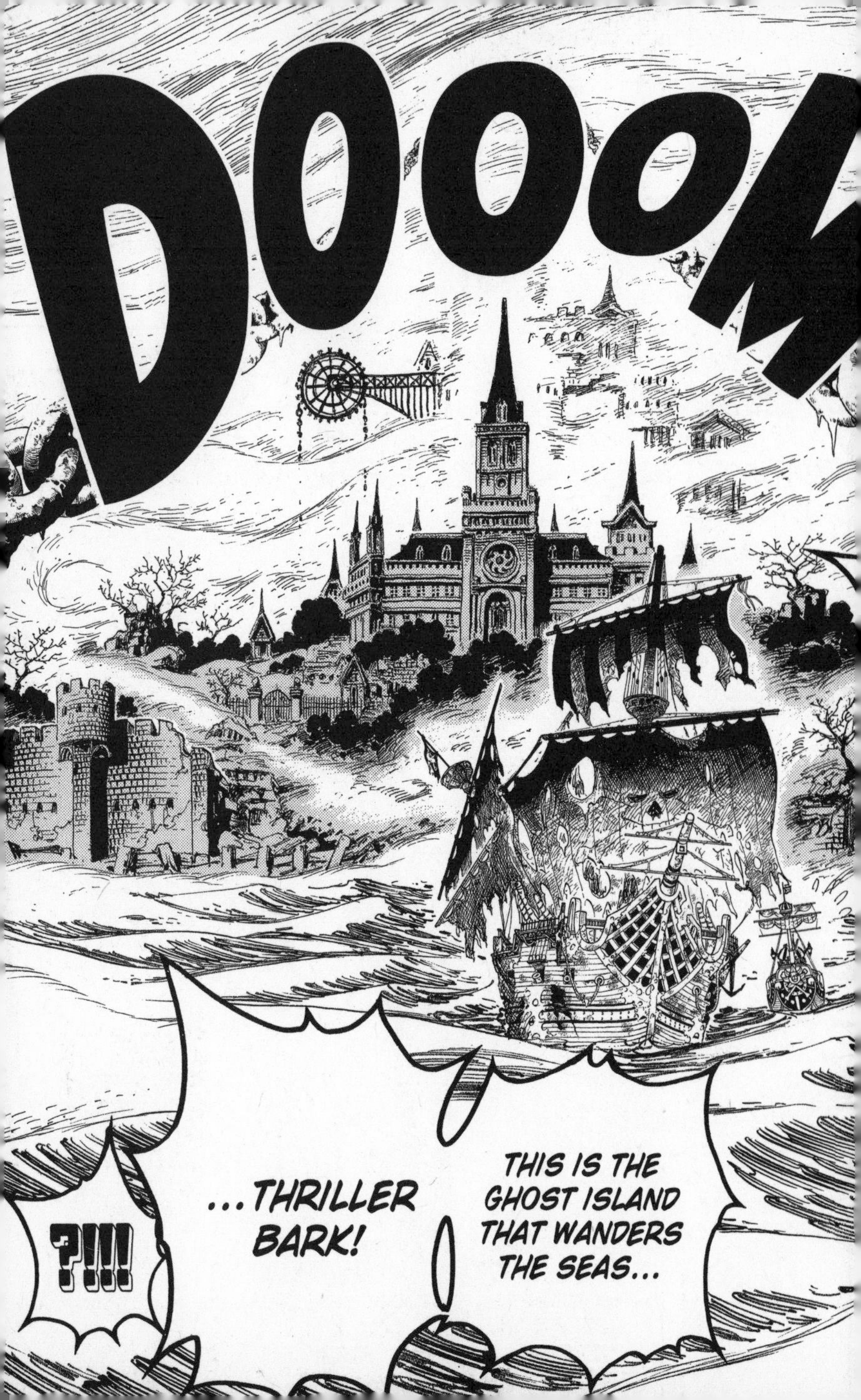
DOOO
THIS IS THE GHOST ISLAND THAT WANDERS THE SEAS...
...THRILLER BARK!
?!!!

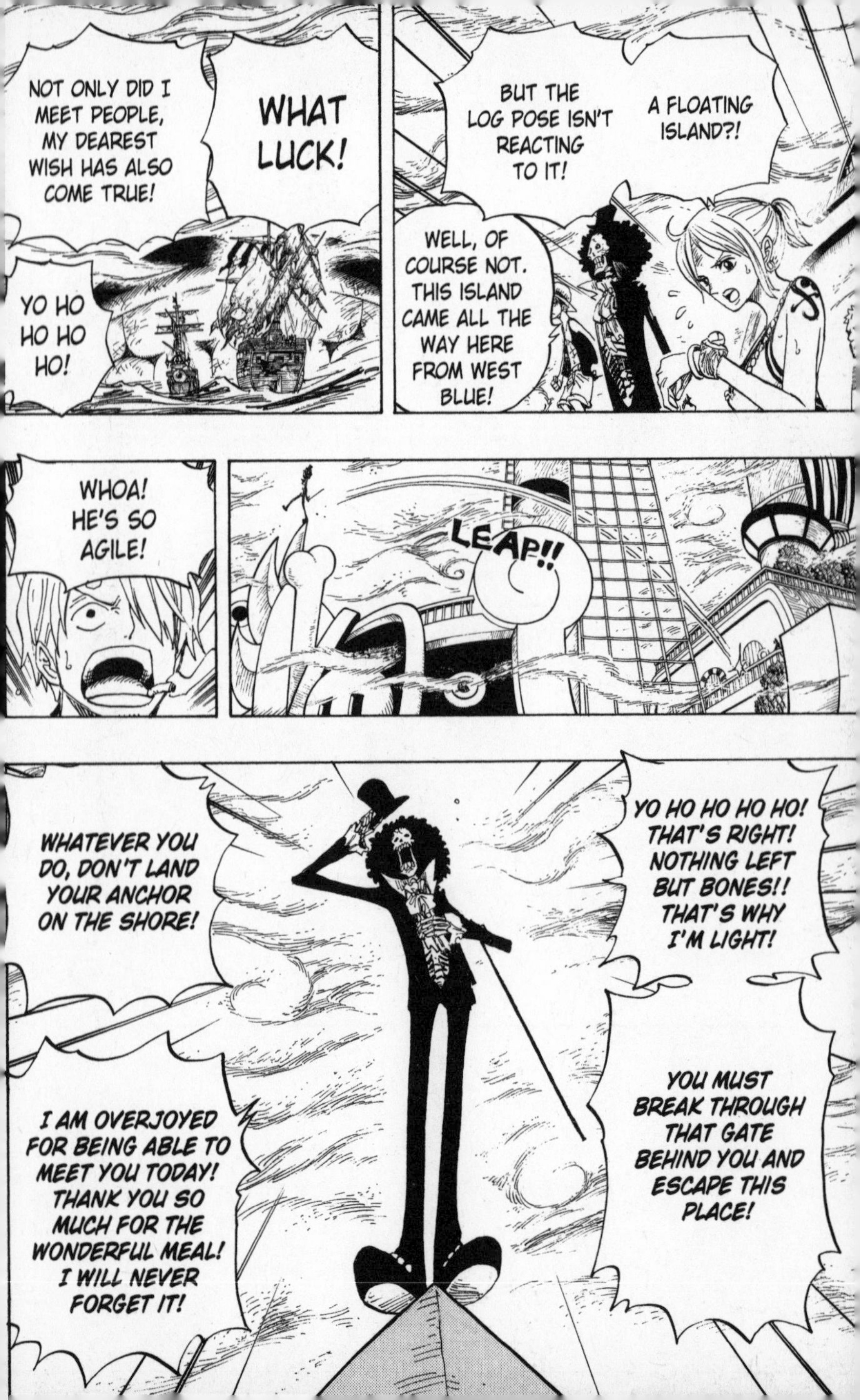
A FLOATING ISLAND?!
BUT THE LOG POSE ISN'T REACTING TO IT!
WELL, OF COURSE NOT. THIS ISLAND CAME ALL THE WAY HERE FROM WEST BLUE!
WHAT LUCK!
NOT ONLY DID I MEET PEOPLE, MY DEAREST WISH HAS ALSO COME TRUE!
YO HO HO HO HO!
LEAP!!
WHOA! HE'S SO AGILE!
YO HO HO HO HO! THAT'S RIGHT! NOTHING LEFT BUT BONES!! THAT'S WHY I'M LIGHT!
WHATEVER YOU DO, DON'T LAND YOUR ANCHOR ON THE SHORE!
YOU MUST BREAK THROUGH THAT GATE BEHIND YOU AND ESCAPE THIS PLACE!
I AM OVERJOYED FOR BEING ABLE TO MEET YOU TODAY! THANK YOU SO MUCH FOR THE WONDERFUL MEAL! I WILL NEVER FORGET IT!

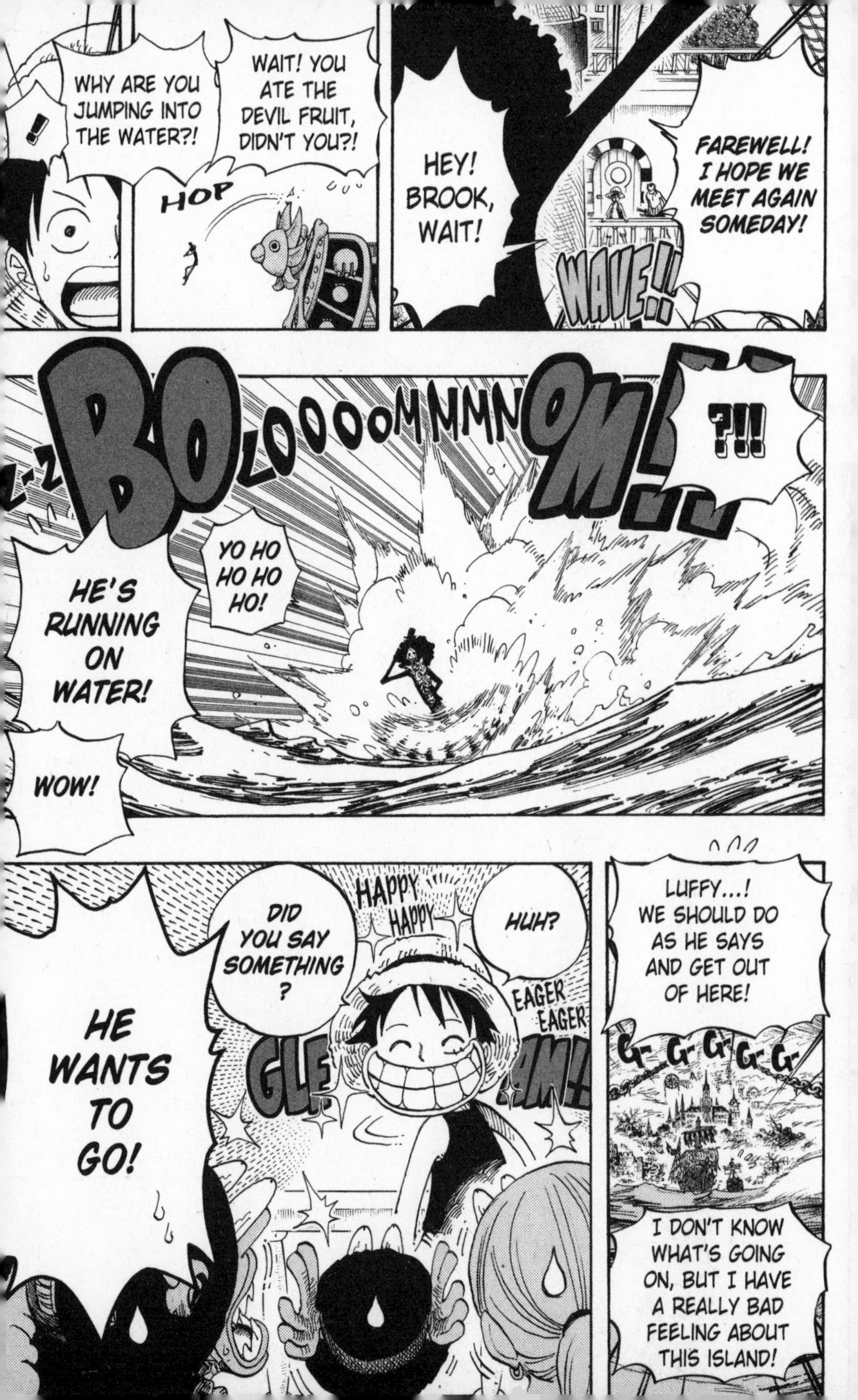
FAREWELL! I HOPE WE MEET AGAIN SOMEDAY!
WAVE!!
HEY! BROOK, WAIT!
WAIT! YOU ATE THE DEVIL FRUIT, DIDN'T YOU?!
HOP
WHY ARE YOU JUMPING INTO THE WATER?!
!
?!!
Z-Z
BOLOOOOMMMNOM!!
YO HO HO HO HO!
HE'S RUNNING ON WATER!
WOW!
LUFFY...! WE SHOULD DO AS HE SAYS AND GET OUT OF HERE!
G-G-G-G-G
I DON'T KNOW WHAT'S GOING ON, BUT I HAVE A REALLY BAD FEELING ABOUT THIS ISLAND!
HUH?
EAGER EAGER
DID YOU SAY SOMETHING?
HAPPY HAPPY
GLEAM!!
HE WANTS TO GO!

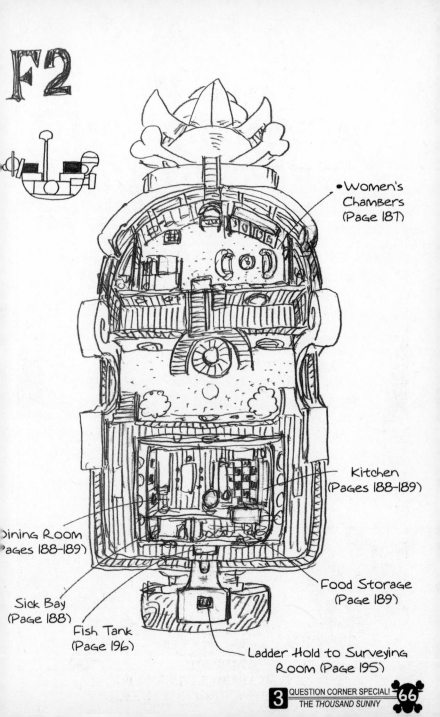

F2

Women's Chambers (Page 187)

Kitchen (Pages 188-189)

Dining Room (Pages 188-189)

Food Storage (Page 189)

Sick Bay (Page 188)

Fish Tank (Page 196)

Ladder Hold to Surveying Room (Page 195)

Chapter 444:
ADVENTURE ON GHOST ISLAND

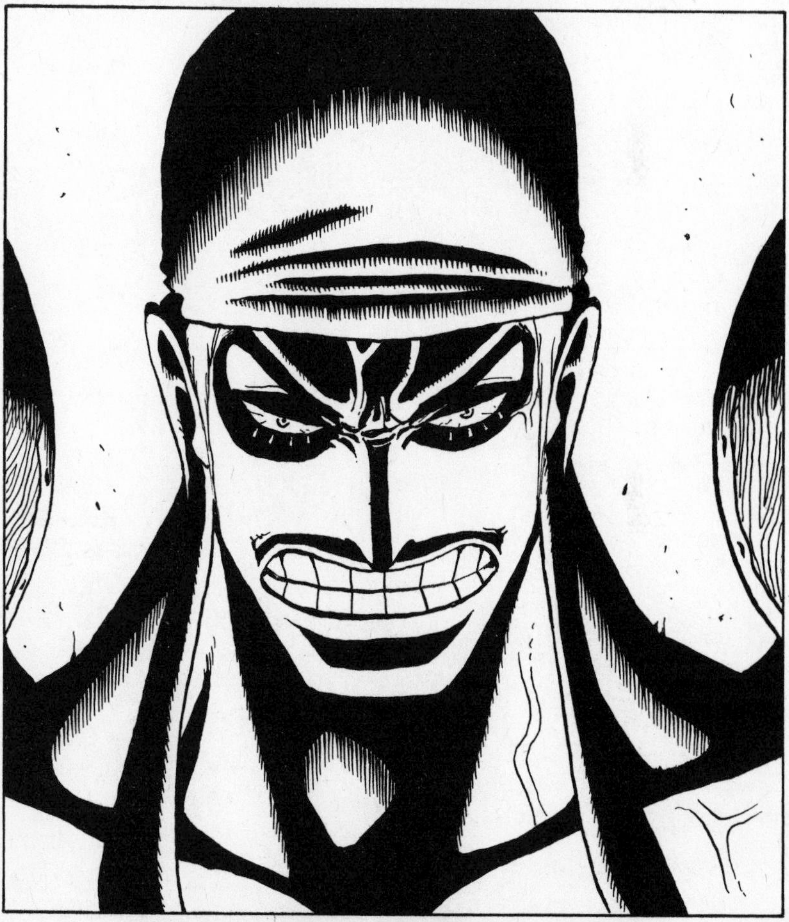

ENERU'S GREAT SPACE MISSION, VOL. 14:
"MY VARSE! UNCONDITIONAL RAGE!"

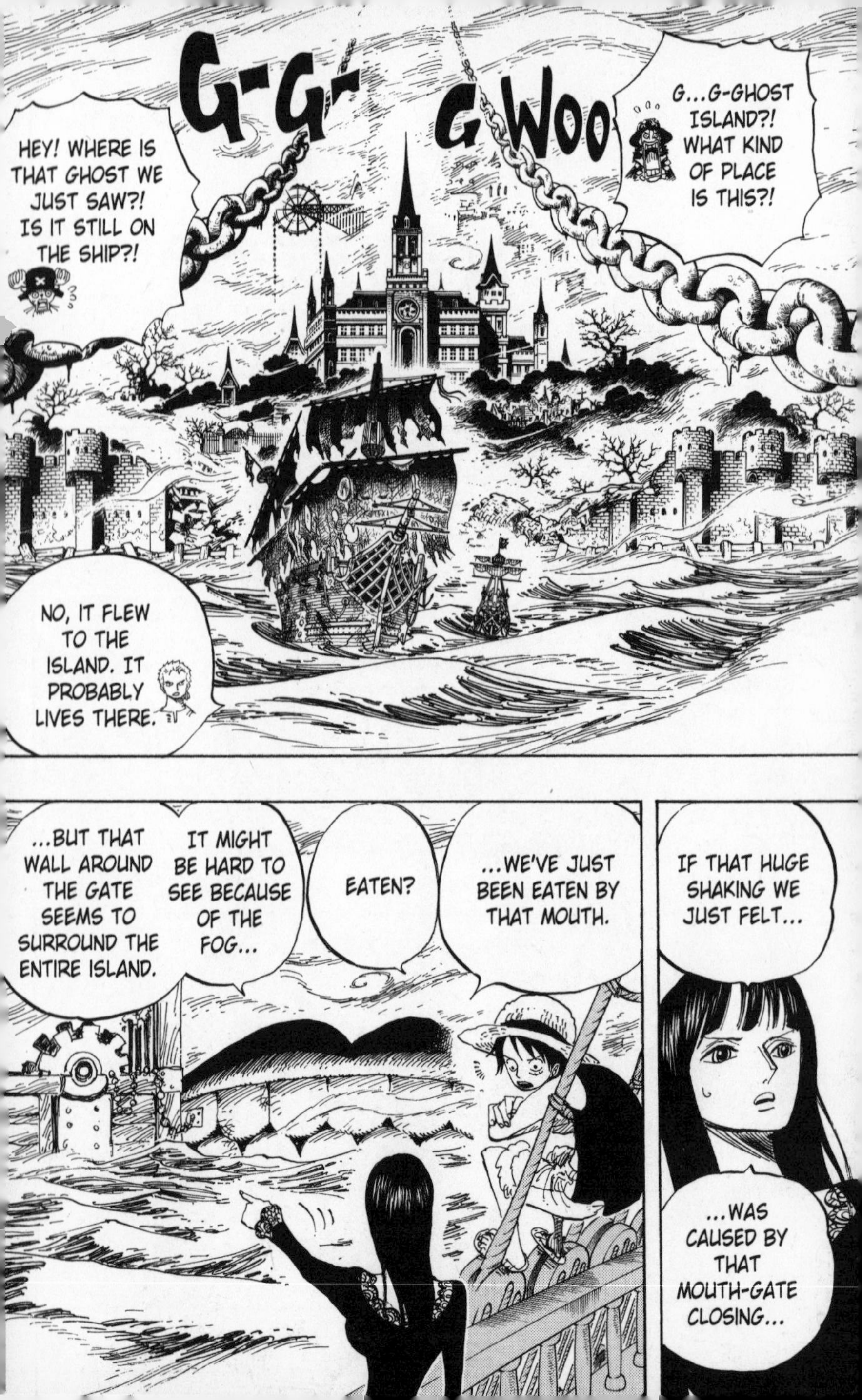
G-G-G WOO
G...G-GHOST ISLAND?! WHAT KIND OF PLACE IS THIS?!
HEY! WHERE IS THAT GHOST WE JUST SAW?! IS IT STILL ON THE SHIP?!
NO, IT FLEW TO THE ISLAND. IT PROBABLY LIVES THERE.
IF THAT HUGE SHAKING WE JUST FELT...
...WAS CAUSED BY THAT MOUTH-GATE CLOSING...
...WE'VE JUST BEEN EATEN BY THAT MOUTH.
EATEN?
IT MIGHT BE HARD TO SEE BECAUSE OF THE FOG...
...BUT THAT WALL AROUND THE GATE SEEMS TO SURROUND THE ENTIRE ISLAND.

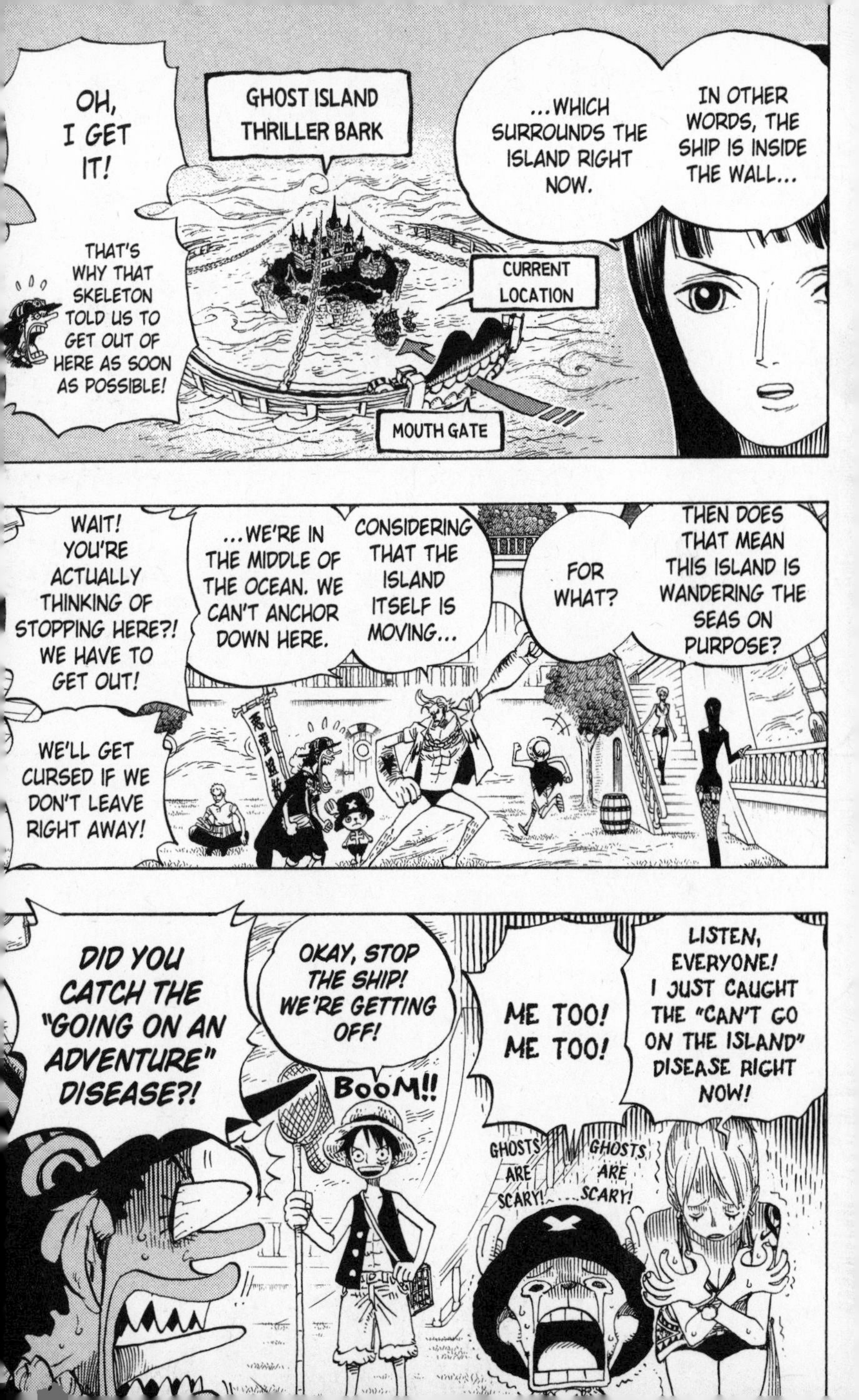
IN OTHER WORDS, THE SHIP IS INSIDE THE WALL...
...WHICH SURROUNDS THE ISLAND RIGHT NOW.
GHOST ISLAND THRILLER BARK
CURRENT LOCATION
MOUTH GATE
OH, I GET IT!
THAT'S WHY THAT SKELETON TOLD US TO GET OUT OF HERE AS SOON AS POSSIBLE!
THEN DOES THAT MEAN THIS ISLAND IS WANDERING THE SEAS ON PURPOSE?
FOR WHAT?
CONSIDERING THAT THE ISLAND ITSELF IS MOVING...
...WE'RE IN THE MIDDLE OF THE OCEAN. WE CAN'T ANCHOR DOWN HERE.
WAIT! YOU'RE ACTUALLY THINKING OF STOPPING HERE?! WE HAVE TO GET OUT!
WE'LL GET CURSED IF WE DON'T LEAVE RIGHT AWAY!
LISTEN, EVERYONE! I JUST CAUGHT THE "CAN'T GO ON THE ISLAND" DISEASE RIGHT NOW!
ME TOO! ME TOO!
GHOSTS ARE SCARY!
GHOSTS ARE SCARY!
OKAY, STOP THE SHIP! WE'RE GETTING OFF!
BOOM!!
DID YOU CATCH THE "GOING ON AN ADVENTURE" DISEASE?!

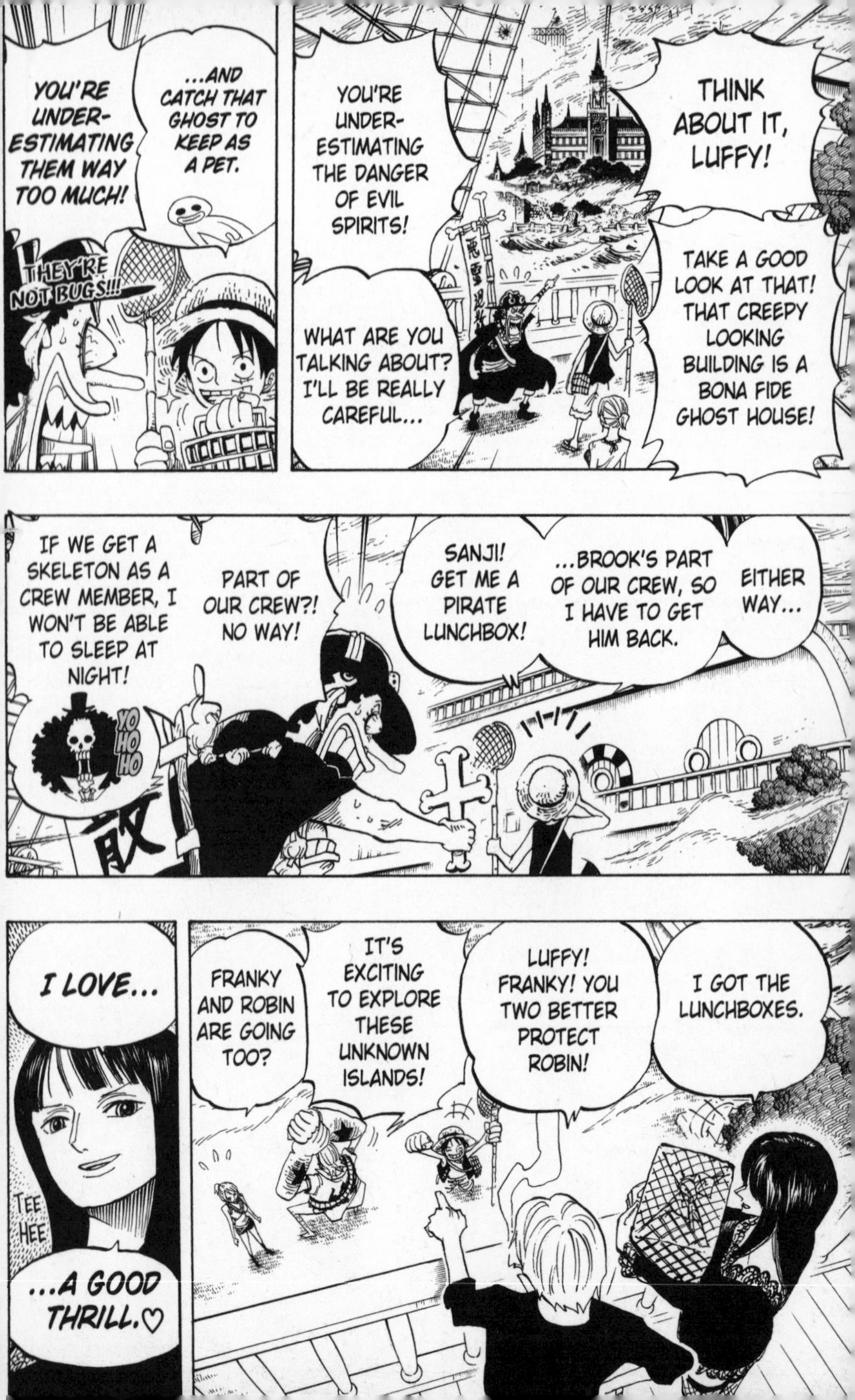
THINK ABOUT IT, LUFFY!
TAKE A GOOD LOOK AT THAT! THAT CREEPY LOOKING BUILDING IS A BONA FIDE GHOST HOUSE!
YOU'RE UNDER-ESTIMATING THE DANGER OF EVIL SPIRITS!
WHAT ARE YOU TALKING ABOUT? I'LL BE REALLY CAREFUL...
...AND CATCH THAT GHOST TO KEEP AS A PET.
YOU'RE UNDER-ESTIMATING THEM WAY TOO MUCH!
THEY'RE NOT BUGS!!!
EITHER WAY...
...BROOK'S PART OF OUR CREW, SO I HAVE TO GET HIM BACK.
SANJI! GET ME A PIRATE LUNCHBOX!
PART OF OUR CREW?! NO WAY!
IF WE GET A SKELETON AS A CREW MEMBER, I WON'T BE ABLE TO SLEEP AT NIGHT!
YO HO HO
I GOT THE LUNCHBOXES.
LUFFY! FRANKY! YOU TWO BETTER PROTECT ROBIN!
IT'S EXCITING TO EXPLORE THESE UNKNOWN ISLANDS!
FRANKY AND ROBIN ARE GOING TOO?
I LOVE...
TEE HEE
...A GOOD THRILL.♡

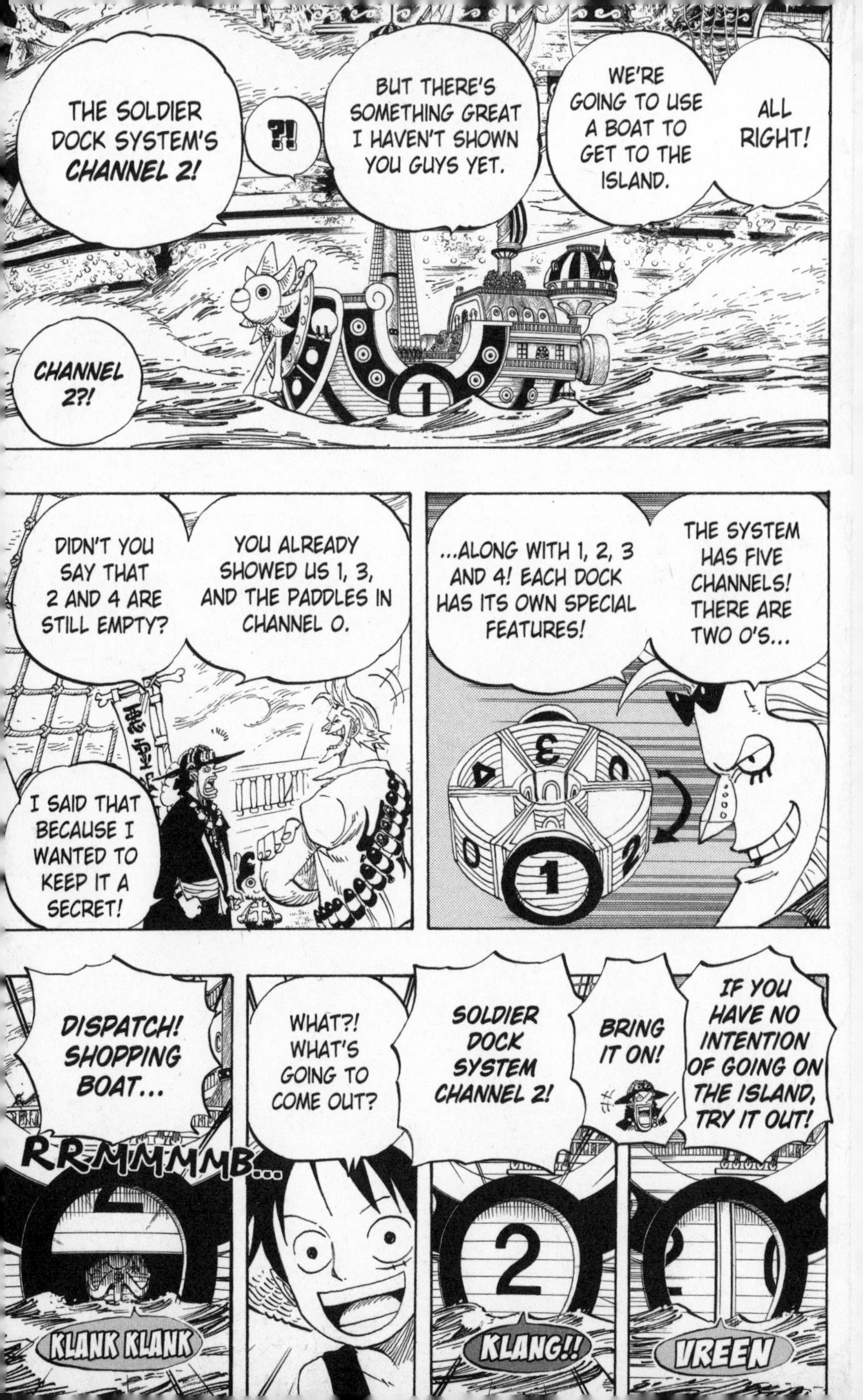
ALL RIGHT!
WE'RE GOING TO USE A BOAT TO GET TO THE ISLAND.
BUT THERE'S SOMETHING GREAT I HAVEN'T SHOWN YOU GUYS YET.
?!
THE SOLDIER DOCK SYSTEM'S CHANNEL 2!
CHANNEL 2?!
1
THE SYSTEM HAS FIVE CHANNELS! THERE ARE TWO 0'S...
...ALONG WITH 1, 2, 3 AND 4! EACH DOCK HAS ITS OWN SPECIAL FEATURES!
YOU ALREADY SHOWED US 1, 3, AND THE PADDLES IN CHANNEL 0.
DIDN'T YOU SAY THAT 2 AND 4 ARE STILL EMPTY?
I SAID THAT BECAUSE I WANTED TO KEEP IT A SECRET!
IF YOU HAVE NO INTENTION OF GOING ON THE ISLAND, TRY IT OUT!
BRING IT ON!
SOLDIER DOCK SYSTEM CHANNEL 2!
WHAT?! WHAT'S GOING TO COME OUT?
DISPATCH! SHOPPING BOAT...
VREEN
2
KLANG!!
RRMMMMB...
KLANK KLANK

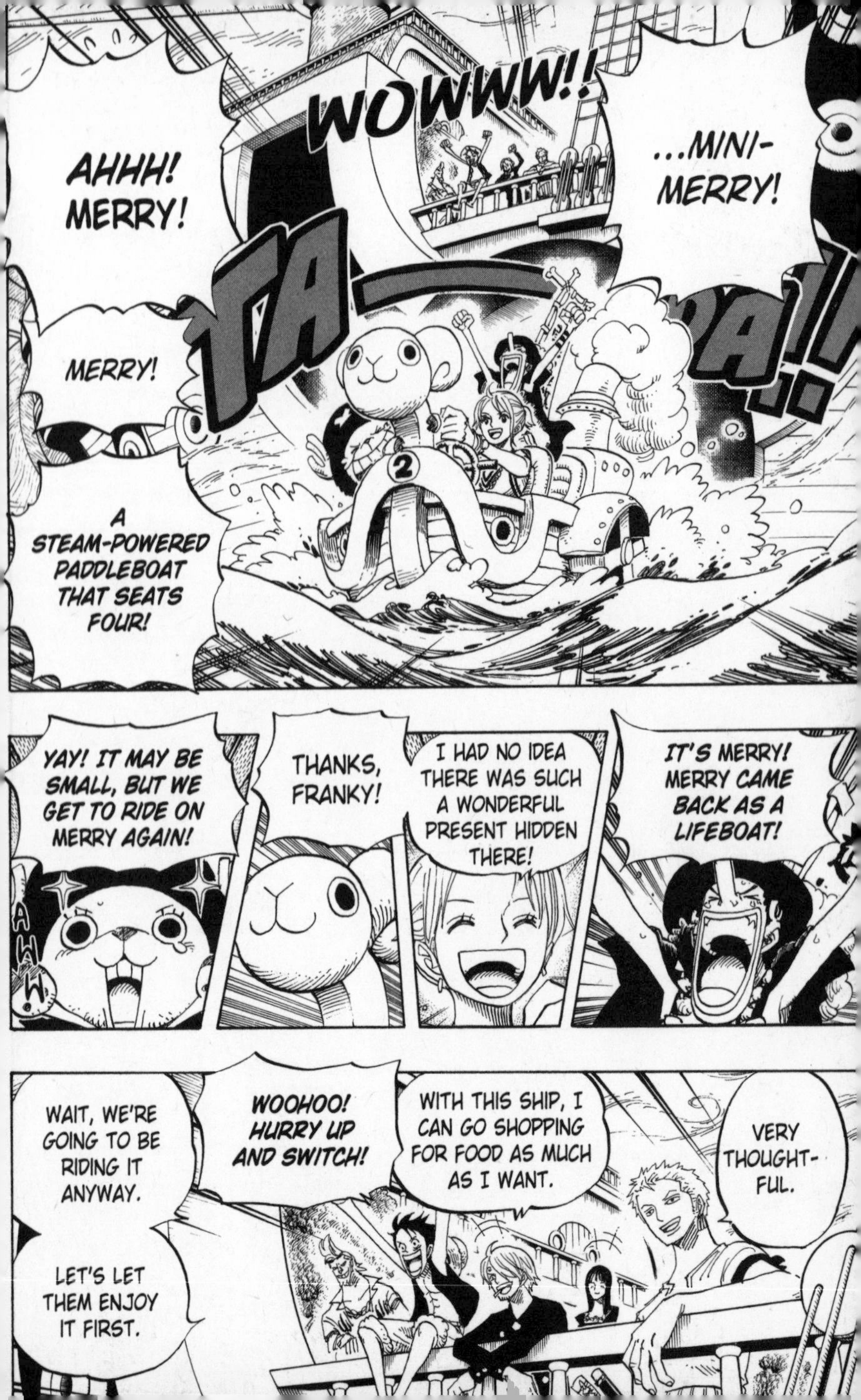
...MINI-MERRY!
WOWWW!!
AHHH! MERRY!
YA—
MERRY!
A STEAM-POWERED PADDLEBOAT THAT SEATS FOUR!
IT'S MERRY! MERRY CAME BACK AS A LIFEBOAT!
I HAD NO IDEA THERE WAS SUCH A WONDERFUL PRESENT HIDDEN THERE!
THANKS, FRANKY!
YAY! IT MAY BE SMALL, BUT WE GET TO RIDE ON MERRY AGAIN!
VERY THOUGHT-FUL.
WITH THIS SHIP, I CAN GO SHOPPING FOR FOOD AS MUCH AS I WANT.
WOOHOO! HURRY UP AND SWITCH!
WAIT, WE'RE GOING TO BE RIDING IT ANYWAY.
LET'S LET THEM ENJOY IT FIRST.

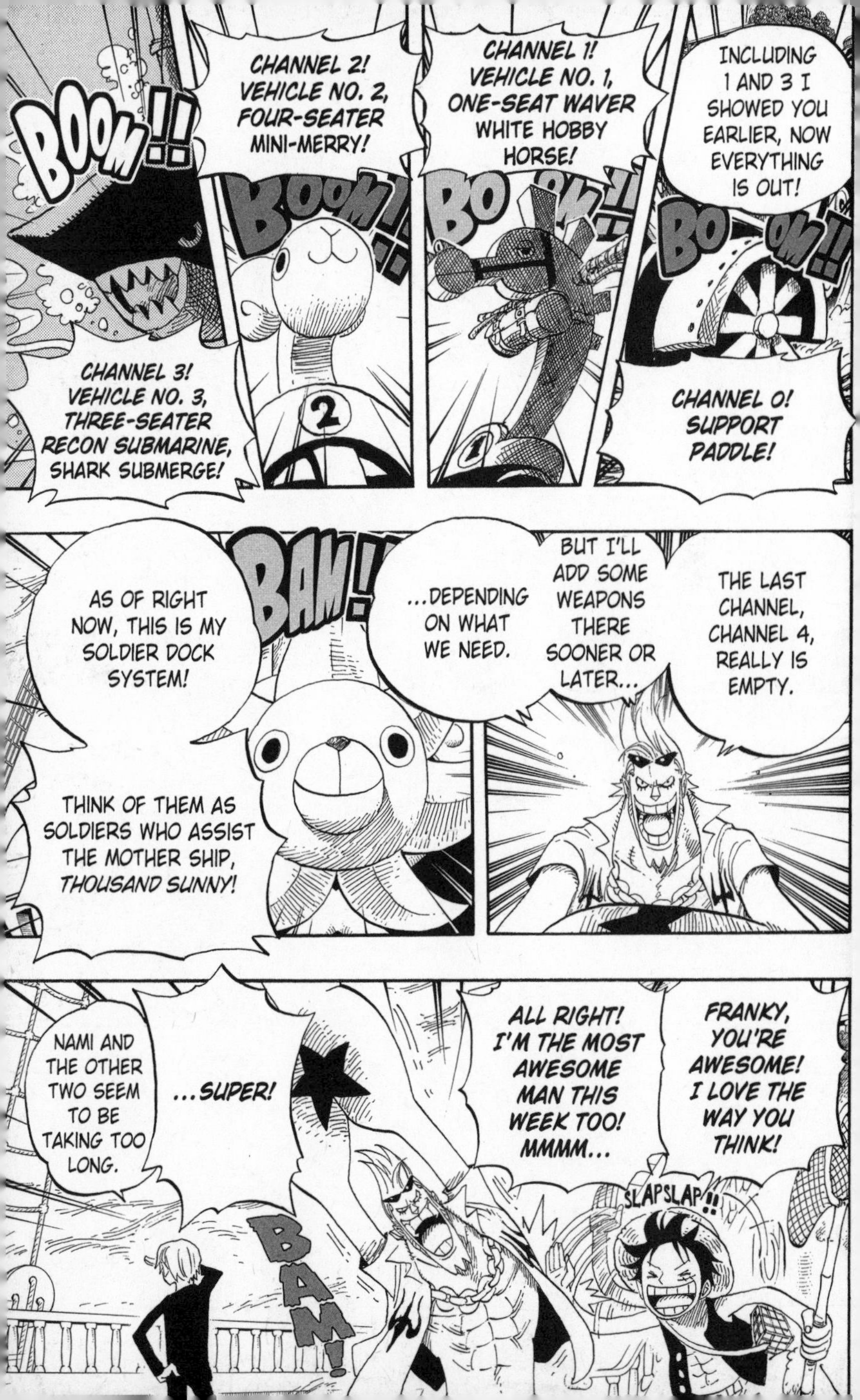
INCLUDING 1 AND 3 I SHOWED YOU EARLIER, NOW EVERYTHING IS OUT!
BOOM!!
CHANNEL 0! SUPPORT PADDLE!
CHANNEL 1! VEHICLE NO. 1, ONE-SEAT WAVER WHITE HOBBY HORSE!
BOOM!!
CHANNEL 2! VEHICLE NO. 2, FOUR-SEATER MINI-MERRY!
BOOM!!
BOOM!!
CHANNEL 3! VEHICLE NO. 3, THREE-SEATER RECON SUBMARINE, SHARK SUBMERGE!
THE LAST CHANNEL, CHANNEL 4, REALLY IS EMPTY.
BUT I'LL ADD SOME WEAPONS THERE SOONER OR LATER...
...DEPENDING ON WHAT WE NEED.
BAM!!
AS OF RIGHT NOW, THIS IS MY SOLDIER DOCK SYSTEM!
THINK OF THEM AS SOLDIERS WHO ASSIST THE MOTHER SHIP, THOUSAND SUNNY!
FRANKY, YOU'RE AWESOME! I LOVE THE WAY YOU THINK!
SLAPSLAP!!
ALL RIGHT! I'M THE MOST AWESOME MAN THIS WEEK TOO! MMMM...
...SUPER!
BAM!
NAMI AND THE OTHER TWO SEEM TO BE TAKING TOO LONG.

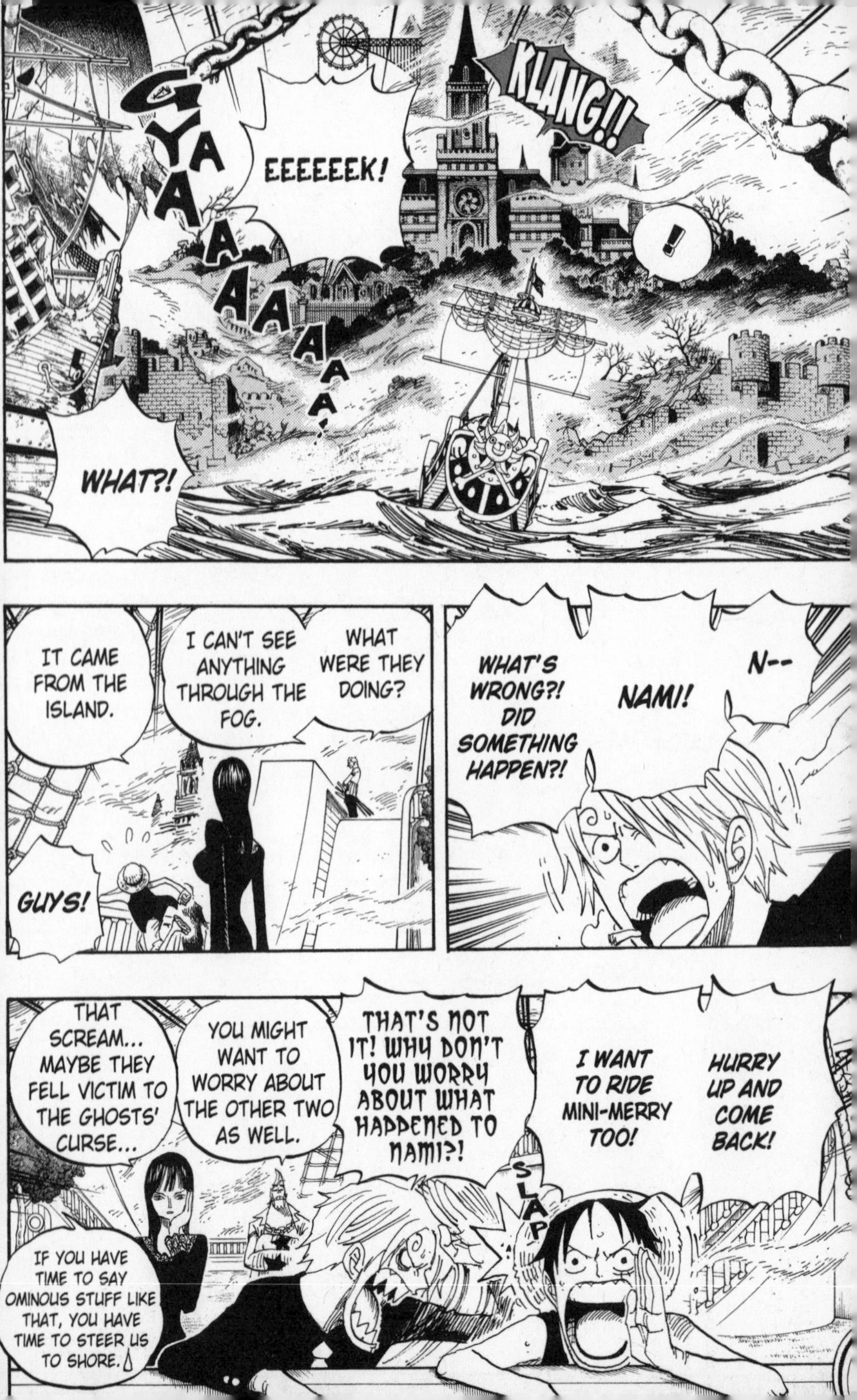
KLANG!!
!
EEEEEEK!
GYAAAAAAAAA!
WHAT?!
N--
NAMI!
WHAT'S WRONG?! DID SOMETHING HAPPEN?!
WHAT WERE THEY DOING?
I CAN'T SEE ANYTHING THROUGH THE FOG.
IT CAME FROM THE ISLAND.
GUYS!
HURRY UP AND COME BACK!
I WANT TO RIDE MINI-MERRY TOO!
SLAP
THAT'S NOT IT! WHY DON'T YOU WORRY ABOUT WHAT HAPPENED TO NAMI?!
YOU MIGHT WANT TO WORRY ABOUT THE OTHER TWO AS WELL.
THAT SCREAM... MAYBE THEY FELL VICTIM TO THE GHOSTS' CURSE...
IF YOU HAVE TIME TO SAY OMINOUS STUFF LIKE THAT, YOU HAVE TIME TO STEER US TO SHORE.

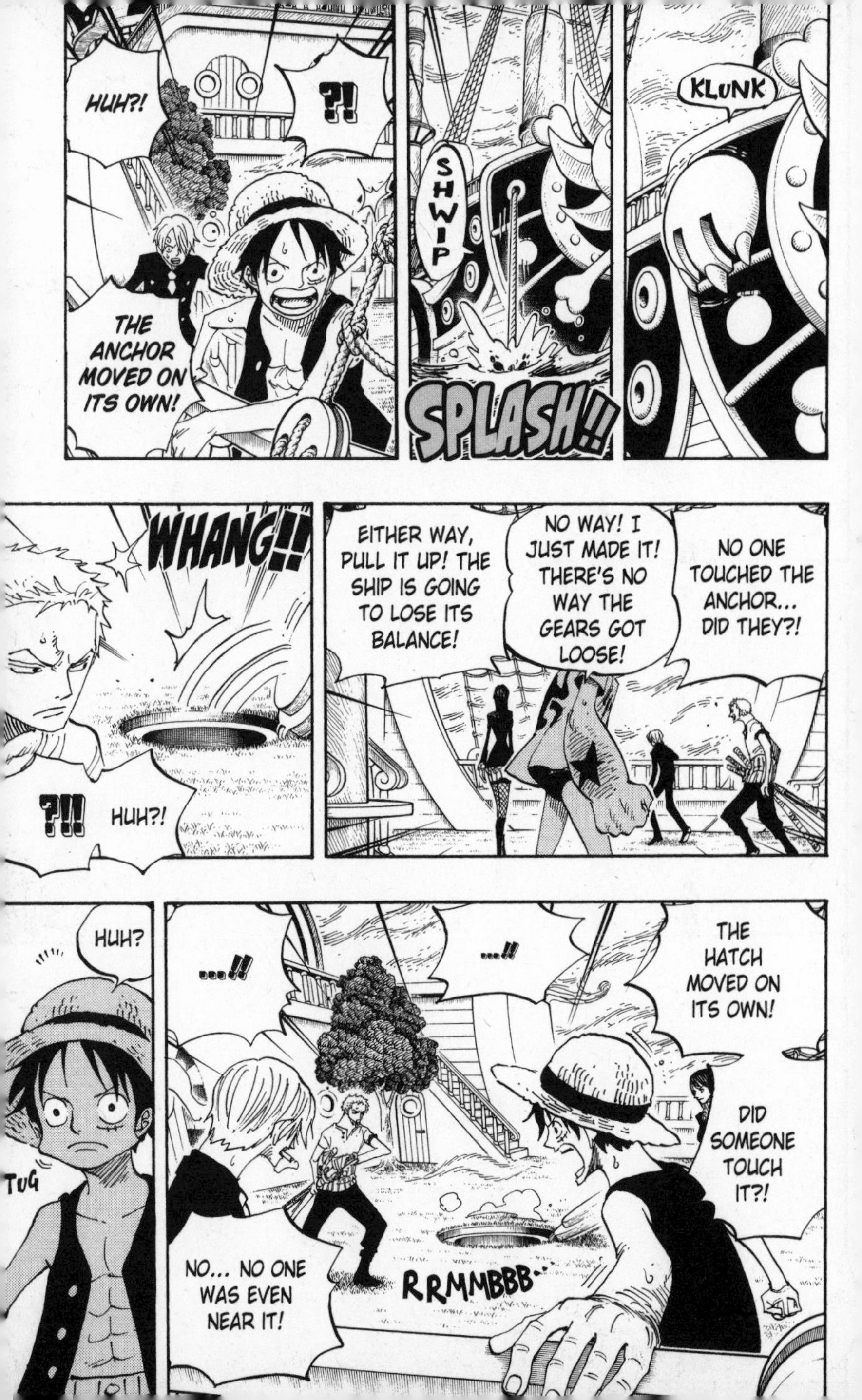
KLUNK
SHWIP
SPLASH!!
?!
HUH?!
THE ANCHOR MOVED ON ITS OWN!
NO ONE TOUCHED THE ANCHOR... DID THEY?!
NO WAY! I JUST MADE IT! THERE'S NO WAY THE GEARS GOT LOOSE!
EITHER WAY, PULL IT UP! THE SHIP IS GOING TO LOSE ITS BALANCE!
WHANG!!
HUH?!
?!!
THE HATCH MOVED ON ITS OWN!
...!!
...!!
DID SOMEONE TOUCH IT?!
RRMMBBB
NO... NO ONE WAS EVEN NEAR IT!
HUH?
TUG

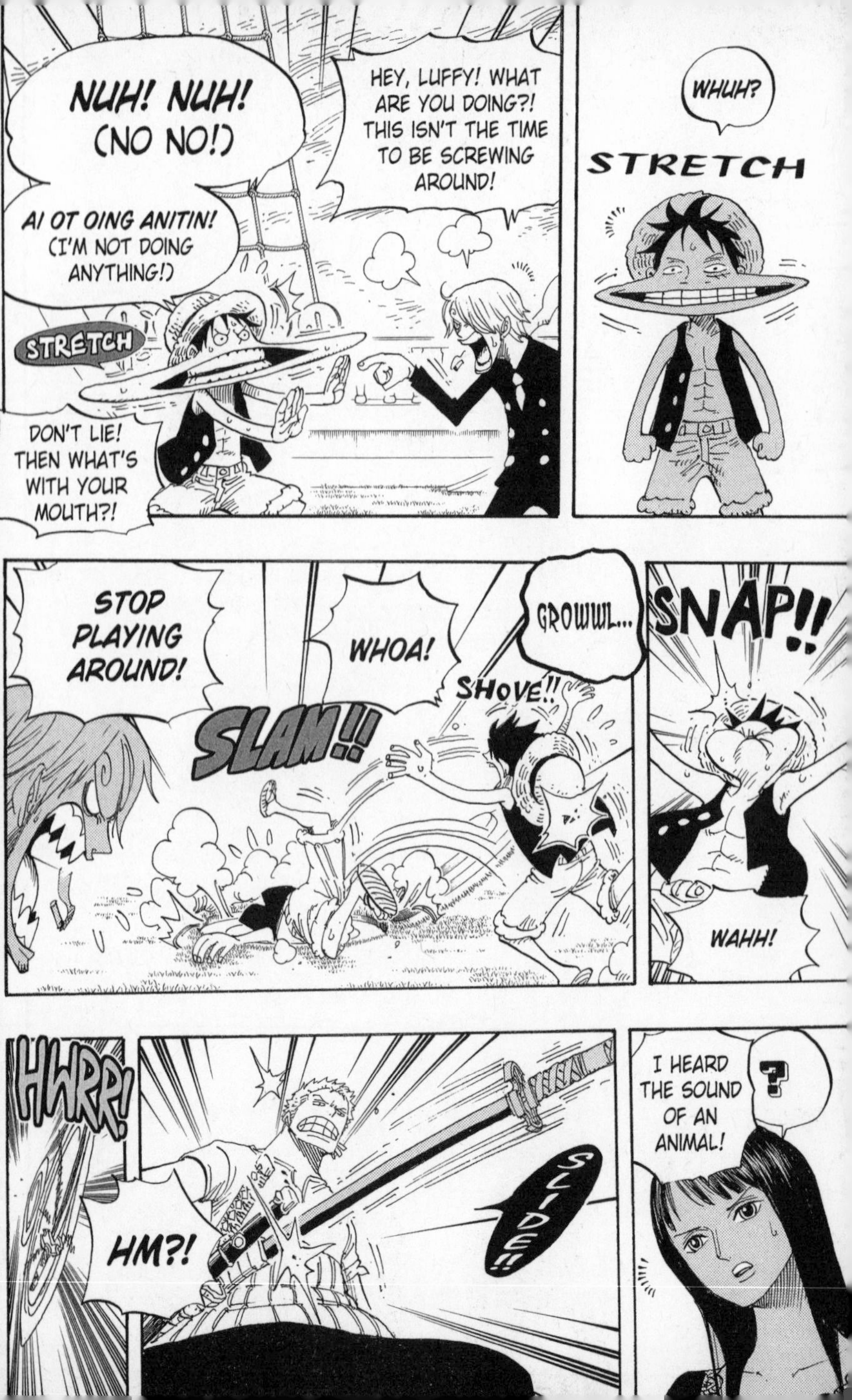
WHUH?
STRETCH
HEY, LUFFY! WHAT ARE YOU DOING?! THIS ISN'T THE TIME TO BE SCREWING AROUND!
NUH! NUH! (NO NO!)
AI OT OING ANITIN! (I'M NOT DOING ANYTHING!)
STRETCH
DON'T LIE! THEN WHAT'S WITH YOUR MOUTH?!
SNAP!!
WAHH!
GROWWL...
SHOVE!!
WHOA!
STOP PLAYING AROUND!
SLAM!!
?
I HEARD THE SOUND OF AN ANIMAL!
SLIDE!!
HM?!
HWRR!

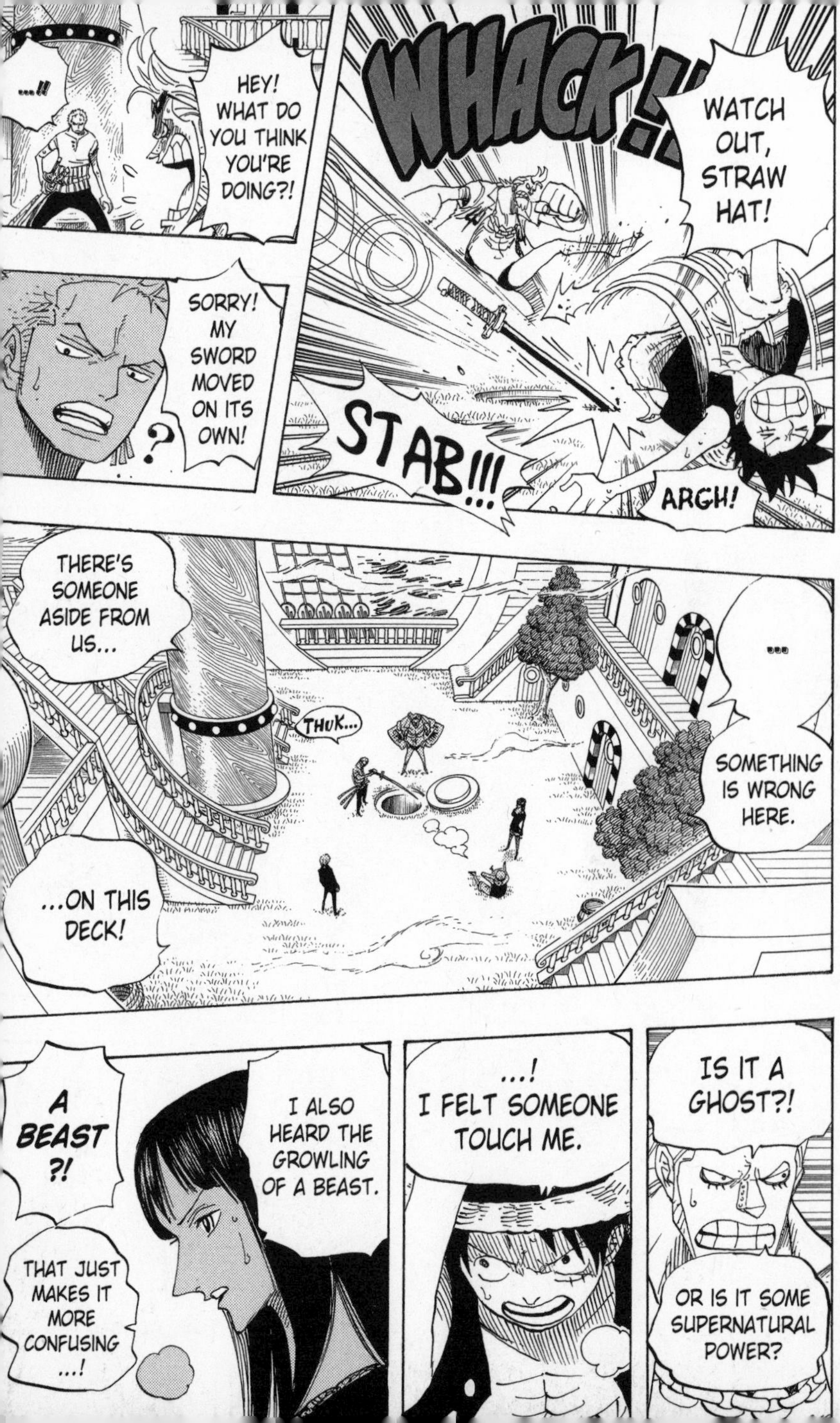

WHACK!!
WATCH OUT, STRAW HAT!
STAB!!!
ARGH!
HEY! WHAT DO YOU THINK YOU'RE DOING?!
...!!
SORRY! MY SWORD MOVED ON ITS OWN!
?
...
THERE'S SOMEONE ASIDE FROM US...
THUK...
SOMETHING IS WRONG HERE.
...ON THIS DECK!
IS IT A GHOST?!
OR IS IT SOME SUPERNATURAL POWER?
...! I FELT SOMEONE TOUCH ME.
I ALSO HEARD THE GROWLING OF A BEAST.
A BEAST ?!
THAT JUST MAKES IT MORE CONFUSING ...!

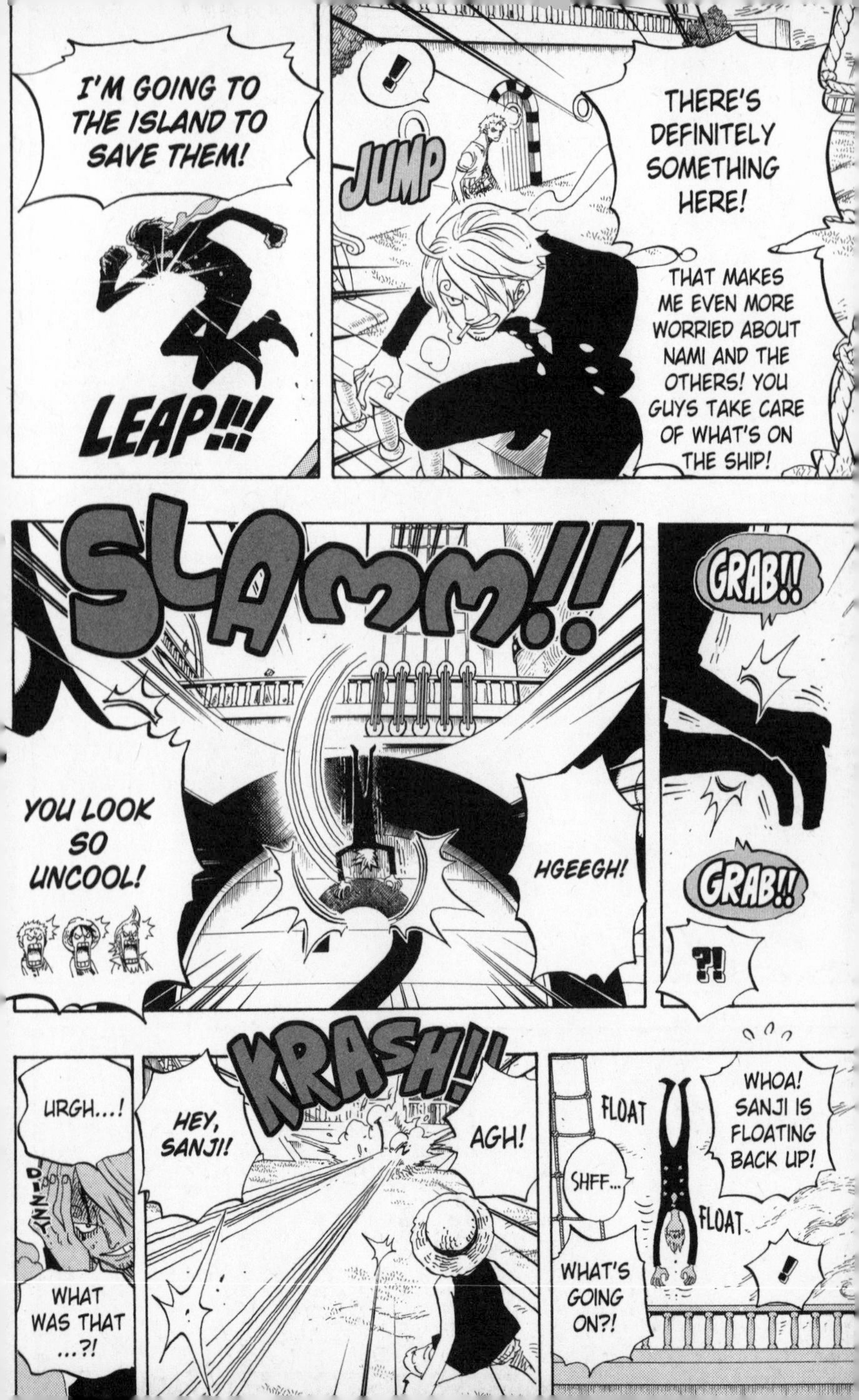
THERE'S DEFINITELY SOMETHING HERE!
!
JUMP
THAT MAKES ME EVEN MORE WORRIED ABOUT NAMI AND THE OTHERS! YOU GUYS TAKE CARE OF WHAT'S ON THE SHIP!
I'M GOING TO THE ISLAND TO SAVE THEM!
LEAP!!!
GRAB!!
GRAB!!
?!
SLAMM!!
HGEEGH!
YOU LOOK SO UNCOOL!
WHOA! SANJI IS FLOATING BACK UP!
FLOAT
SHFF...
FLOAT
!
WHAT'S GOING ON?!
KRASH!!
AGH!
HEY, SANJI!
URGH...!
WHAT WAS THAT ...?!

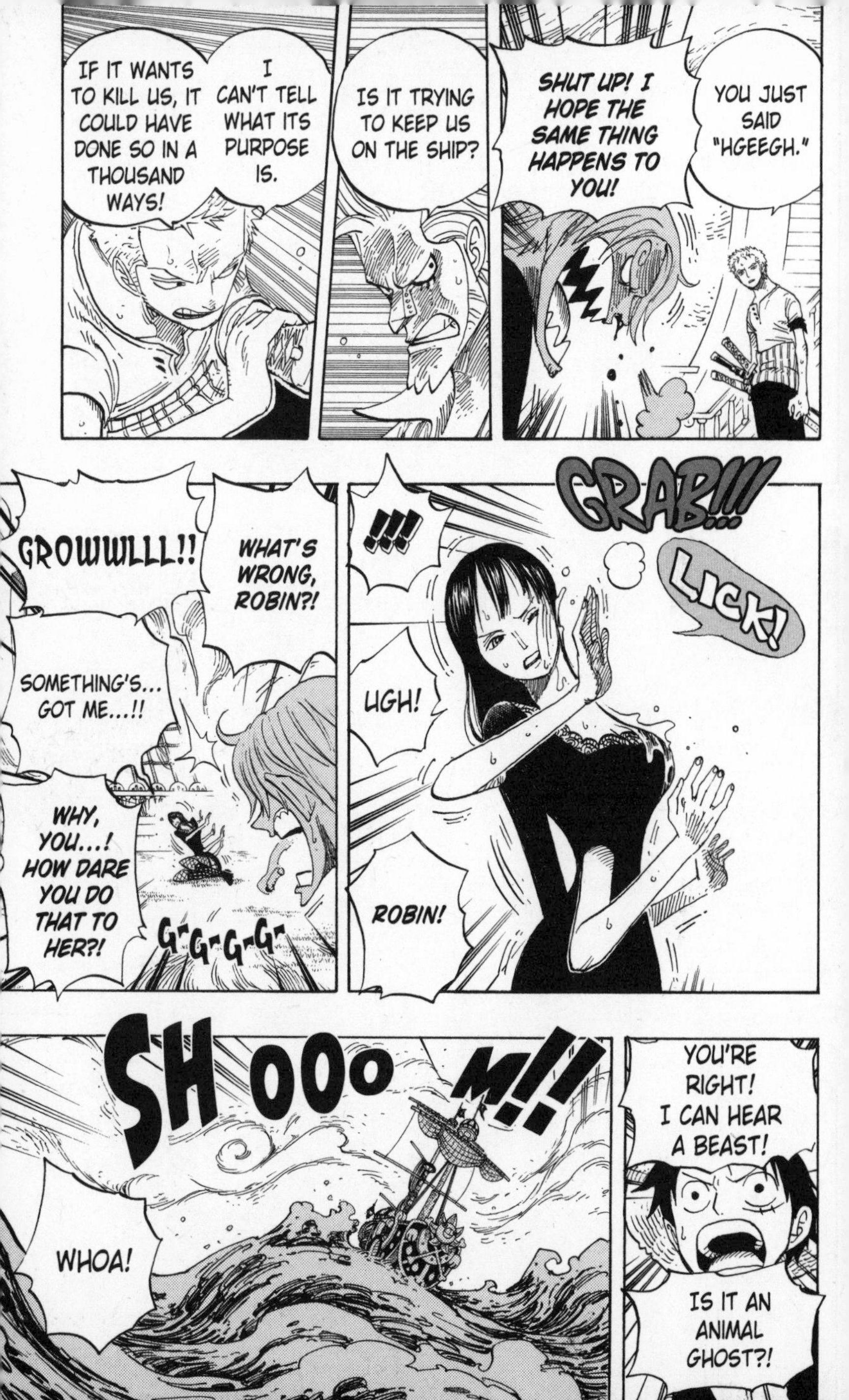
YOU JUST SAID "HGEEGH."
SHUT UP! I HOPE THE SAME THING HAPPENS TO YOU!
IS IT TRYING TO KEEP US ON THE SHIP?
I CAN'T TELL WHAT ITS PURPOSE IS.
IF IT WANTS TO KILL US, IT COULD HAVE DONE SO IN A THOUSAND WAYS!
GRAB!!!...
LICK!
!!!
UGH!
ROBIN!
WHAT'S WRONG, ROBIN?!
GROWWLLL!!
SOMETHING'S... GOT ME...!!
WHY, YOU...! HOW DARE YOU DO THAT TO HER?!
GrGrGrGr
YOU'RE RIGHT! I CAN HEAR A BEAST!
IS IT AN ANIMAL GHOST?!
SHOOOM!!
WHOA!

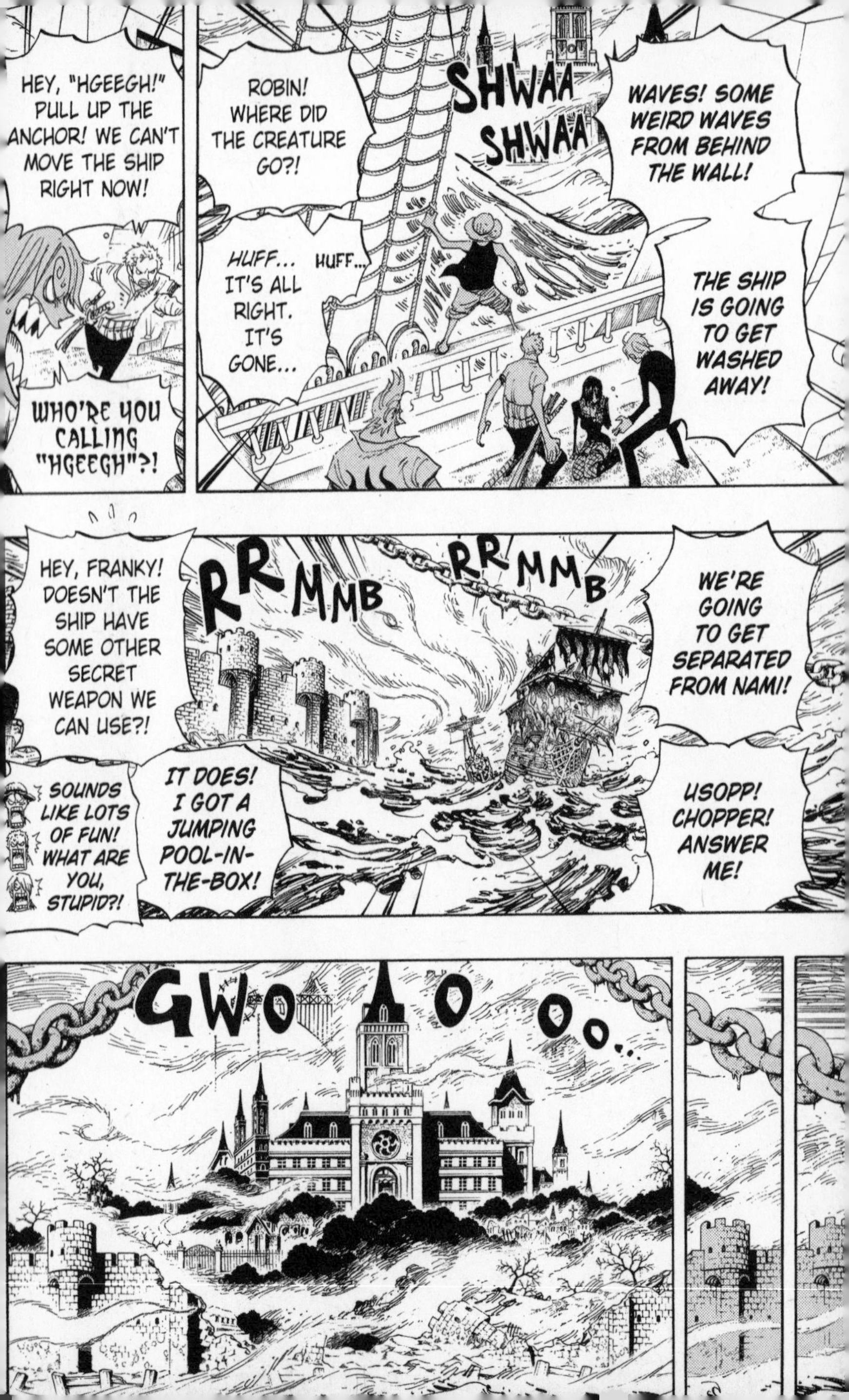
WAVES! SOME WEIRD WAVES FROM BEHIND THE WALL!
SHWAA SHWAA
ROBIN! WHERE DID THE CREATURE GO?!
THE SHIP IS GOING TO GET WASHED AWAY!
HUFF...
HUFF... IT'S ALL RIGHT. IT'S GONE...
HEY, "HGEEGH!" PULL UP THE ANCHOR! WE CAN'T MOVE THE SHIP RIGHT NOW!
WHO'RE YOU CALLING "HGEEGH"?!
WE'RE GOING TO GET SEPARATED FROM NAMI!
RRMMB
RRMMB
USOPP! CHOPPER! ANSWER ME!
HEY, FRANKY! DOESN'T THE SHIP HAVE SOME OTHER SECRET WEAPON WE CAN USE?!
IT DOES! I GOT A JUMPING POOL-IN-THE-BOX!
SOUNDS LIKE LOTS OF FUN! WHAT ARE YOU, STUPID?!
GWOOOO...

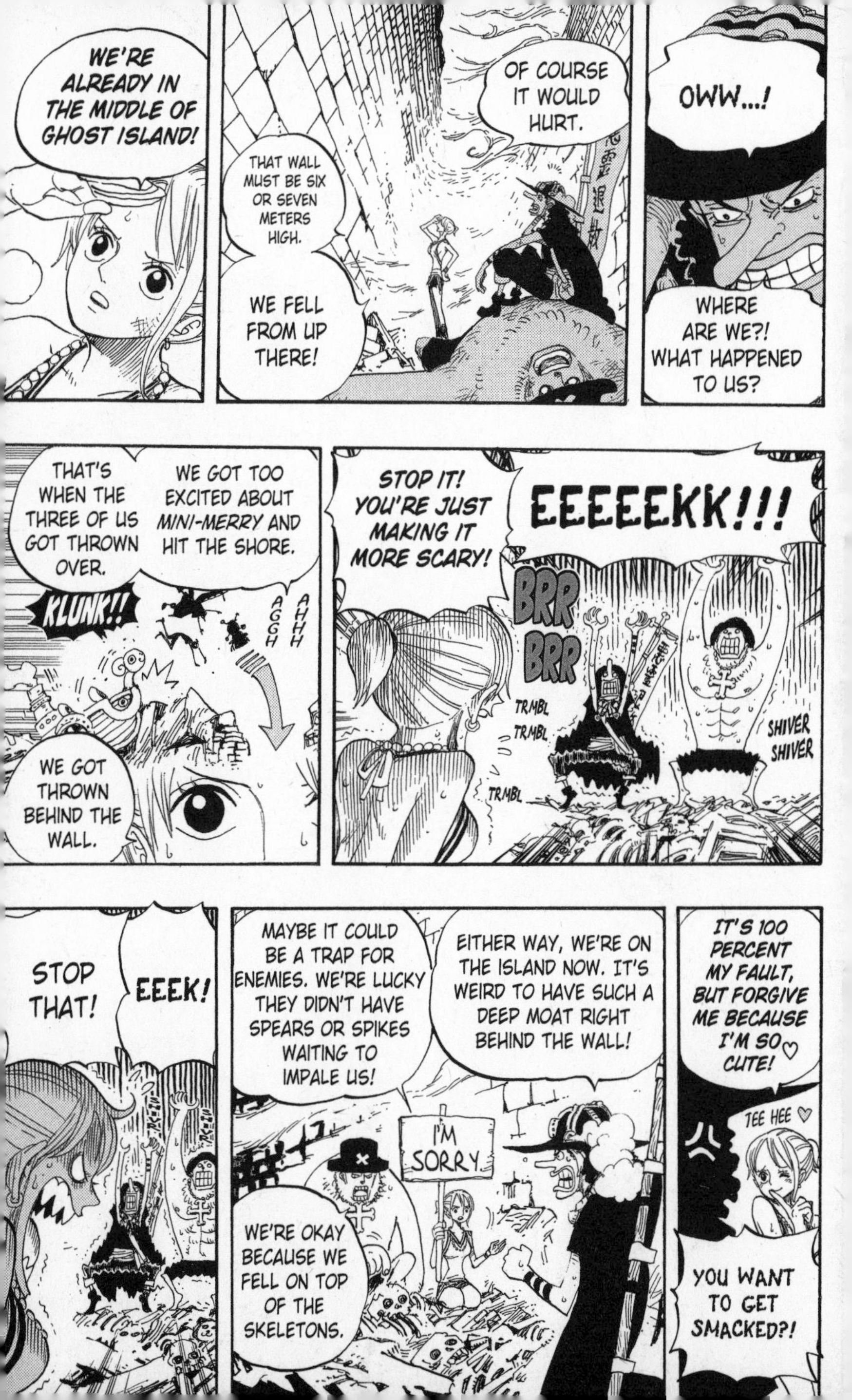
OWW...!
WHERE ARE WE?! WHAT HAPPENED TO US?
OF COURSE IT WOULD HURT.
THAT WALL MUST BE SIX OR SEVEN METERS HIGH.
WE FELL FROM UP THERE!
WE'RE ALREADY IN THE MIDDLE OF GHOST ISLAND!
EEEEEKK!!!
STOP IT! YOU'RE JUST MAKING IT MORE SCARY!
BRR BRR
TRMBL TRMBL
TRMBL
SHIVER SHIVER
WE GOT TOO EXCITED ABOUT MINI-MERRY AND HIT THE SHORE.
THAT'S WHEN THE THREE OF US GOT THROWN OVER.
AHHH
AGGH
KLUNK!!
WE GOT THROWN BEHIND THE WALL.
IT'S 100 PERCENT MY FAULT, BUT FORGIVE ME BECAUSE I'M SO CUTE! ♡
TEE HEE ♡
YOU WANT TO GET SMACKED?!
EITHER WAY, WE'RE ON THE ISLAND NOW. IT'S WEIRD TO HAVE SUCH A DEEP MOAT RIGHT BEHIND THE WALL!
MAYBE IT COULD BE A TRAP FOR ENEMIES. WE'RE LUCKY THEY DIDN'T HAVE SPEARS OR SPIKES WAITING TO IMPALE US!
I'M SORRY.
WE'RE OKAY BECAUSE WE FELL ON TOP OF THE SKELETONS.
EEEK!
STOP THAT!

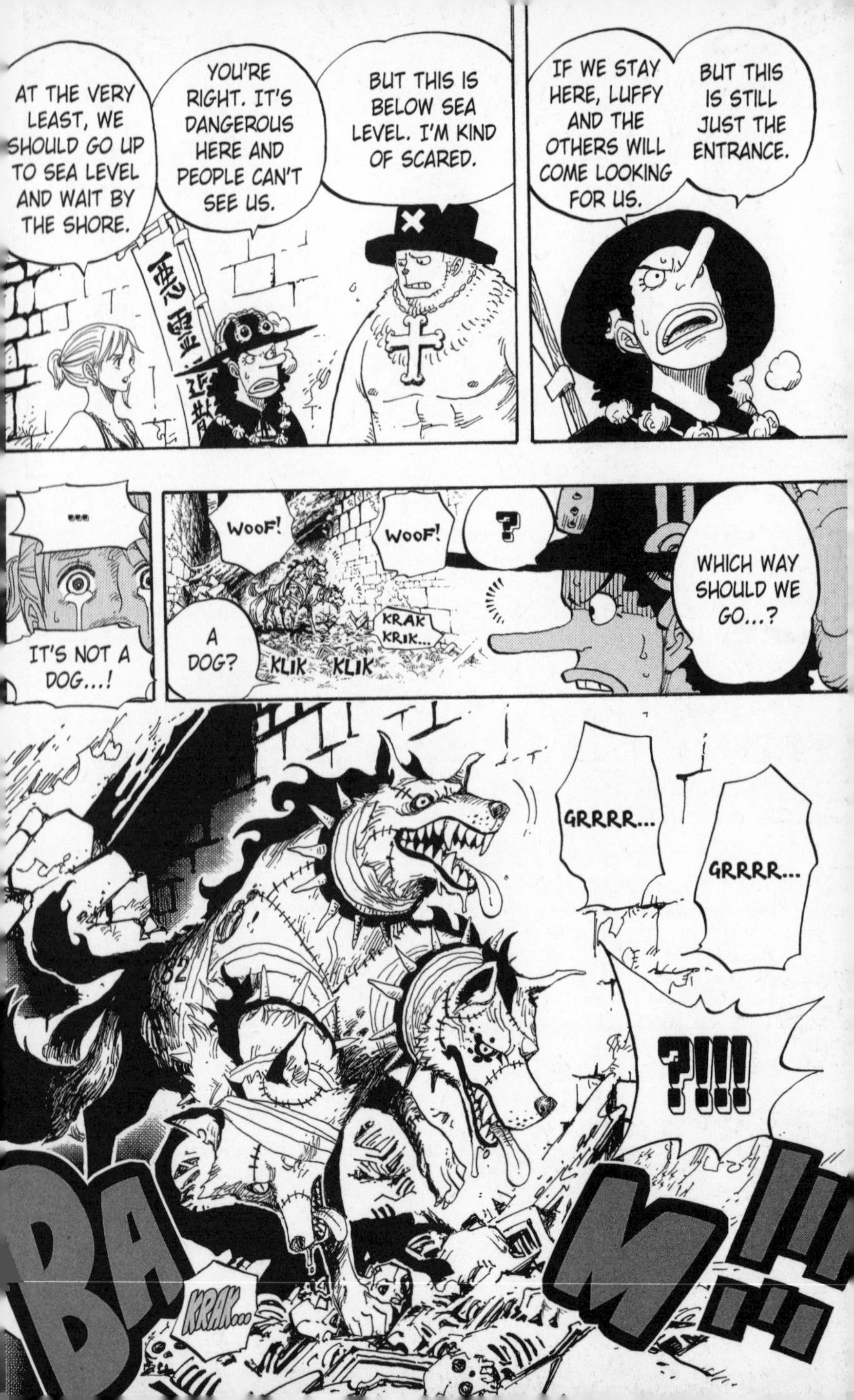
BUT THIS IS STILL JUST THE ENTRANCE.
IF WE STAY HERE, LUFFY AND THE OTHERS WILL COME LOOKING FOR US.
BUT THIS IS BELOW SEA LEVEL. I'M KIND OF SCARED.
YOU'RE RIGHT. IT'S DANGEROUS HERE AND PEOPLE CAN'T SEE US.
AT THE VERY LEAST, WE SHOULD GO UP TO SEA LEVEL AND WAIT BY THE SHORE.
WHICH WAY SHOULD WE GO...?
?
WOOF!
WOOF!
KRAK KRIK...
A DOG?
KLIK KLIK
...
IT'S NOT A DOG...!
GRRRR...
GRRRR...
?!!!
BAM!!
KRAK...

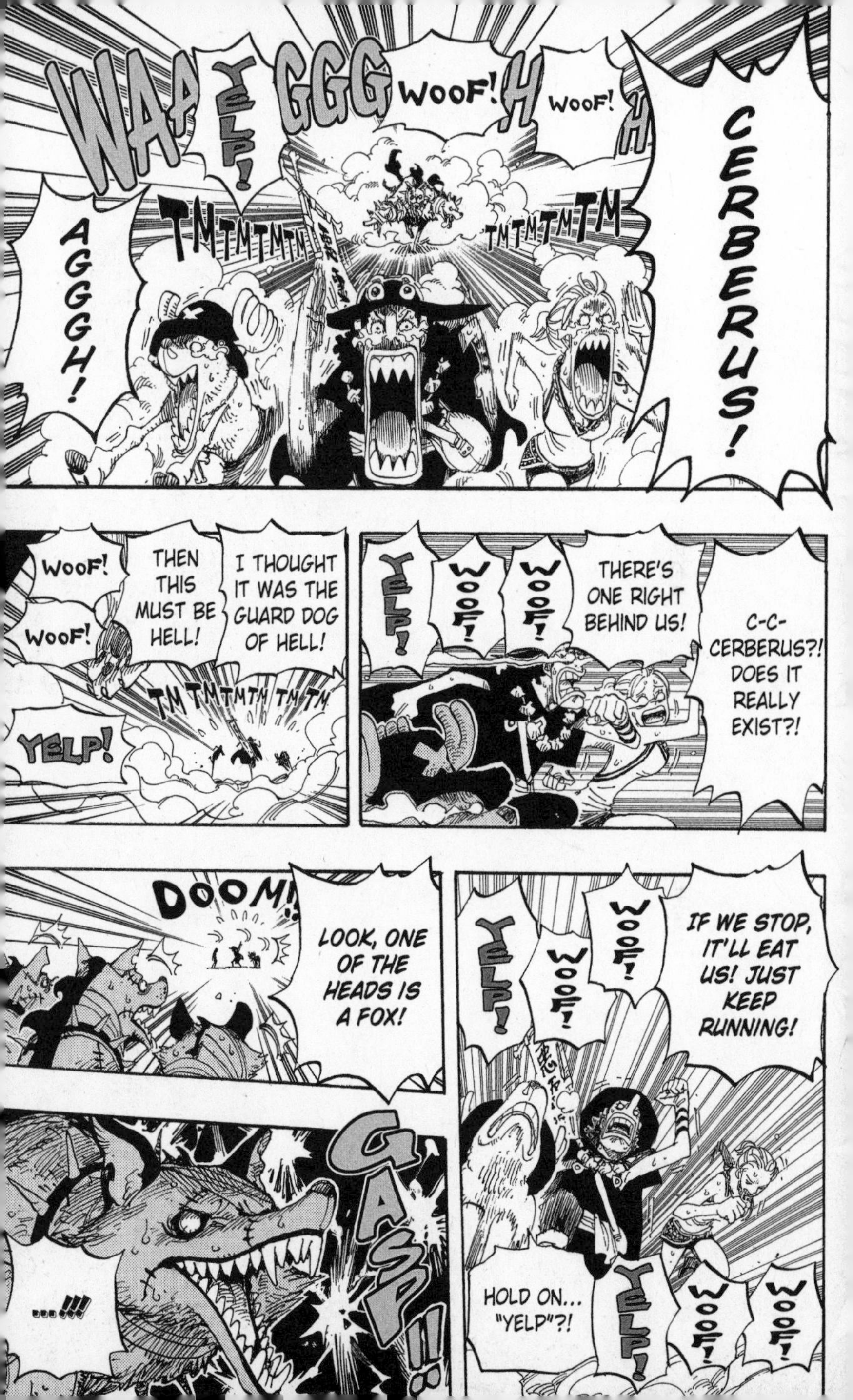
CERBERUS!
WOOF!
WOOF!
WAAGGGHH
YELP!
TMTMTMTM
TMTMTMTM
AGGGH!
C-C-CERBERUS?! DOES IT REALLY EXIST?!
THERE'S ONE RIGHT BEHIND US!
WOOF!
WOOF!
YELP!
I THOUGHT IT WAS THE GUARD DOG OF HELL!
THEN THIS MUST BE HELL!
WOOF!
WOOF!
TMTMTMTMTMTM
YELP!
IF WE STOP, IT'LL EAT US! JUST KEEP RUNNING!
WOOF!
WOOF!
YELP!
HOLD ON... "YELP"?!
WOOF!
WOOF!
YELP!
LOOK, ONE OF THE HEADS IS A FOX!
DOOM!!
GASP!!
...!!!

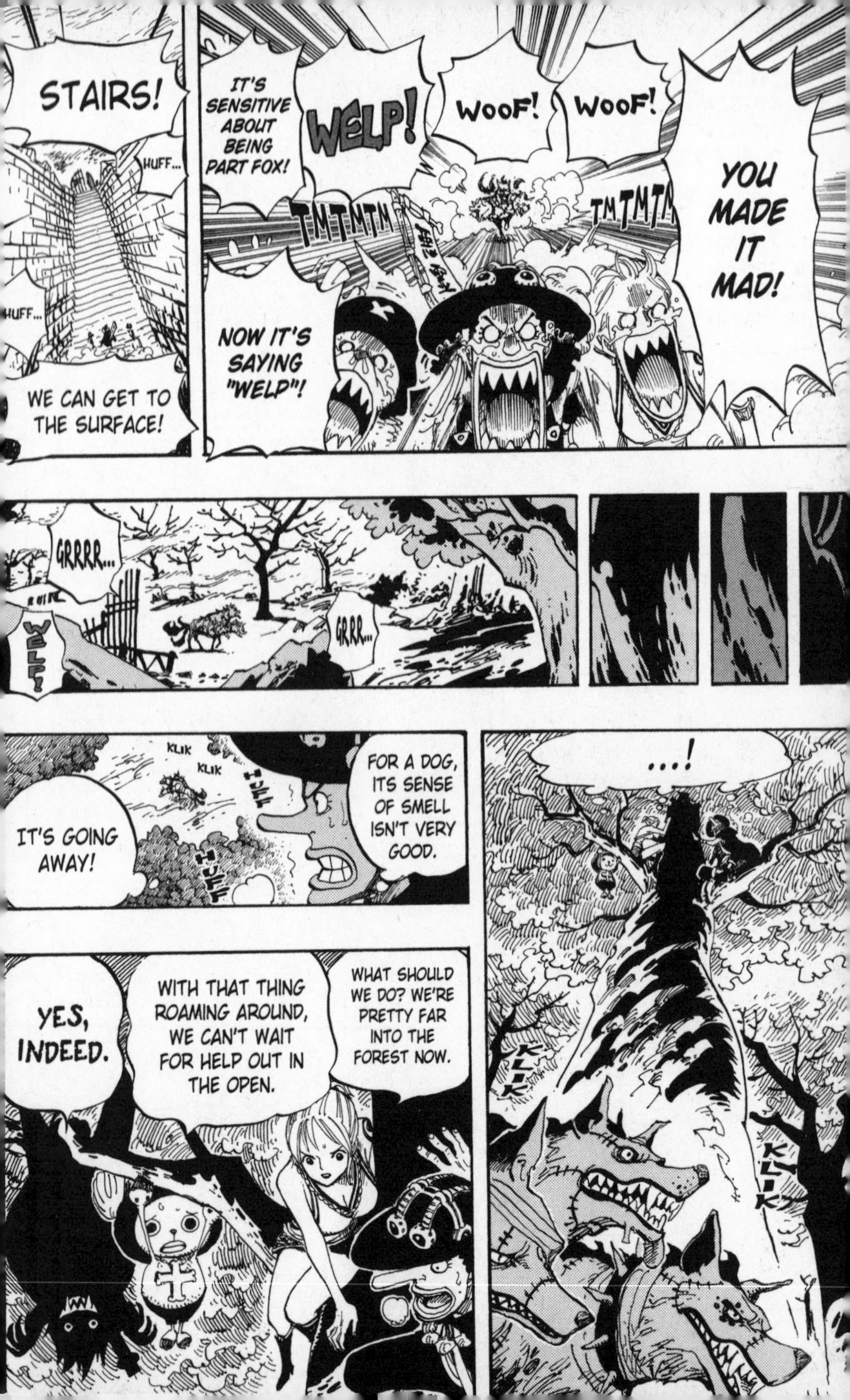
YOU MADE IT MAD!
WOOF!
WOOF!
WELP!
IT'S SENSITIVE ABOUT BEING PART FOX!
TMTMTM
TMTMTM
NOW IT'S SAYING "WELP"!
STAIRS!
HUFF...
HUFF...
WE CAN GET TO THE SURFACE!
GRRR...
GRRRR...
WELP!
...!
KLIK
KLIK
FOR A DOG, ITS SENSE OF SMELL ISN'T VERY GOOD.
HUFF
HUFF
KLIK
KLIK
IT'S GOING AWAY!
WHAT SHOULD WE DO? WE'RE PRETTY FAR INTO THE FOREST NOW.
WITH THAT THING ROAMING AROUND, WE CAN'T WAIT FOR HELP OUT IN THE OPEN.
YES, INDEED.

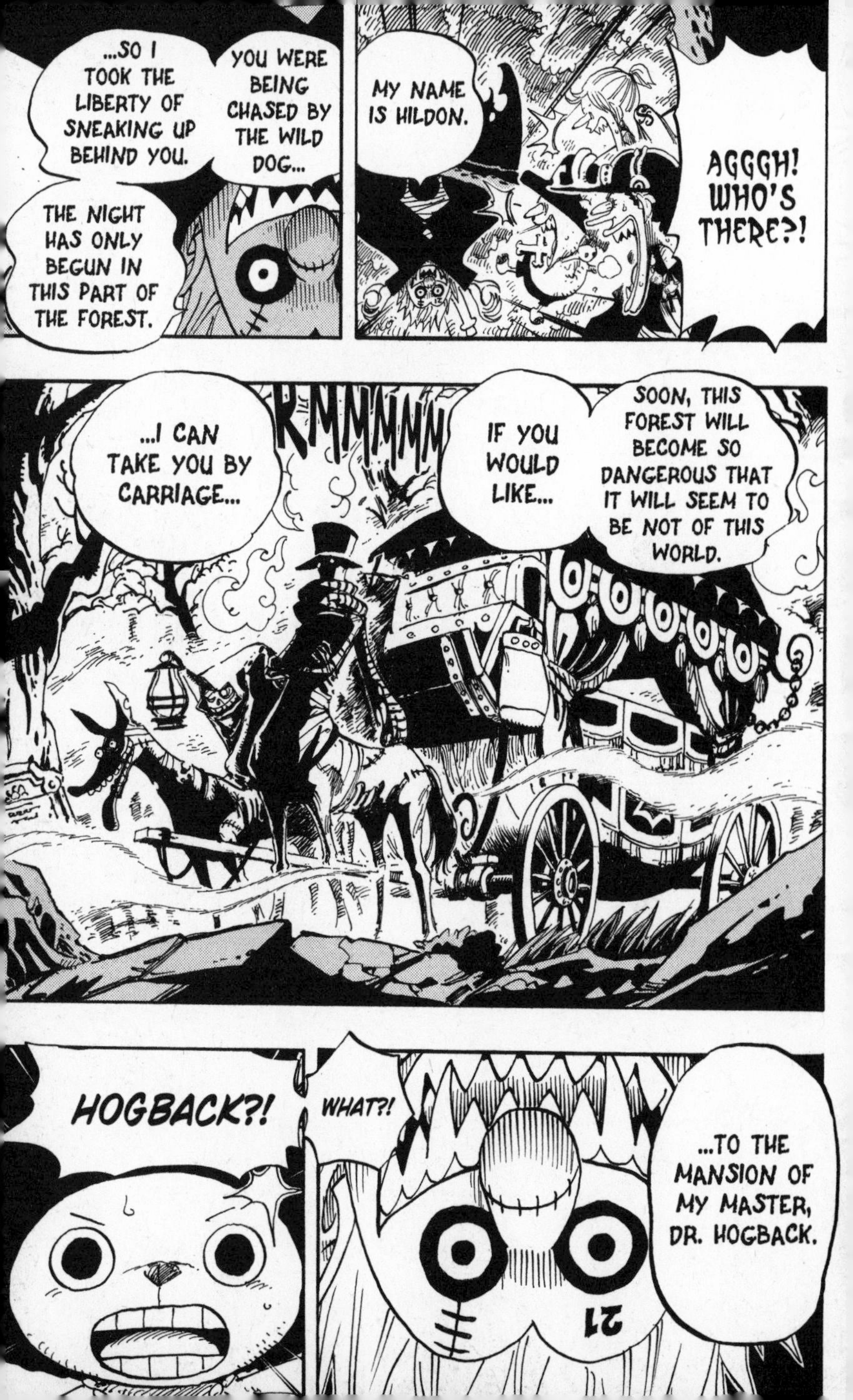
AGGGH! WHO'S THERE?!
MY NAME IS HILDON.
YOU WERE BEING CHASED BY THE WILD DOG...
...SO I TOOK THE LIBERTY OF SNEAKING UP BEHIND YOU.
THE NIGHT HAS ONLY BEGUN IN THIS PART OF THE FOREST.
SOON, THIS FOREST WILL BECOME SO DANGEROUS THAT IT WILL SEEM TO BE NOT OF THIS WORLD.
IF YOU WOULD LIKE...
RMMMMN
...I CAN TAKE YOU BY CARRIAGE...
...TO THE MANSION OF MY MASTER, DR. HOGBACK.
21
WHAT?!
HOGBACK?!

F1

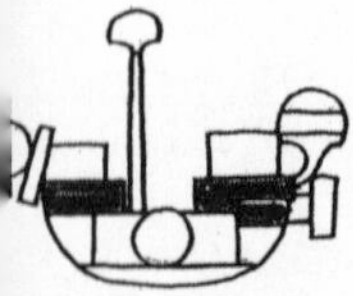

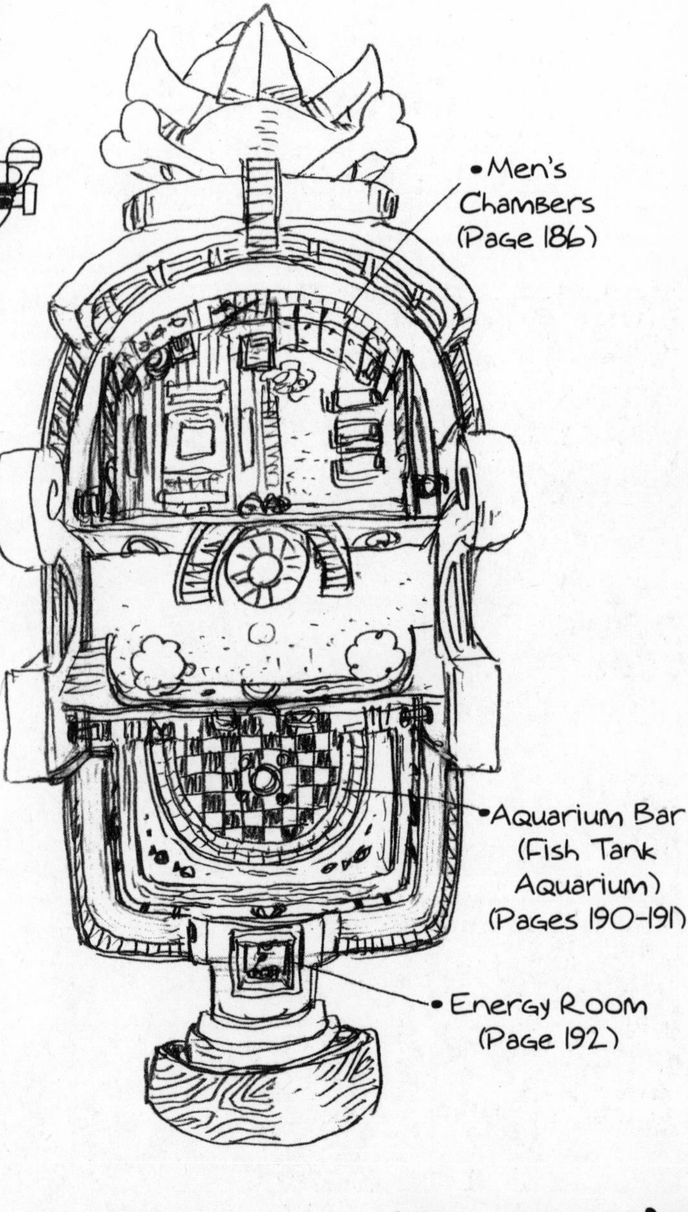

•Men's Chambers (Page 186)
•Aquarium Bar (Fish Tank Aquarium) (Pages 190-191)
•Energy Room (Page 192)

Chapter 445:
ZOMBIES

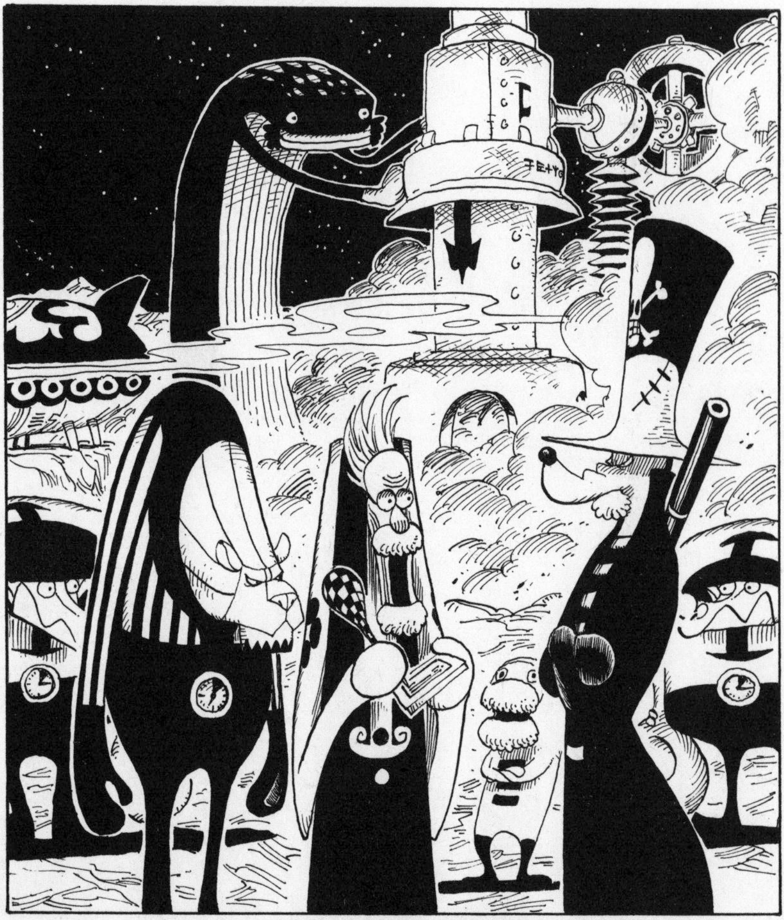

ENERU'S GREAT SPACE MISSION, VOL. 15:
"THE SPACE PIRATES' MOON RUINS EXCAVATION PLAN"

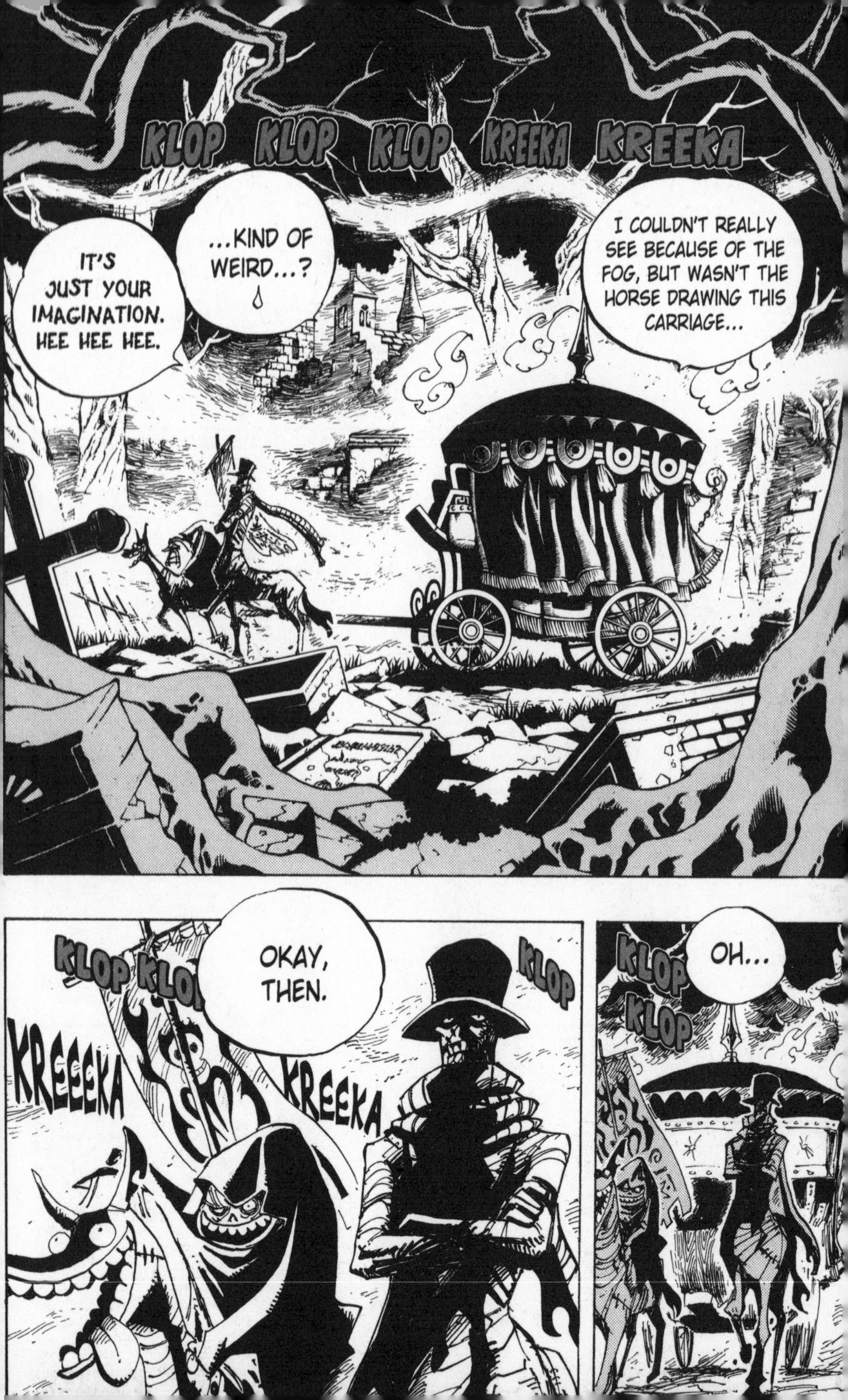
KLOP KLOP KLOP KREEKA KREEKA
I COULDN'T REALLY SEE BECAUSE OF THE FOG, BUT WASN'T THE HORSE DRAWING THIS CARRIAGE...
...KIND OF WEIRD...?
IT'S JUST YOUR IMAGINATION. HEE HEE HEE.
KLOP KLOP
OH...
KLOP
OKAY, THEN.
KLOP KLOP
KREEKA
KREEEKA

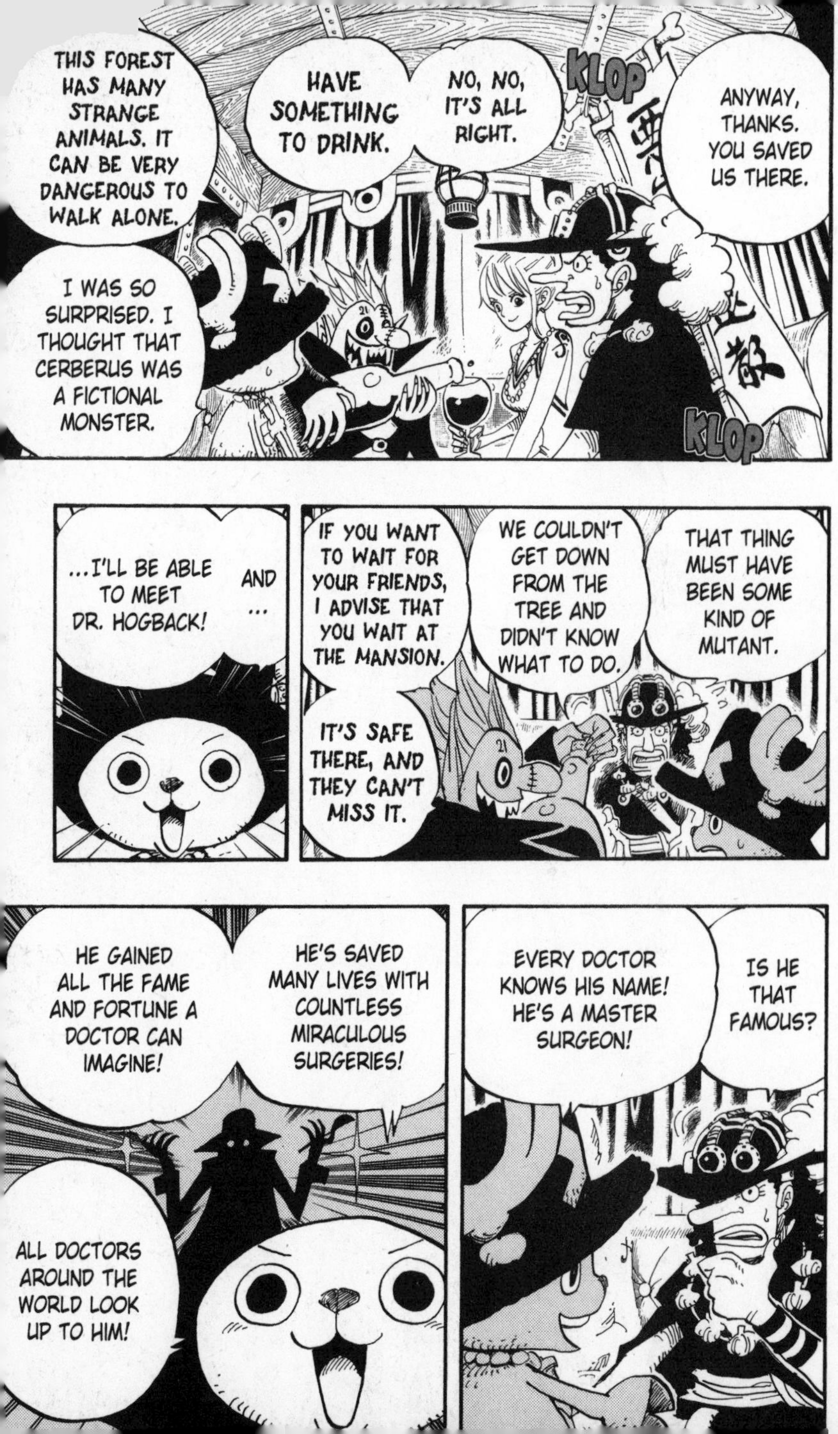
KLOP
ANYWAY, THANKS. YOU SAVED US THERE.
NO, NO, IT'S ALL RIGHT.
HAVE SOMETHING TO DRINK.
THIS FOREST HAS MANY STRANGE ANIMALS. IT CAN BE VERY DANGEROUS TO WALK ALONE.
I WAS SO SURPRISED. I THOUGHT THAT CERBERUS WAS A FICTIONAL MONSTER.
KLOP
THAT THING MUST HAVE BEEN SOME KIND OF MUTANT.
WE COULDN'T GET DOWN FROM THE TREE AND DIDN'T KNOW WHAT TO DO.
IF YOU WANT TO WAIT FOR YOUR FRIENDS, I ADVISE THAT YOU WAIT AT THE MANSION.
IT'S SAFE THERE, AND THEY CAN'T MISS IT.
AND ...
...I'LL BE ABLE TO MEET DR. HOGBACK!
IS HE THAT FAMOUS?
EVERY DOCTOR KNOWS HIS NAME! HE'S A MASTER SURGEON!
HE'S SAVED MANY LIVES WITH COUNTLESS MIRACULOUS SURGERIES!
HE GAINED ALL THE FAME AND FORTUNE A DOCTOR CAN IMAGINE!
ALL DOCTORS AROUND THE WORLD LOOK UP TO HIM!

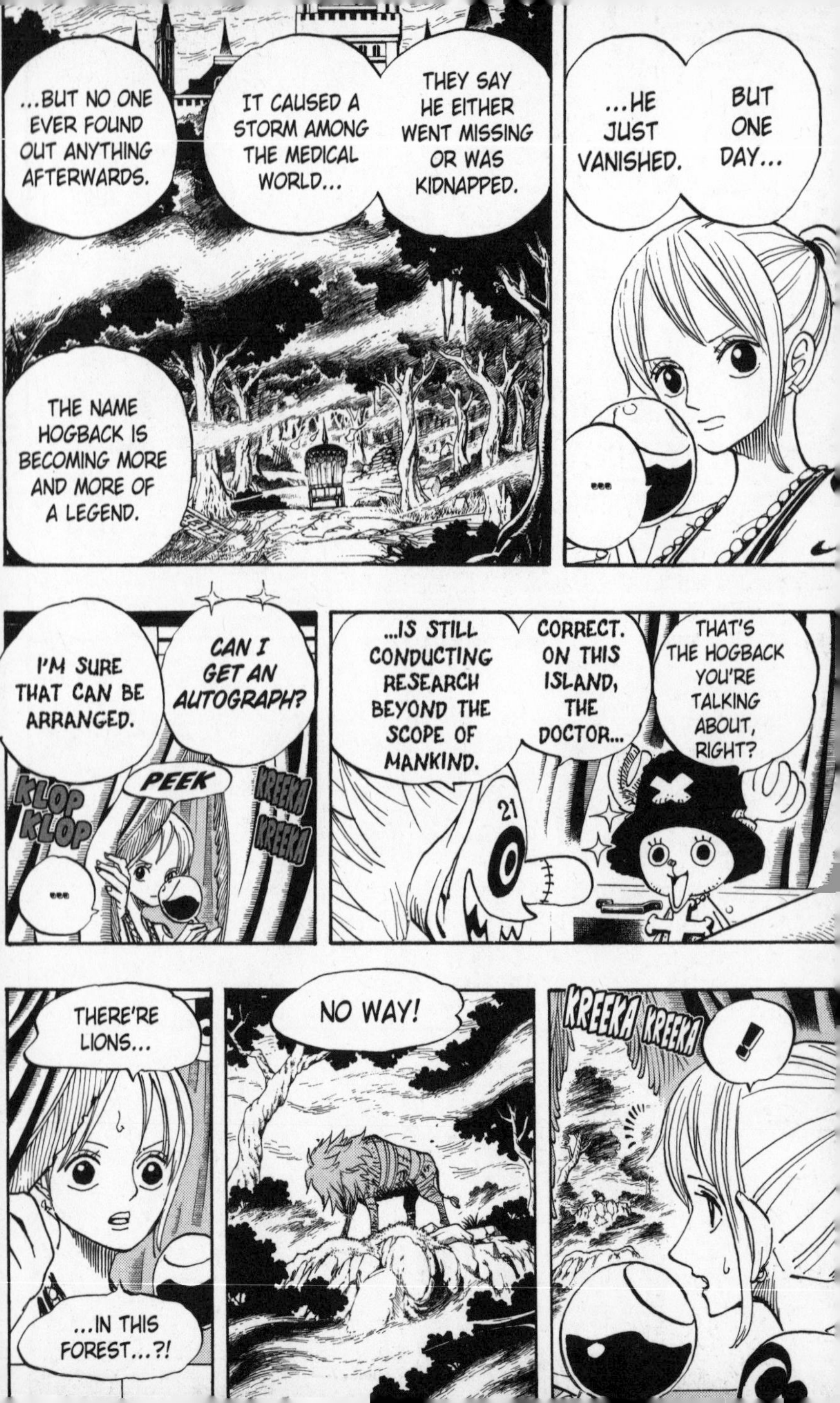
BUT ONE DAY...
...HE JUST VANISHED.
...
THEY SAY HE EITHER WENT MISSING OR WAS KIDNAPPED.
IT CAUSED A STORM AMONG THE MEDICAL WORLD...
...BUT NO ONE EVER FOUND OUT ANYTHING AFTERWARDS.
THE NAME HOGBACK IS BECOMING MORE AND MORE OF A LEGEND.
THAT'S THE HOGBACK YOU'RE TALKING ABOUT, RIGHT?
CORRECT. ON THIS ISLAND, THE DOCTOR...
...IS STILL CONDUCTING RESEARCH BEYOND THE SCOPE OF MANKIND.
21
CAN I GET AN AUTOGRAPH?
I'M SURE THAT CAN BE ARRANGED.
KREEKA KREEKA
PEEK
KLOP KLOP
...
KREEKA KREEKA
!
NO WAY!
THERE'RE LIONS...
...IN THIS FOREST...?!

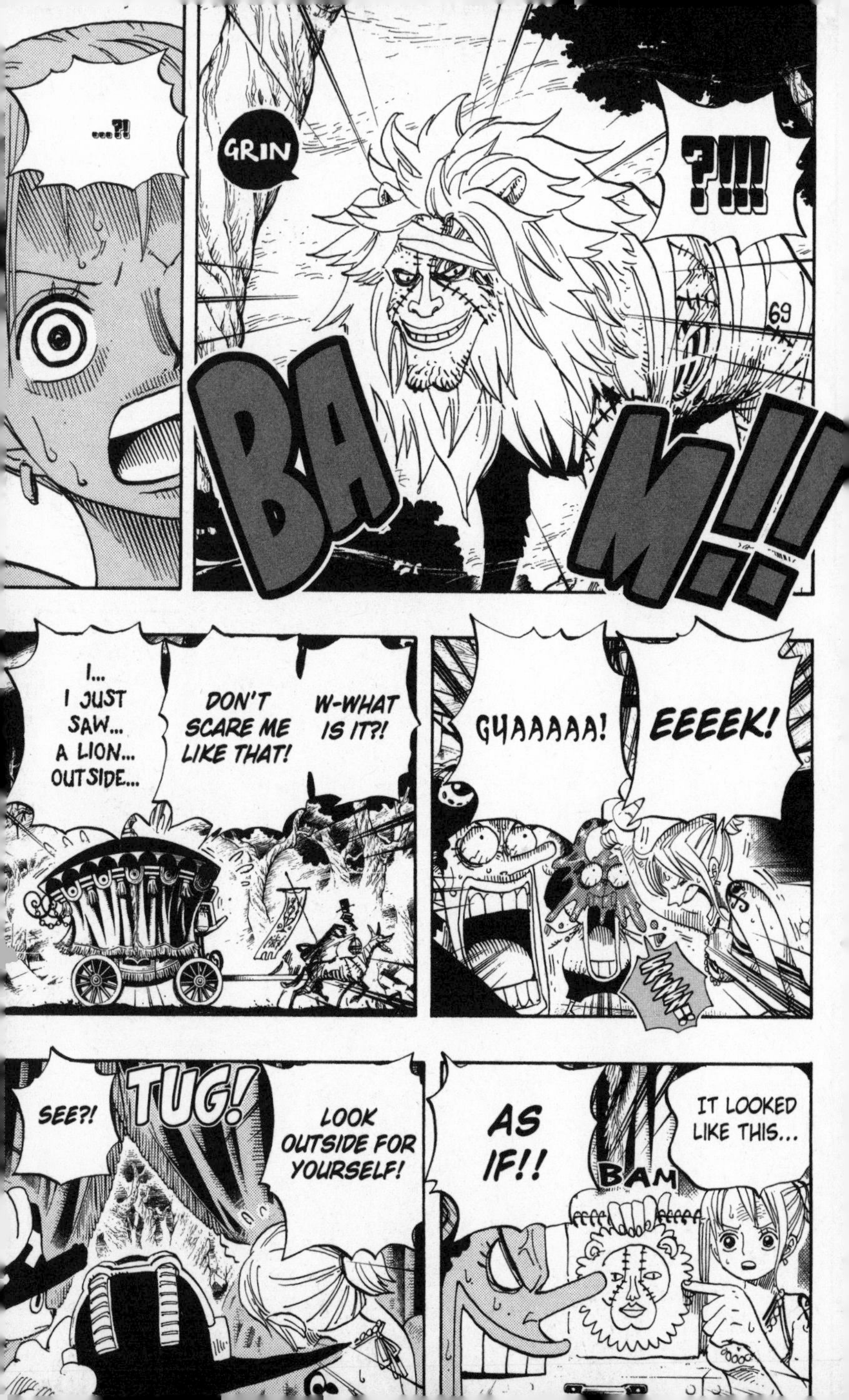
?!!!
GRIN
BAM!!
...?!
EEEEK!
GUAAAAA!
W-WHAT IS IT?!
DON'T SCARE ME LIKE THAT!
I... I JUST SAW... A LION... OUTSIDE...
IT LOOKED LIKE THIS...
AS IF!!
BAM
LOOK OUTSIDE FOR YOURSELF!
TUG!
SEE?!

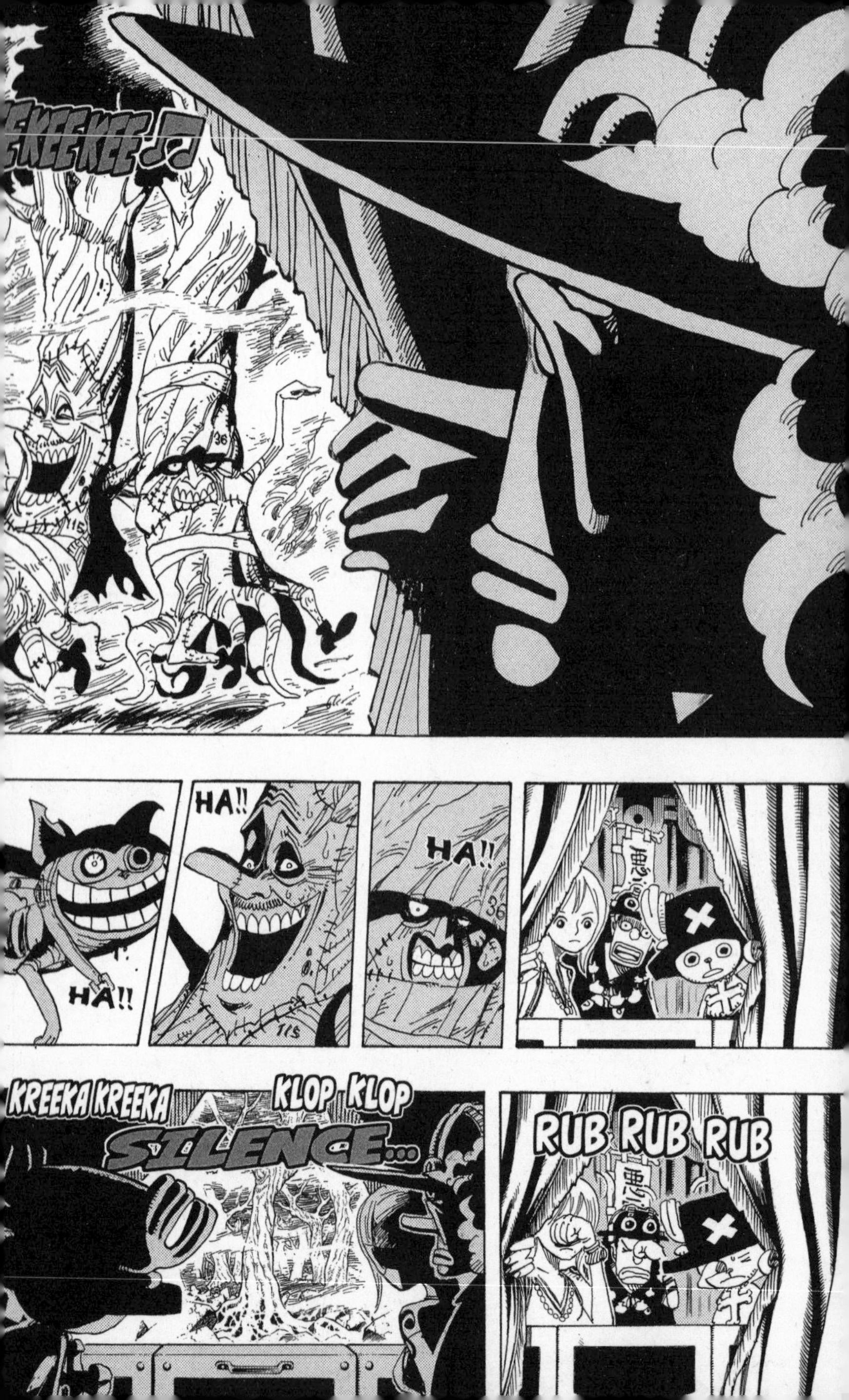
KEE KEE ♪♫
HA!!
HA!!
HA!!
RUB RUB RUB
KLOP KLOP
KREEKA KREEKA
SILENCE...

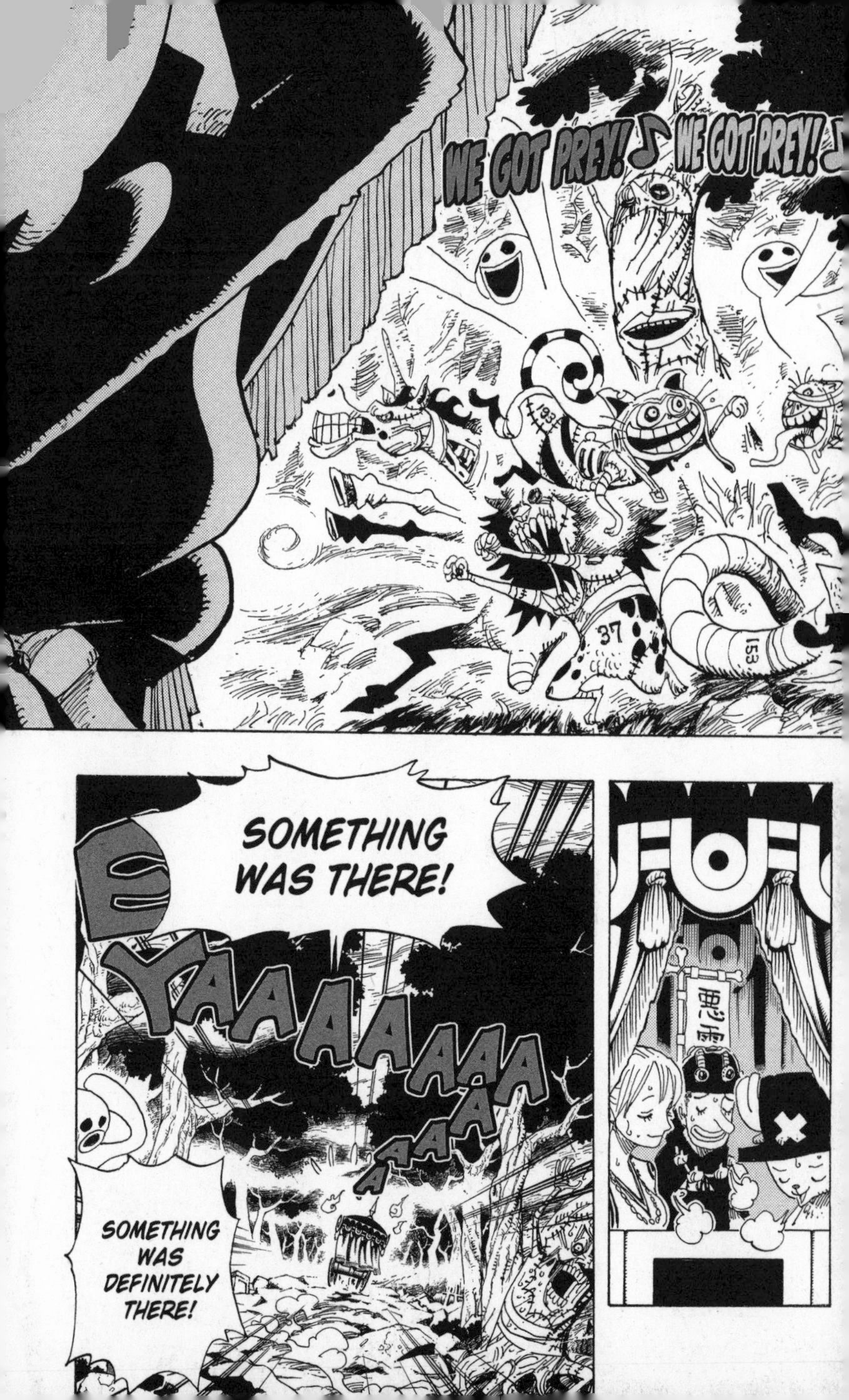
WE GOT PREY!♪ WE GOT PREY!♪
SOMETHING WAS THERE!
EYAAAAAAAAAAA
SOMETHING WAS DEFINITELY THERE!

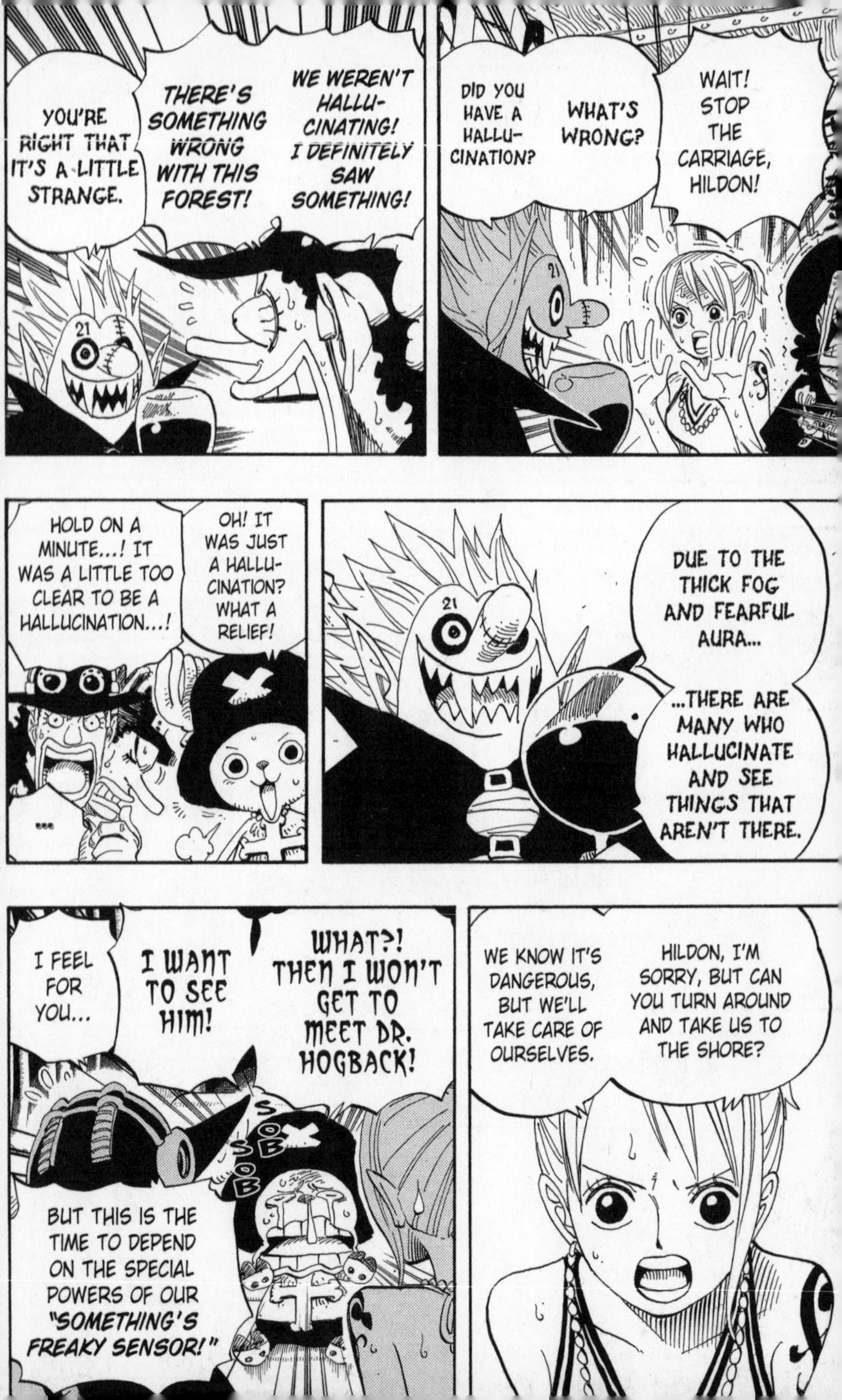
WAIT! STOP THE CARRIAGE, HILDON!
WHAT'S WRONG?
DID YOU HAVE A HALLU-CINATION?
WE WEREN'T HALLU-CINATING! I DEFINITELY SAW SOMETHING!
THERE'S SOMETHING WRONG WITH THIS FOREST!
YOU'RE RIGHT THAT IT'S A LITTLE STRANGE.
DUE TO THE THICK FOG AND FEARFUL AURA...
...THERE ARE MANY WHO HALLUCINATE AND SEE THINGS THAT AREN'T THERE.
OH! IT WAS JUST A HALLU-CINATION? WHAT A RELIEF!
HOLD ON A MINUTE...! IT WAS A LITTLE TOO CLEAR TO BE A HALLUCINATION...!
...
HILDON, I'M SORRY, BUT CAN YOU TURN AROUND AND TAKE US TO THE SHORE?
WE KNOW IT'S DANGEROUS, BUT WE'LL TAKE CARE OF OURSELVES.
WHAT?! THEN I WON'T GET TO MEET DR. HOGBACK!
I WANT TO SEE HIM!
I FEEL FOR YOU...
SOB SOB
BUT THIS IS THE TIME TO DEPEND ON THE SPECIAL POWERS OF OUR "SOMETHING'S FREAKY SENSOR!"

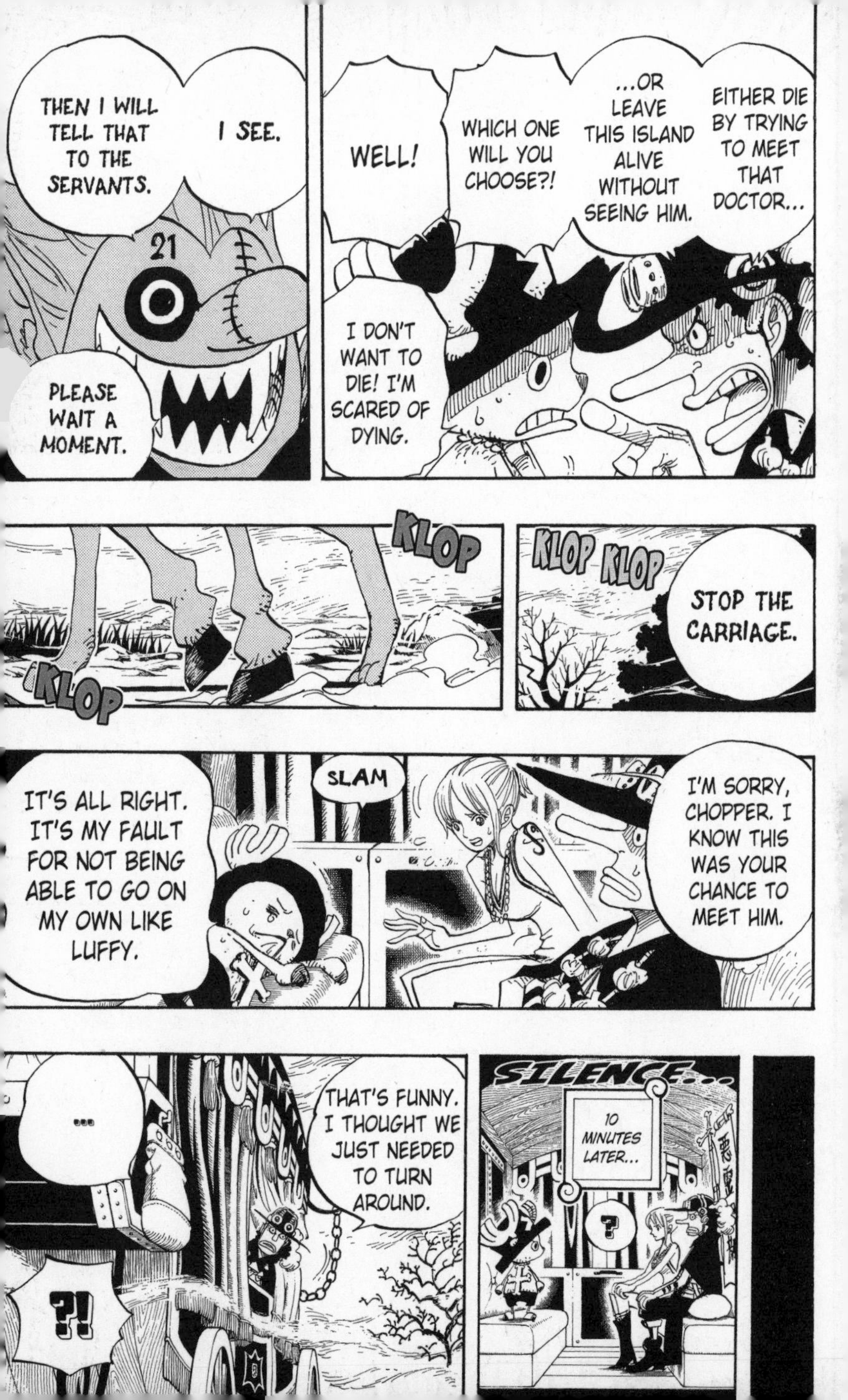
EITHER DIE BY TRYING TO MEET THAT DOCTOR...
...OR LEAVE THIS ISLAND ALIVE WITHOUT SEEING HIM.
WHICH ONE WILL YOU CHOOSE?!
WELL!
I DON'T WANT TO DIE! I'M SCARED OF DYING.
I SEE.
THEN I WILL TELL THAT TO THE SERVANTS.
21
PLEASE WAIT A MOMENT.
KLOP KLOP
STOP THE CARRIAGE.
KLOP
KLOP
I'M SORRY, CHOPPER. I KNOW THIS WAS YOUR CHANCE TO MEET HIM.
SLAM
IT'S ALL RIGHT. IT'S MY FAULT FOR NOT BEING ABLE TO GO ON MY OWN LIKE LUFFY.
SILENCE...
10 MINUTES LATER...
?
THAT'S FUNNY. I THOUGHT WE JUST NEEDED TO TURN AROUND.
...
?!

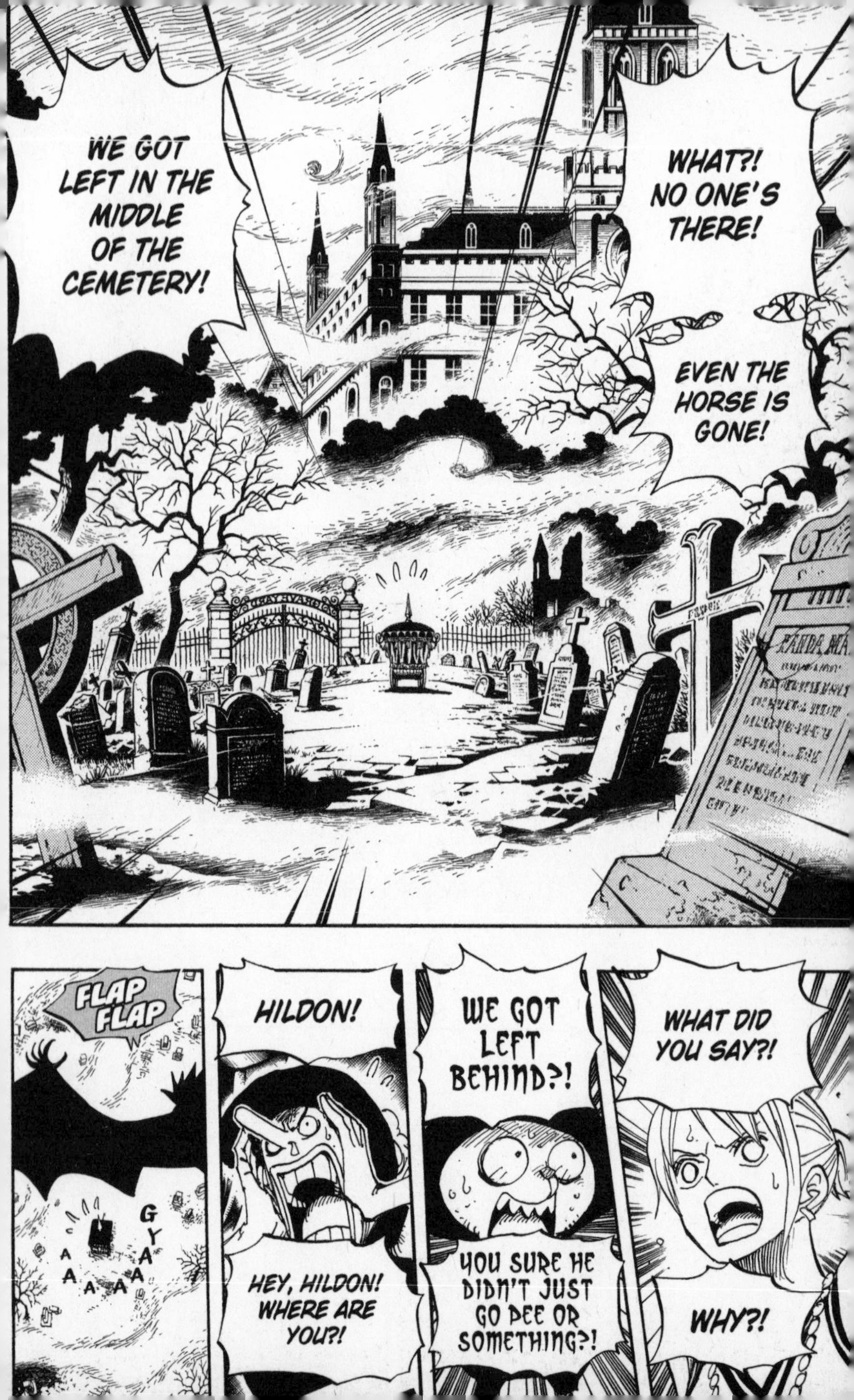

WHAT?! NO ONE'S THERE!
EVEN THE HORSE IS GONE!
WE GOT LEFT IN THE MIDDLE OF THE CEMETERY!
WHAT DID YOU SAY?!
WHY?!
WE GOT LEFT BEHIND?!
YOU SURE HE DIDN'T JUST GO PEE OR SOMETHING?!
HILDON!
HEY, HILDON! WHERE ARE YOU?!
FLAP FLAP
GYAAAAAAA

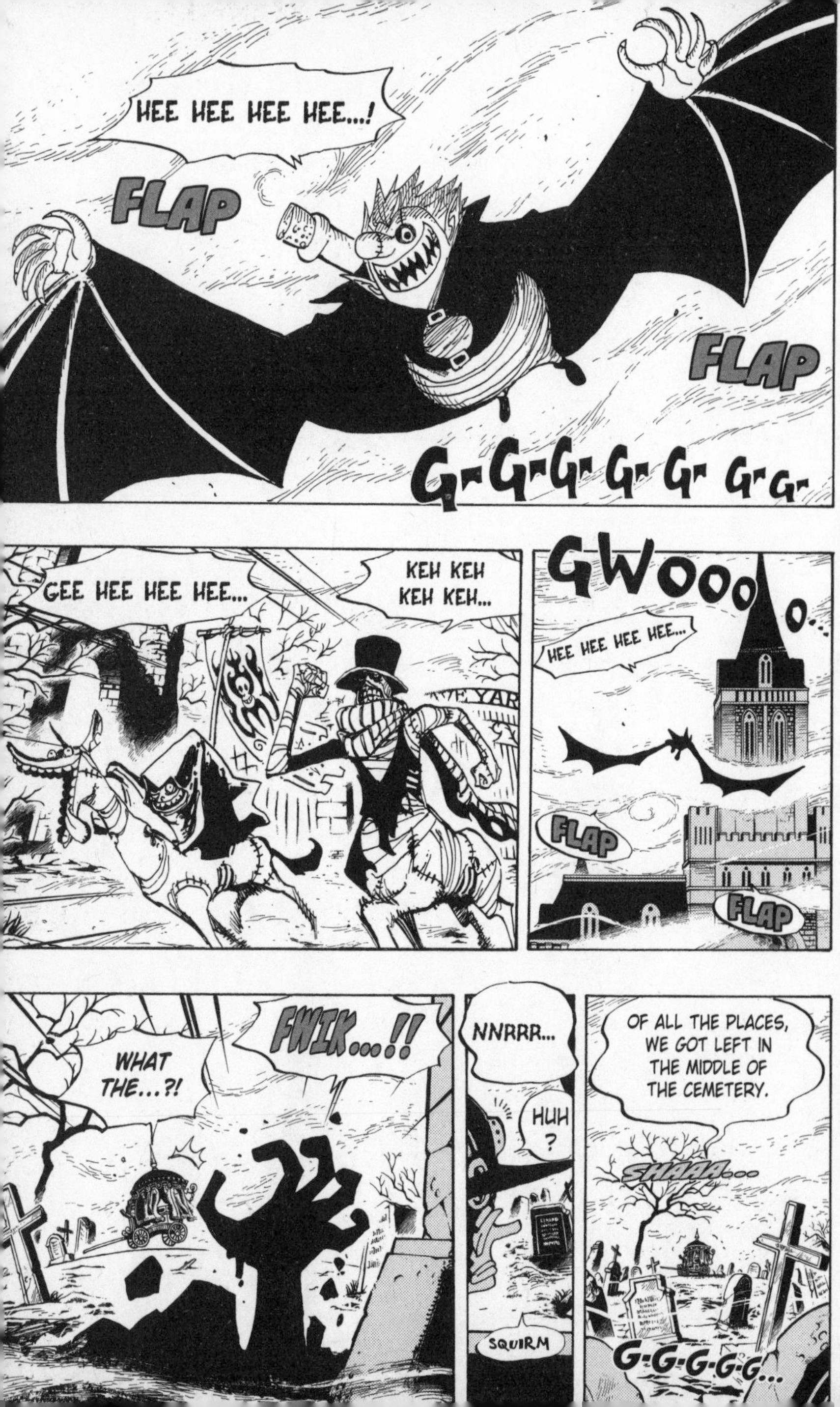
HEE HEE HEE HEE...!
FLAP
FLAP
G-G-G-G-G-G-G-
GWOOOO O...
HEE HEE HEE HEE...
FLAP
FLAP
KEH KEH KEH KEH...
GEE HEE HEE HEE...
OF ALL THE PLACES, WE GOT LEFT IN THE MIDDLE OF THE CEMETERY.
SHAAA...
G-G-G-G-G...
NNRRR...
HUH ?
SQUIRM
FWIK...!!
WHAT THE...?!

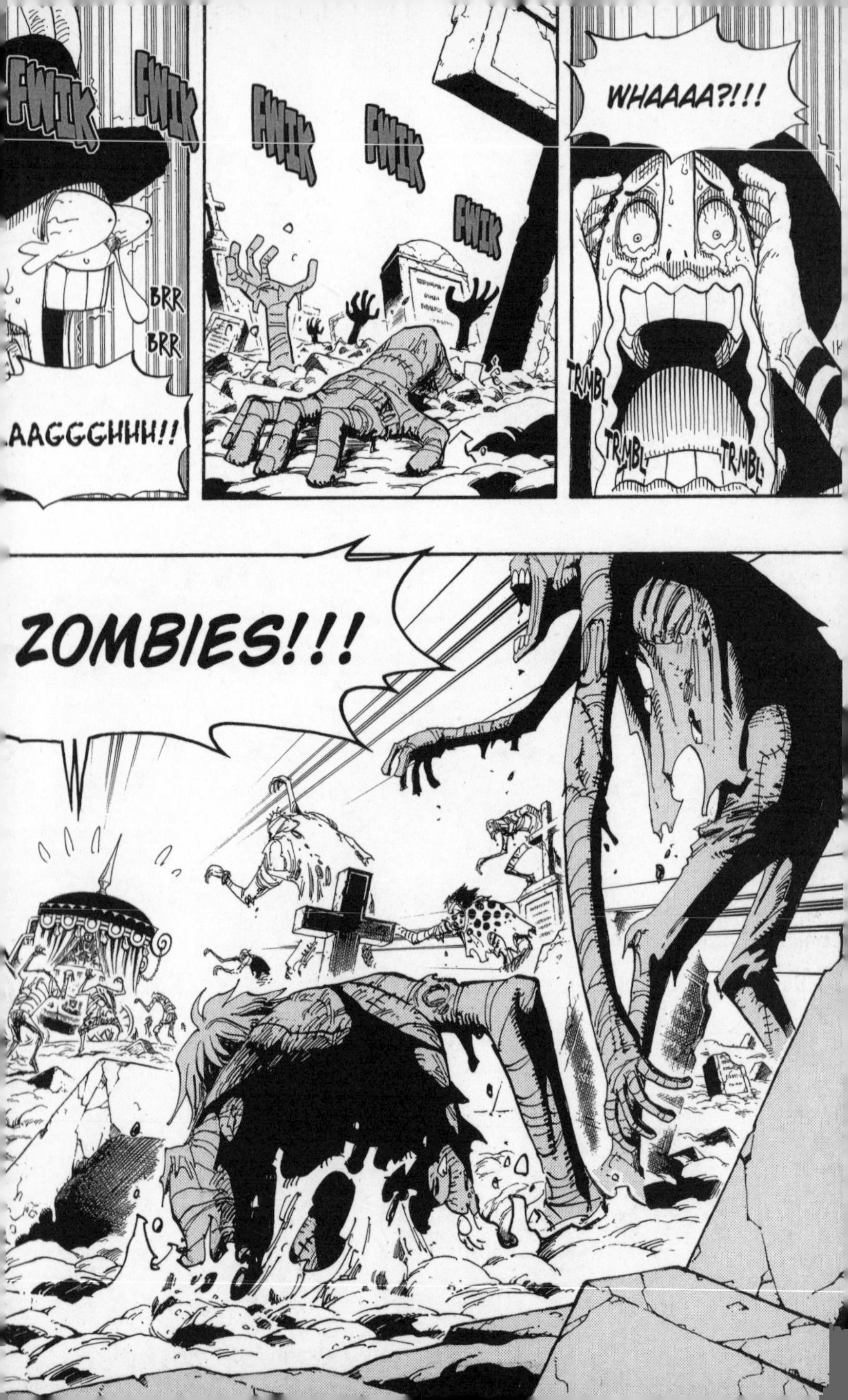
WHAAAA?!!!
TRMBL
TRMBL
TRMBL
FWIK
FWIK
FWIK
FWIK
FWIK
BRR
BRR
AAGGGHHH!!
ZOMBIES!!!

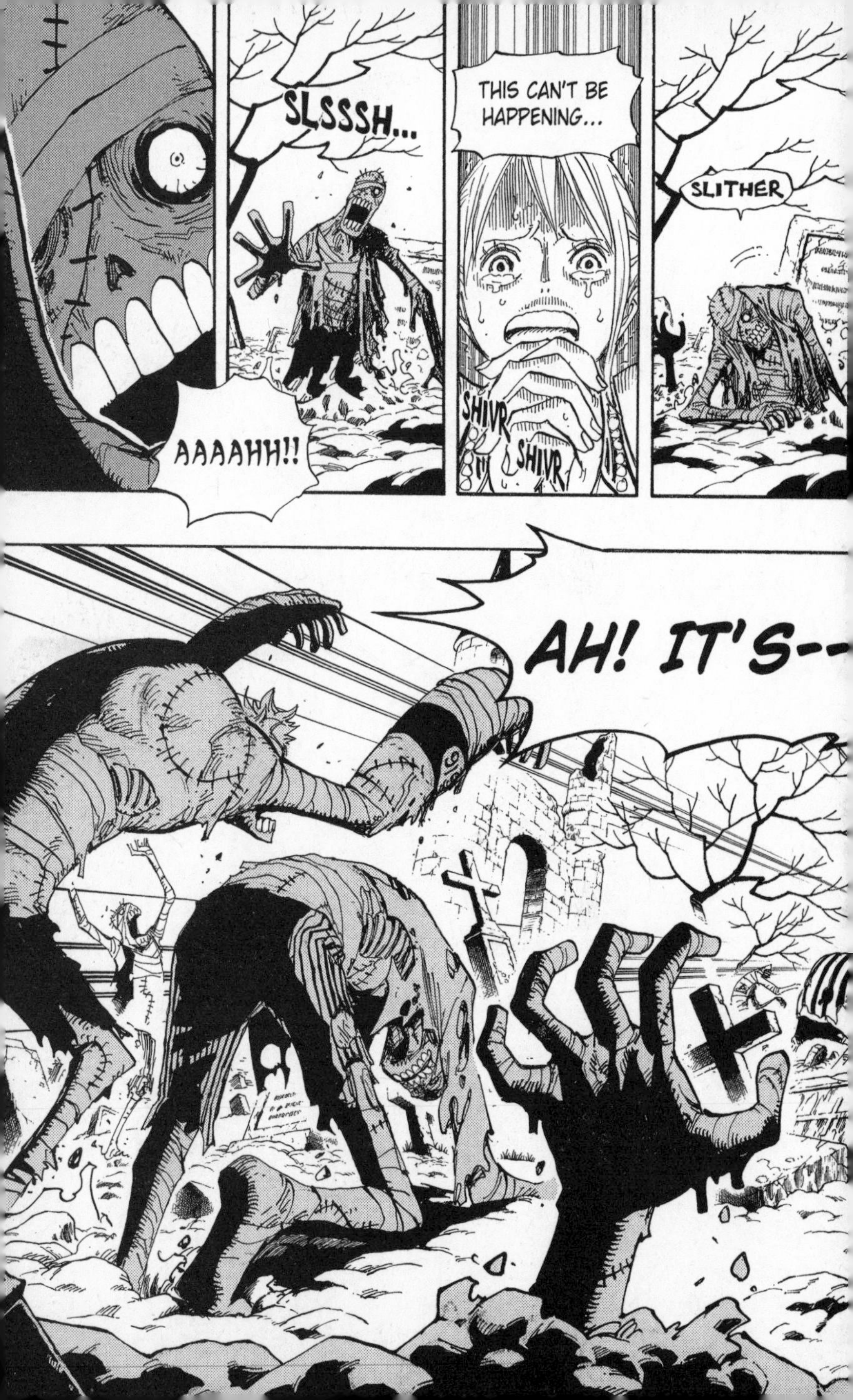

SLITHER
THIS CAN'T BE HAPPENING...
SHIVR
SHIVR
SLSSSH...
AAAAHH!!
AH! IT'S---

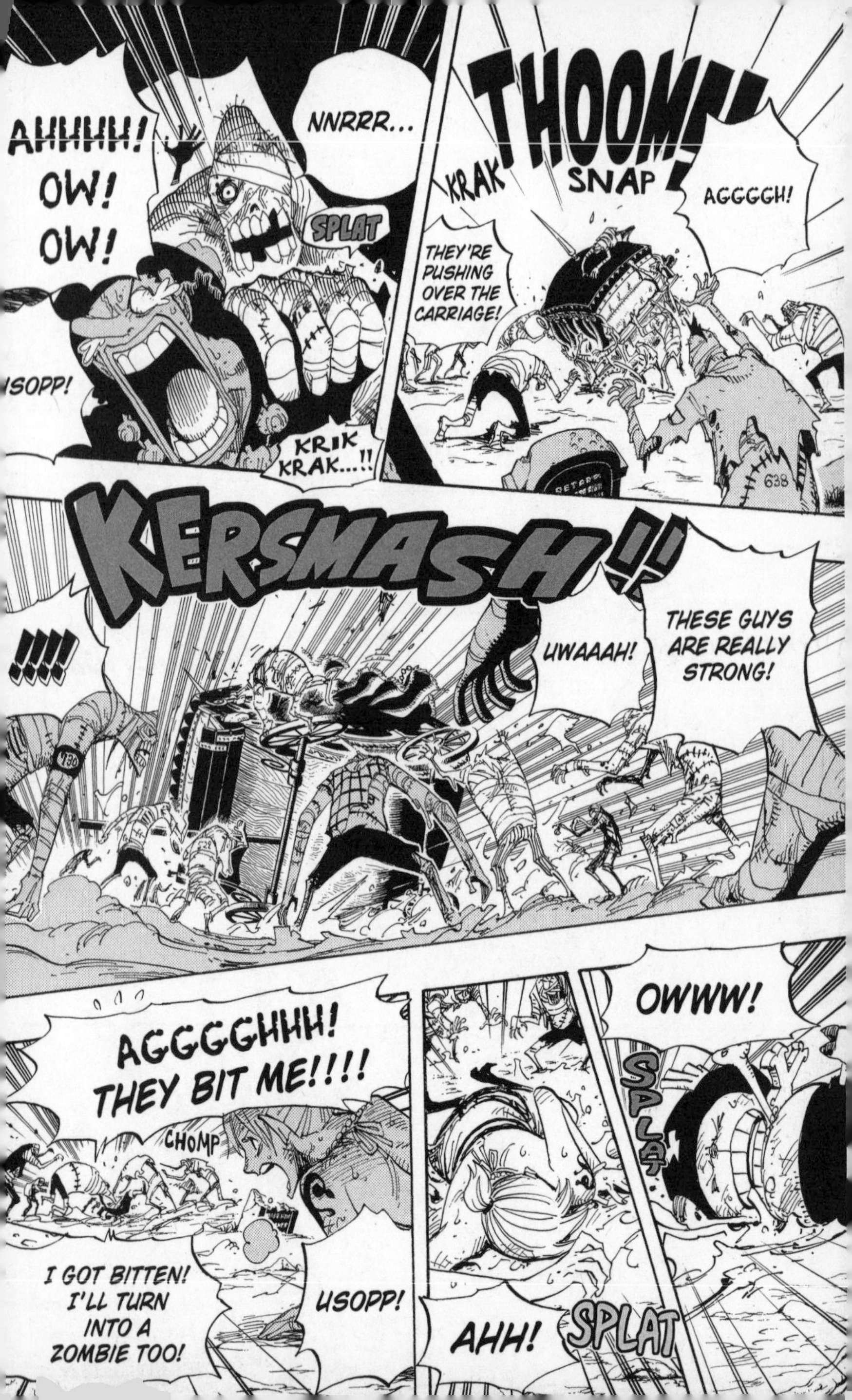
AGGGGH!
THOOM!!
SNAP
KRAK
THEY'RE PUSHING OVER THE CARRIAGE!
NNRRR...
SPLAT
AHHHH! OW! OW!
SOPP!
KRIK KRAK...!!
KERSMASH!!
THESE GUYS ARE REALLY STRONG!
UWAAAH!
!!!!!
OWWW!
SPLAT
AHH!
SPLAT
AGGGGHHH! THEY BIT ME!!!!
CHOMP
USOPP!
I GOT BITTEN! I'LL TURN INTO A ZOMBIE TOO!

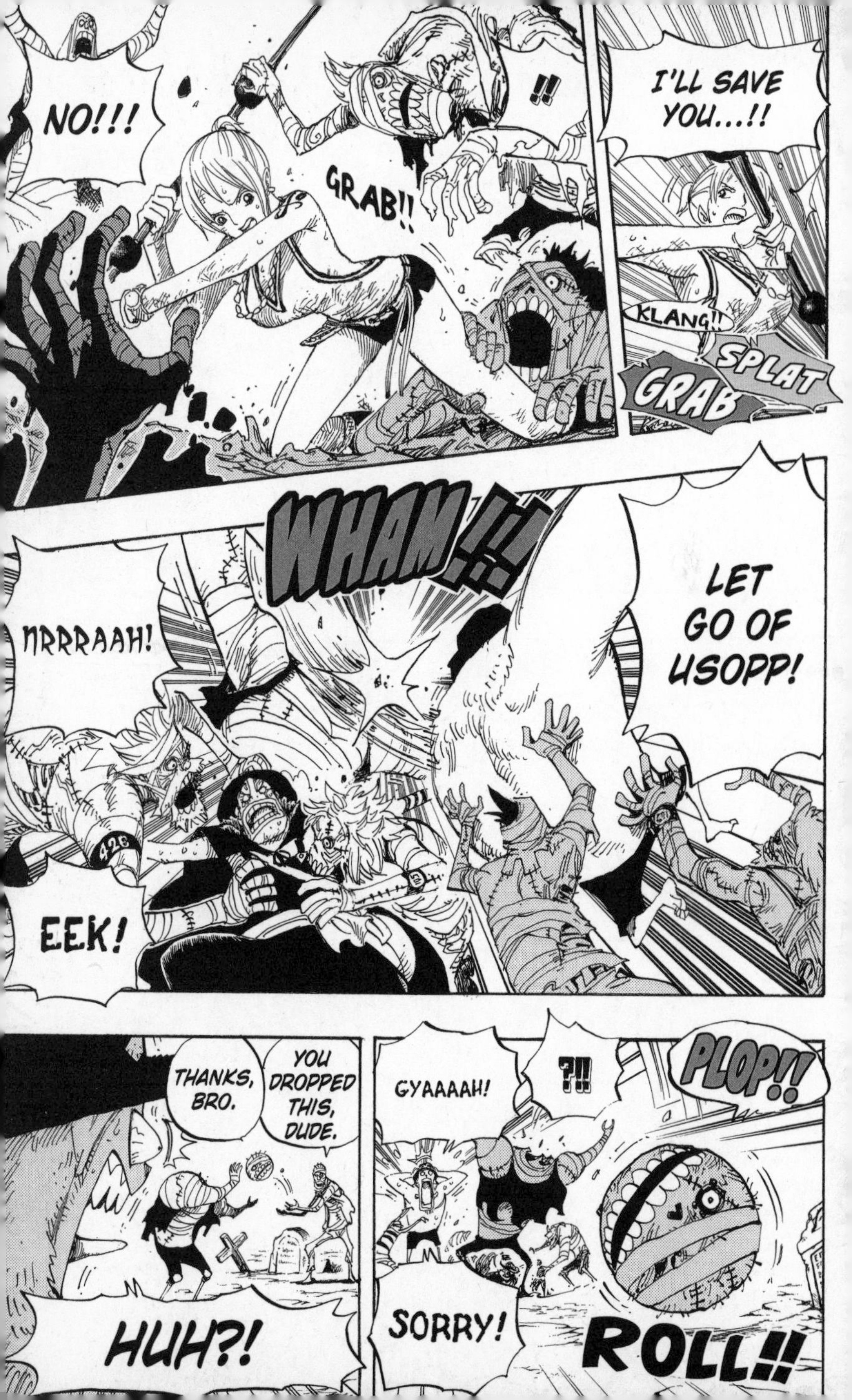
I'LL SAVE YOU...!!
KLANG!!
SPLAT
GRAB
!!
NO!!!
GRAB!!
WHAM!!!
LET GO OF USOPP!
NRRRAAH!
EEK!
PLOP!!
?!!
GYAAAAH!
ROLL!!
SORRY!
YOU DROPPED THIS, DUDE.
THANKS, BRO.
HUH?!

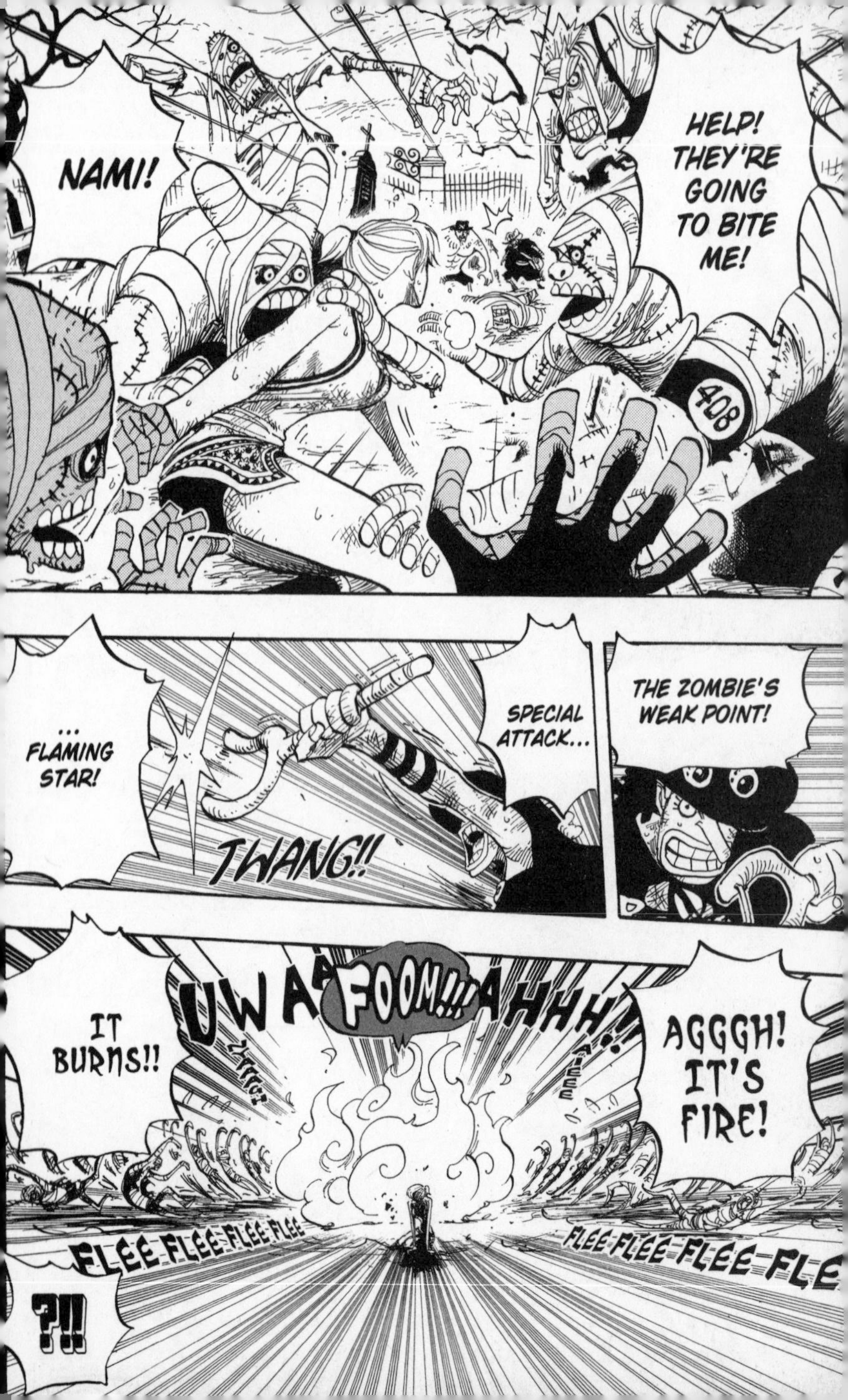
HELP! THEY'RE GOING TO BITE ME!
NAMI!
THE ZOMBIE'S WEAK POINT!
SPECIAL ATTACK...
TWANG!!
... FLAMING STAR!
AGGGH! IT'S FIRE!
UWAAHHH!!
FOOM!!!
IT BURNS!!
FLEE FLEE FLEE FLE
FLEE FLEE FLEE FLEE
?!!

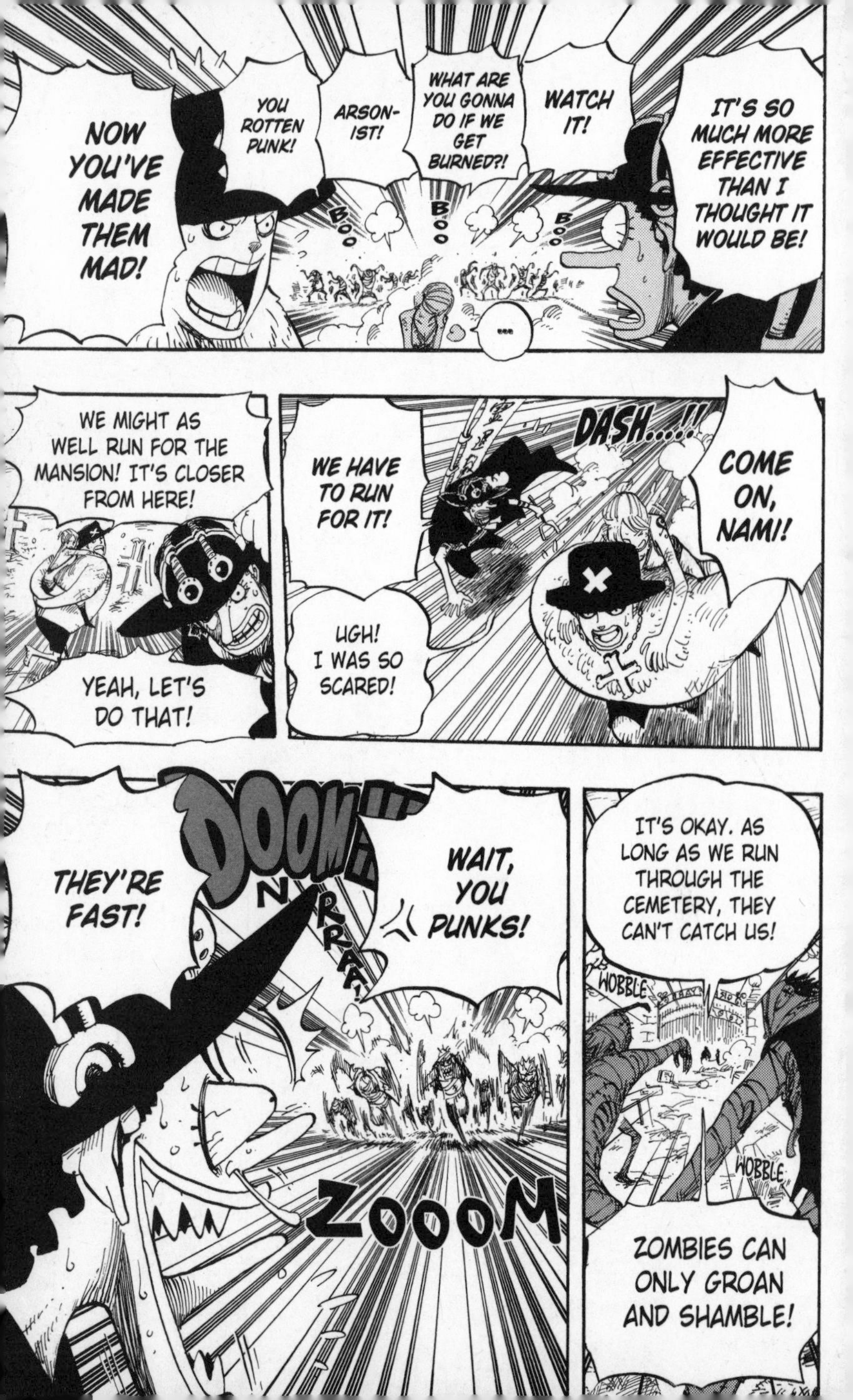
IT'S SO MUCH MORE EFFECTIVE THAN I THOUGHT IT WOULD BE!
WATCH IT!
WHAT ARE YOU GONNA DO IF WE GET BURNED?!
ARSON-IST!
YOU ROTTEN PUNK!
NOW YOU'VE MADE THEM MAD!
BOO
BOO
BOO
...
DASH...!!
COME ON, NAMI!
WE HAVE TO RUN FOR IT!
UGH! I WAS SO SCARED!
WE MIGHT AS WELL RUN FOR THE MANSION! IT'S CLOSER FROM HERE!
YEAH, LET'S DO THAT!
IT'S OKAY. AS LONG AS WE RUN THROUGH THE CEMETERY, THEY CAN'T CATCH US!
WOBBLE
WOBBLE
ZOMBIES CAN ONLY GROAN AND SHAMBLE!
DOOM!!!
WAIT, YOU PUNKS!
NRRAA!
THEY'RE FAST!
ZOOOM

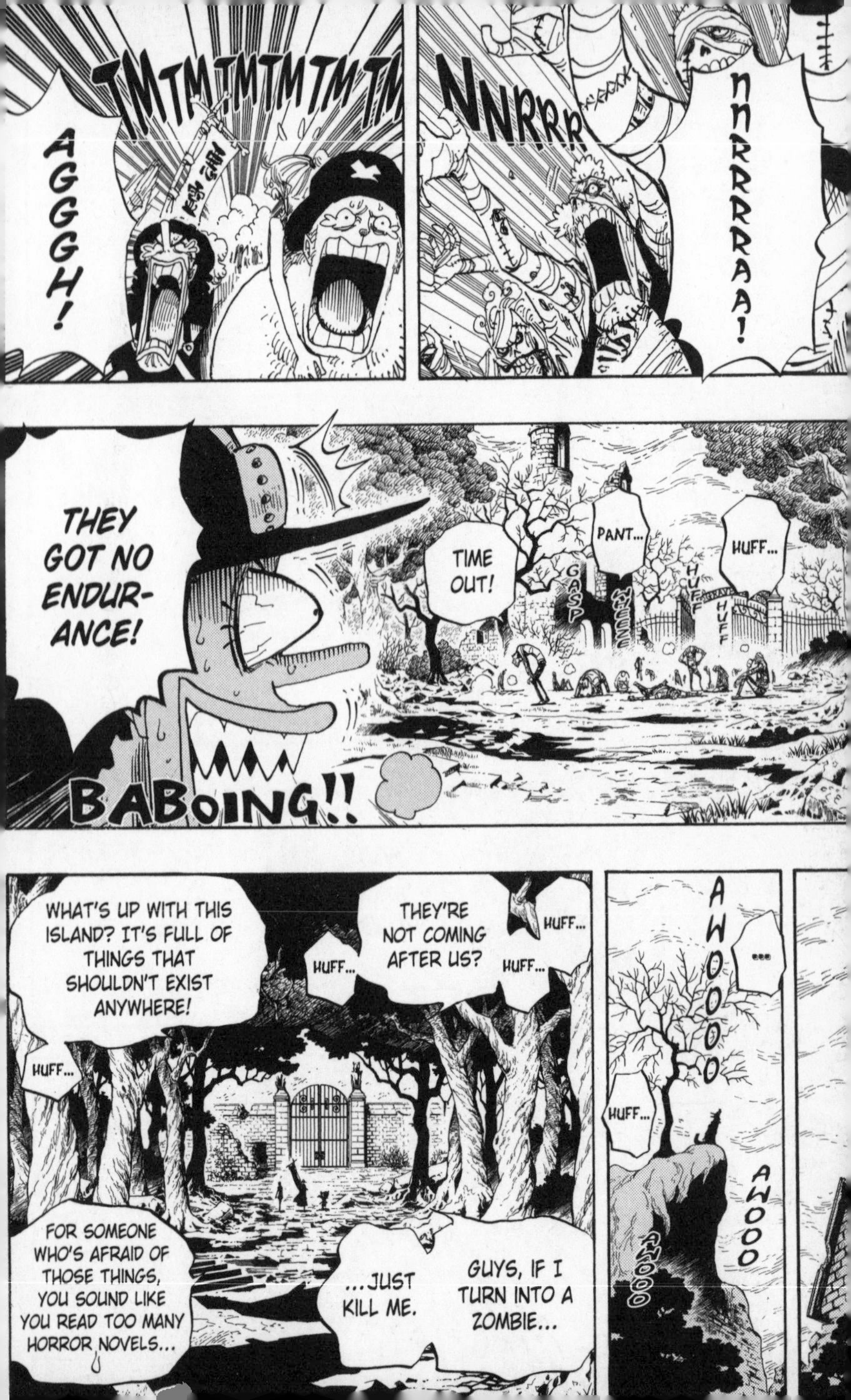
NNRRRR
nnRRRRRAA!
TMTMTMTMTMTMTM
AGGGH!
HUFF...
HUFF
HUFF
PANT...
WHEEZE
GASP
TIME OUT!
THEY GOT NO ENDUR-ANCE!
BABOING!!
...
AWOOOO
HUFF...
AWOOO
AWOOO
THEY'RE NOT COMING AFTER US?
HUFF...
HUFF...
HUFF...
WHAT'S UP WITH THIS ISLAND? IT'S FULL OF THINGS THAT SHOULDN'T EXIST ANYWHERE!
HUFF...
GUYS, IF I TURN INTO A ZOMBIE...
...JUST KILL ME.
FOR SOMEONE WHO'S AFRAID OF THOSE THINGS, YOU SOUND LIKE YOU READ TOO MANY HORROR NOVELS...

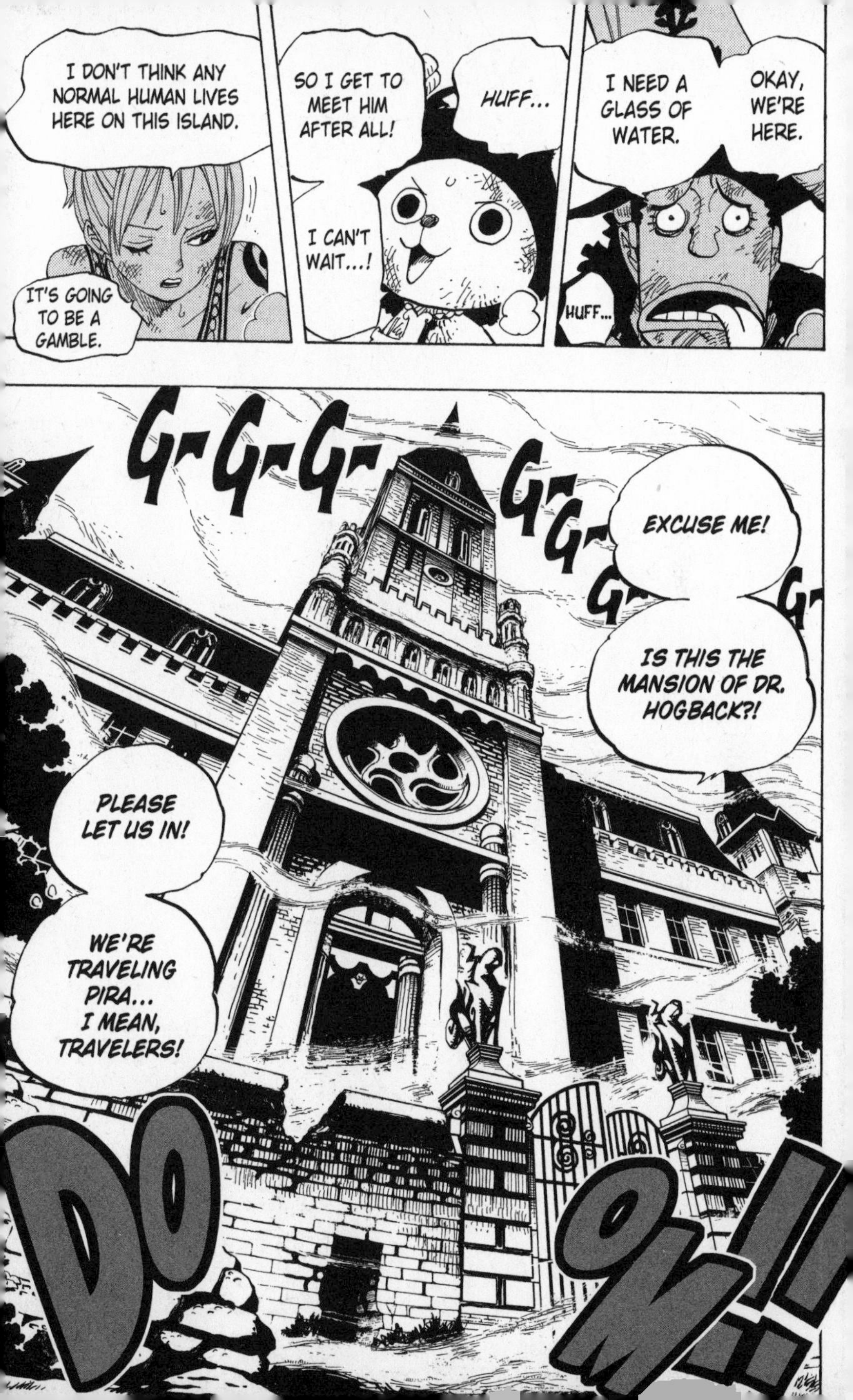
OKAY, WE'RE HERE.
I NEED A GLASS OF WATER.
HUFF...
HUFF...
SO I GET TO MEET HIM AFTER ALL!
I CAN'T WAIT...!
I DON'T THINK ANY NORMAL HUMAN LIVES HERE ON THIS ISLAND.
IT'S GOING TO BE A GAMBLE.
G-G-G-
G-G-G- G-
EXCUSE ME!
IS THIS THE MANSION OF DR. HOGBACK?!
PLEASE LET US IN!
WE'RE TRAVELING PIRA... I MEAN, TRAVELERS!
DOOM!!

DOCTOR HOGBACK

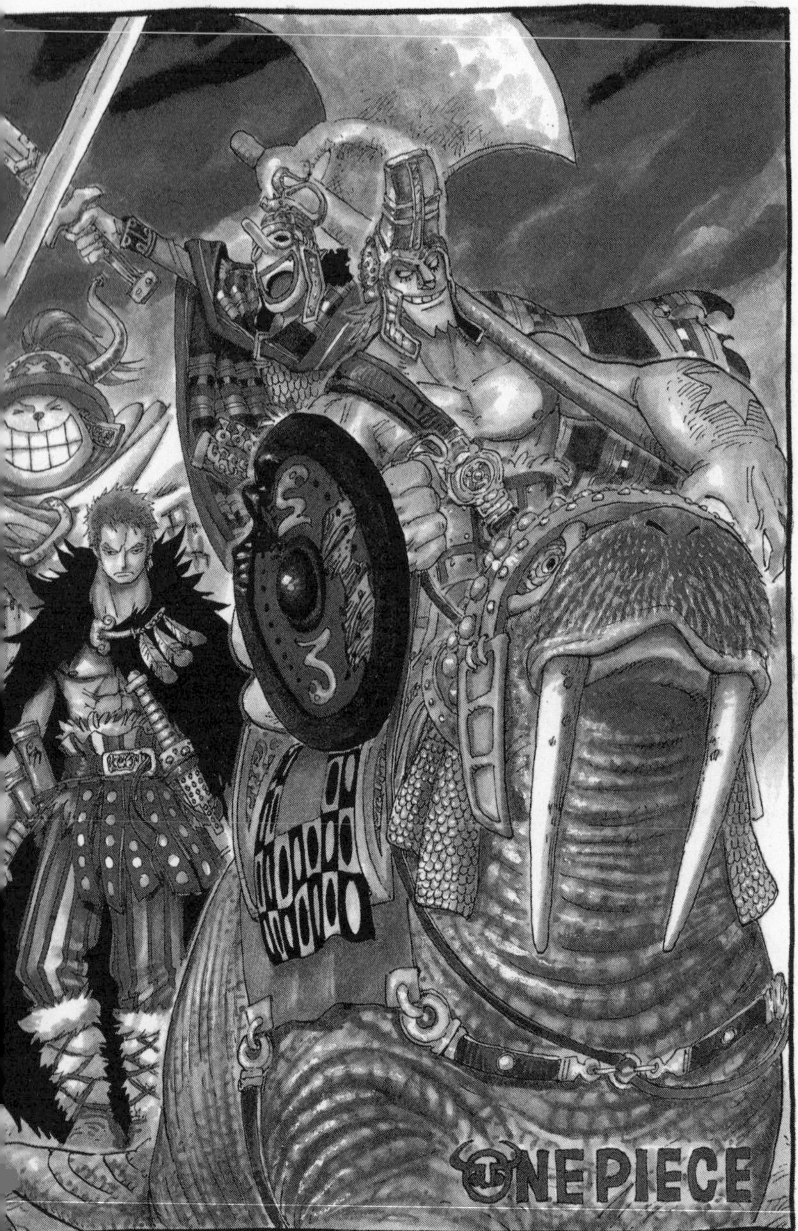
ONE PIECE

Chapter 446:

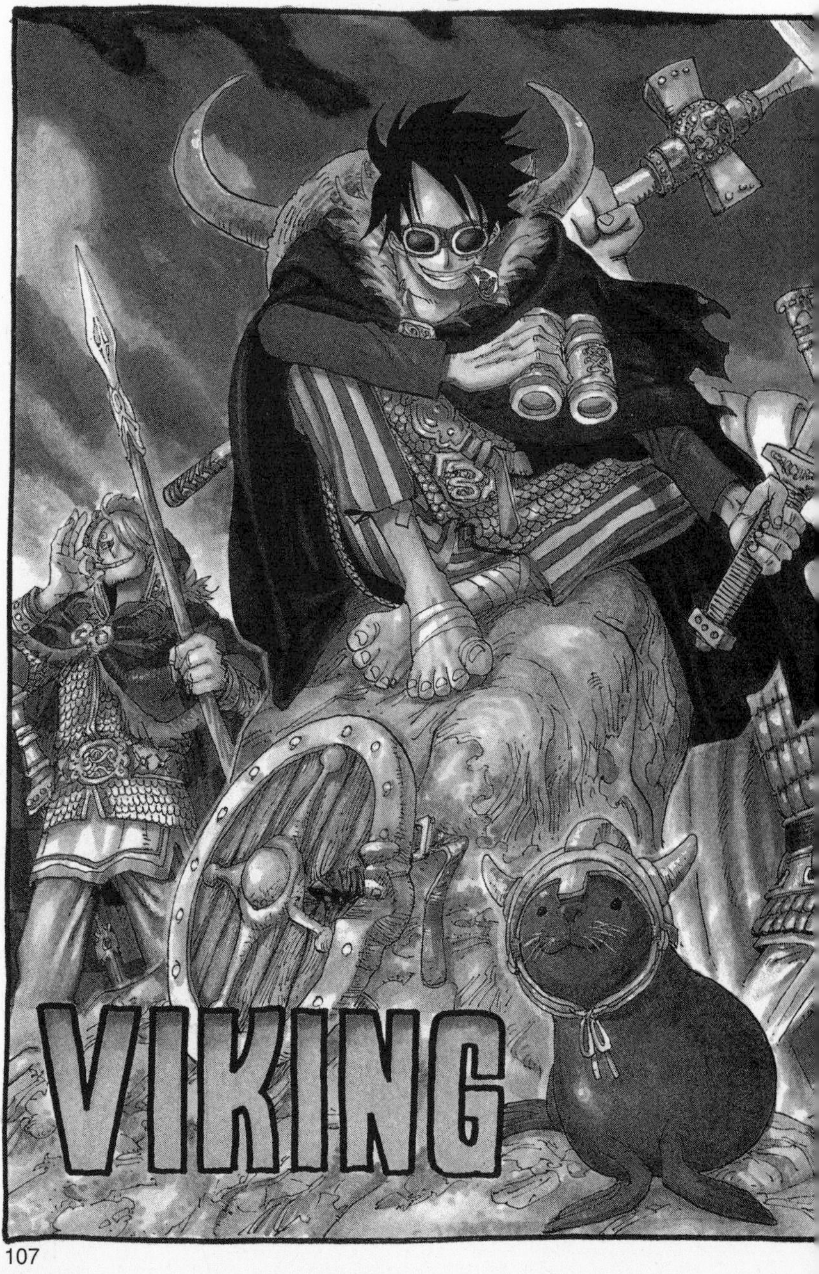
VIKING

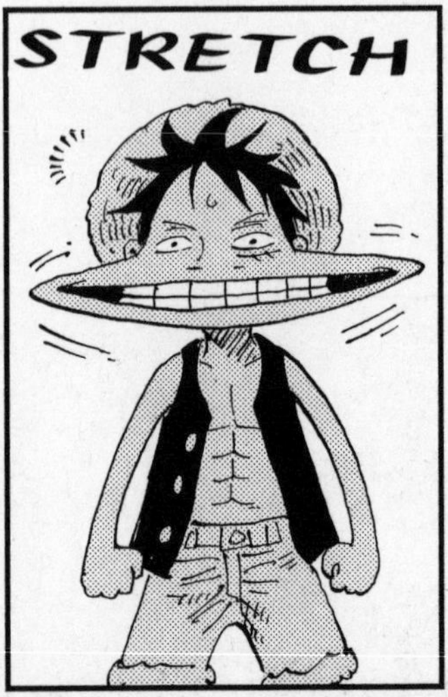
STRETCH

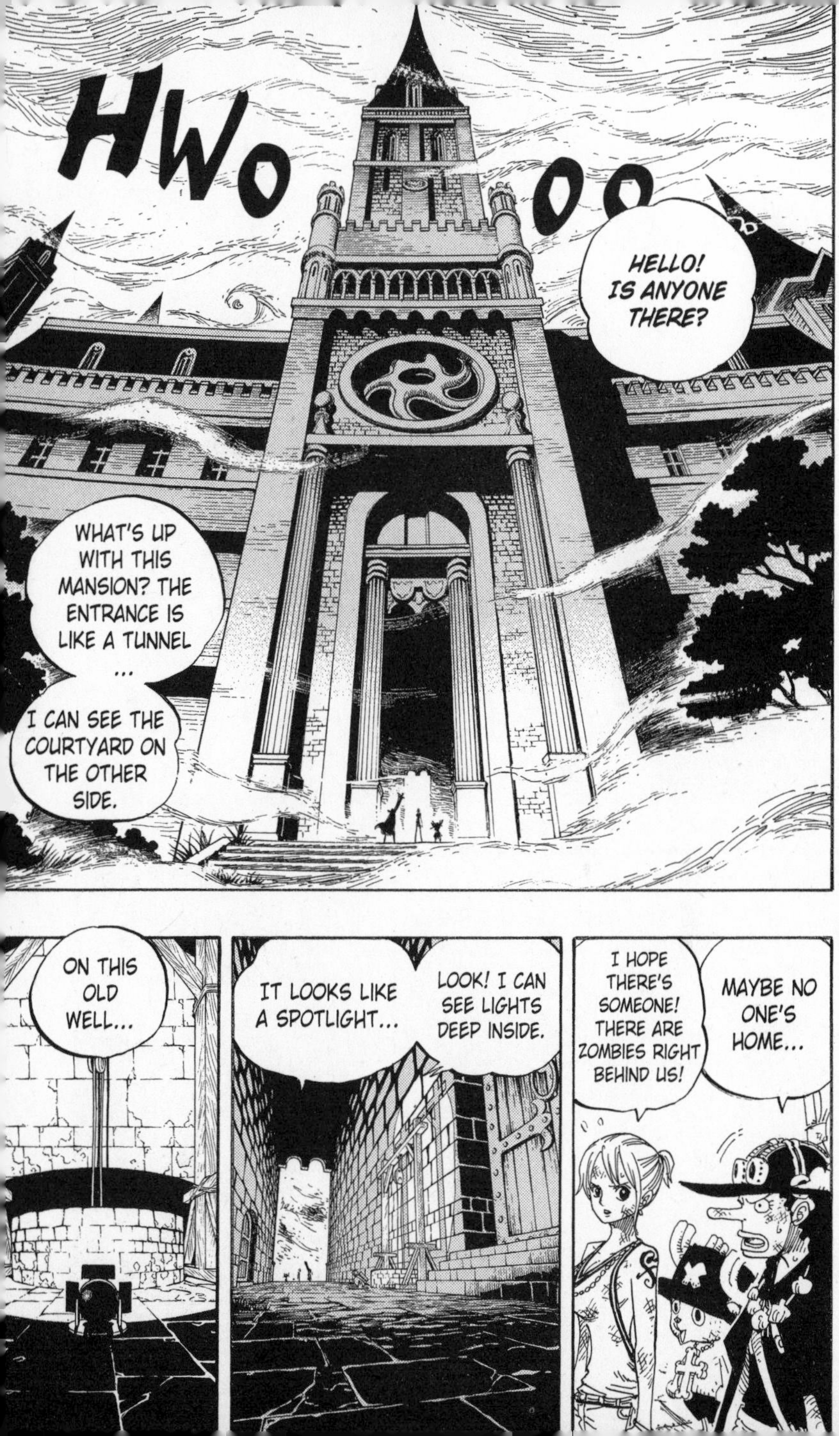
HWOOO
HELLO! IS ANYONE THERE?
WHAT'S UP WITH THIS MANSION? THE ENTRANCE IS LIKE A TUNNEL ...
I CAN SEE THE COURTYARD ON THE OTHER SIDE.
MAYBE NO ONE'S HOME...
I HOPE THERE'S SOMEONE! THERE ARE ZOMBIES RIGHT BEHIND US!
LOOK! I CAN SEE LIGHTS DEEP INSIDE.
IT LOOKS LIKE A SPOTLIGHT...
ON THIS OLD WELL...

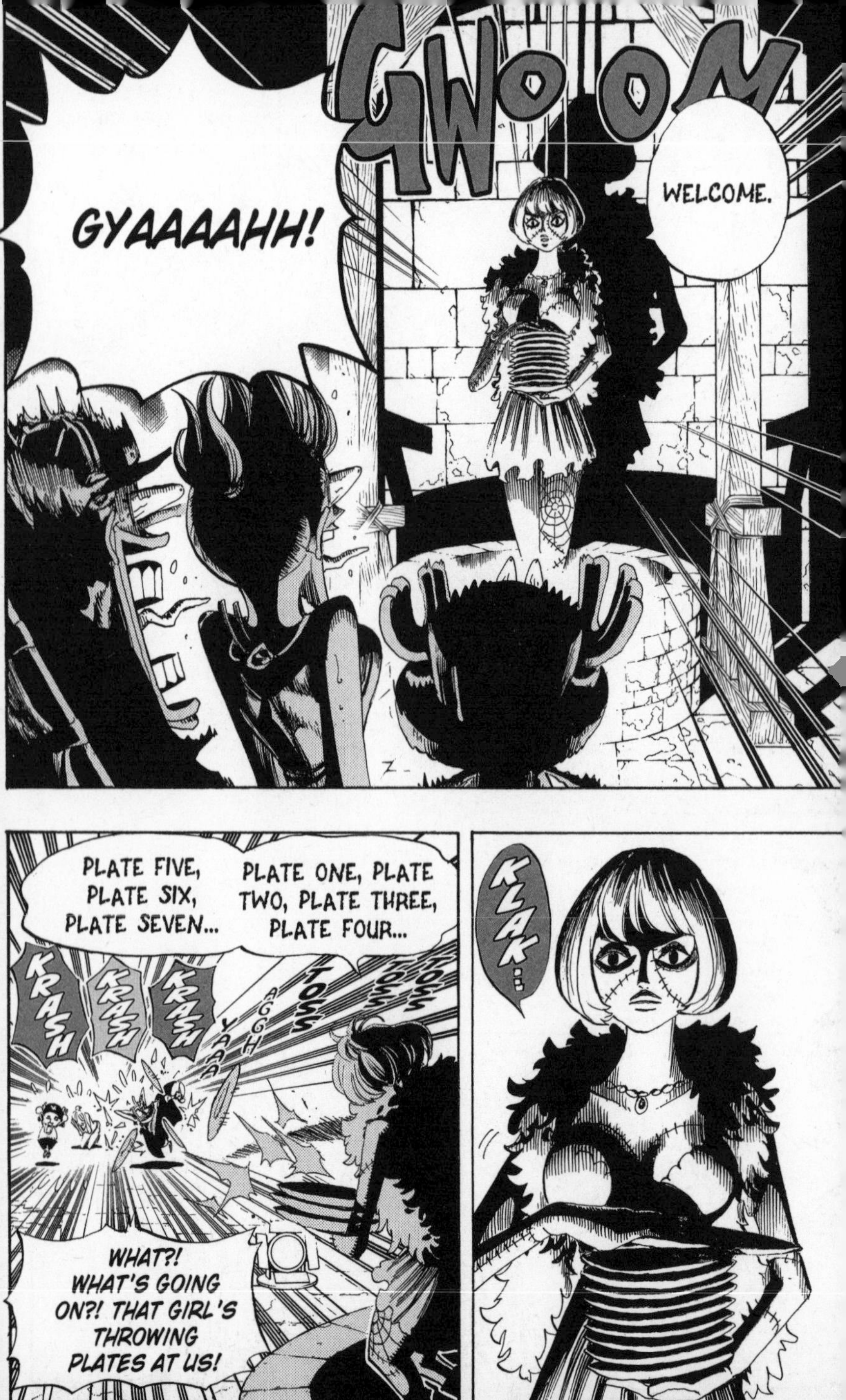
GWOOM
WELCOME.
GYAAAAHH!
KLAK...
PLATE ONE, PLATE TWO, PLATE THREE, PLATE FOUR...
PLATE FIVE, PLATE SIX, PLATE SEVEN...
TOSS
TOSS
TOSS
AGGH
YAAAA
KRASH
KRASH
KRASH
WHAT?! WHAT'S GOING ON?! THAT GIRL'S THROWING PLATES AT US!

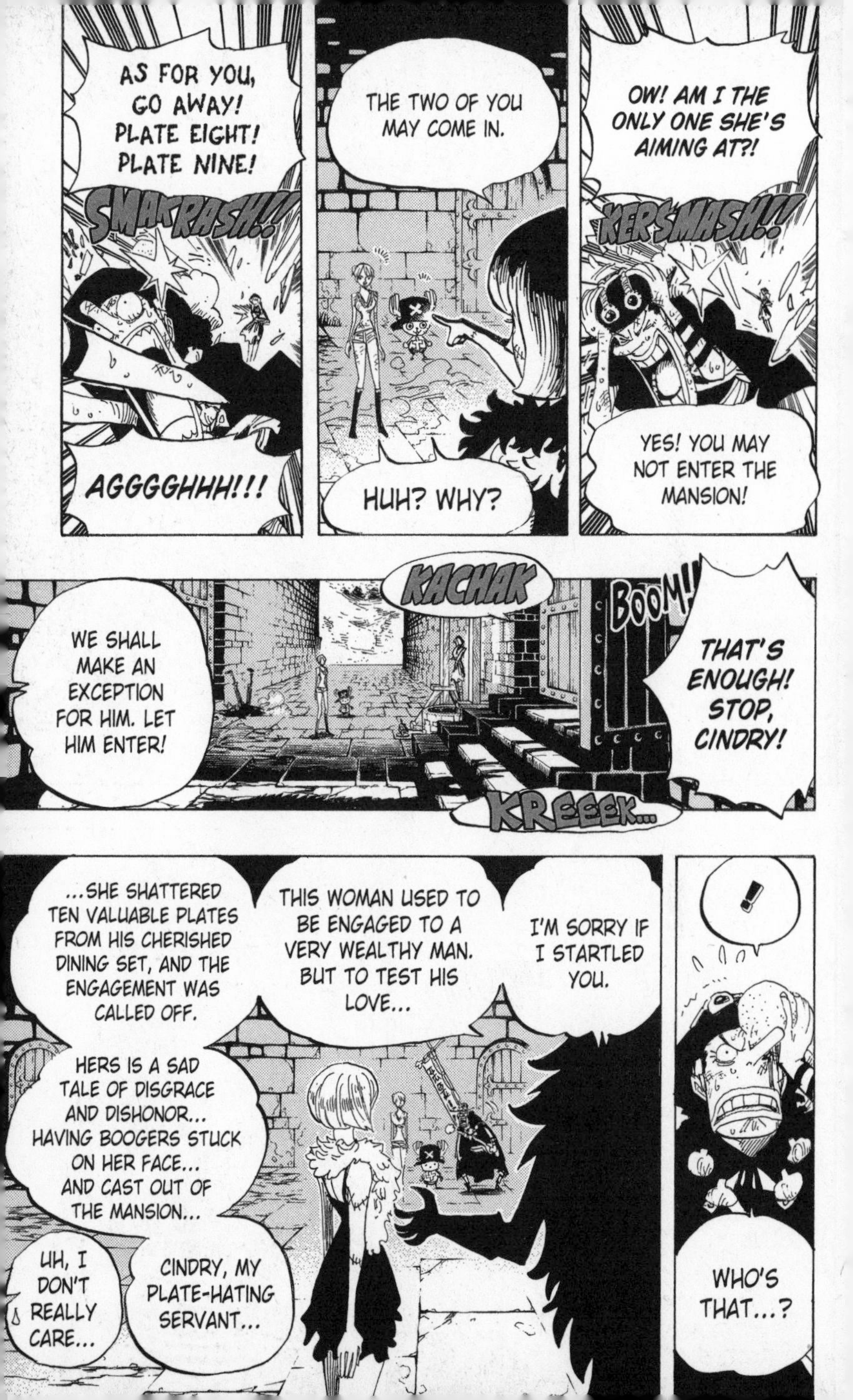
OW! AM I THE ONLY ONE SHE'S AIMING AT?!
KERSMASH!!
YES! YOU MAY NOT ENTER THE MANSION!
THE TWO OF YOU MAY COME IN.
HUH? WHY?
AS FOR YOU, GO AWAY! PLATE EIGHT! PLATE NINE!
SMAKRASH!!
AGGGGHHH!!!
BOOM!!
THAT'S ENOUGH! STOP, CINDRY!
KREEEK...
KACHAK
WE SHALL MAKE AN EXCEPTION FOR HIM. LET HIM ENTER!
!
WHO'S THAT...?
I'M SORRY IF I STARTLED YOU.
THIS WOMAN USED TO BE ENGAGED TO A VERY WEALTHY MAN. BUT TO TEST HIS LOVE...
...SHE SHATTERED TEN VALUABLE PLATES FROM HIS CHERISHED DINING SET, AND THE ENGAGEMENT WAS CALLED OFF.
HERS IS A SAD TALE OF DISGRACE AND DISHONOR... HAVING BOOGERS STUCK ON HER FACE... AND CAST OUT OF THE MANSION...
CINDRY, MY PLATE-HATING SERVANT...
UH, I DON'T REALLY CARE...

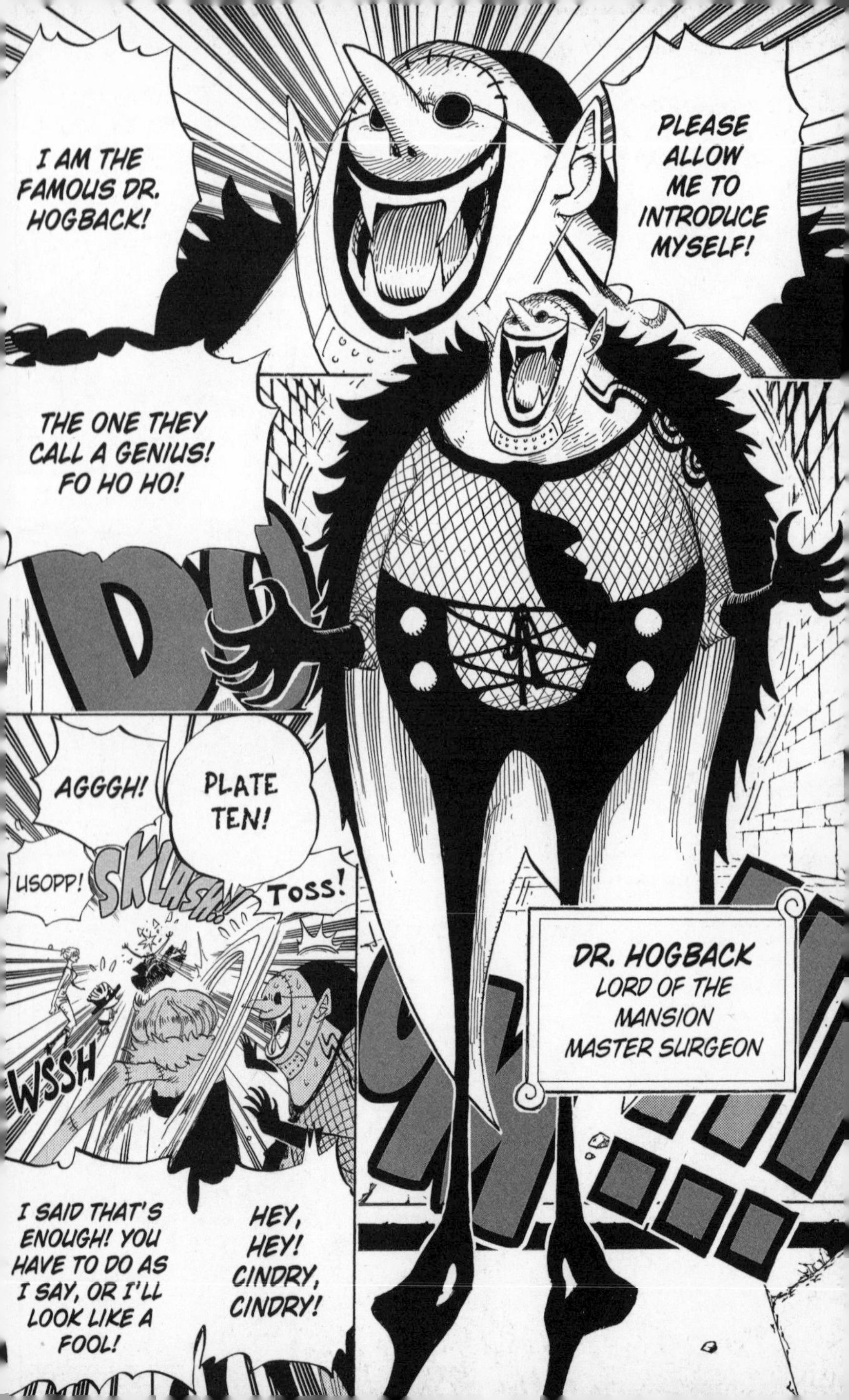
PLEASE ALLOW ME TO INTRODUCE MYSELF!
I AM THE FAMOUS DR. HOGBACK!
THE ONE THEY CALL A GENIUS! FO HO HO!
DR. HOGBACK
LORD OF THE MANSION
MASTER SURGEON
PLATE TEN!
AGGGH!
USOPP!
SKLASH!!
TOSS!
WSSH
HEY, HEY! CINDRY, CINDRY!
I SAID THAT'S ENOUGH! YOU HAVE TO DO AS I SAY, OR I'LL LOOK LIKE A FOOL!

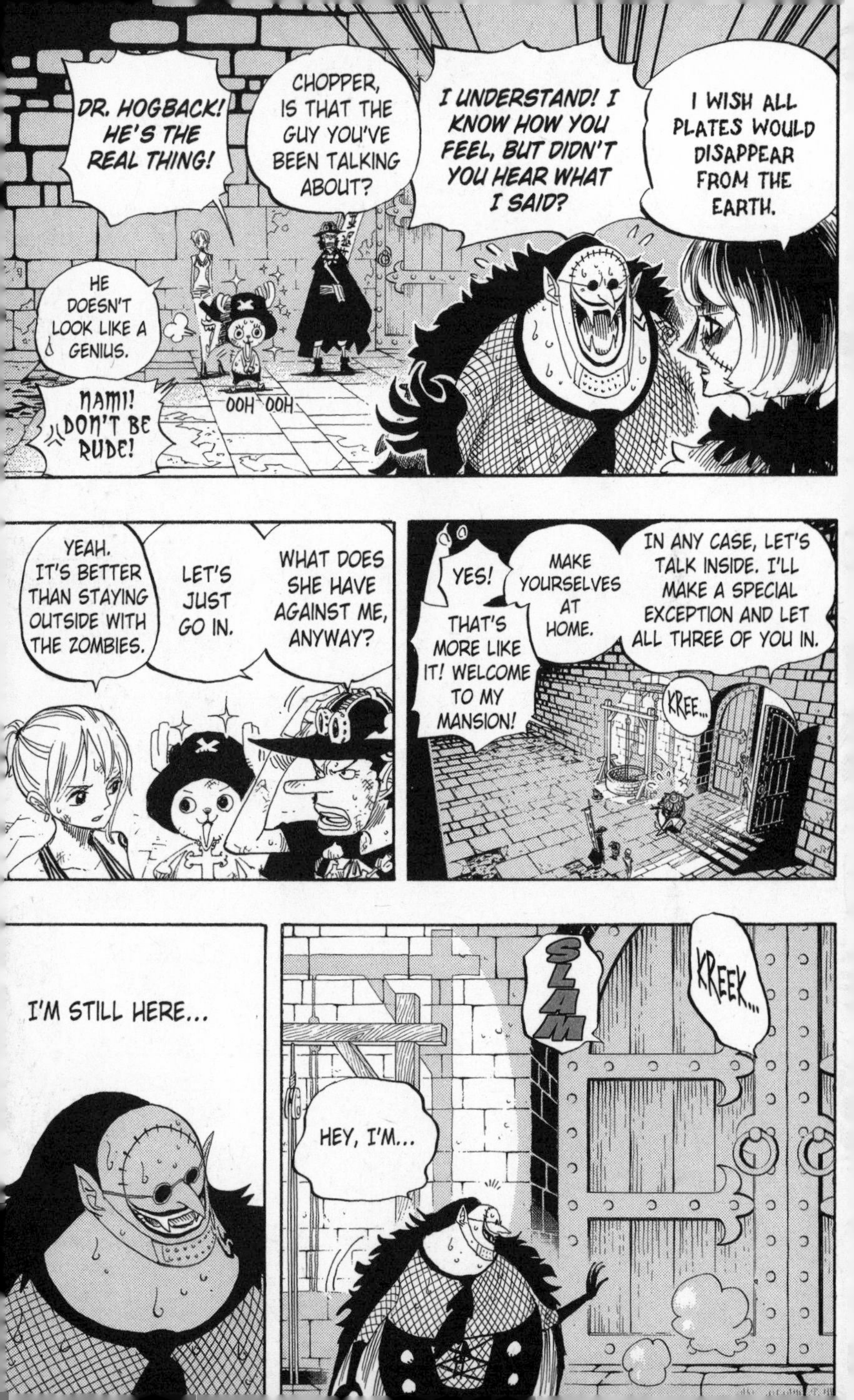
I WISH ALL PLATES WOULD DISAPPEAR FROM THE EARTH.
I UNDERSTAND! I KNOW HOW YOU FEEL, BUT DIDN'T YOU HEAR WHAT I SAID?
CHOPPER, IS THAT THE GUY YOU'VE BEEN TALKING ABOUT?
DR. HOGBACK! HE'S THE REAL THING!
HE DOESN'T LOOK LIKE A GENIUS.
OOH OOH
NAMI! DON'T BE RUDE!
IN ANY CASE, LET'S TALK INSIDE. I'LL MAKE A SPECIAL EXCEPTION AND LET ALL THREE OF YOU IN.
MAKE YOURSELVES AT HOME.
YES!
THAT'S MORE LIKE IT! WELCOME TO MY MANSION!
KREE...
WHAT DOES SHE HAVE AGAINST ME, ANYWAY?
LET'S JUST GO IN.
YEAH. IT'S BETTER THAN STAYING OUTSIDE WITH THE ZOMBIES.
KREEK...
SLAM
HEY, I'M...
I'M STILL HERE...

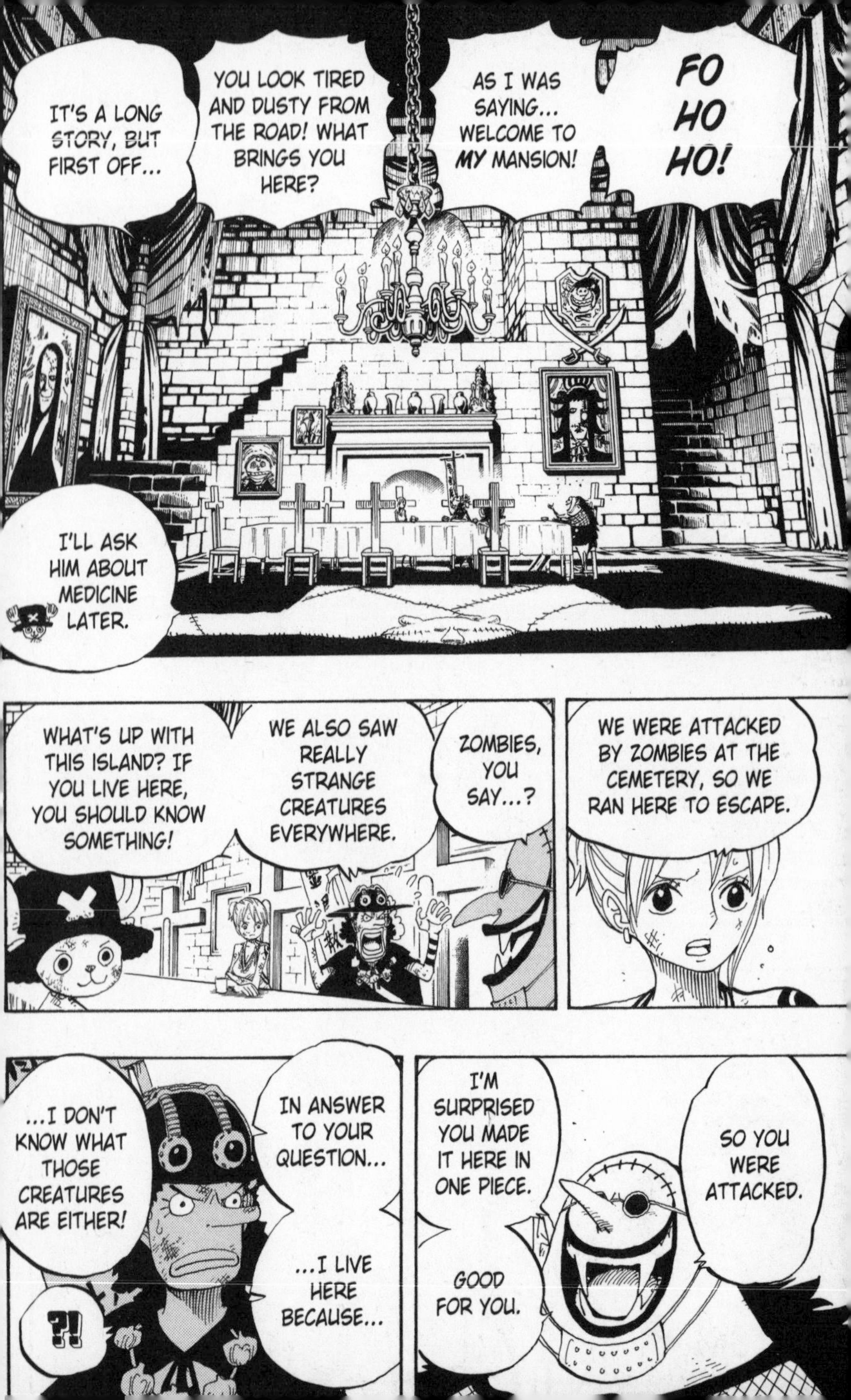
FO HO HO!
AS I WAS SAYING... WELCOME TO MY MANSION!
YOU LOOK TIRED AND DUSTY FROM THE ROAD! WHAT BRINGS YOU HERE?
IT'S A LONG STORY, BUT FIRST OFF...
I'LL ASK HIM ABOUT MEDICINE LATER.
WE WERE ATTACKED BY ZOMBIES AT THE CEMETERY, SO WE RAN HERE TO ESCAPE.
ZOMBIES, YOU SAY...?
WE ALSO SAW REALLY STRANGE CREATURES EVERYWHERE.
WHAT'S UP WITH THIS ISLAND? IF YOU LIVE HERE, YOU SHOULD KNOW SOMETHING!
SO YOU WERE ATTACKED.
I'M SURPRISED YOU MADE IT HERE IN ONE PIECE.
GOOD FOR YOU.
IN ANSWER TO YOUR QUESTION...
...I DON'T KNOW WHAT THOSE CREATURES ARE EITHER!
...I LIVE HERE BECAUSE...
?!

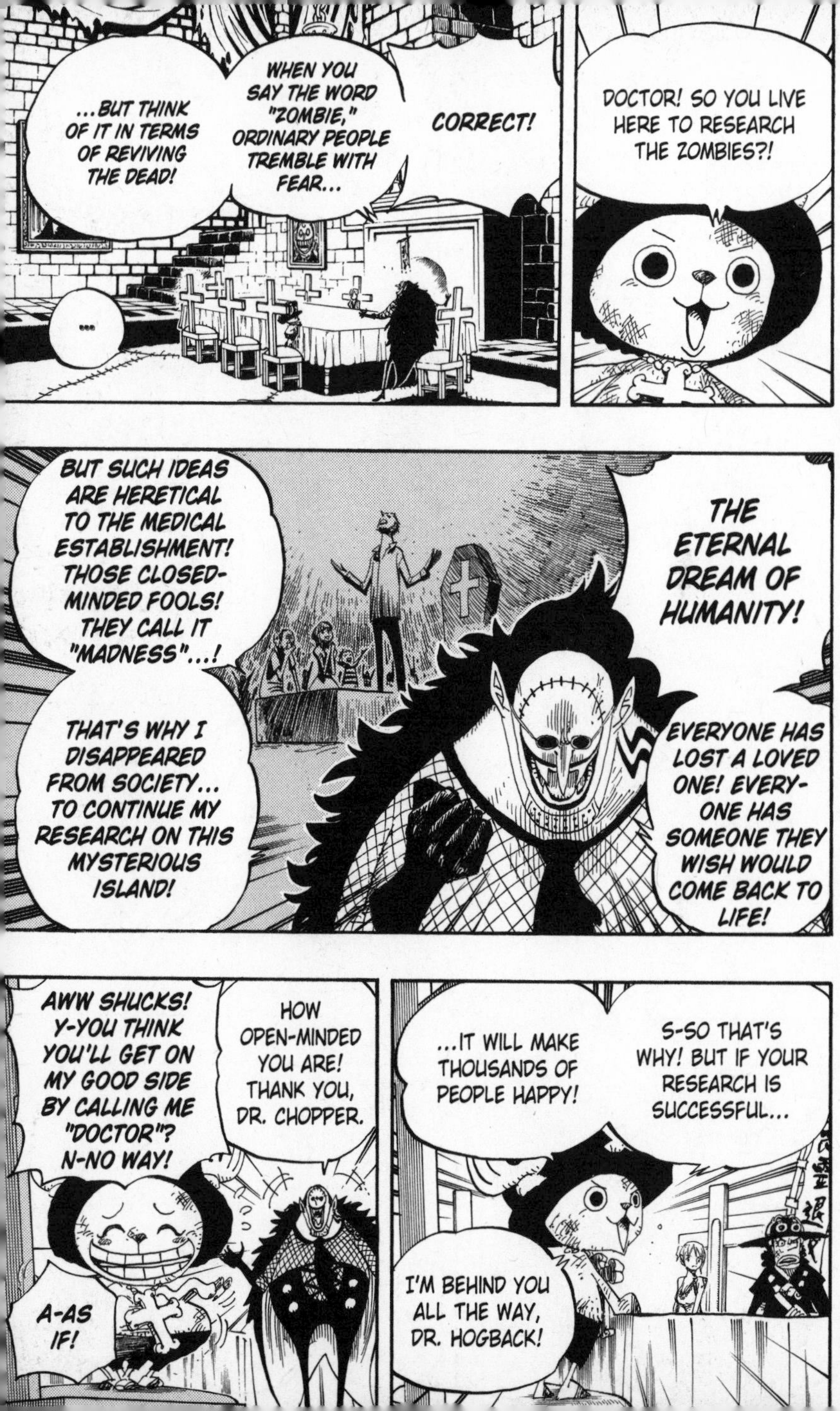
DOCTOR! SO YOU LIVE HERE TO RESEARCH THE ZOMBIES?!
CORRECT!
WHEN YOU SAY THE WORD "ZOMBIE," ORDINARY PEOPLE TREMBLE WITH FEAR...
...BUT THINK OF IT IN TERMS OF REVIVING THE DEAD!
...
THE ETERNAL DREAM OF HUMANITY!
EVERYONE HAS LOST A LOVED ONE! EVERY-ONE HAS SOMEONE THEY WISH WOULD COME BACK TO LIFE!
BUT SUCH IDEAS ARE HERETICAL TO THE MEDICAL ESTABLISHMENT! THOSE CLOSED-MINDED FOOLS! THEY CALL IT "MADNESS"...!
THAT'S WHY I DISAPPEARED FROM SOCIETY... TO CONTINUE MY RESEARCH ON THIS MYSTERIOUS ISLAND!
S-SO THAT'S WHY! BUT IF YOUR RESEARCH IS SUCCESSFUL...
...IT WILL MAKE THOUSANDS OF PEOPLE HAPPY!
I'M BEHIND YOU ALL THE WAY, DR. HOGBACK!
HOW OPEN-MINDED YOU ARE! THANK YOU, DR. CHOPPER.
AWW SHUCKS! Y-YOU THINK YOU'LL GET ON MY GOOD SIDE BY CALLING ME "DOCTOR"? N-NO WAY!
A-AS IF!

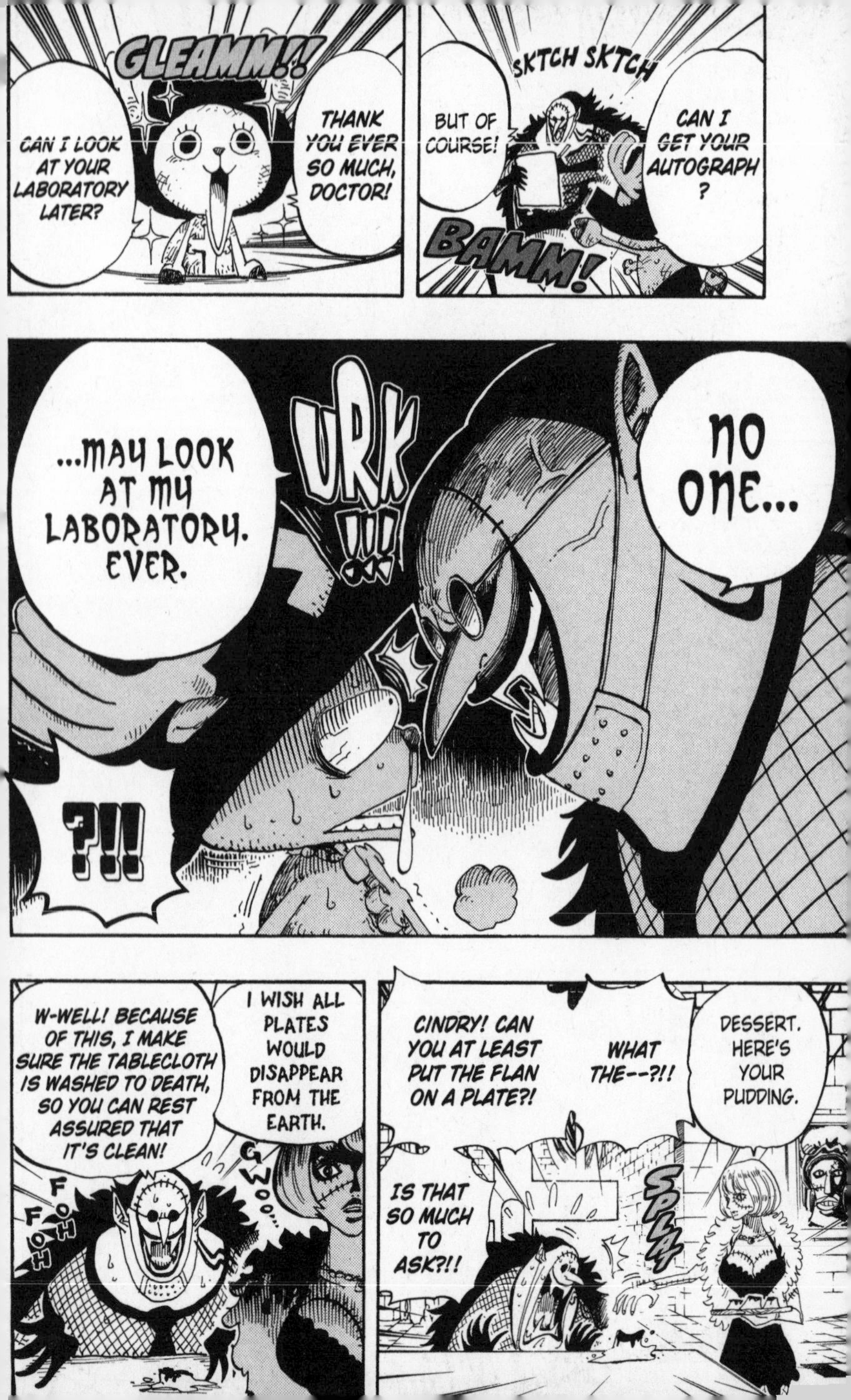
CAN I GET YOUR AUTOGRAPH ?
SKTCH SKTCH
BUT OF COURSE!
BAMM!
THANK YOU EVER SO MUCH, DOCTOR!
GLEAMM!!
CAN I LOOK AT YOUR LABORATORY LATER?
NO ONE...
URK!!!
...MAY LOOK AT MY LABORATORY. EVER.
?!!
DESSERT. HERE'S YOUR PUDDING.
WHAT THE--?!!
CINDRY! CAN YOU AT LEAST PUT THE FLAN ON A PLATE?!
SPLAT
IS THAT SO MUCH TO ASK?!!
I WISH ALL PLATES WOULD DISAPPEAR FROM THE EARTH.
W-WELL! BECAUSE OF THIS, I MAKE SURE THE TABLECLOTH IS WASHED TO DEATH, SO YOU CAN REST ASSURED THAT IT'S CLEAN!
GWOO...
FOH FOH

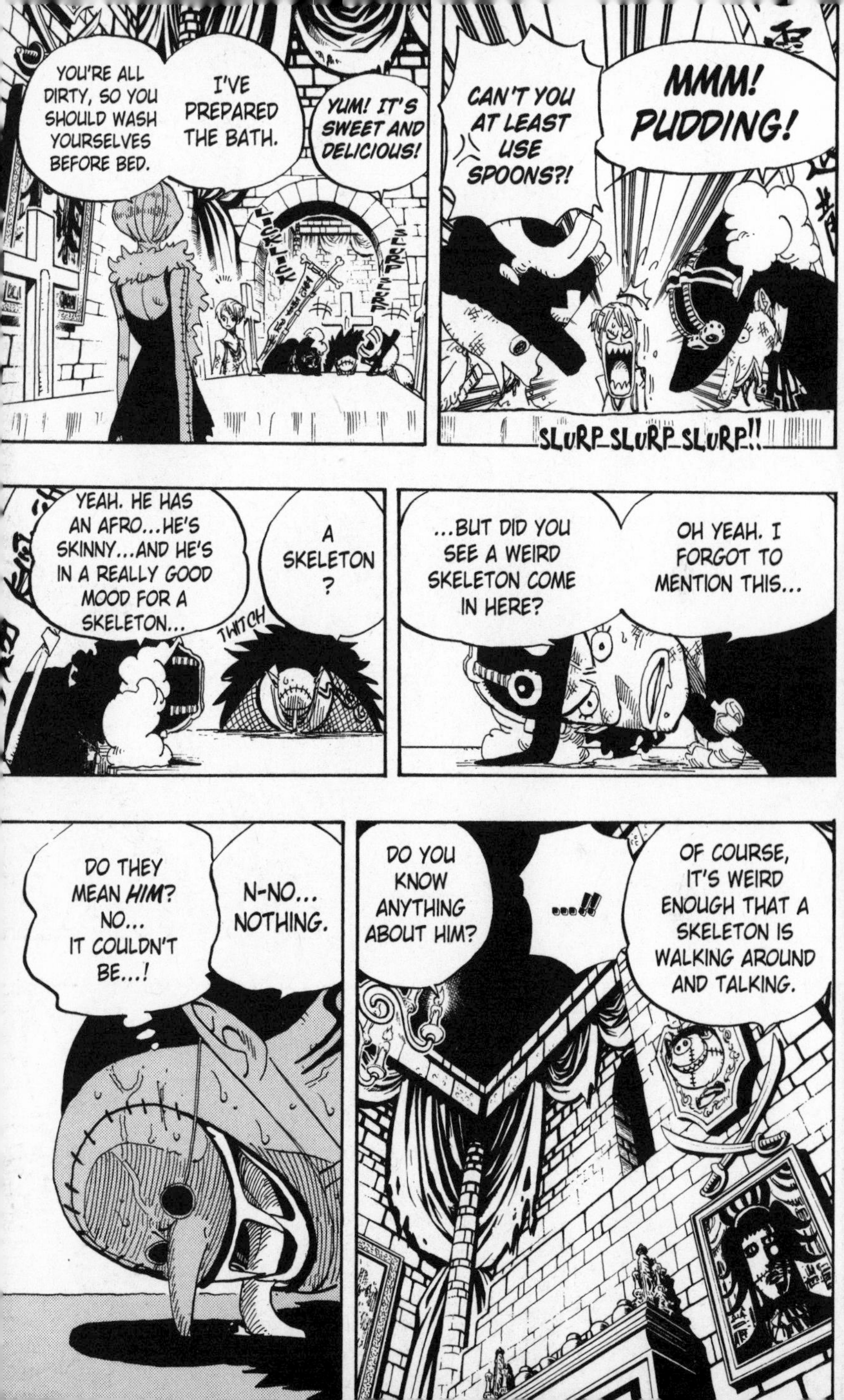
MMM! PUDDING!
CAN'T YOU AT LEAST USE SPOONS?!
SLURP SLURP SLURP!!
YUM! IT'S SWEET AND DELICIOUS!
I'VE PREPARED THE BATH.
YOU'RE ALL DIRTY, SO YOU SHOULD WASH YOURSELVES BEFORE BED.
SLURP SLURP
LICK LICK
OH YEAH. I FORGOT TO MENTION THIS...
...BUT DID YOU SEE A WEIRD SKELETON COME IN HERE?
A SKELETON?
TWITCH
YEAH. HE HAS AN AFRO...HE'S SKINNY...AND HE'S IN A REALLY GOOD MOOD FOR A SKELETON...
OF COURSE, IT'S WEIRD ENOUGH THAT A SKELETON IS WALKING AROUND AND TALKING.
...!!
DO YOU KNOW ANYTHING ABOUT HIM?
N-NO... NOTHING.
DO THEY MEAN *HIM*? NO... IT COULDN'T BE...!

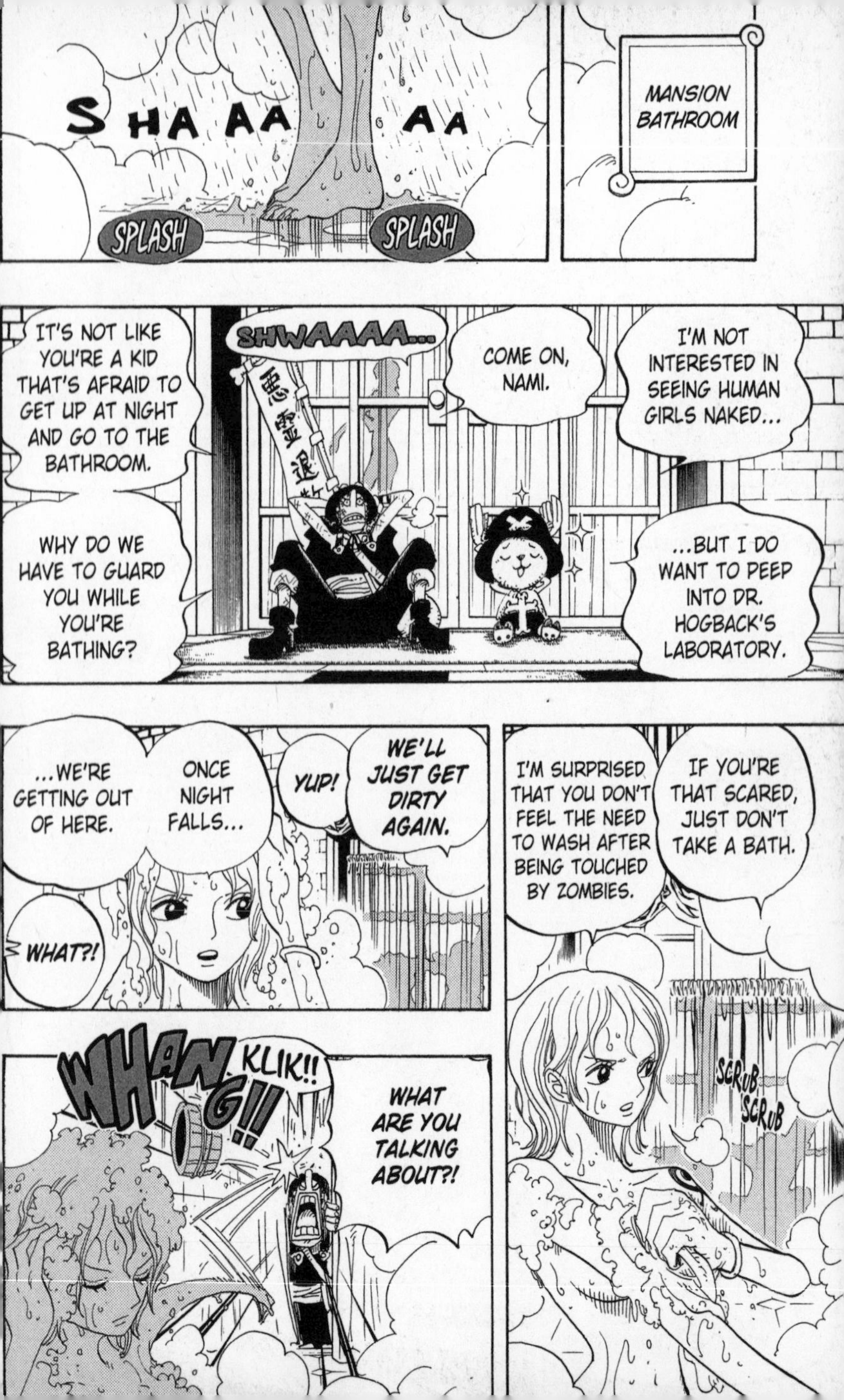
MANSION BATHROOM
SHAAAAA
SPLASH
SPLASH
I'M NOT INTERESTED IN SEEING HUMAN GIRLS NAKED...
...BUT I DO WANT TO PEEP INTO DR. HOGBACK'S LABORATORY.
COME ON, NAMI.
SHWAAAAA...
IT'S NOT LIKE YOU'RE A KID THAT'S AFRAID TO GET UP AT NIGHT AND GO TO THE BATHROOM.
WHY DO WE HAVE TO GUARD YOU WHILE YOU'RE BATHING?
IF YOU'RE THAT SCARED, JUST DON'T TAKE A BATH.
I'M SURPRISED THAT YOU DON'T FEEL THE NEED TO WASH AFTER BEING TOUCHED BY ZOMBIES.
SCRUB SCRUB
WE'LL JUST GET DIRTY AGAIN.
YUP!
ONCE NIGHT FALLS...
...WE'RE GETTING OUT OF HERE.
WHAT?!
WHAT ARE YOU TALKING ABOUT?!
KLIK!!
WHANG!!

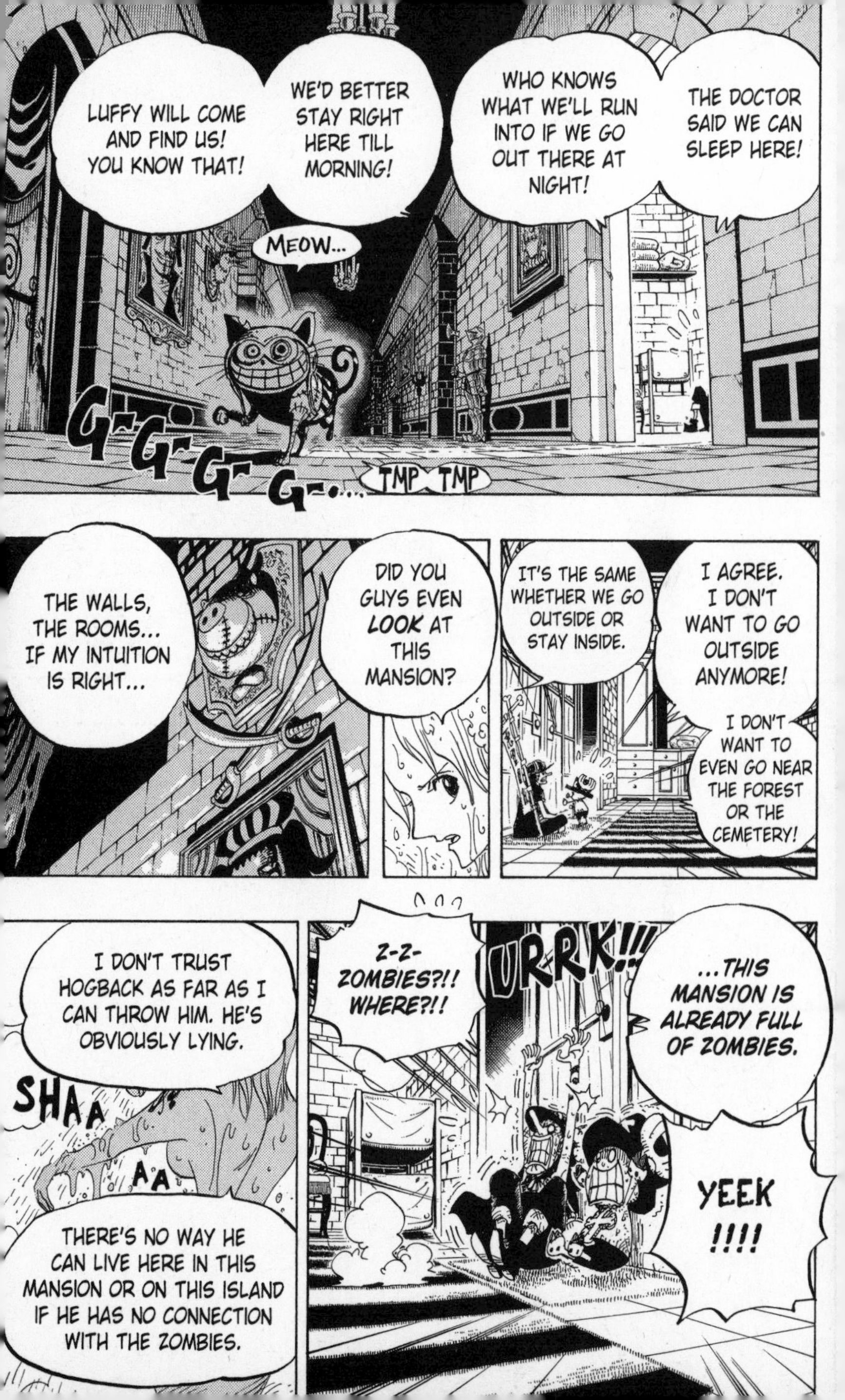
THE DOCTOR SAID WE CAN SLEEP HERE!
WHO KNOWS WHAT WE'LL RUN INTO IF WE GO OUT THERE AT NIGHT!
WE'D BETTER STAY RIGHT HERE TILL MORNING!
LUFFY WILL COME AND FIND US! YOU KNOW THAT!
MEOW...
G-G-G-G-...
TMP TMP
I AGREE. I DON'T WANT TO GO OUTSIDE ANYMORE!
I DON'T WANT TO EVEN GO NEAR THE FOREST OR THE CEMETERY!
IT'S THE SAME WHETHER WE GO OUTSIDE OR STAY INSIDE.
DID YOU GUYS EVEN *LOOK* AT THIS MANSION?
THE WALLS, THE ROOMS... IF MY INTUITION IS RIGHT...
...THIS MANSION IS ALREADY FULL OF ZOMBIES.
URRK!!!
Z-Z-ZOMBIES?!! WHERE?!!
YEEK !!!!
I DON'T TRUST HOGBACK AS FAR AS I CAN THROW HIM. HE'S OBVIOUSLY LYING.
SHAA
AA
THERE'S NO WAY HE CAN LIVE HERE IN THIS MANSION OR ON THIS ISLAND IF HE HAS NO CONNECTION WITH THE ZOMBIES.

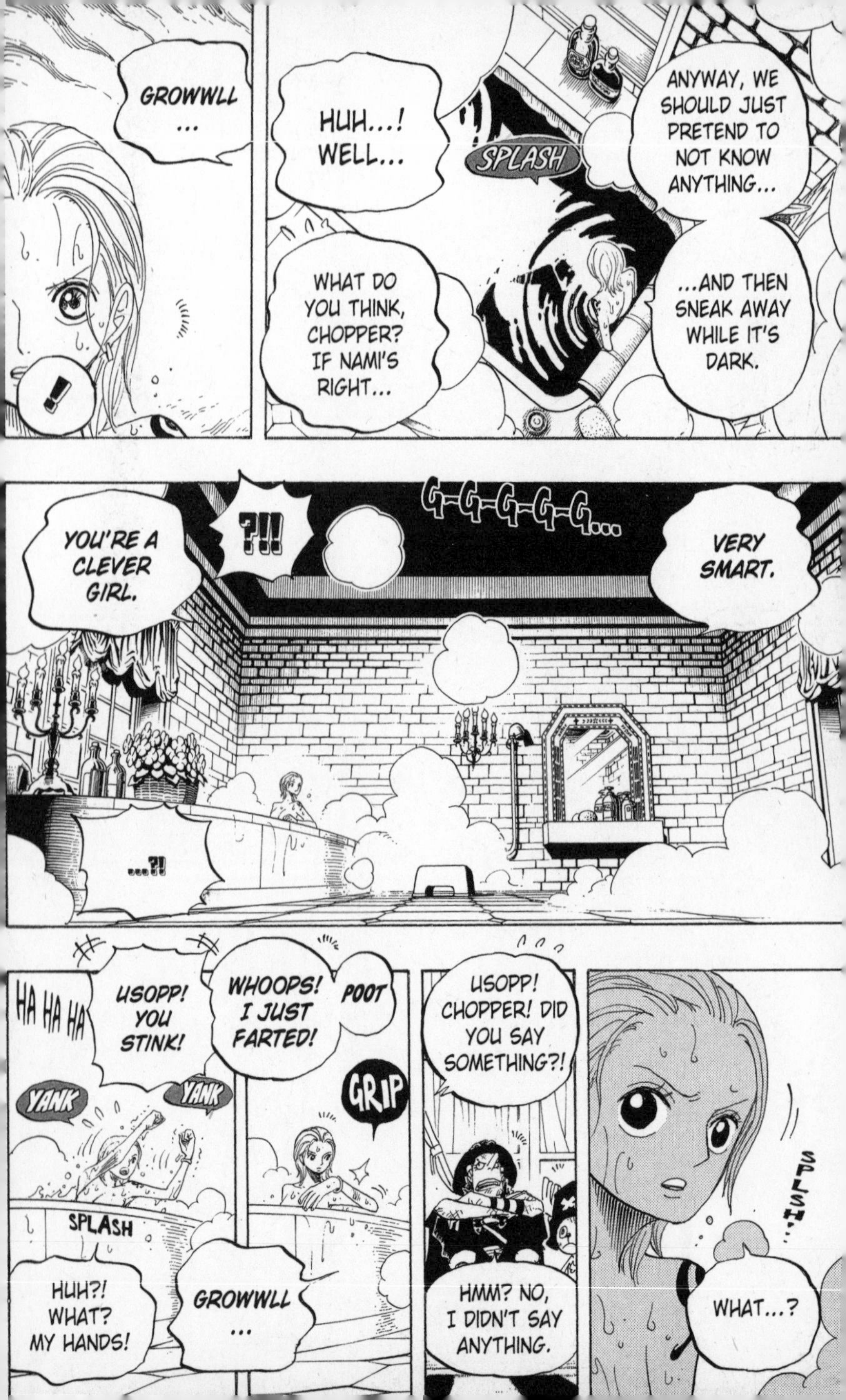
ANYWAY, WE SHOULD JUST PRETEND TO NOT KNOW ANYTHING...
...AND THEN SNEAK AWAY WHILE IT'S DARK.
SPLASH
HUH...! WELL...
WHAT DO YOU THINK, CHOPPER? IF NAMI'S RIGHT...
GROWWLL ...
!
VERY SMART.
G-G-G-G-G...
?!!
YOU'RE A CLEVER GIRL.
...?!
SPLASH...
WHAT...?
USOPP! CHOPPER! DID YOU SAY SOMETHING?!
HMM? NO, I DIDN'T SAY ANYTHING.
POOT
WHOOPS! I JUST FARTED!
GRIP
GROWWLL ...
USOPP! YOU STINK!
HA HA HA
YANK
YANK
SPLASH
HUH?! WHAT? MY HANDS!

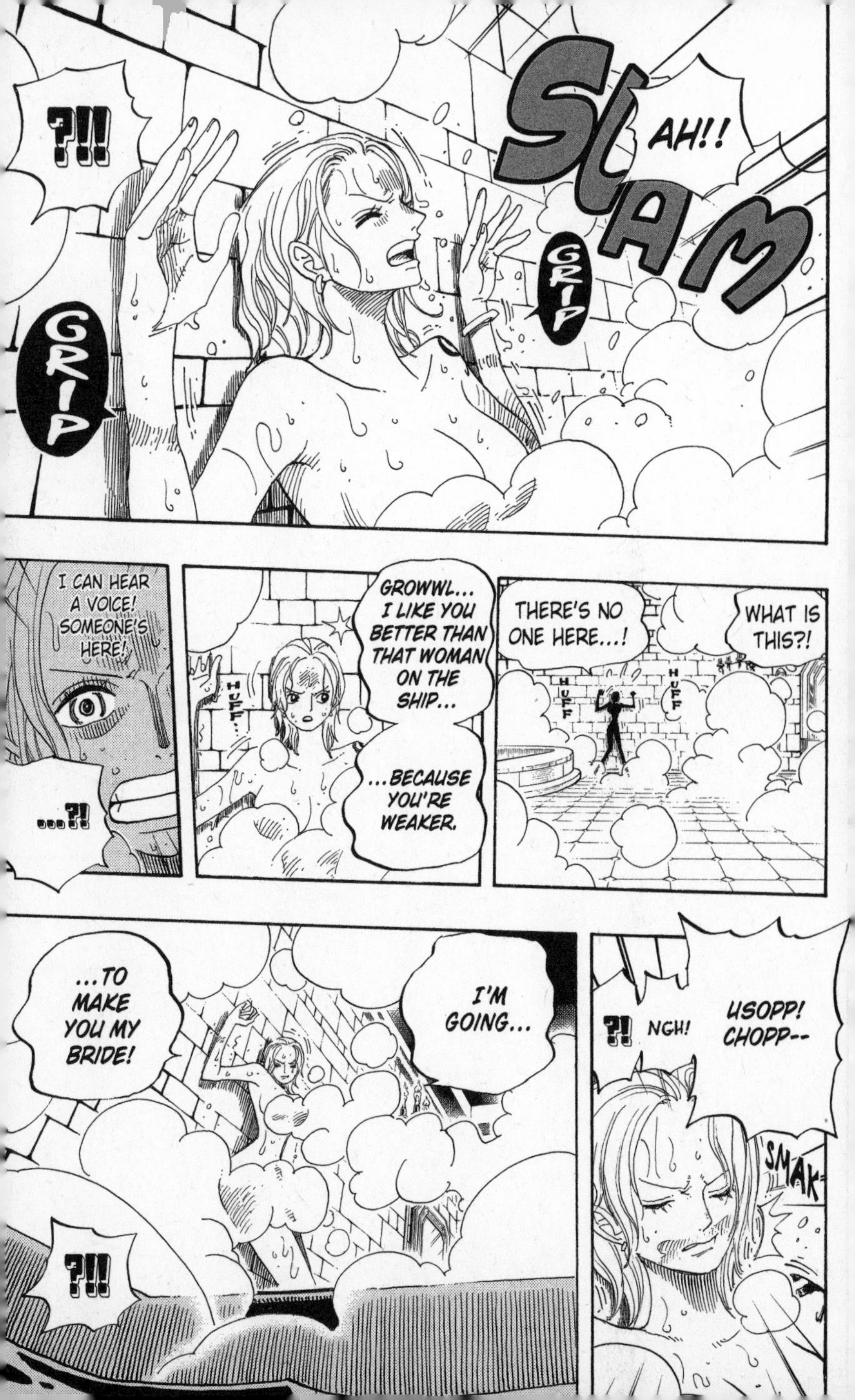
SLAM
AH!!
GRIP
?!!
GRIP
WHAT IS THIS?!
THERE'S NO ONE HERE...!
HUFF
HUFF
GROWWL... I LIKE YOU BETTER THAN THAT WOMAN ON THE SHIP...
...BECAUSE YOU'RE WEAKER.
HUFF...
I CAN HEAR A VOICE! SOMEONE'S HERE!
...?!
USOPP! CHOPP--
NGH!
?!
SMAK
I'M GOING...
...TO MAKE YOU MY BRIDE!
?!!

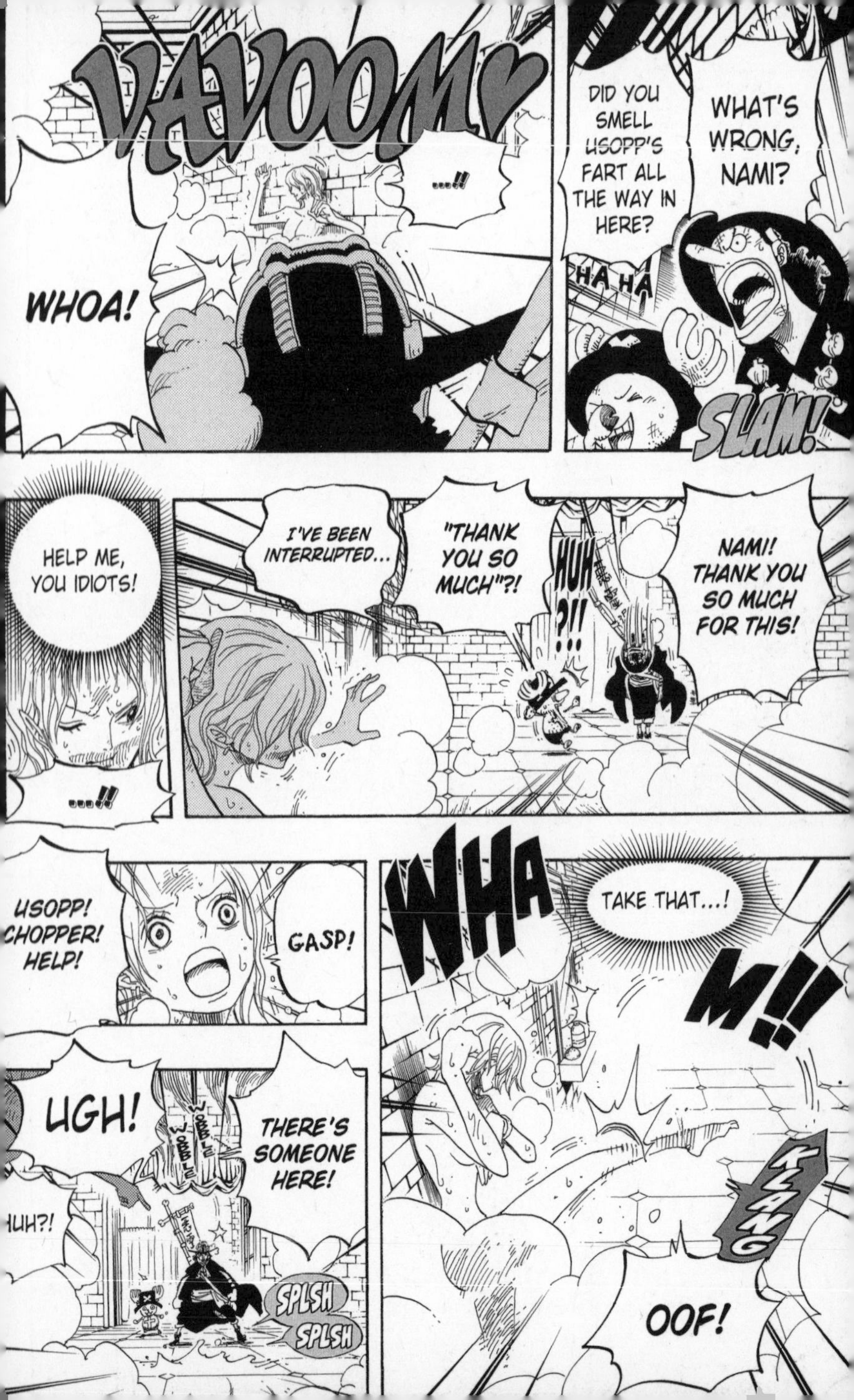
WHAT'S WRONG, NAMI?
DID YOU SMELL USOPP'S FART ALL THE WAY IN HERE?
HA HA
SLAM!
VAVOOM♥
...!!
WHOA!
NAMI! THANK YOU SO MUCH FOR THIS!
HUH ?!!
"THANK YOU SO MUCH"?!
I'VE BEEN INTERRUPTED...
HELP ME, YOU IDIOTS!
...!!
WHAM!!
TAKE THAT...!
KLANG
OOF!
GASP!
USOPP! CHOPPER! HELP!
THERE'S SOMEONE HERE!
WOBBLE
WOBBLE
UGH!
HUH?!
SPLSH
SPLSH

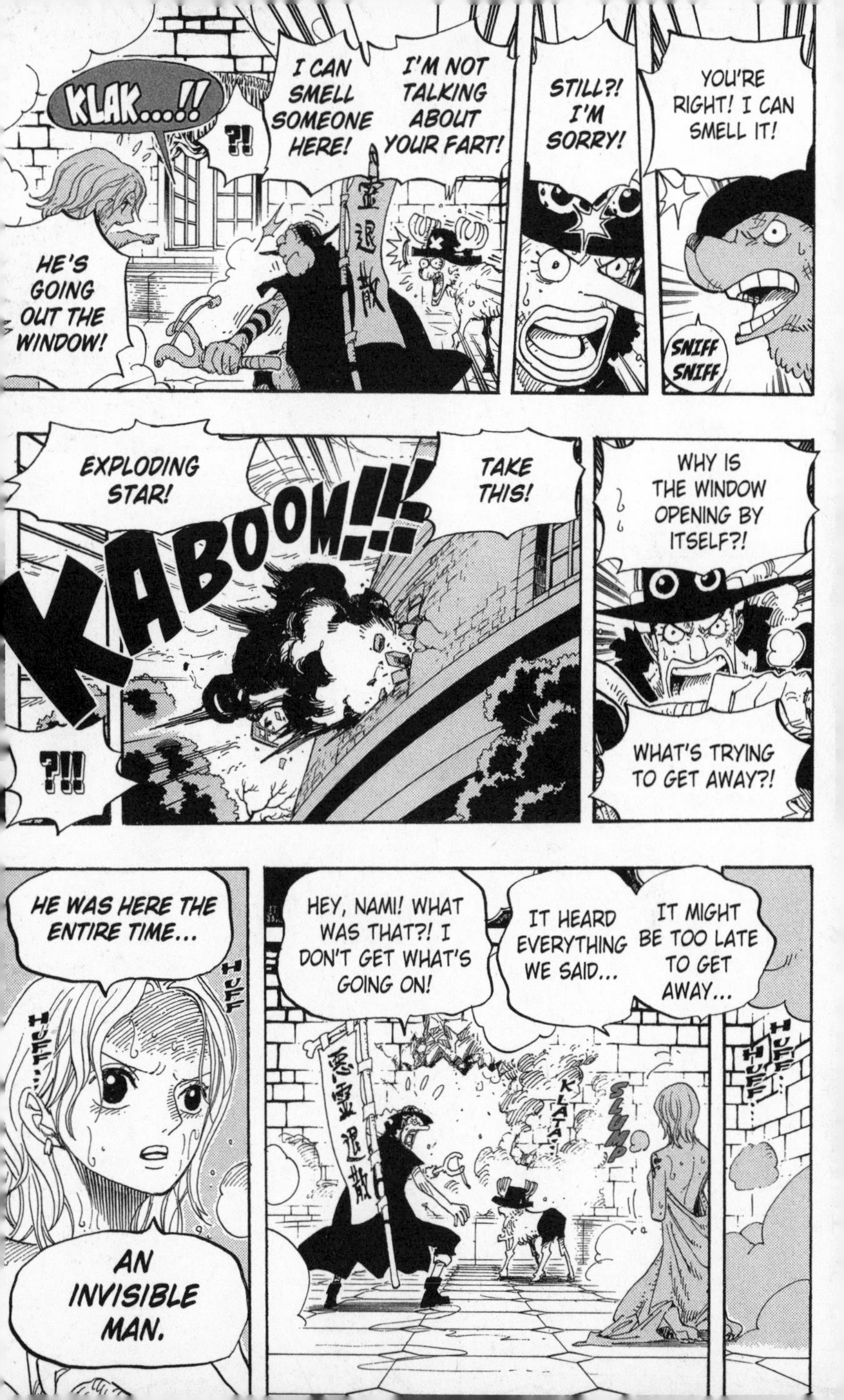

YOU'RE RIGHT! I CAN SMELL IT!
SNIFF SNIFF
STILL?! I'M SORRY!
I'M NOT TALKING ABOUT YOUR FART!
I CAN SMELL SOMEONE HERE!
KLAK...!!
?!
HE'S GOING OUT THE WINDOW!
WHY IS THE WINDOW OPENING BY ITSELF?!
WHAT'S TRYING TO GET AWAY?!
TAKE THIS!
EXPLODING STAR!
KABOOM!!!
?!!
IT MIGHT BE TOO LATE TO GET AWAY...
IT HEARD EVERYTHING WE SAID...
HEY, NAMI! WHAT WAS THAT?! I DON'T GET WHAT'S GOING ON!
HUFF HUFF...
KLATA...
SLUMP
HE WAS HERE THE ENTIRE TIME...
HUFF HUFF...
AN INVISIBLE MAN.

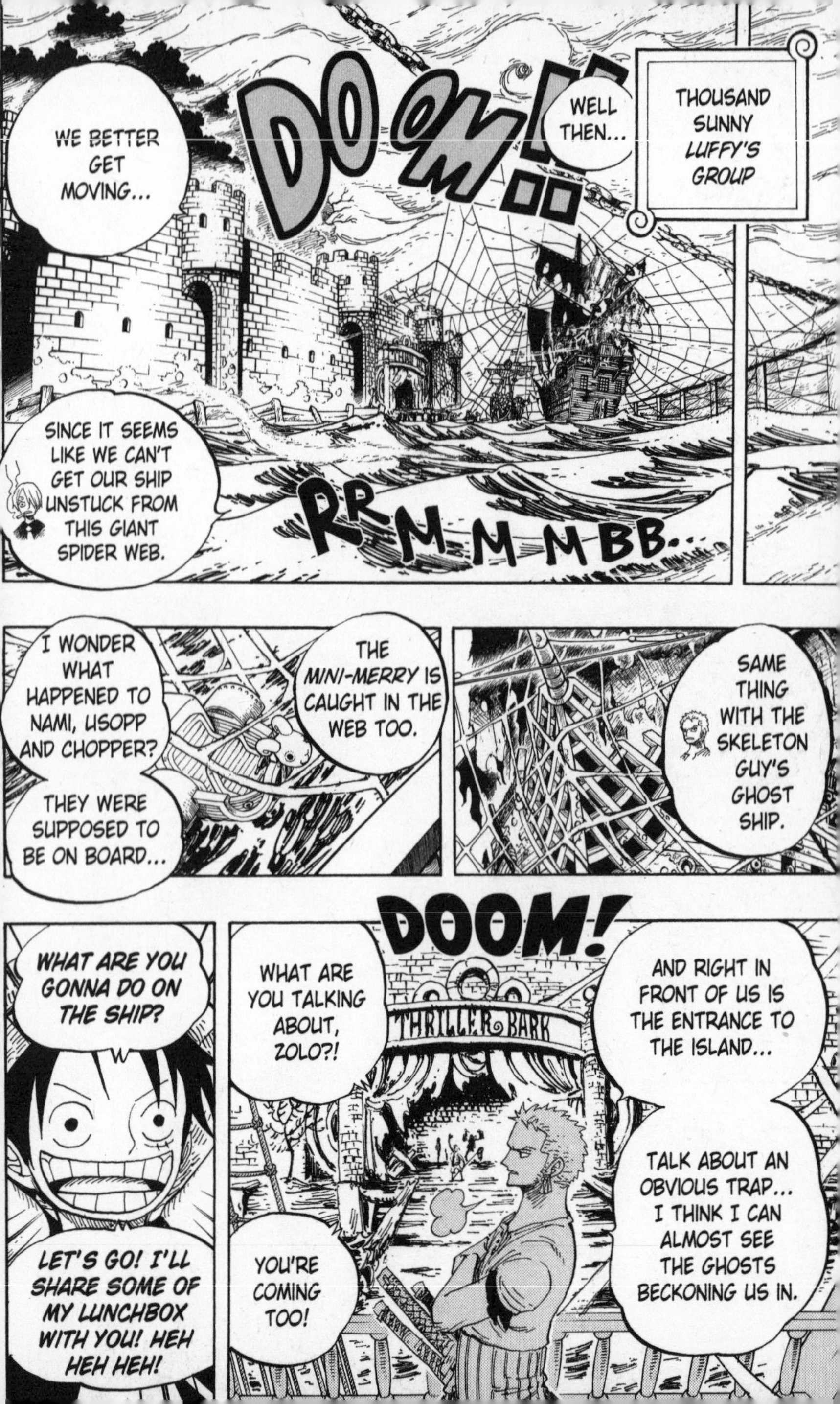

THOUSAND SUNNY *LUFFY'S GROUP*
WELL THEN...
DOOM!!
WE BETTER GET MOVING...
RRMMMBB...
SINCE IT SEEMS LIKE WE CAN'T GET OUR SHIP UNSTUCK FROM THIS GIANT SPIDER WEB.
SAME THING WITH THE SKELETON GUY'S GHOST SHIP.
THE *MINI-MERRY* IS CAUGHT IN THE WEB TOO.
I WONDER WHAT HAPPENED TO NAMI, USOPP AND CHOPPER?
THEY WERE SUPPOSED TO BE ON BOARD...
DOOM!
AND RIGHT IN FRONT OF US IS THE ENTRANCE TO THE ISLAND...
THRILLER BARK
WHAT ARE YOU TALKING ABOUT, ZOLO?!
TALK ABOUT AN OBVIOUS TRAP... I THINK I CAN ALMOST SEE THE GHOSTS BECKONING US IN.
YOU'RE COMING TOO!
WHAT ARE YOU GONNA DO ON THE SHIP?
LET'S GO! I'LL SHARE SOME OF MY LUNCHBOX WITH YOU! HEH HEH HEH!

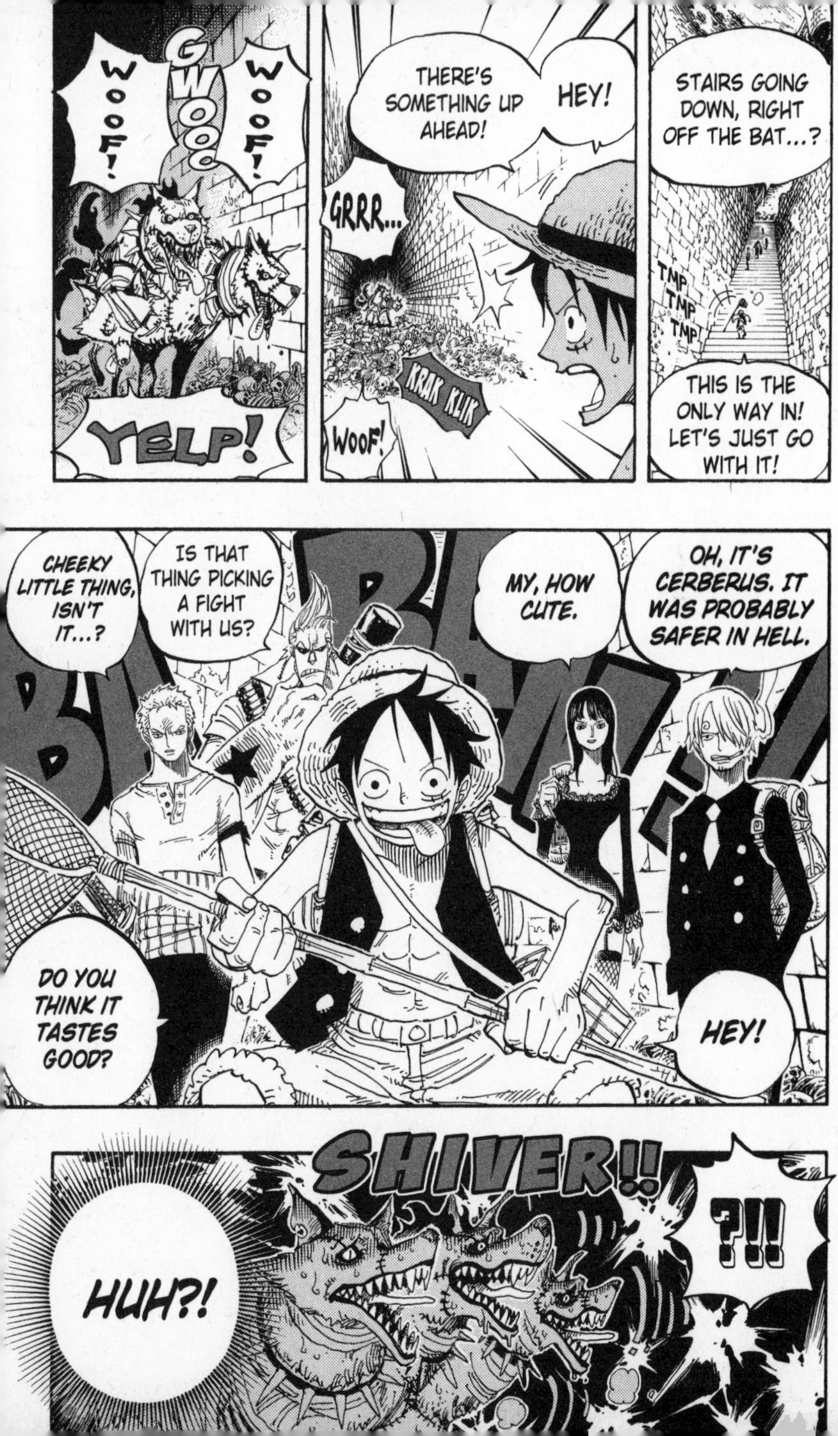
STAIRS GOING DOWN, RIGHT OFF THE BAT...?
TMP TMP TMP
THIS IS THE ONLY WAY IN! LET'S JUST GO WITH IT!
HEY!
THERE'S SOMETHING UP AHEAD!
GRRR...
KRAK KLIK
WOOF!
WOOF!
GWOOO
WOOF!
YELP!
OH, IT'S CERBERUS. IT WAS PROBABLY SAFER IN HELL.
MY, HOW CUTE.
IS THAT THING PICKING A FIGHT WITH US?
CHEEKY LITTLE THING, ISN'T IT...?
HEY!
DO YOU THINK IT TASTES GOOD?
?!!
SHIVER!!
HUH?!

B1

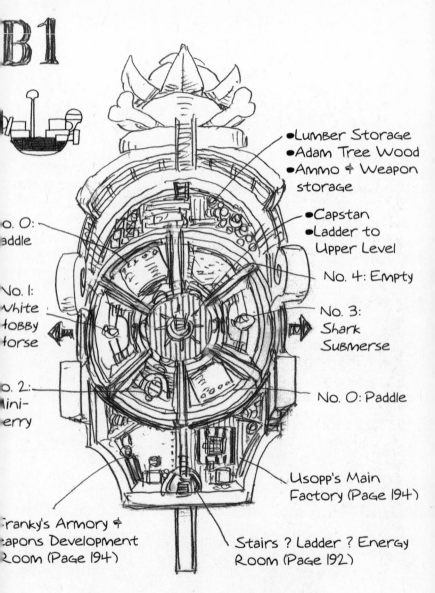

- Lumber Storage
- Adam Tree Wood
- Ammo & Weapon storage

- Capstan
- Ladder to Upper Level

No. 4: Empty

No. 3: Shark Submerse

No. O: Paddle

No. O: Paddle

No. I: White Hobby Horse

No. 2: Mini-Merry

Usopp's Main Factory (Page 194)

Franky's Armory & Weapons Development Room (Page 194)

Stairs ? Ladder ? Energy Room (Page 192)

Soldier Dock System (Page 193)

Chapter 447:
ZOMBIE-IN-THE-BOX

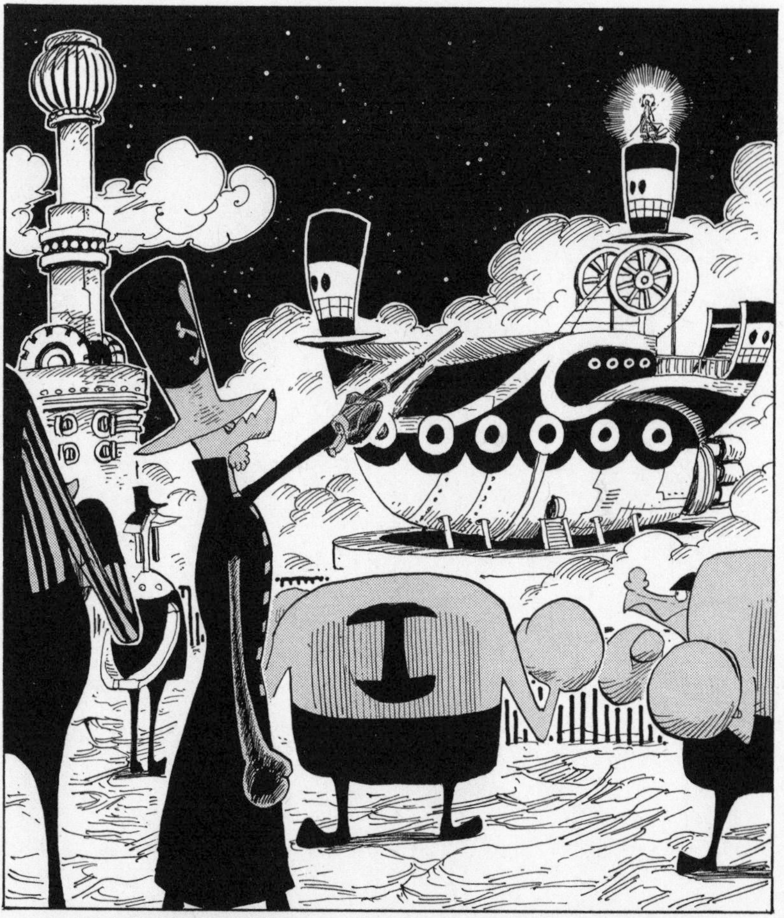

ENERU'S GREAT SPACE MISSION, VOL. 16: "DESCENT"

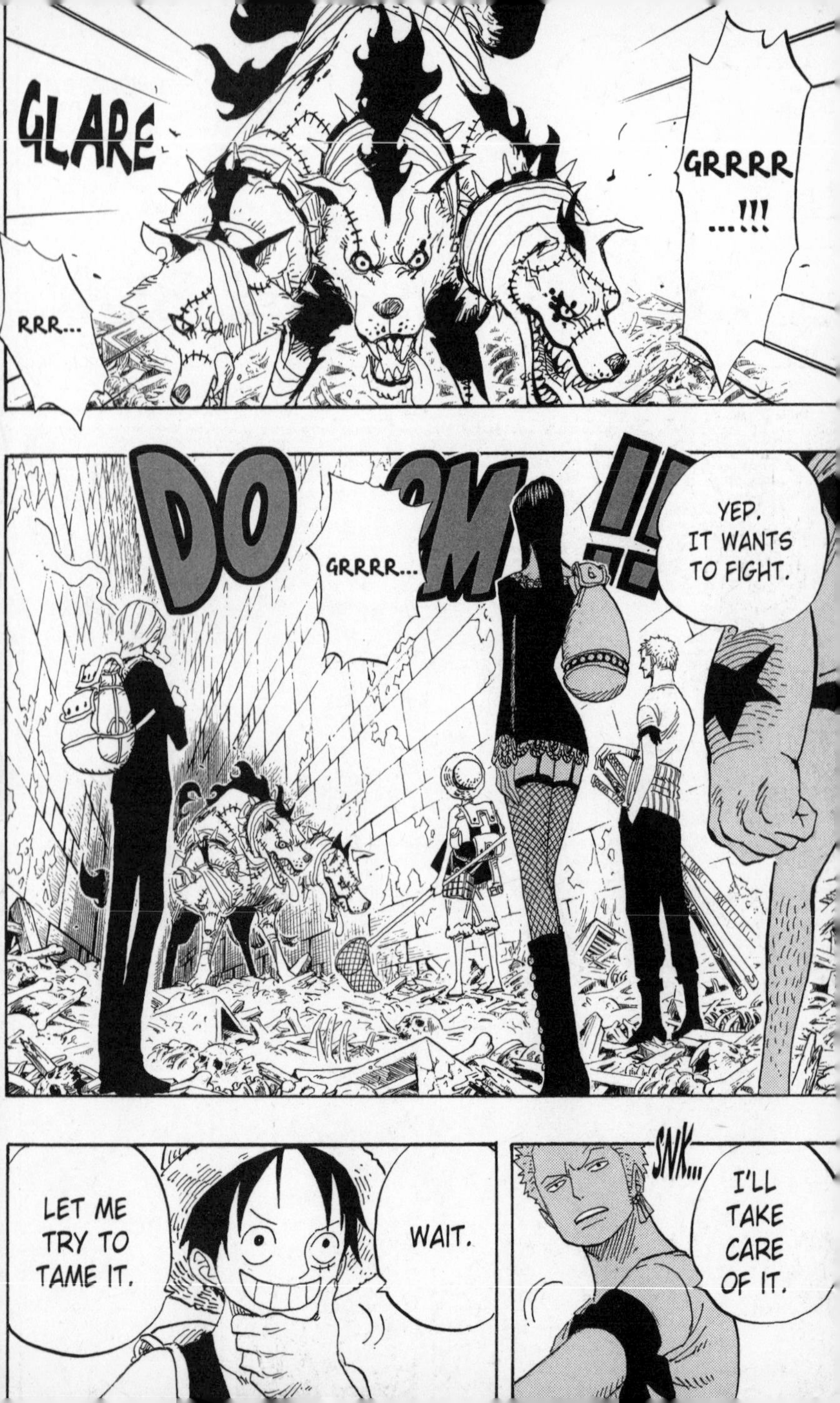
GRRRR ...!!!
GLARE
RRR...
YEP. IT WANTS TO FIGHT.
DO OM!!
GRRRR...
SNK...
I'LL TAKE CARE OF IT.
WAIT.
LET ME TRY TO TAME IT.

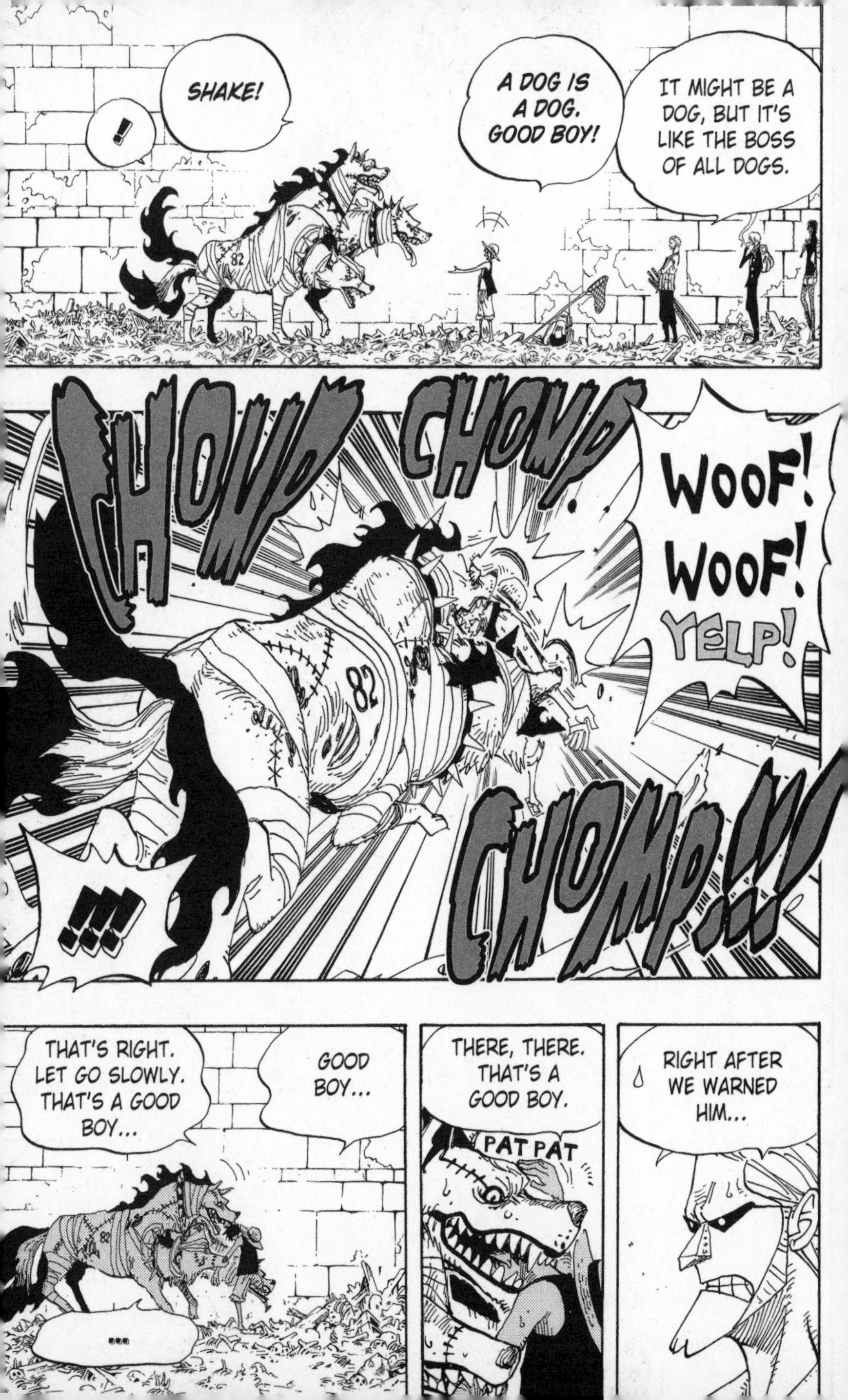
IT MIGHT BE A DOG, BUT IT'S LIKE THE BOSS OF ALL DOGS.
A DOG IS A DOG. GOOD BOY!
SHAKE!
!
WOOF! WOOF! YELP!
CHOMP
CHOMP
CHOMP!!
!!!
RIGHT AFTER WE WARNED HIM...
THERE, THERE. THAT'S A GOOD BOY.
PAT PAT
GOOD BOY...
THAT'S RIGHT. LET GO SLOWLY. THAT'S A GOOD BOY...
...

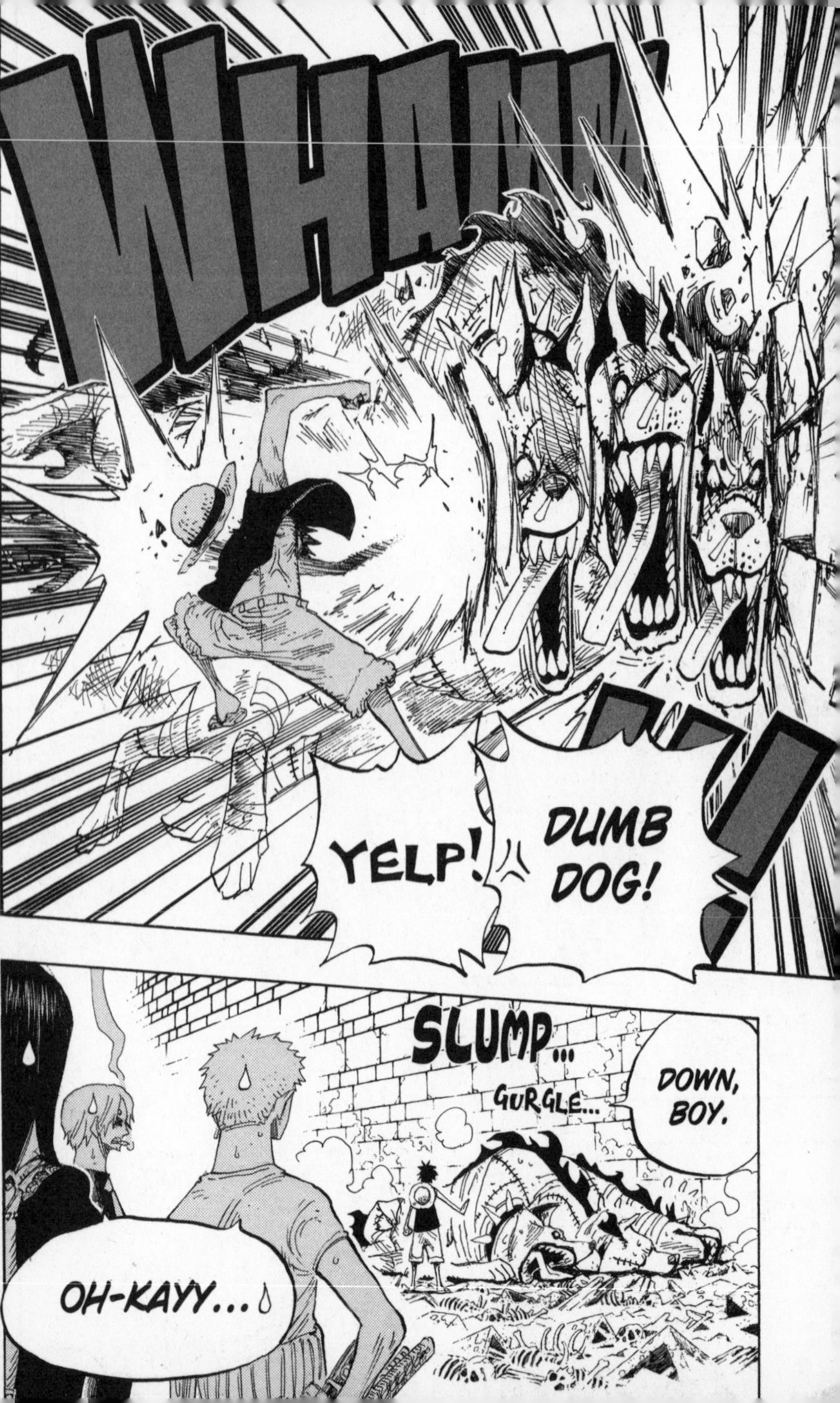
WHAM
DUMB DOG!
YELP!
DOWN, BOY.
SLUMP...
GURGLE...
OH-KAYY...

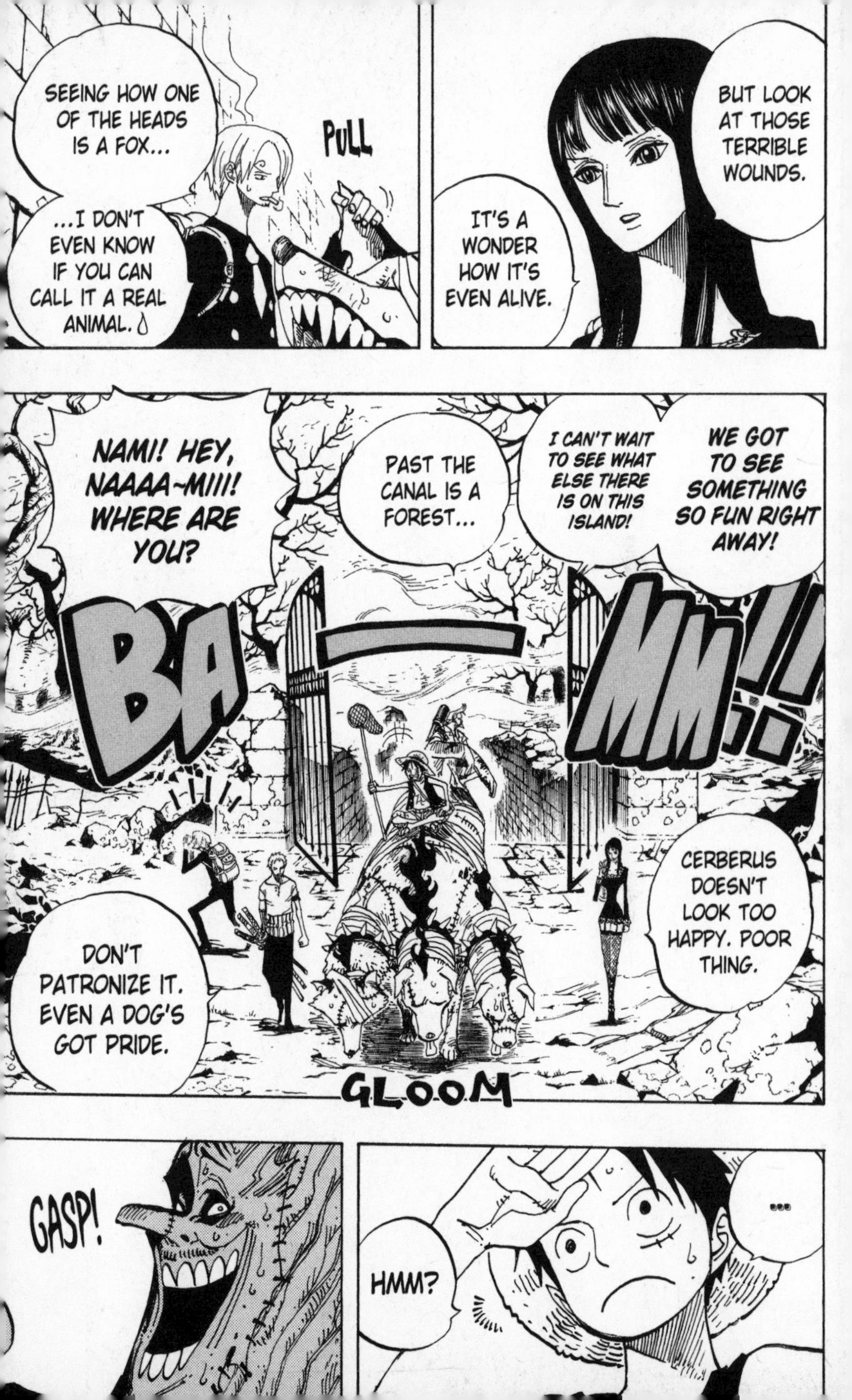
BUT LOOK AT THOSE TERRIBLE WOUNDS.
IT'S A WONDER HOW IT'S EVEN ALIVE.
SEEING HOW ONE OF THE HEADS IS A FOX...
PULL
...I DON'T EVEN KNOW IF YOU CAN CALL IT A REAL ANIMAL.
WE GOT TO SEE SOMETHING SO FUN RIGHT AWAY!
I CAN'T WAIT TO SEE WHAT ELSE THERE IS ON THIS ISLAND!
PAST THE CANAL IS A FOREST...
NAMI! HEY, NAAAA~MIIII! WHERE ARE YOU?
BA—MM!!
CERBERUS DOESN'T LOOK TOO HAPPY. POOR THING.
DON'T PATRONIZE IT. EVEN A DOG'S GOT PRIDE.
GLOOM
...
HMM?
GASP!

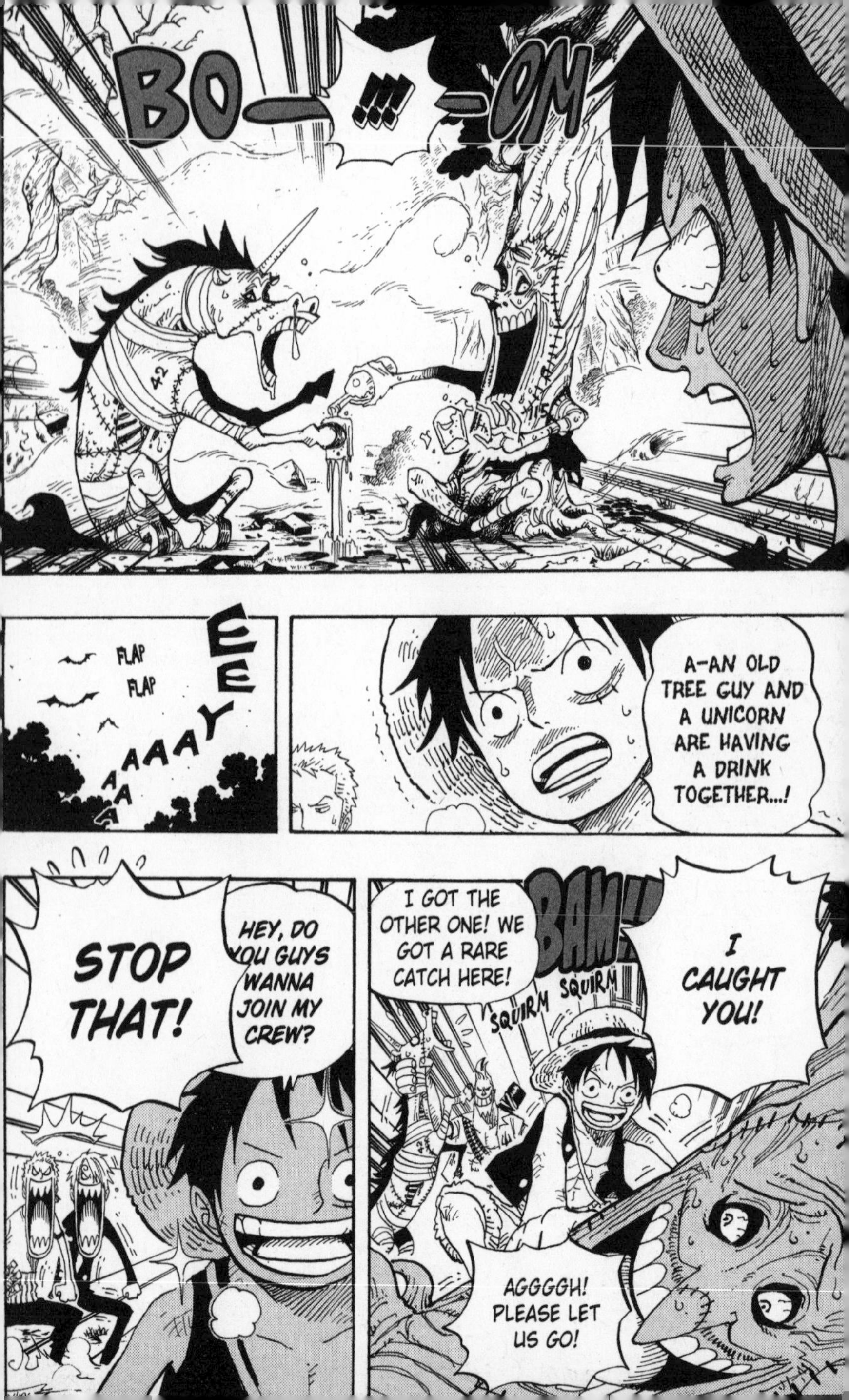
BO—!!! —OM
A-AN OLD TREE GUY AND A UNICORN ARE HAVING A DRINK TOGETHER...!
FLAP
FLAP
AAAAAAYEE
I CAUGHT YOU!
BAM!!
I GOT THE OTHER ONE! WE GOT A RARE CATCH HERE!
SQUIRM SQUIRM
AGGGGH! PLEASE LET US GO!
HEY, DO YOU GUYS WANNA JOIN MY CREW?
STOP THAT!

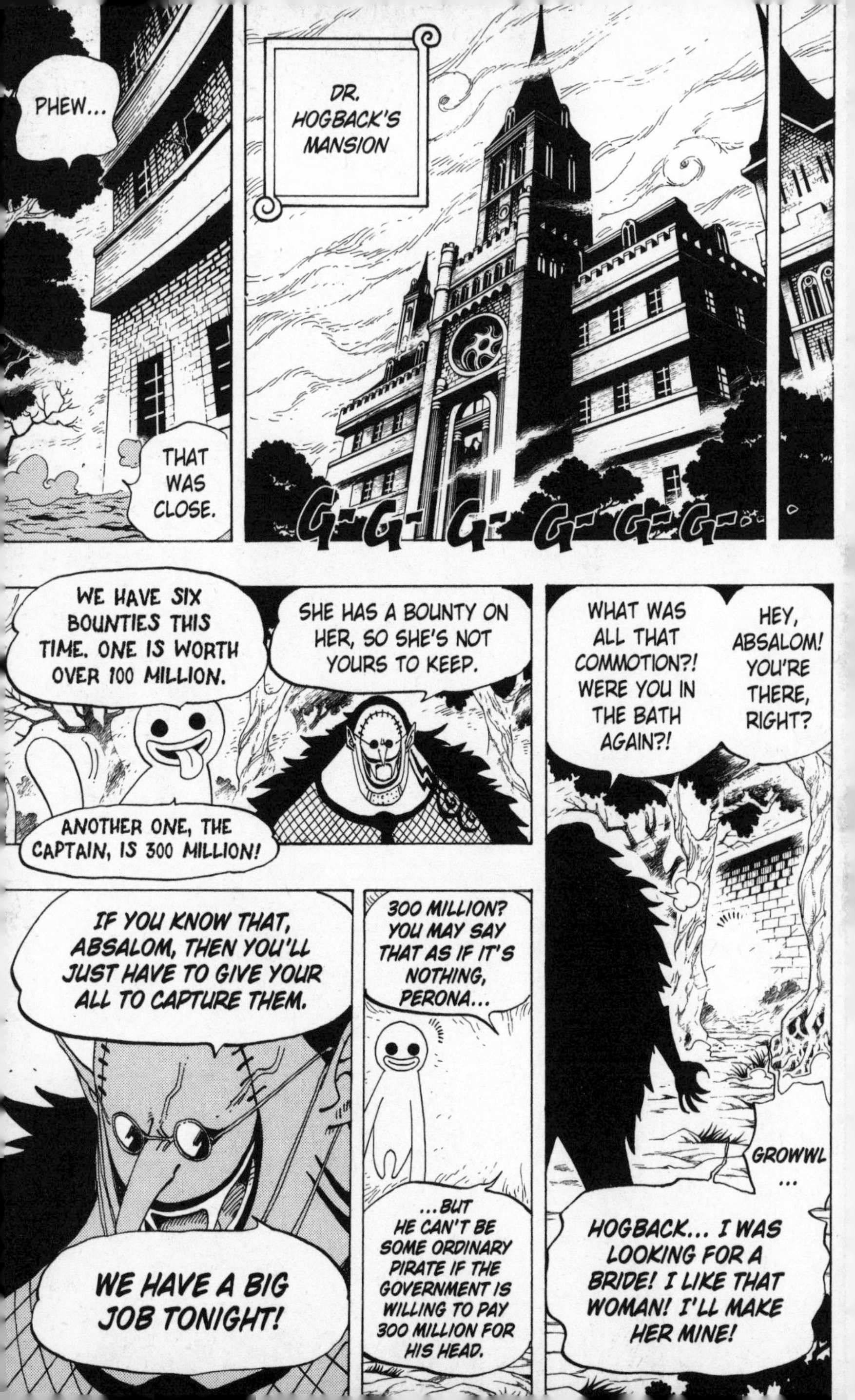
DR. HOGBACK'S MANSION
G-G-G-G-G-G-...
PHEW...
THAT WAS CLOSE.
HEY, ABSALOM! YOU'RE THERE, RIGHT?
WHAT WAS ALL THAT COMMOTION?! WERE YOU IN THE BATH AGAIN?!
GROWWL...
HOGBACK... I WAS LOOKING FOR A BRIDE! I LIKE THAT WOMAN! I'LL MAKE HER MINE!
SHE HAS A BOUNTY ON HER, SO SHE'S NOT YOURS TO KEEP.
WE HAVE SIX BOUNTIES THIS TIME. ONE IS WORTH OVER 100 MILLION.
ANOTHER ONE, THE CAPTAIN, IS 300 MILLION!
300 MILLION? YOU MAY SAY THAT AS IF IT'S NOTHING, PERONA...
...BUT HE CAN'T BE SOME ORDINARY PIRATE IF THE GOVERNMENT IS WILLING TO PAY 300 MILLION FOR HIS HEAD.
IF YOU KNOW THAT, ABSALOM, THEN YOU'LL JUST HAVE TO GIVE YOUR ALL TO CAPTURE THEM.
WE HAVE A BIG JOB TONIGHT!

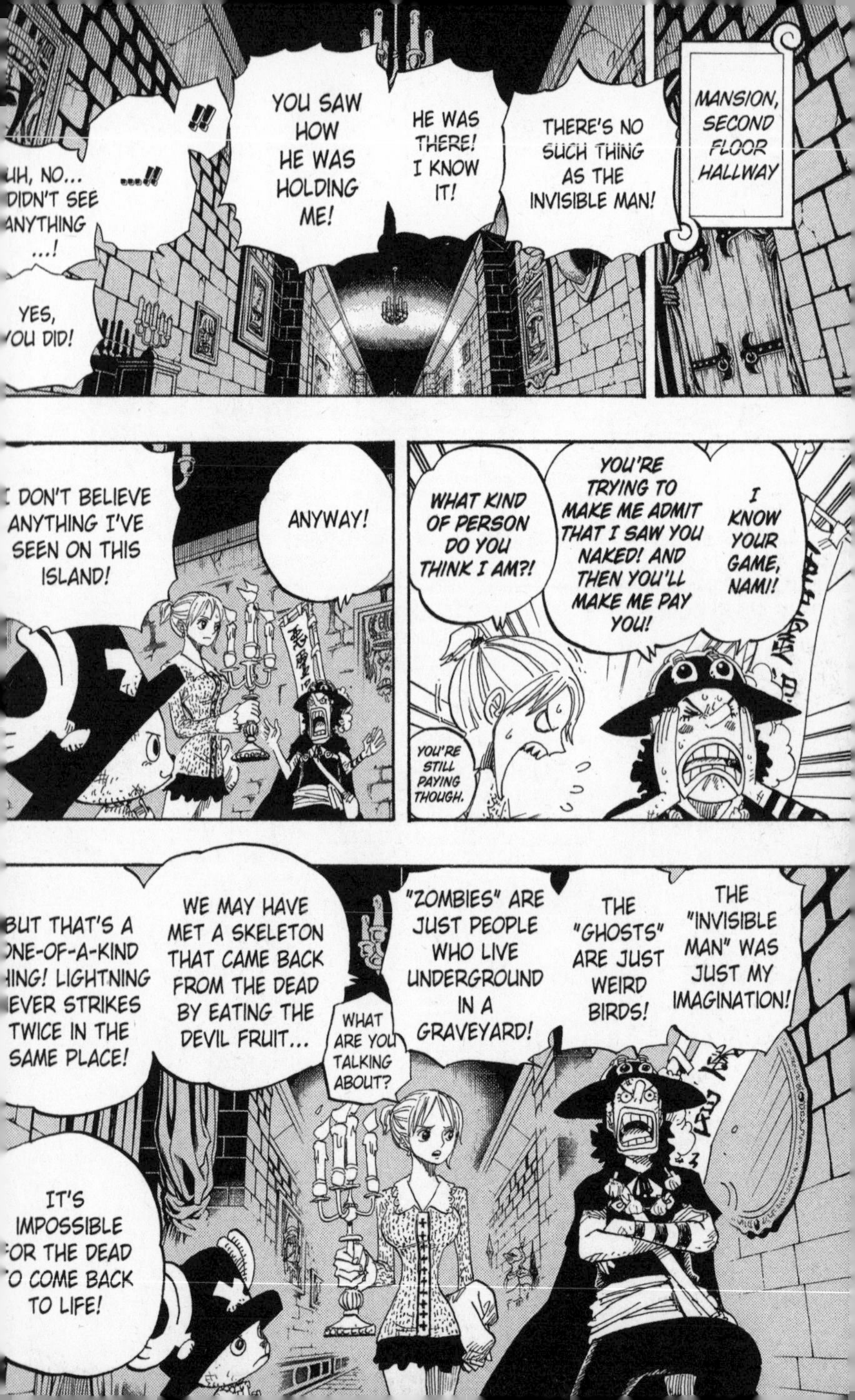
MANSION, SECOND FLOOR HALLWAY
THERE'S NO SUCH THING AS THE INVISIBLE MAN!
HE WAS THERE! I KNOW IT!
YOU SAW HOW HE WAS HOLDING ME!
!!
...!!
UH, NO... DIDN'T SEE ANYTHING ...!
YES, YOU DID!
I KNOW YOUR GAME, NAMI!
YOU'RE TRYING TO MAKE ME ADMIT THAT I SAW YOU NAKED! AND THEN YOU'LL MAKE ME PAY YOU!
WHAT KIND OF PERSON DO YOU THINK I AM?!
YOU'RE STILL PAYING THOUGH.
ANYWAY!
DON'T BELIEVE ANYTHING I'VE SEEN ON THIS ISLAND!
THE "INVISIBLE MAN" WAS JUST MY IMAGINATION!
THE "GHOSTS" ARE JUST WEIRD BIRDS!
"ZOMBIES" ARE JUST PEOPLE WHO LIVE UNDERGROUND IN A GRAVEYARD!
WHAT ARE YOU TALKING ABOUT?
WE MAY HAVE MET A SKELETON THAT CAME BACK FROM THE DEAD BY EATING THE DEVIL FRUIT...
BUT THAT'S A NE-OF-A-KIND HING! LIGHTNING EVER STRIKES TWICE IN THE SAME PLACE!
IT'S IMPOSSIBLE OR THE DEAD O COME BACK TO LIFE!

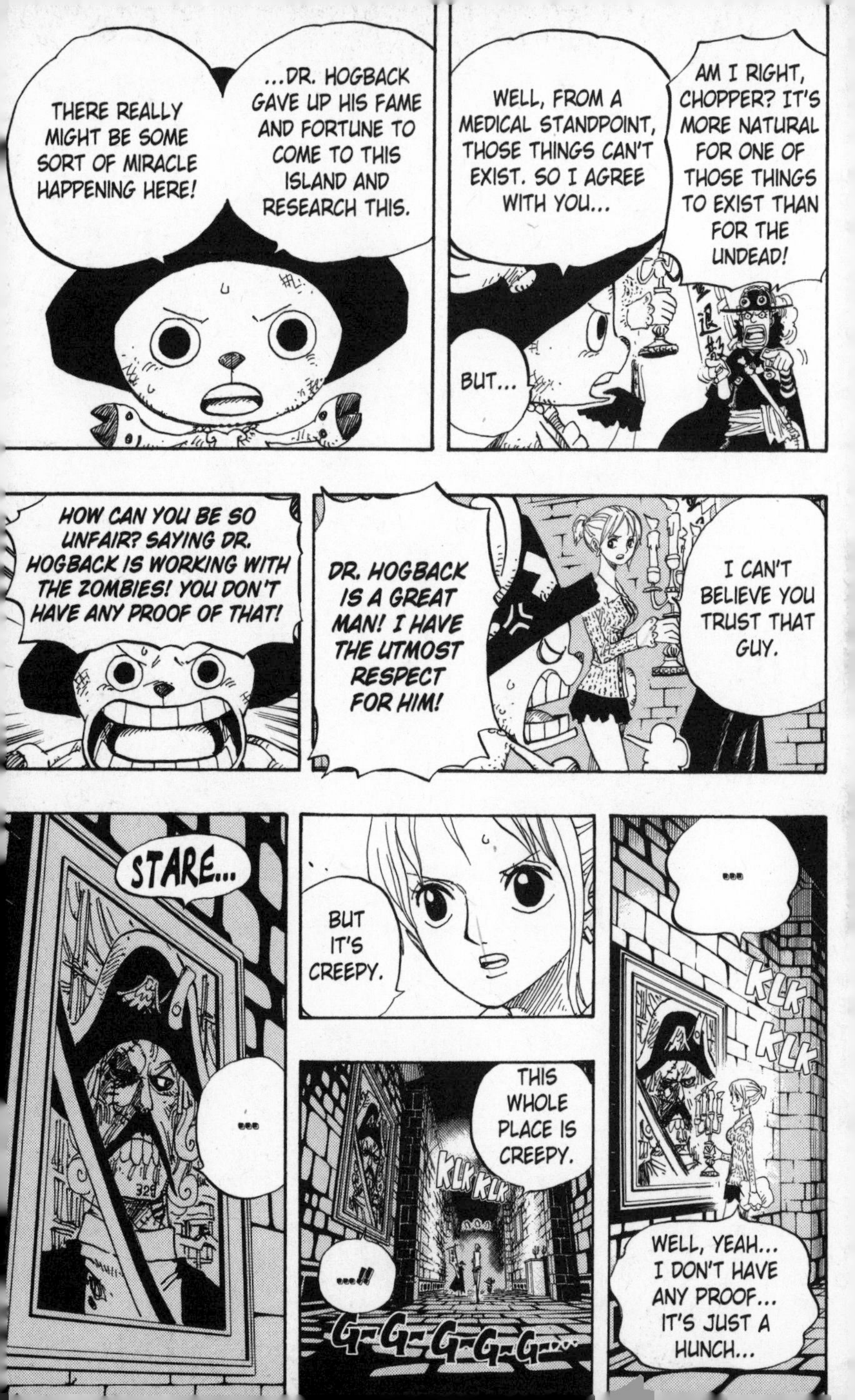
AM I RIGHT, CHOPPER? IT'S MORE NATURAL FOR ONE OF THOSE THINGS TO EXIST THAN FOR THE UNDEAD!
WELL, FROM A MEDICAL STANDPOINT, THOSE THINGS CAN'T EXIST. SO I AGREE WITH YOU...
BUT...
...DR. HOGBACK GAVE UP HIS FAME AND FORTUNE TO COME TO THIS ISLAND AND RESEARCH THIS.
THERE REALLY MIGHT BE SOME SORT OF MIRACLE HAPPENING HERE!
I CAN'T BELIEVE YOU TRUST THAT GUY.
DR. HOGBACK IS A GREAT MAN! I HAVE THE UTMOST RESPECT FOR HIM!
HOW CAN YOU BE SO UNFAIR? SAYING DR. HOGBACK IS WORKING WITH THE ZOMBIES! YOU DON'T HAVE ANY PROOF OF THAT!
...
KLK
KLK
WELL, YEAH... I DON'T HAVE ANY PROOF... IT'S JUST A HUNCH...
BUT IT'S CREEPY.
THIS WHOLE PLACE IS CREEPY.
KLK KLK
...!!
G-G-G-G-G...
STARE...
...

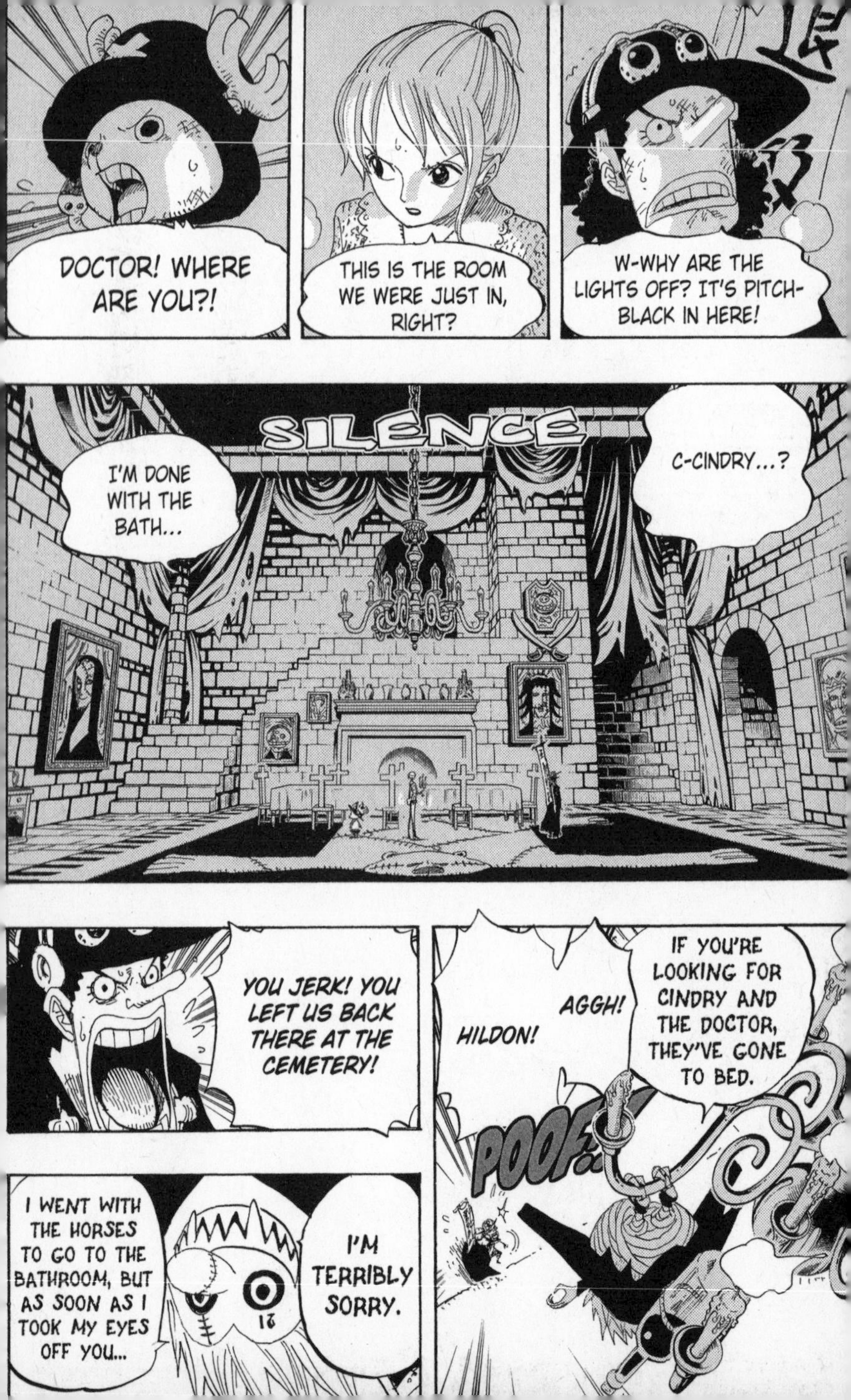
W-WHY ARE THE LIGHTS OFF? IT'S PITCH-BLACK IN HERE!
THIS IS THE ROOM WE WERE JUST IN, RIGHT?
DOCTOR! WHERE ARE YOU?!
C-CINDRY...?
SILENCE
I'M DONE WITH THE BATH...
IF YOU'RE LOOKING FOR CINDRY AND THE DOCTOR, THEY'VE GONE TO BED.
AGGH!
HILDON!
POOF
YOU JERK! YOU LEFT US BACK THERE AT THE CEMETERY!
I'M TERRIBLY SORRY.
I WENT WITH THE HORSES TO GO TO THE BATHROOM, BUT AS SOON AS I TOOK MY EYES OFF YOU...

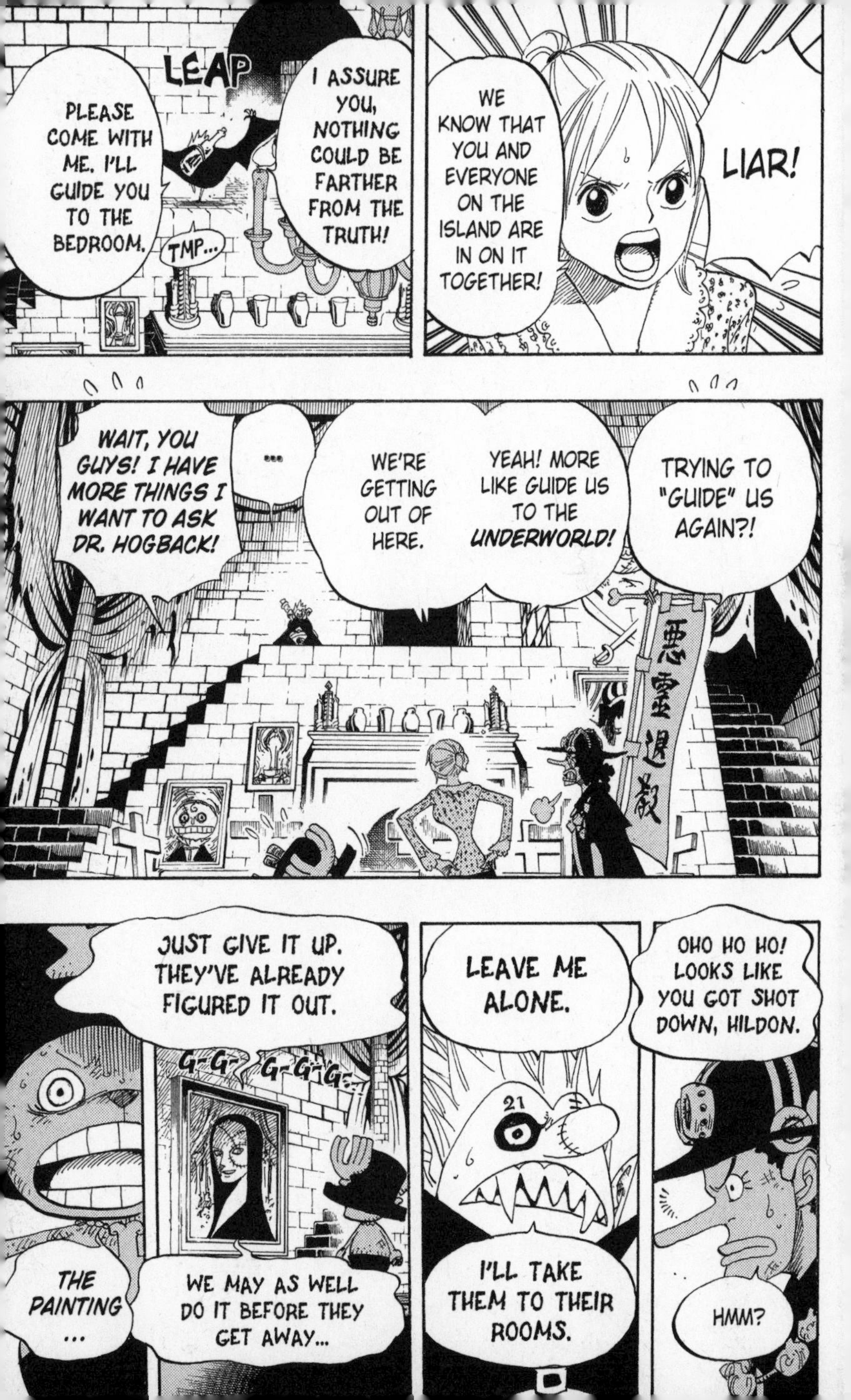
LIAR!
WE KNOW THAT YOU AND EVERYONE ON THE ISLAND ARE IN ON IT TOGETHER!
I ASSURE YOU, NOTHING COULD BE FARTHER FROM THE TRUTH!
LEAP
PLEASE COME WITH ME. I'LL GUIDE YOU TO THE BEDROOM.
TMP...
TRYING TO "GUIDE" US AGAIN?!
YEAH! MORE LIKE GUIDE US TO THE *UNDERWORLD!*
WE'RE GETTING OUT OF HERE.
...
WAIT, YOU GUYS! I HAVE MORE THINGS I WANT TO ASK DR. HOGBACK!
悪霊退散
OHO HO HO! LOOKS LIKE YOU GOT SHOT DOWN, HILDON.
HMM?
LEAVE ME ALONE.
I'LL TAKE THEM TO THEIR ROOMS.
JUST GIVE IT UP. THEY'VE ALREADY FIGURED IT OUT.
G-G- G-G-G...
WE MAY AS WELL DO IT BEFORE THEY GET AWAY...
THE PAINTING ...

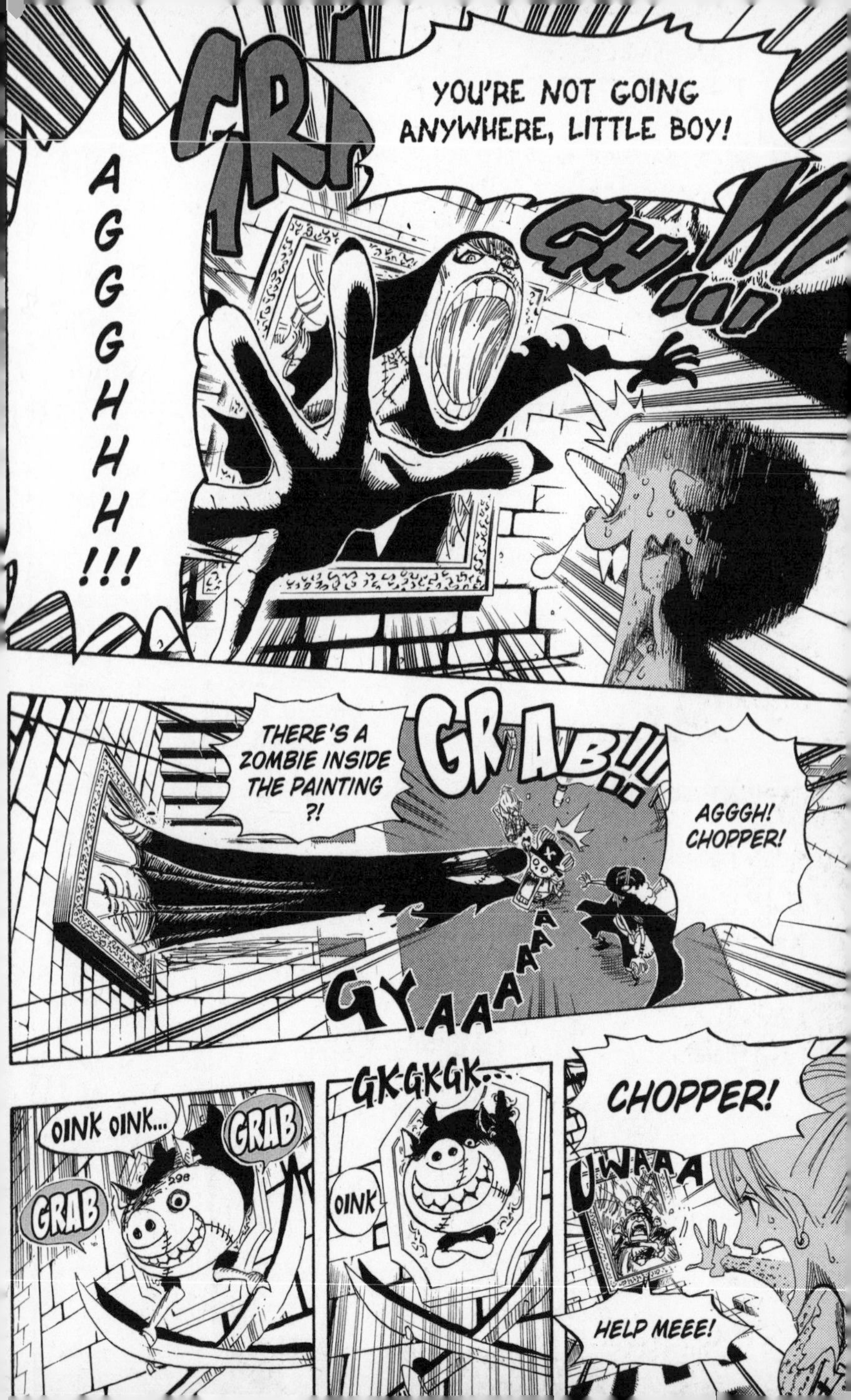

YOU'RE NOT GOING ANYWHERE, LITTLE BOY!
GR
GH...!!
AGGGHHH!!!
AGGGH! CHOPPER!
GRAB!!
THERE'S A ZOMBIE INSIDE THE PAINTING ?!
GYAAAAAA
CHOPPER!
UWAAA
HELP MEEE!
GKGKGK...
OINK
OINK OINK...
GRAB
GRAB

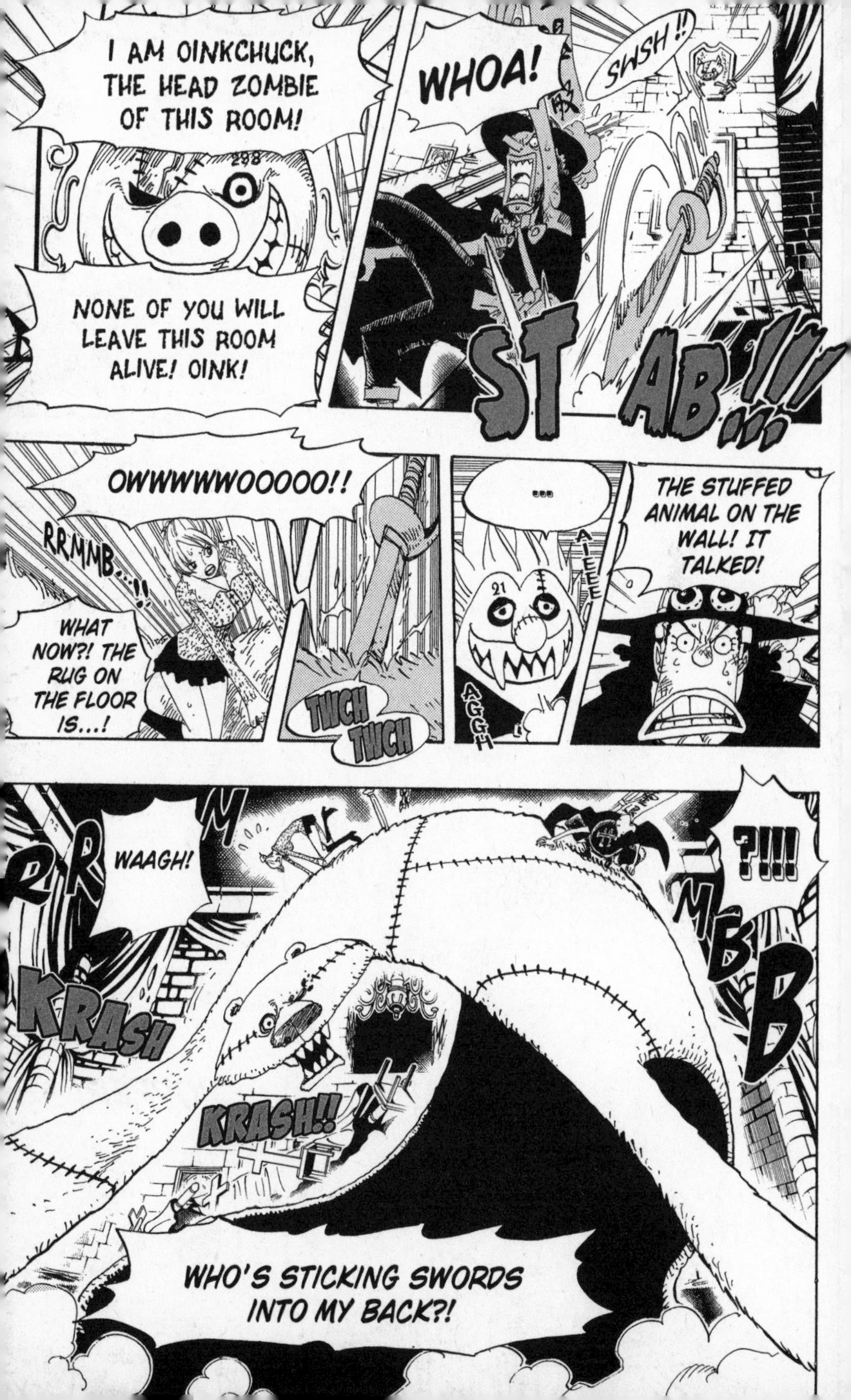
SWSH!!
WHOA!
STAB!!!
I AM OINKCHUCK, THE HEAD ZOMBIE OF THIS ROOM!
298
NONE OF YOU WILL LEAVE THIS ROOM ALIVE! OINK!
THE STUFFED ANIMAL ON THE WALL! IT TALKED!
...
AIEEE
21
AGGH
TWCH TWCH
OWWWWWOOOOO!!
RRMMB...!!
WHAT NOW?! THE RUG ON THE FLOOR IS...!
?!!!
RRRMMBB
WAAGH!
KRASH
KRASH!!
WHO'S STICKING SWORDS INTO MY BACK?!

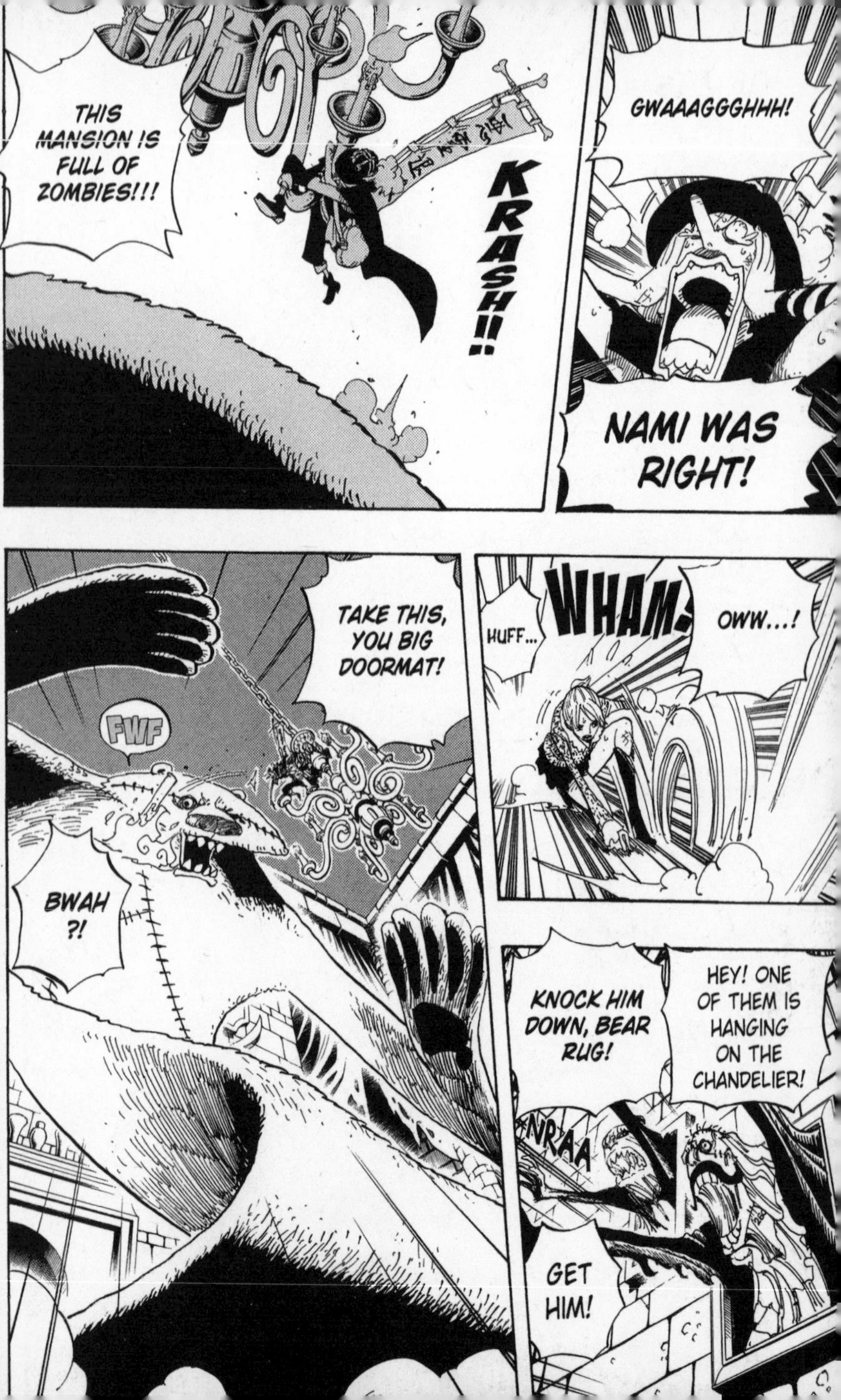
GWAAAGGGHHH!
NAMI WAS RIGHT!
THIS MANSION IS FULL OF ZOMBIES!!!
KRASH!!
OWW...!
WHAM!
HUFF...
HEY! ONE OF THEM IS HANGING ON THE CHANDELIER!
KNOCK HIM DOWN, BEAR RUG!
NRAA
GET HIM!
TAKE THIS, YOU BIG DOORMAT!
FWF
BWAH ?!

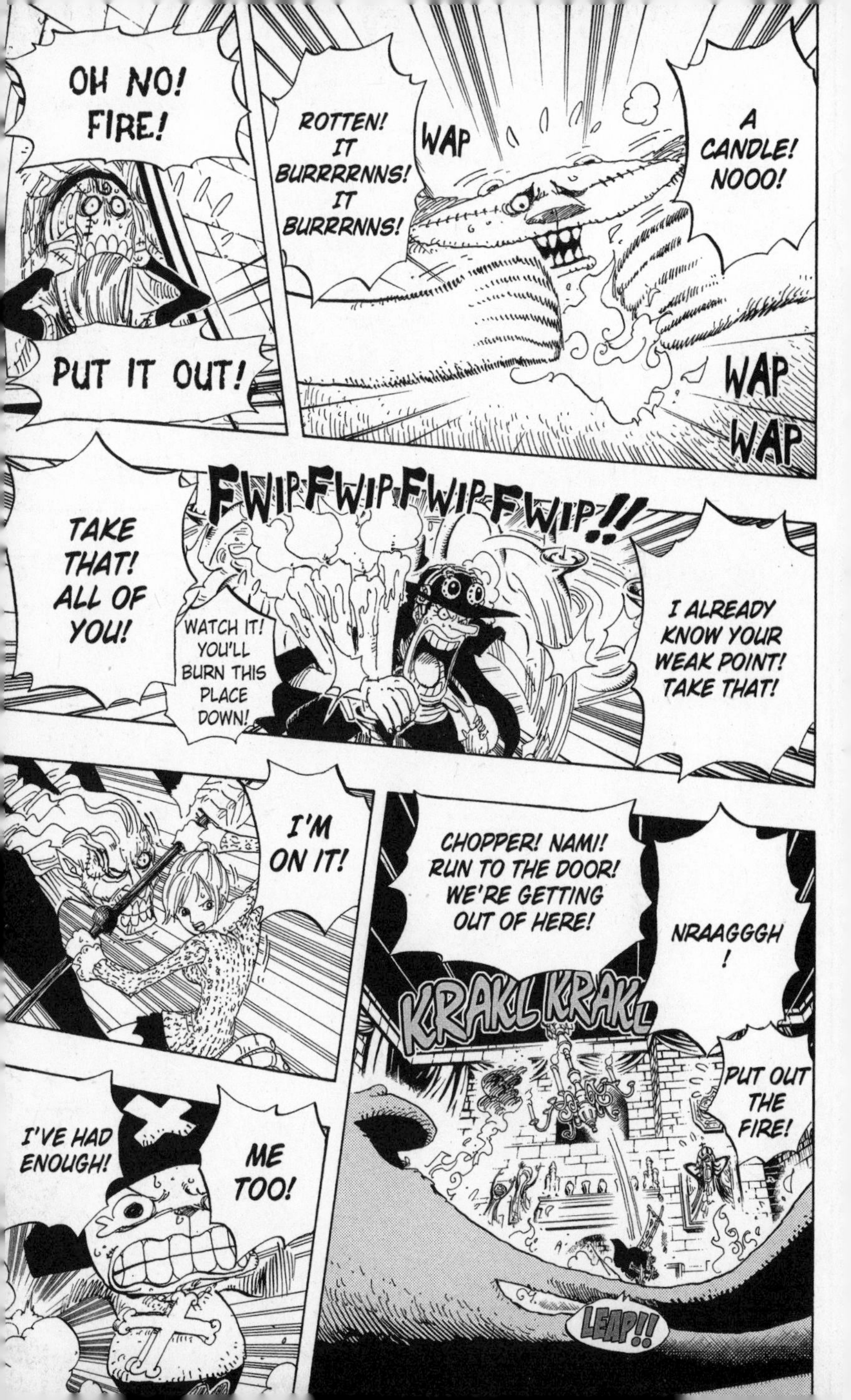
A CANDLE! NOOO!
WAP
ROTTEN! IT BURRRRNNS! IT BURRRNNS!
WAP WAP
OH NO! FIRE!
PUT IT OUT!
I ALREADY KNOW YOUR WEAK POINT! TAKE THAT!
FWIP FWIP FWIP FWIP!!
WATCH IT! YOU'LL BURN THIS PLACE DOWN!
TAKE THAT! ALL OF YOU!
NRAAGGGH!
CHOPPER! NAMI! RUN TO THE DOOR! WE'RE GETTING OUT OF HERE!
KRAKL KRAKL
PUT OUT THE FIRE!
LEAP!!
I'M ON IT!
ME TOO!
I'VE HAD ENOUGH!

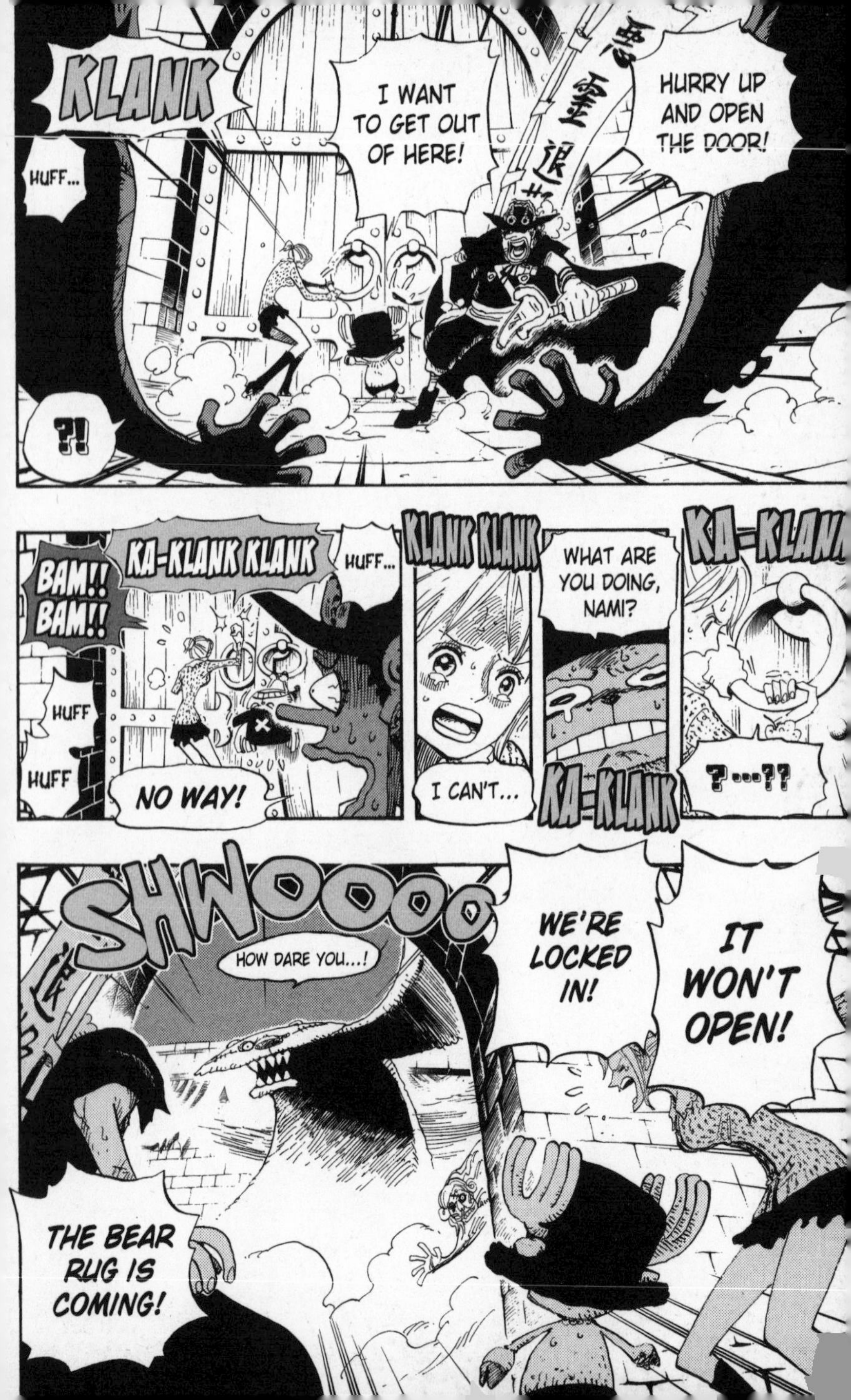

HURRY UP AND OPEN THE DOOR!
I WANT TO GET OUT OF HERE!
KLANK
HUFF...
?!
KA-KLANK
?...??
WHAT ARE YOU DOING, NAMI?
KA-KLANK
KLANK KLANK
I CAN'T...
HUFF...
KA-KLANK KLANK
BAM!! BAM!!
HUFF
HUFF
NO WAY!
IT WON'T OPEN!
WE'RE LOCKED IN!
SHWOOOO
HOW DARE YOU...!
THE BEAR RUG IS COMING!

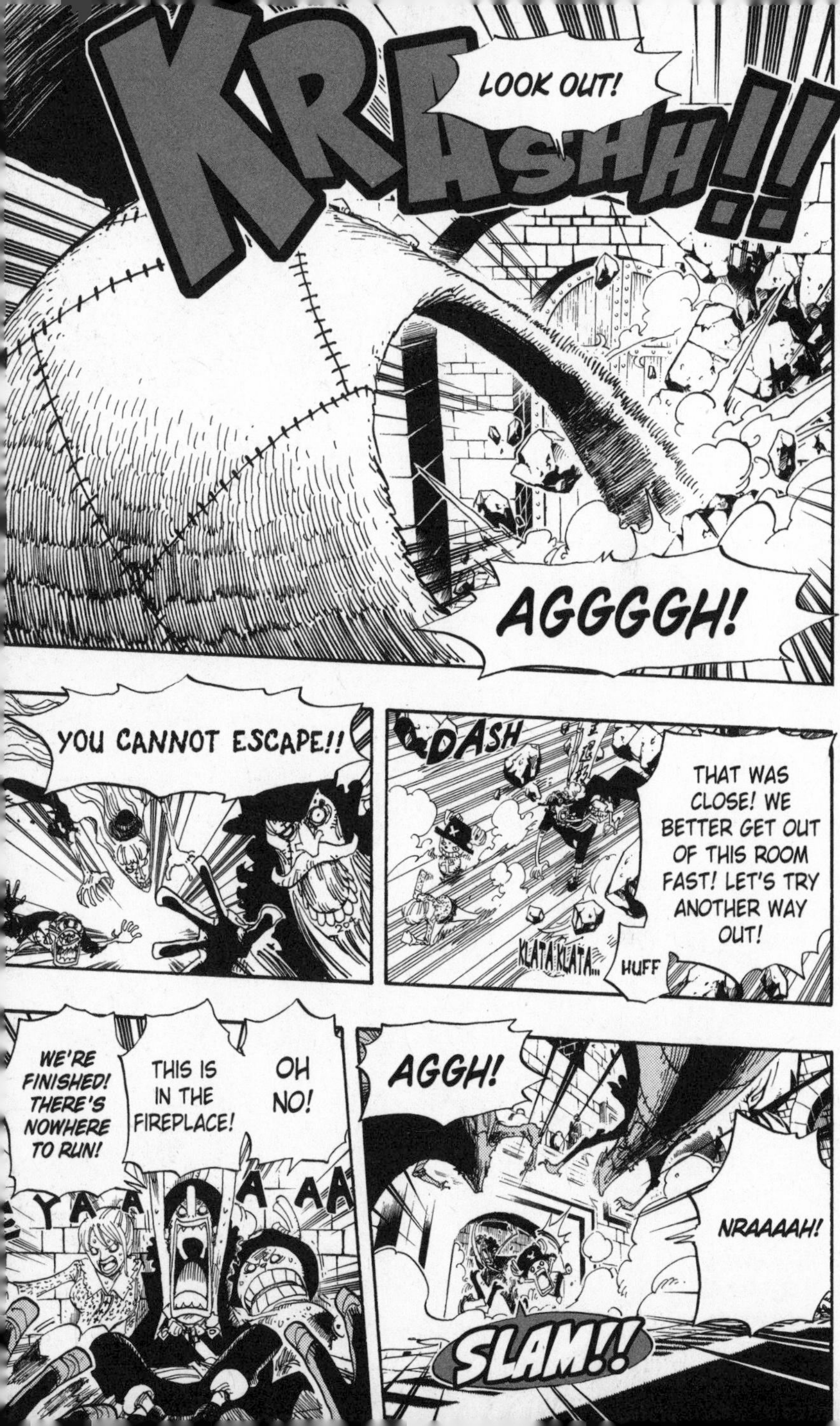
KRASHH!!
LOOK OUT!
AGGGGH!
DASH
THAT WAS CLOSE! WE BETTER GET OUT OF THIS ROOM FAST! LET'S TRY ANOTHER WAY OUT!
KLATA KLATA...
HUFF
YOU CANNOT ESCAPE!!
AGGH!
NRAAAAH!
SLAM!!
OH NO!
THIS IS IN THE FIREPLACE!
WE'RE FINISHED! THERE'S NOWHERE TO RUN!
YAAAAA

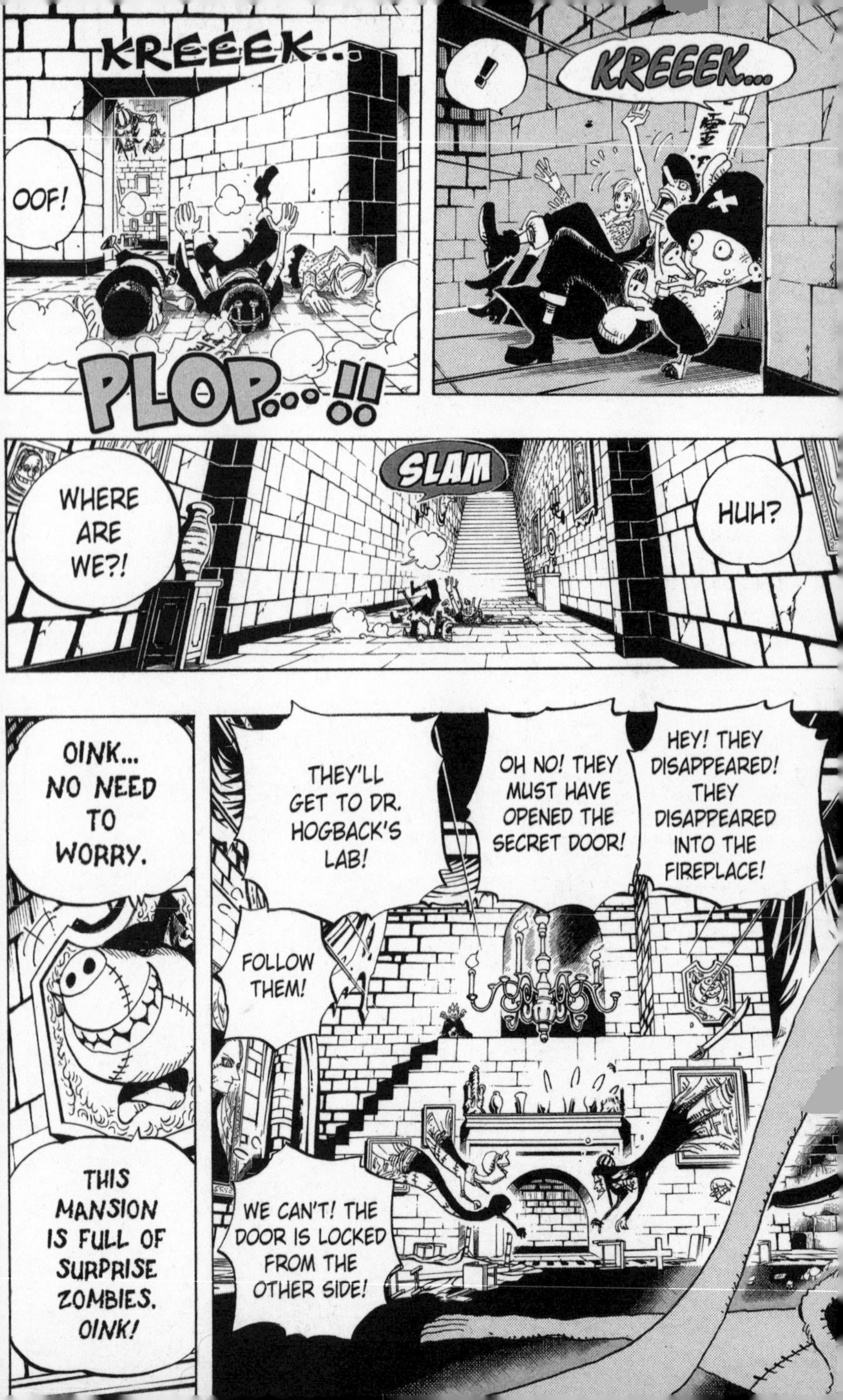
!
KREEEK...
KREEEK...
OOF!
PLOP...!!
HUH?
SLAM
WHERE ARE WE?!
HEY! THEY DISAPPEARED! THEY DISAPPEARED INTO THE FIREPLACE!
OH NO! THEY MUST HAVE OPENED THE SECRET DOOR!
THEY'LL GET TO DR. HOGBACK'S LAB!
FOLLOW THEM!
WE CAN'T! THE DOOR IS LOCKED FROM THE OTHER SIDE!
OINK... NO NEED TO WORRY.
THIS MANSION IS FULL OF SURPRISE ZOMBIES. OINK!

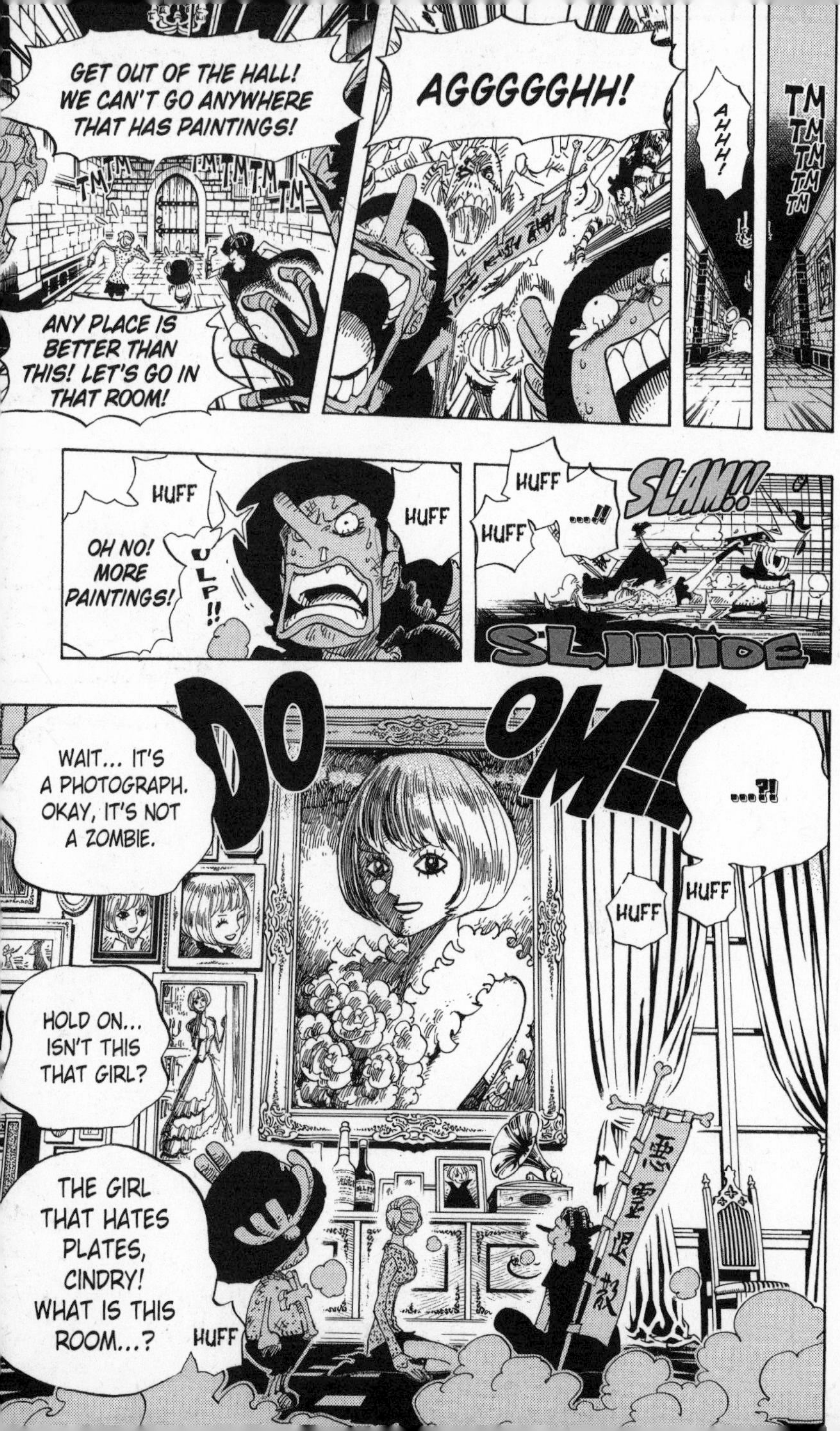
TMTMTMTMTMTM
AHHH!
AGGGGGHH!
GET OUT OF THE HALL! WE CAN'T GO ANYWHERE THAT HAS PAINTINGS!
TMTMTMTMTMTM
ANY PLACE IS BETTER THAN THIS! LET'S GO IN THAT ROOM!
SLAM!!
HUFF
HUFF
...!!
SLIIIIDE
HUFF
HUFF
OH NO! MORE PAINTINGS!
ULP!!
DOOM!!
...?!
HUFF
HUFF
WAIT... IT'S A PHOTOGRAPH. OKAY, IT'S NOT A ZOMBIE.
HOLD ON... ISN'T THIS THAT GIRL?
THE GIRL THAT HATES PLATES, CINDRY! WHAT IS THIS ROOM...?
HUFF

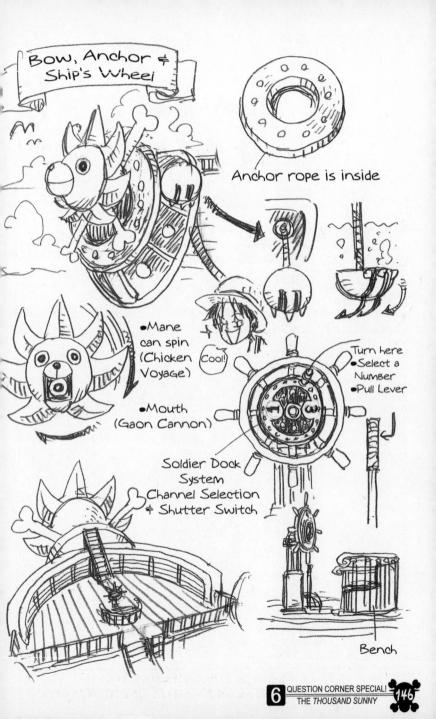

Bow, Anchor &
Ship's Wheel

Anchor rope is inside

•Mane
can spin
(Chicken
Voyage)

Cool!

•Mouth
(Gaon Cannon)

Turn here
•Select a
Number
•Pull Lever

Soldier Dock
System
Channel Selection
& Shutter Switch

Bench

Chapter 447:
MORIA

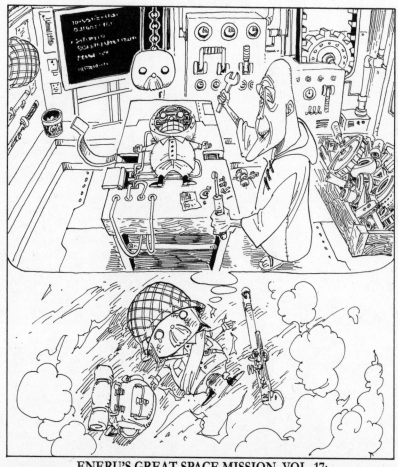

ENERU'S GREAT SPACE MISSION, VOL. 17:
"FLASHBACK––MACHINE ISLAND, THE DAY HE WAS BORN"

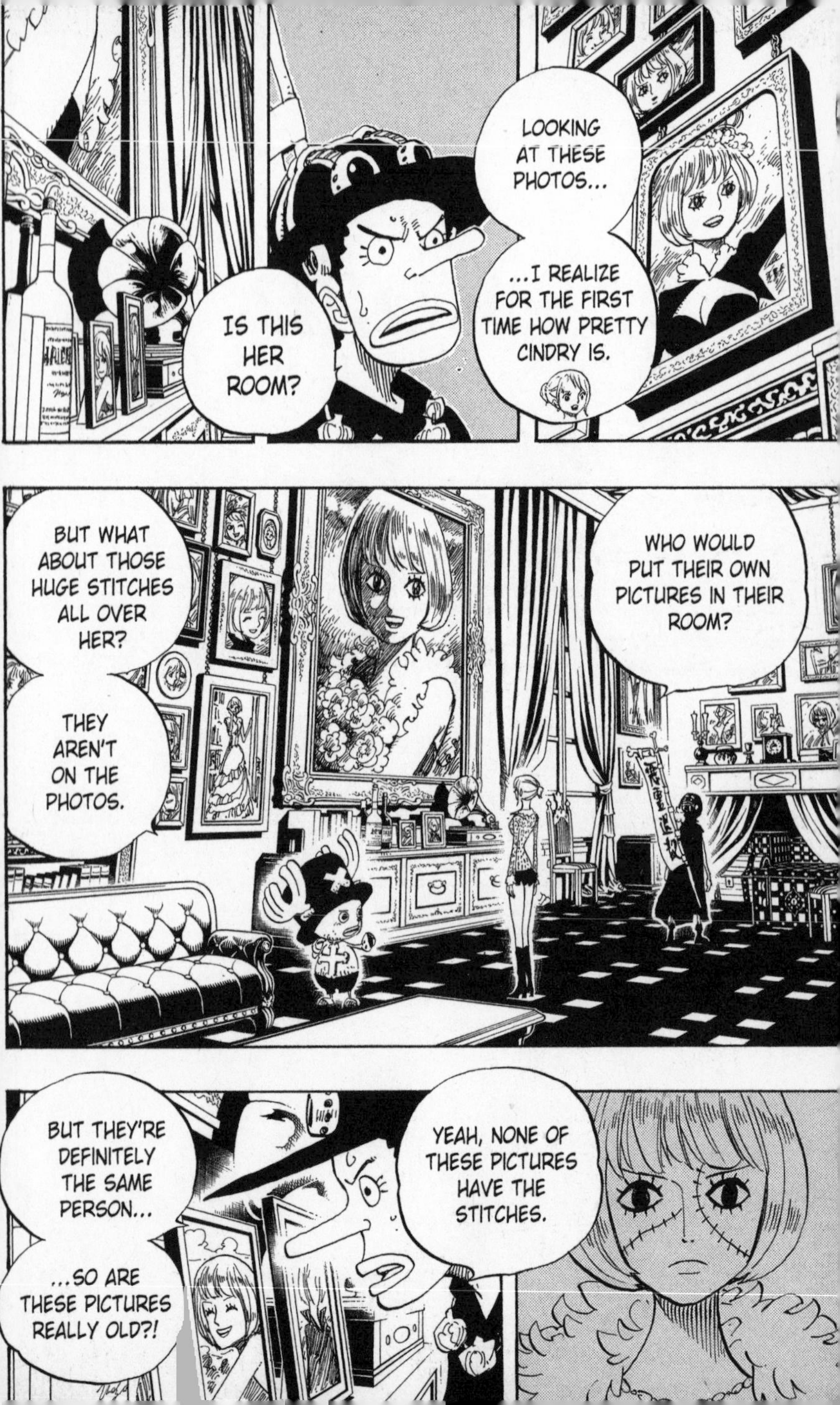
LOOKING AT THESE PHOTOS...
...I REALIZE FOR THE FIRST TIME HOW PRETTY CINDRY IS.
IS THIS HER ROOM?
WHO WOULD PUT THEIR OWN PICTURES IN THEIR ROOM?
BUT WHAT ABOUT THOSE HUGE STITCHES ALL OVER HER?
THEY AREN'T ON THE PHOTOS.
YEAH, NONE OF THESE PICTURES HAVE THE STITCHES.
BUT THEY'RE DEFINITELY THE SAME PERSON...
...SO ARE THESE PICTURES REALLY OLD?!

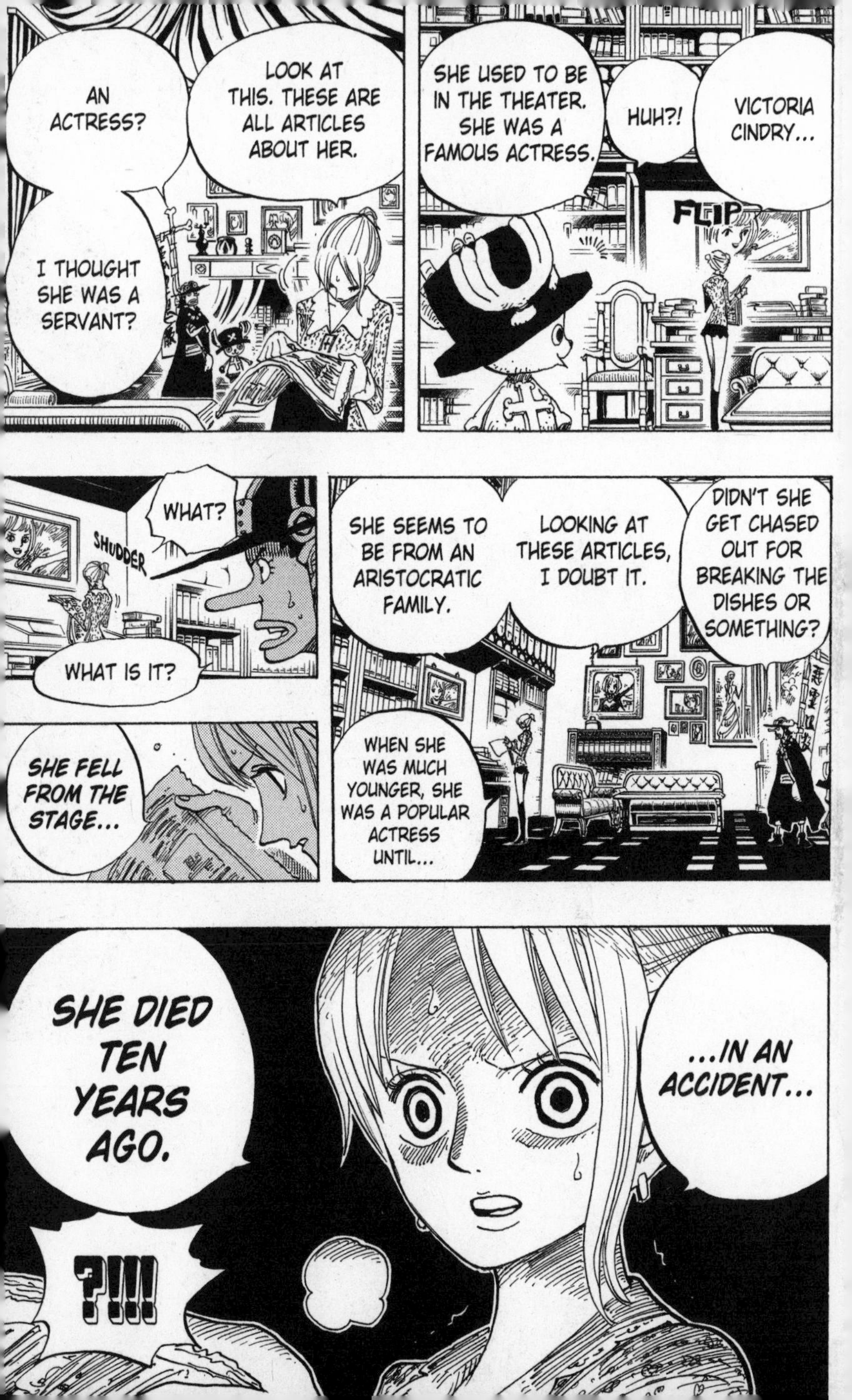
VICTORIA CINDRY...
HUH?!
SHE USED TO BE IN THE THEATER. SHE WAS A FAMOUS ACTRESS.
FLIP
LOOK AT THIS. THESE ARE ALL ARTICLES ABOUT HER.
AN ACTRESS?
I THOUGHT SHE WAS A SERVANT?
DIDN'T SHE GET CHASED OUT FOR BREAKING THE DISHES OR SOMETHING?
LOOKING AT THESE ARTICLES, I DOUBT IT.
SHE SEEMS TO BE FROM AN ARISTOCRATIC FAMILY.
WHEN SHE WAS MUCH YOUNGER, SHE WAS A POPULAR ACTRESS UNTIL...
WHAT?
SHUDDER
WHAT IS IT?
SHE FELL FROM THE STAGE...
...IN AN ACCIDENT...
SHE DIED TEN YEARS AGO.
?!!!

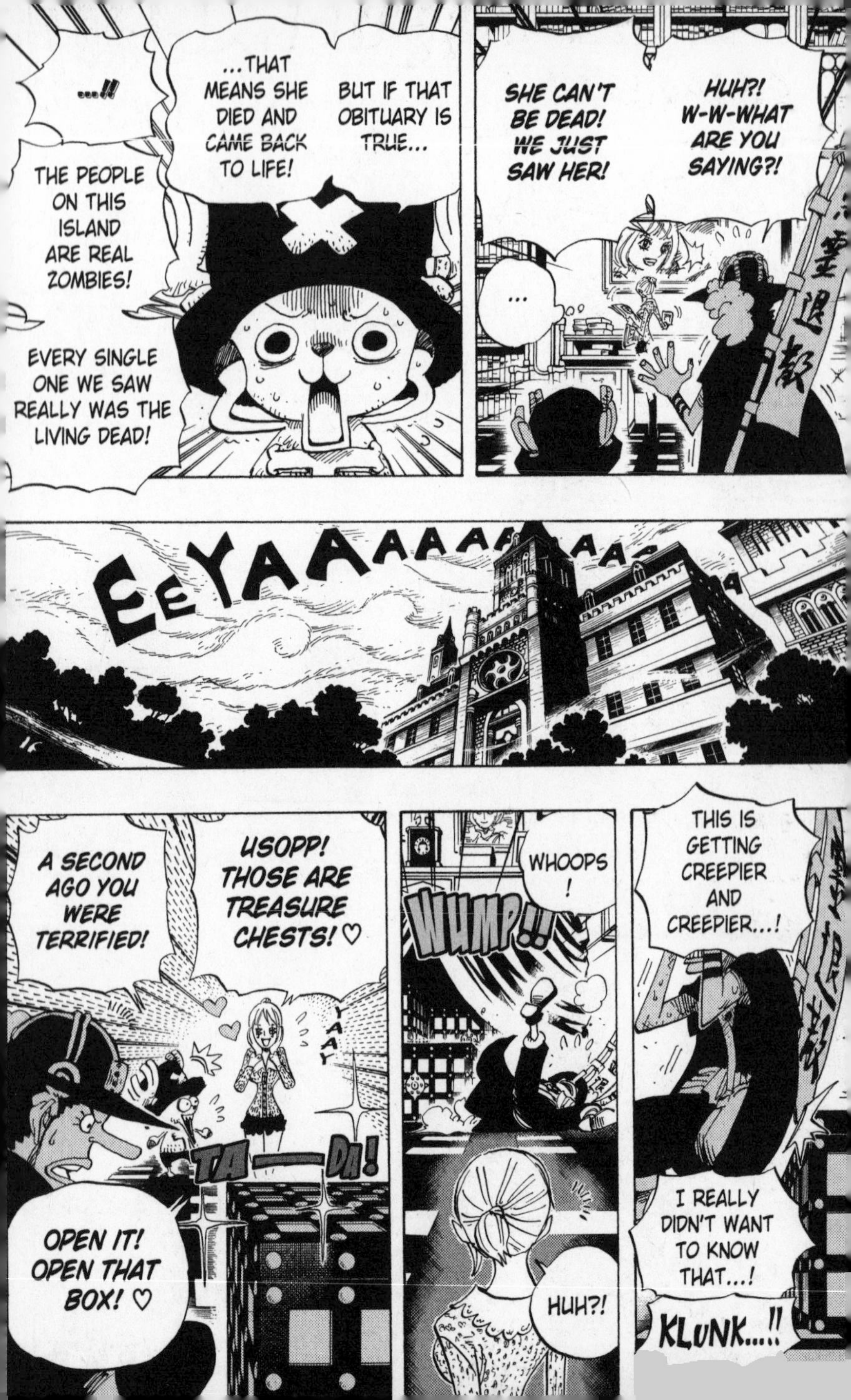
HUH?! W-W-WHAT ARE YOU SAYING?!
SHE CAN'T BE DEAD! WE JUST SAW HER!
...
BUT IF THAT OBITUARY IS TRUE...
...THAT MEANS SHE DIED AND CAME BACK TO LIFE!
...!!
THE PEOPLE ON THIS ISLAND ARE REAL ZOMBIES!
EVERY SINGLE ONE WE SAW REALLY WAS THE LIVING DEAD!
EEYAAAAAAAAAA
THIS IS GETTING CREEPIER AND CREEPIER...!
I REALLY DIDN'T WANT TO KNOW THAT...!
KLUNK...!!
WHOOPS!
WUMP!!
HUH?!
USOPP! THOSE ARE TREASURE CHESTS! ♡
A SECOND AGO YOU WERE TERRIFIED!
YAAAY
TA——DA!
OPEN IT! OPEN THAT BOX! ♡

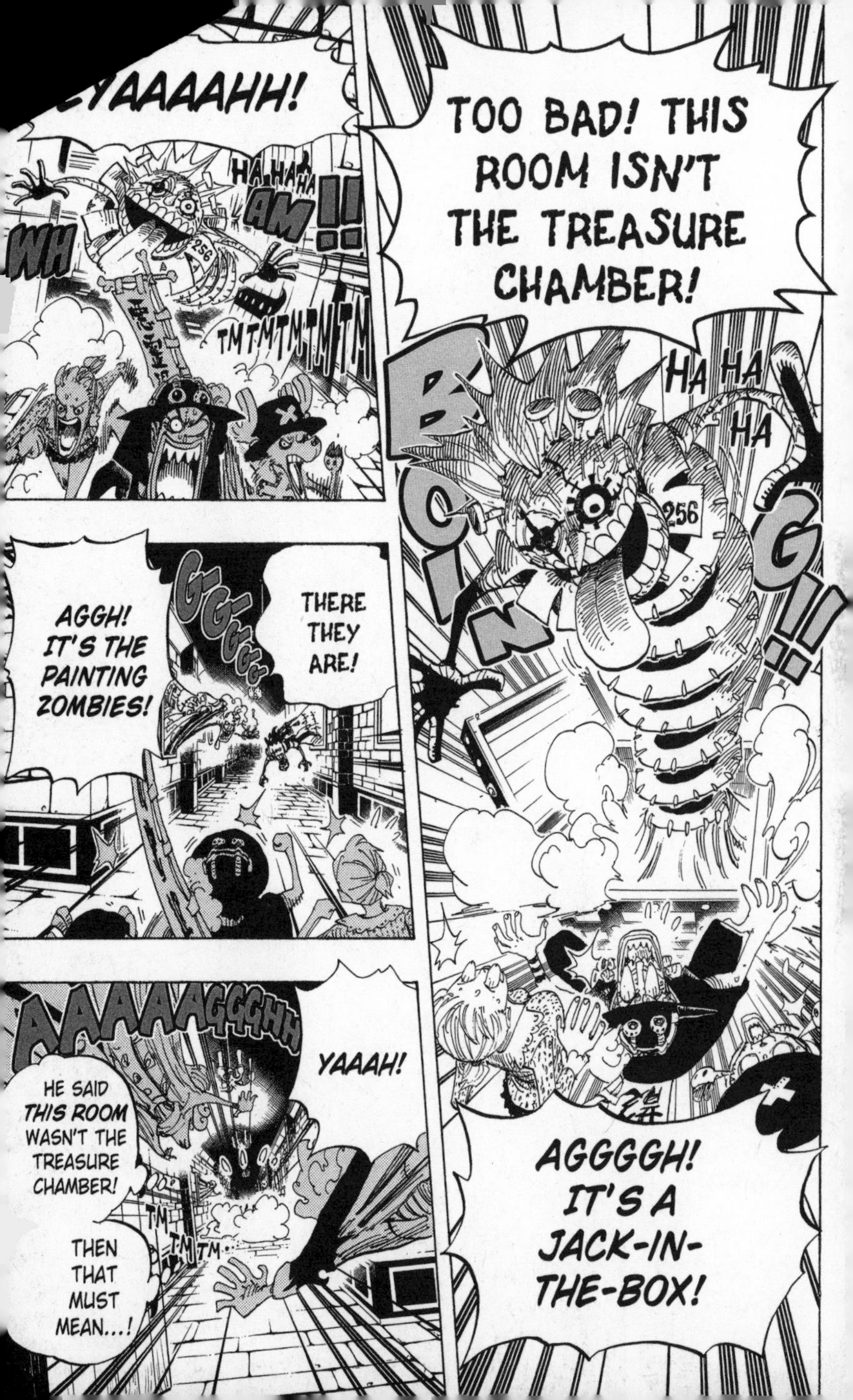
TOO BAD! THIS ROOM ISN'T THE TREASURE CHAMBER!
BOING!!
HA HA HA
256
AGGGGH! IT'S A JACK-IN-THE-BOX!
EYAAAAAHH!
HA HA HA
WHAM!!
256
TMTMTMTMTMTM
THERE THEY ARE!
AGGH! IT'S THE PAINTING ZOMBIES!
G-GGGGG
YAAAH!
AAAAAGGGHH
HE SAID THIS ROOM WASN'T THE TREASURE CHAMBER!
THEN THAT MUST MEAN...!
TM TM TM

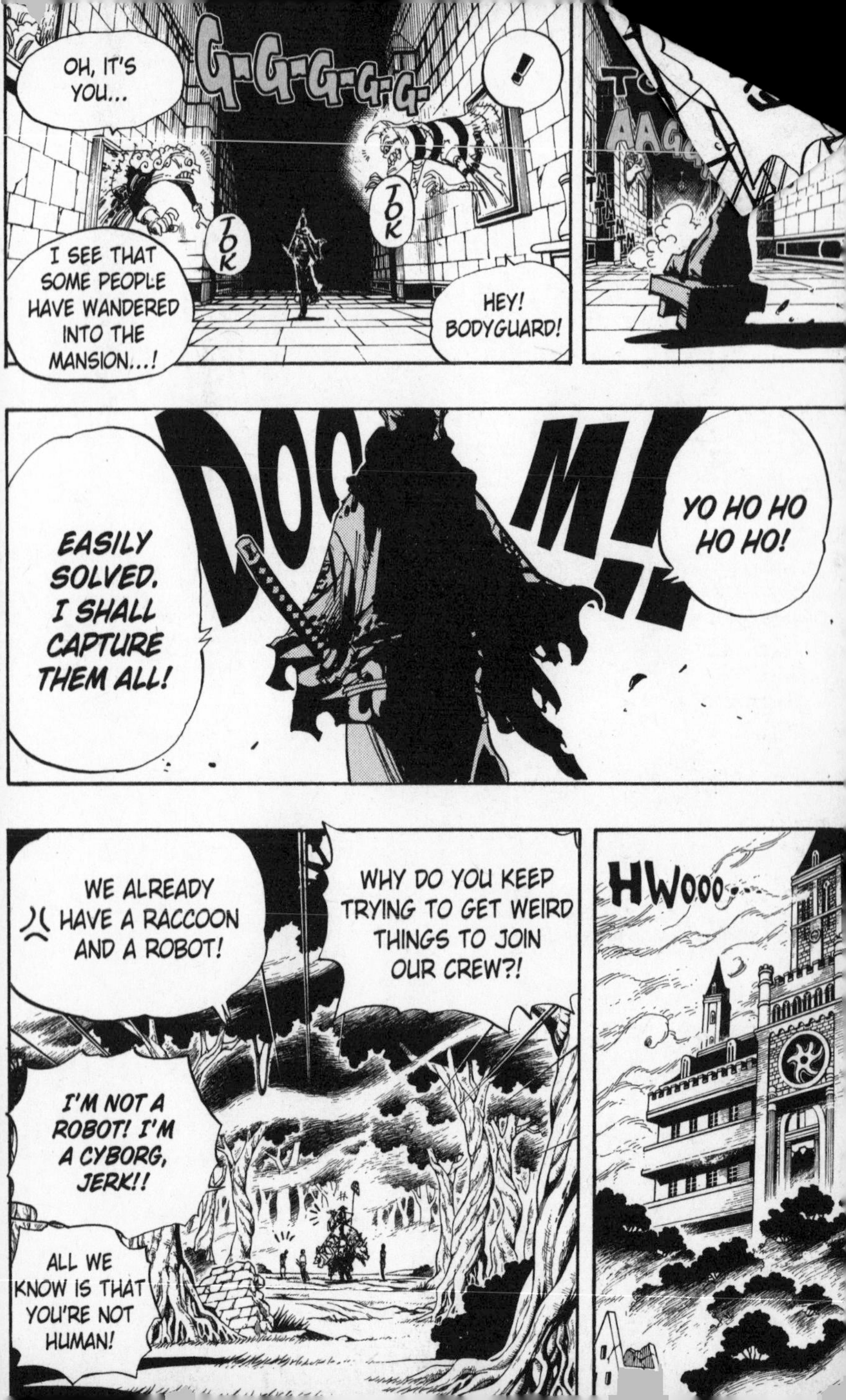
!
G-G-G-G-G-
OH, IT'S YOU...
TOK
TOK
HEY! BODYGUARD!
I SEE THAT SOME PEOPLE HAVE WANDERED INTO THE MANSION...!
YO HO HO HO HO!
EASILY SOLVED. I SHALL CAPTURE THEM ALL!
HWOOO
WHY DO YOU KEEP TRYING TO GET WEIRD THINGS TO JOIN OUR CREW?!
WE ALREADY HAVE A RACCOON AND A ROBOT!
I'M NOT A ROBOT! I'M A CYBORG, JERK!!
ALL WE KNOW IS THAT YOU'RE NOT HUMAN!

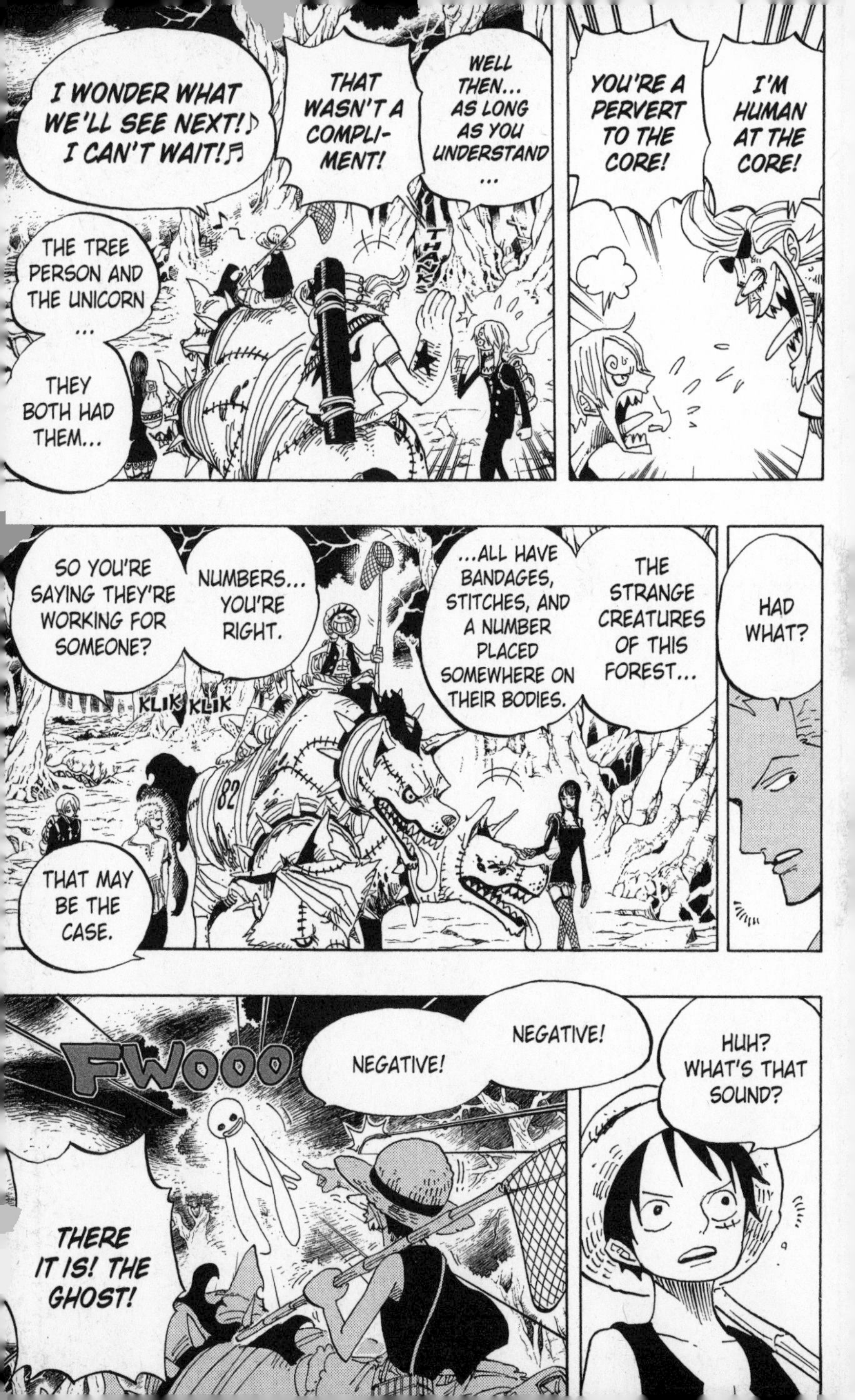
I'M HUMAN AT THE CORE!
YOU'RE A PERVERT TO THE CORE!
WELL THEN... AS LONG AS YOU UNDERSTAND ...
THANKS
THAT WASN'T A COMPLI-MENT!
I WONDER WHAT WE'LL SEE NEXT!♪ I CAN'T WAIT!♬
THE TREE PERSON AND THE UNICORN ...
THEY BOTH HAD THEM...
HAD WHAT?
THE STRANGE CREATURES OF THIS FOREST...
...ALL HAVE BANDAGES, STITCHES, AND A NUMBER PLACED SOMEWHERE ON THEIR BODIES.
NUMBERS... YOU'RE RIGHT.
SO YOU'RE SAYING THEY'RE WORKING FOR SOMEONE?
KLIK KLIK
82
THAT MAY BE THE CASE.
HUH? WHAT'S THAT SOUND?
NEGATIVE!
NEGATIVE!
FWOOO
THERE IT IS! THE GHOST!

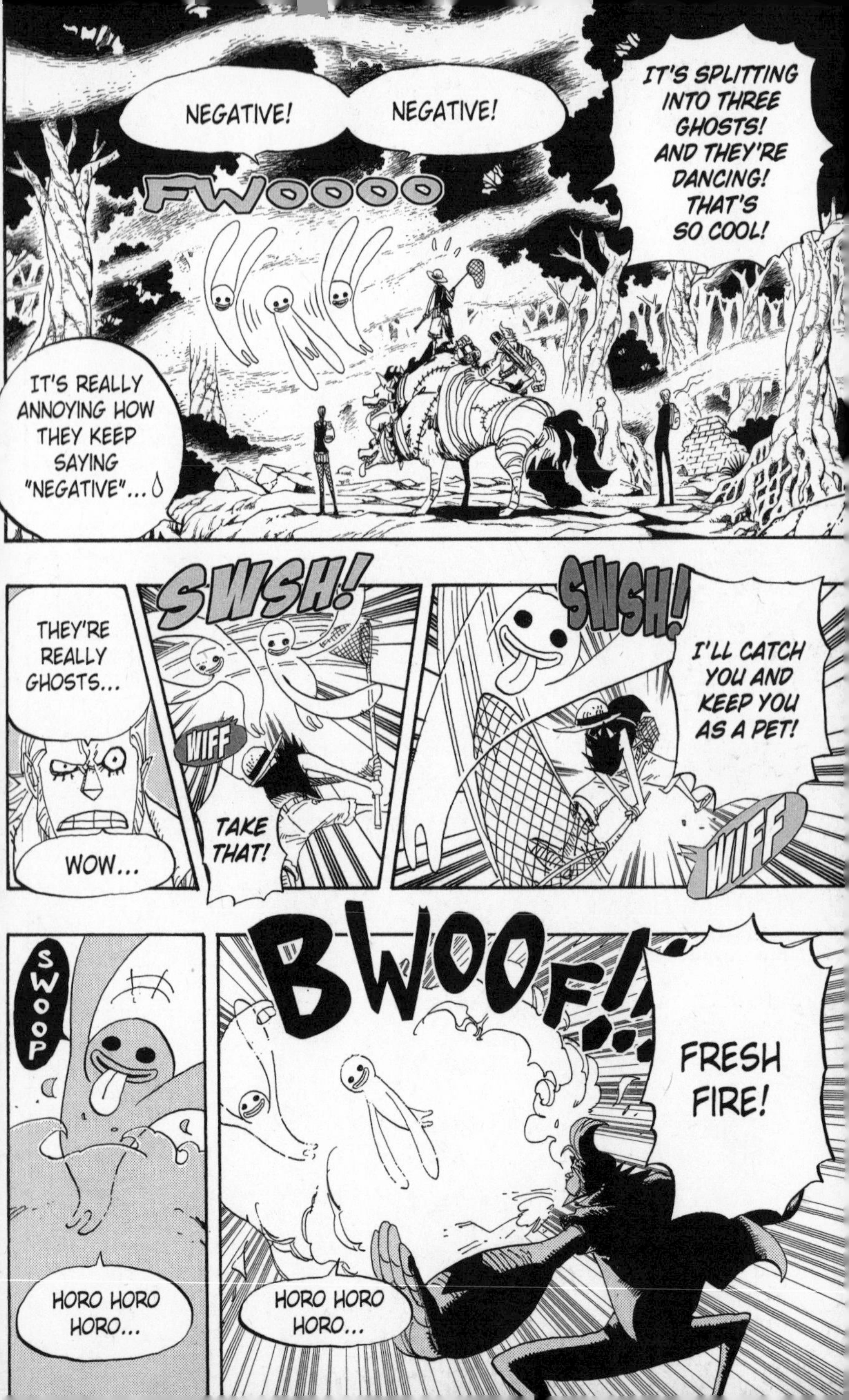
IT'S SPLITTING INTO THREE GHOSTS! AND THEY'RE DANCING! THAT'S SO COOL!
NEGATIVE!
NEGATIVE!
FWOOOO
IT'S REALLY ANNOYING HOW THEY KEEP SAYING "NEGATIVE"...
SWSH!
I'LL CATCH YOU AND KEEP YOU AS A PET!
WIFF
SWSH!
WIFF
TAKE THAT!
THEY'RE REALLY GHOSTS...
WOW...
BWOOF!!
FRESH FIRE!
HORO HORO HORO...
SWOOP
HORO HORO HORO...

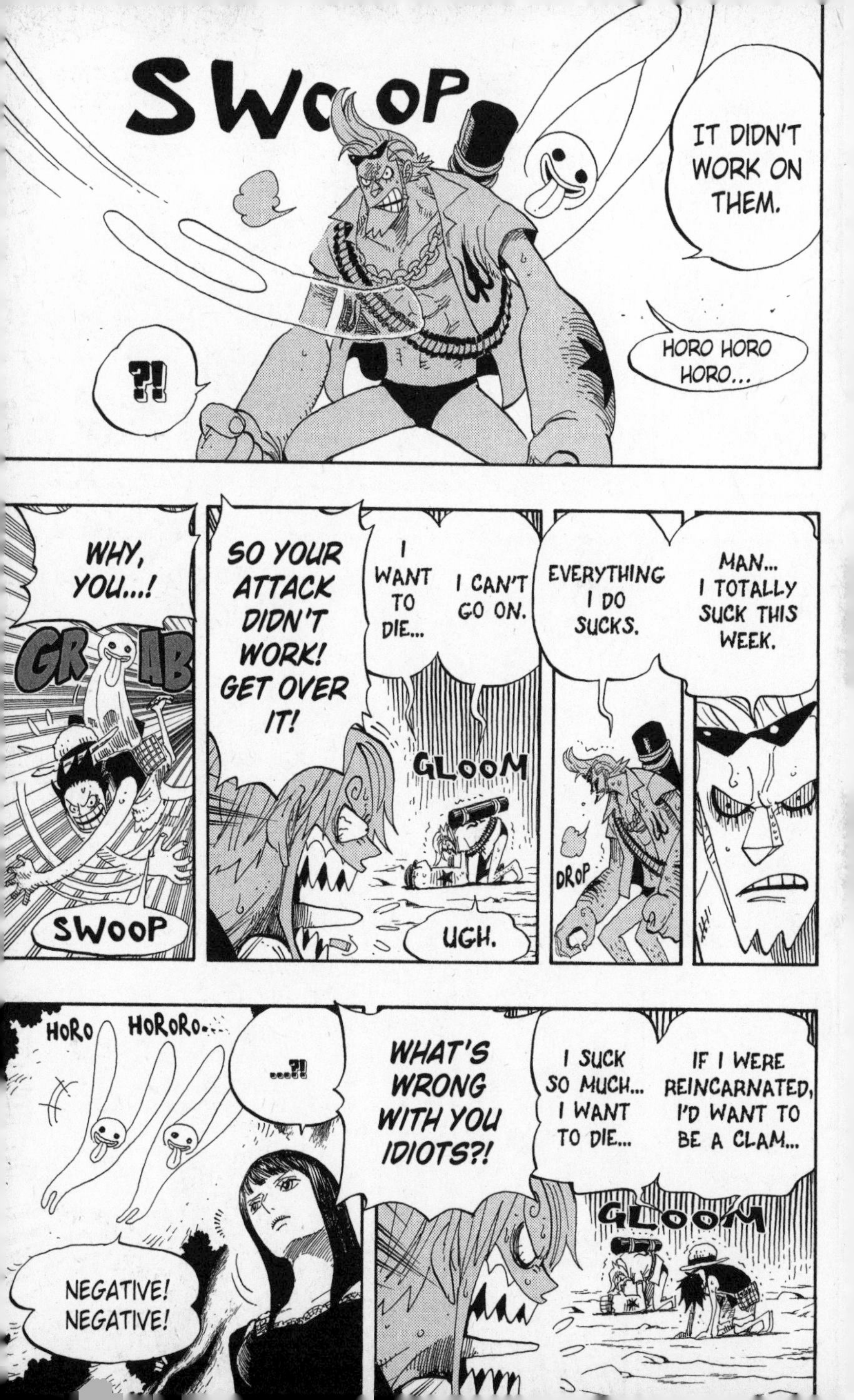
IT DIDN'T WORK ON THEM.
SWOOP
HORO HORO HORO...
?!
MAN... I TOTALLY SUCK THIS WEEK.
EVERYTHING I DO SUCKS.
DROP
I CAN'T GO ON.
I WANT TO DIE...
SO YOUR ATTACK DIDN'T WORK! GET OVER IT!
GLOOM
UGH.
WHY, YOU...!
GRAB
SWOOP
IF I WERE REINCARNATED, I'D WANT TO BE A CLAM...
I SUCK SO MUCH... I WANT TO DIE...
GLOOM
WHAT'S WRONG WITH YOU IDIOTS?!
...?!
HORO HORORO...
NEGATIVE! NEGATIVE!

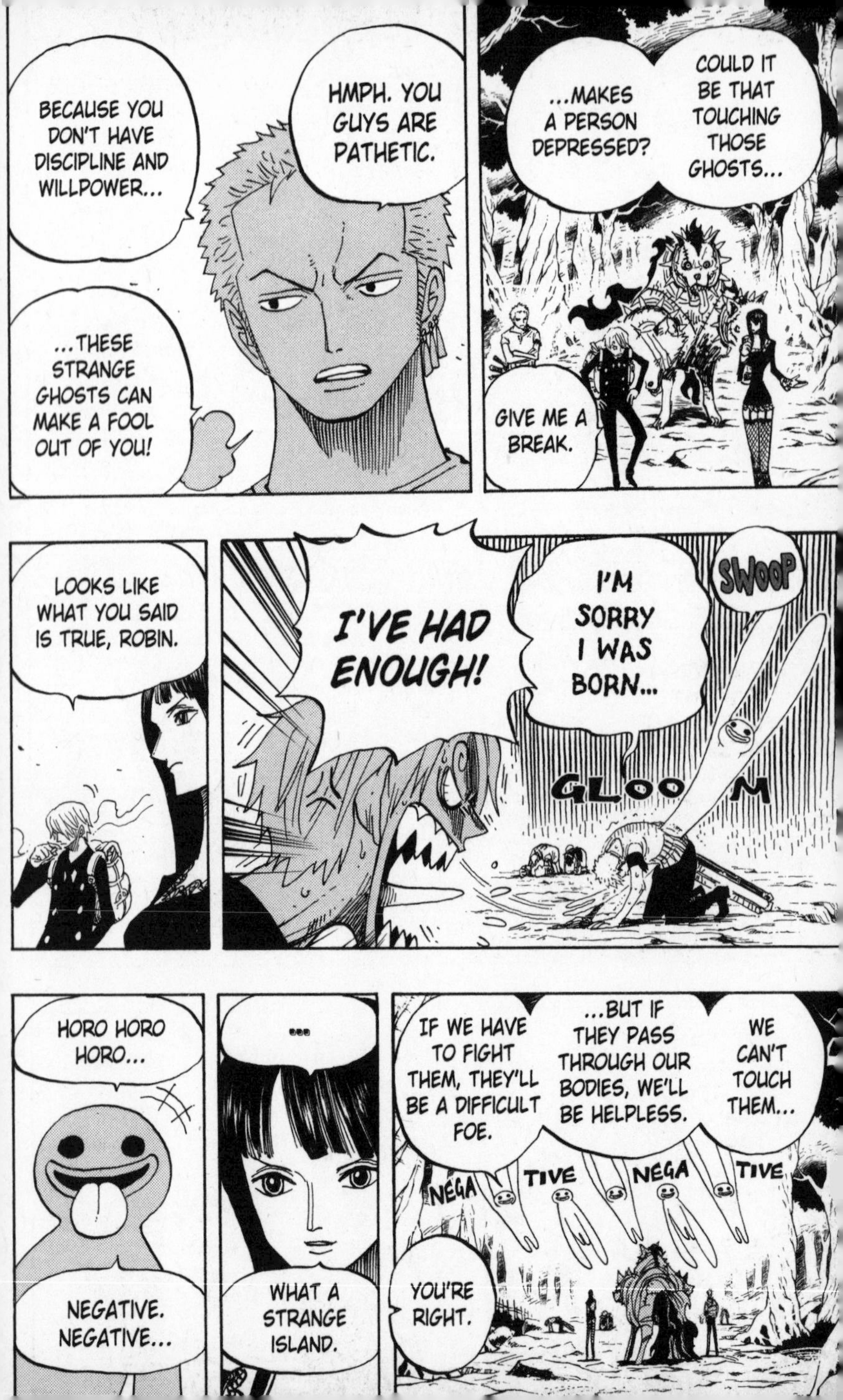
COULD IT BE THAT TOUCHING THOSE GHOSTS...
...MAKES A PERSON DEPRESSED?
GIVE ME A BREAK.
HMPH. YOU GUYS ARE PATHETIC.
BECAUSE YOU DON'T HAVE DISCIPLINE AND WILLPOWER...
...THESE STRANGE GHOSTS CAN MAKE A FOOL OUT OF YOU!
SWOOP
I'M SORRY I WAS BORN...
I'VE HAD ENOUGH!
GLOOM
LOOKS LIKE WHAT YOU SAID IS TRUE, ROBIN.
WE CAN'T TOUCH THEM...
...BUT IF THEY PASS THROUGH OUR BODIES, WE'LL BE HELPLESS.
IF WE HAVE TO FIGHT THEM, THEY'LL BE A DIFFICULT FOE.
NEGA TIVE NEGA TIVE
YOU'RE RIGHT.
...
WHAT A STRANGE ISLAND.
HORO HORO HORO...
NEGATIVE. NEGATIVE...

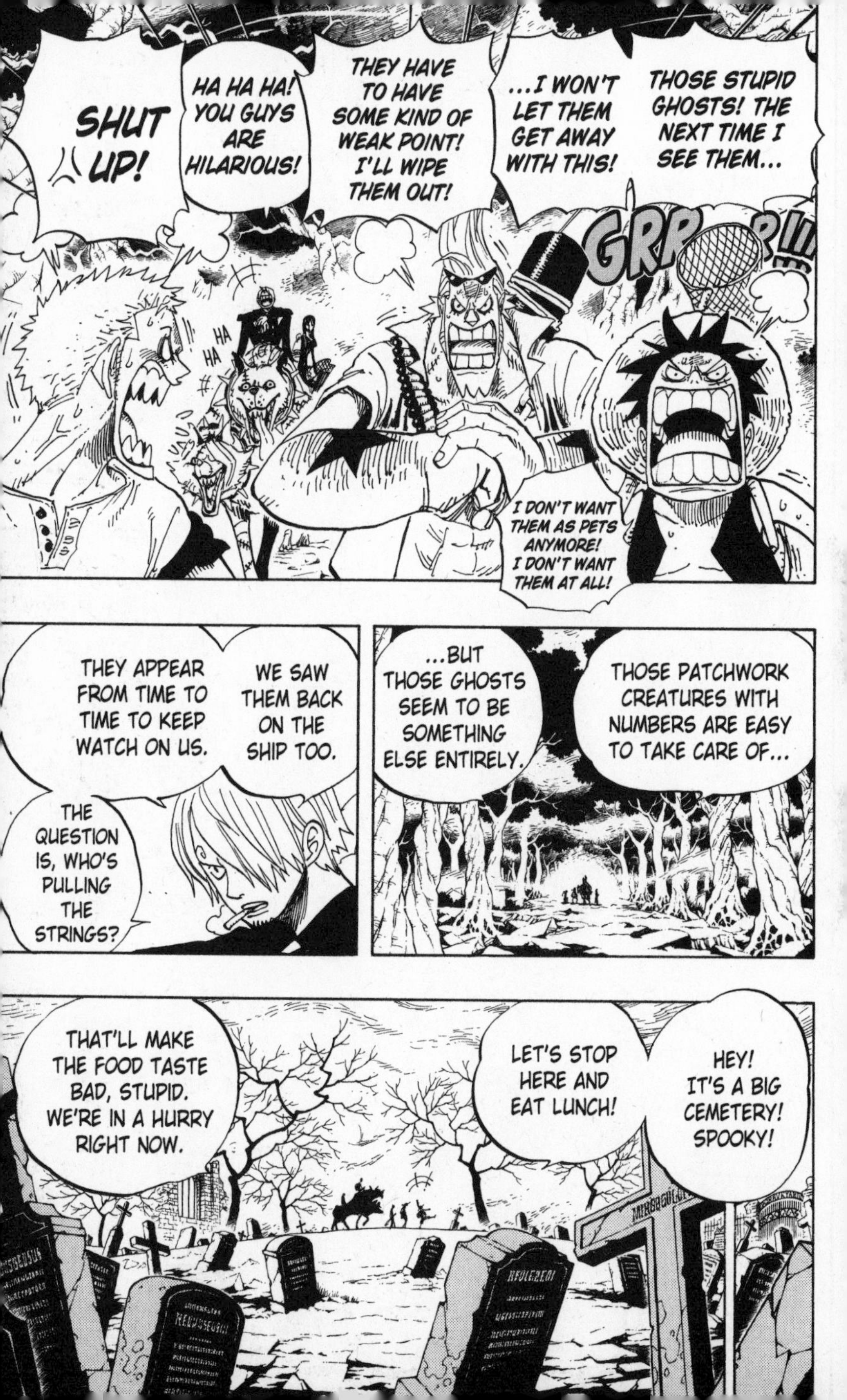
THOSE STUPID GHOSTS! THE NEXT TIME I SEE THEM...
...I WON'T LET THEM GET AWAY WITH THIS!
THEY HAVE TO HAVE SOME KIND OF WEAK POINT! I'LL WIPE THEM OUT!
HA HA HA! YOU GUYS ARE HILARIOUS!
SHUT UP!
HA HA
I DON'T WANT THEM AS PETS ANYMORE! I DON'T WANT THEM AT ALL!
THOSE PATCHWORK CREATURES WITH NUMBERS ARE EASY TO TAKE CARE OF...
...BUT THOSE GHOSTS SEEM TO BE SOMETHING ELSE ENTIRELY.
WE SAW THEM BACK ON THE SHIP TOO.
THEY APPEAR FROM TIME TO TIME TO KEEP WATCH ON US.
THE QUESTION IS, WHO'S PULLING THE STRINGS?
HEY! IT'S A BIG CEMETERY! SPOOKY!
LET'S STOP HERE AND EAT LUNCH!
THAT'LL MAKE THE FOOD TASTE BAD, STUPID. WE'RE IN A HURRY RIGHT NOW.

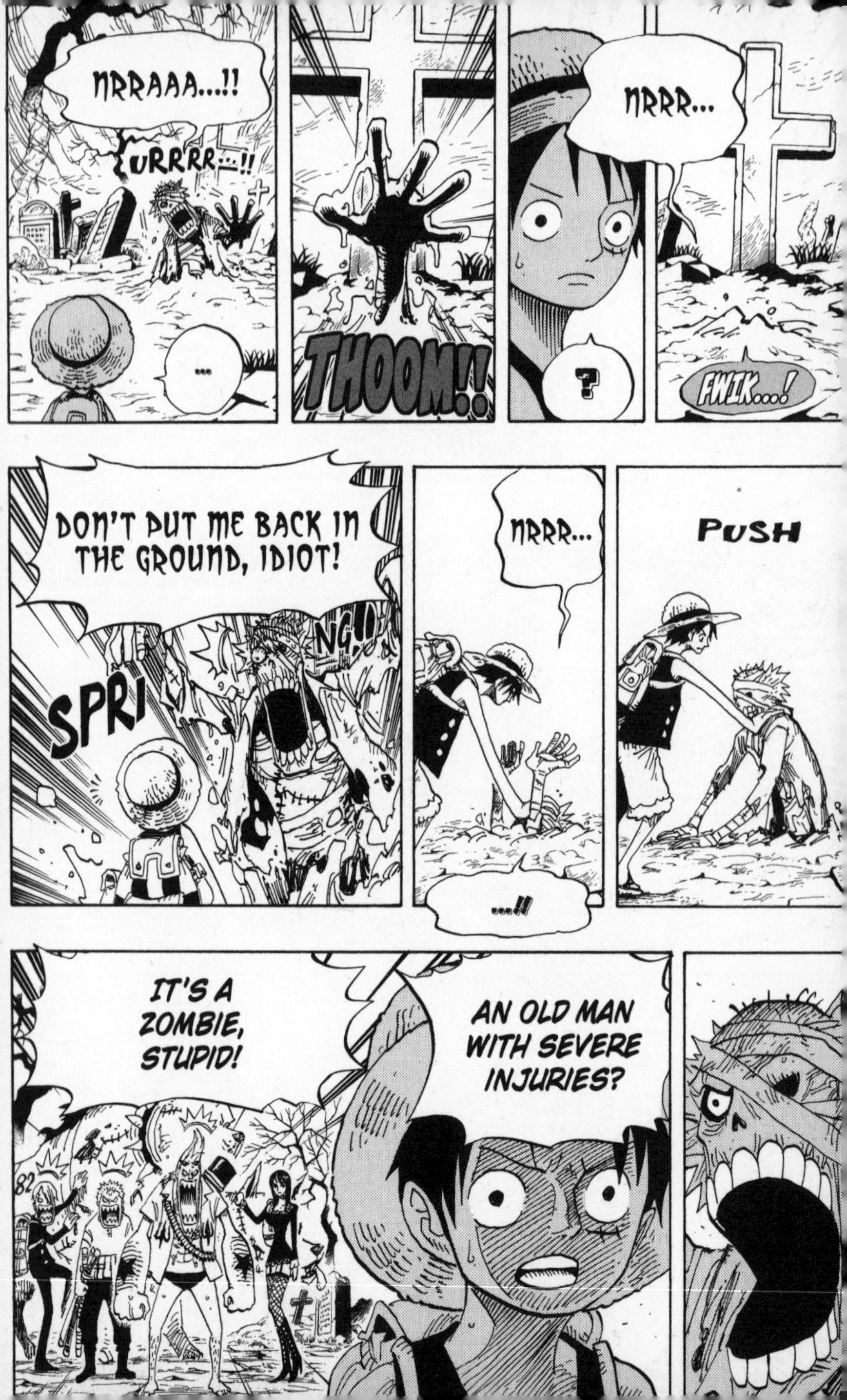
FWIK...!
NRRR...
?
THOOM!!
NRRAAA...!!
URRRR...!!
...
PUSH
NRRR...
...!!
DON'T PUT ME BACK IN THE GROUND, IDIOT!
SPRI
NG!!
AN OLD MAN WITH SEVERE INJURIES?
IT'S A ZOMBIE, STUPID!

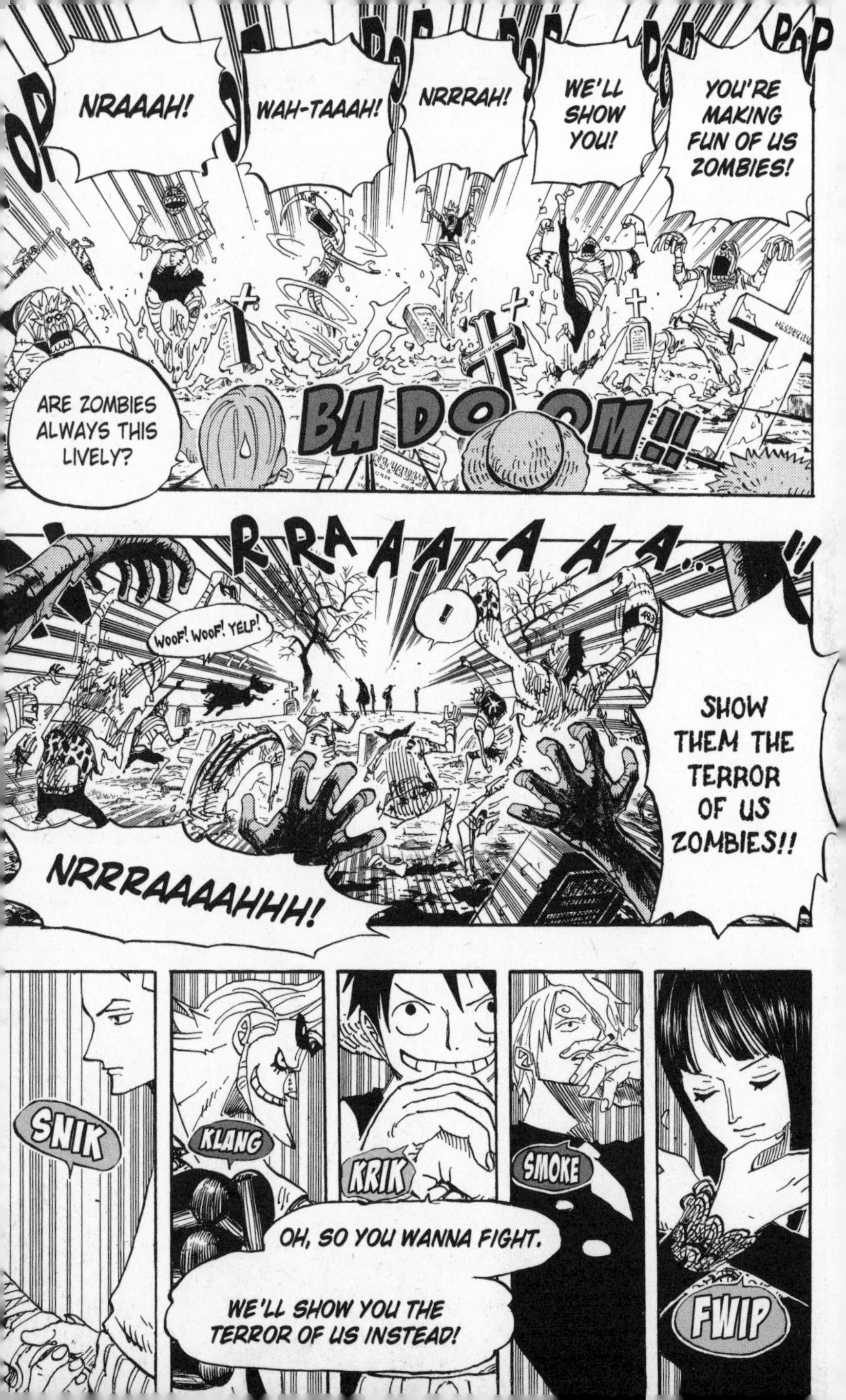
POP
YOU'RE MAKING FUN OF US ZOMBIES!
WE'LL SHOW YOU!
NRRRAH!
WAH-TAAAH!
NRAAAH!
BADOOOM!!
ARE ZOMBIES ALWAYS THIS LIVELY?
SHOW THEM THE TERROR OF US ZOMBIES!!
RRAAAAAA...!!
!
WOOF! WOOF! YELP!
NRRRAAAAAHHHH!
FWIP
SMOKE
KRIK
OH, SO YOU WANNA FIGHT.
WE'LL SHOW YOU THE TERROR OF US INSTEAD!
KLANG
SNIK

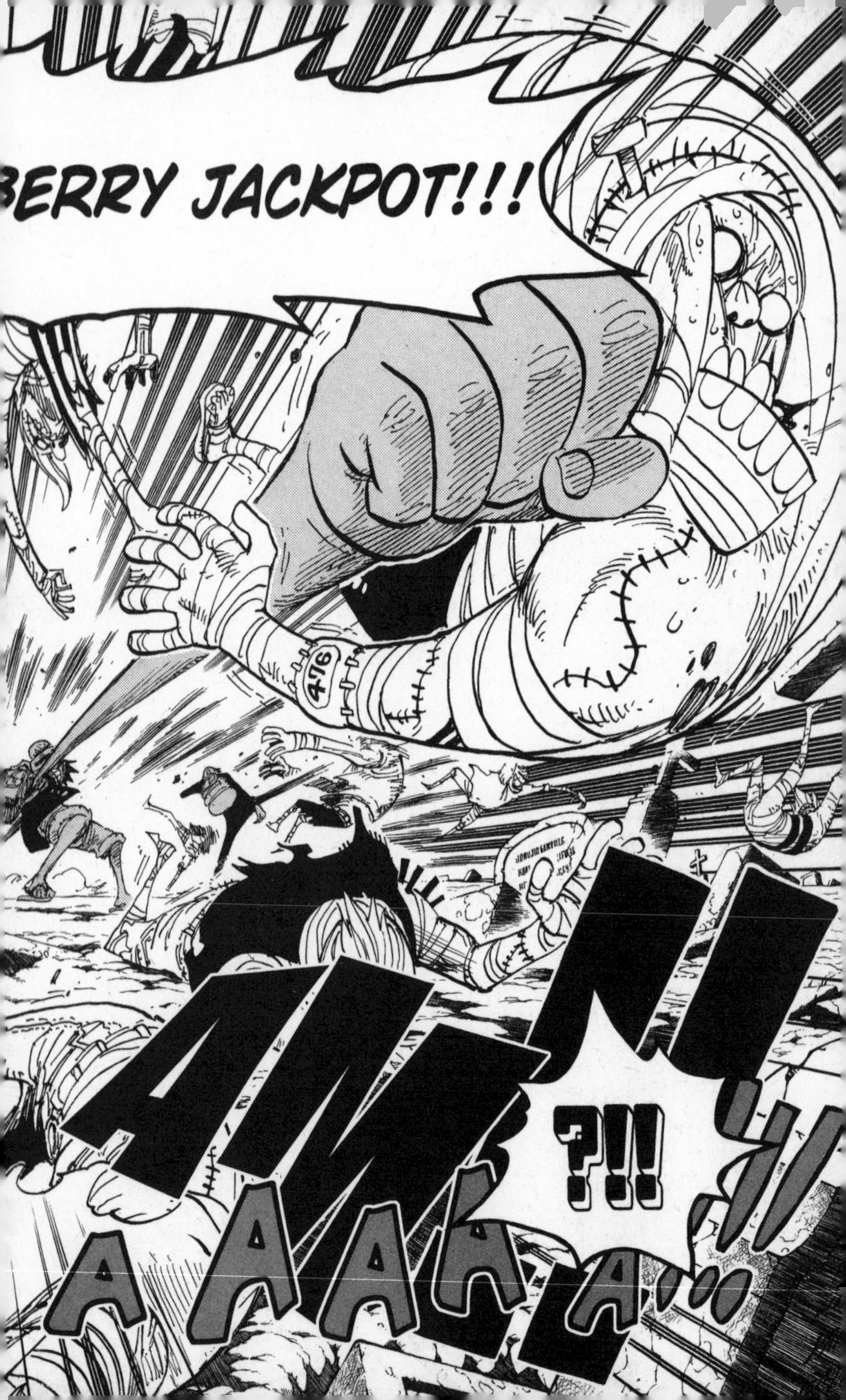
BERRY JACKPOT!!!
?!!

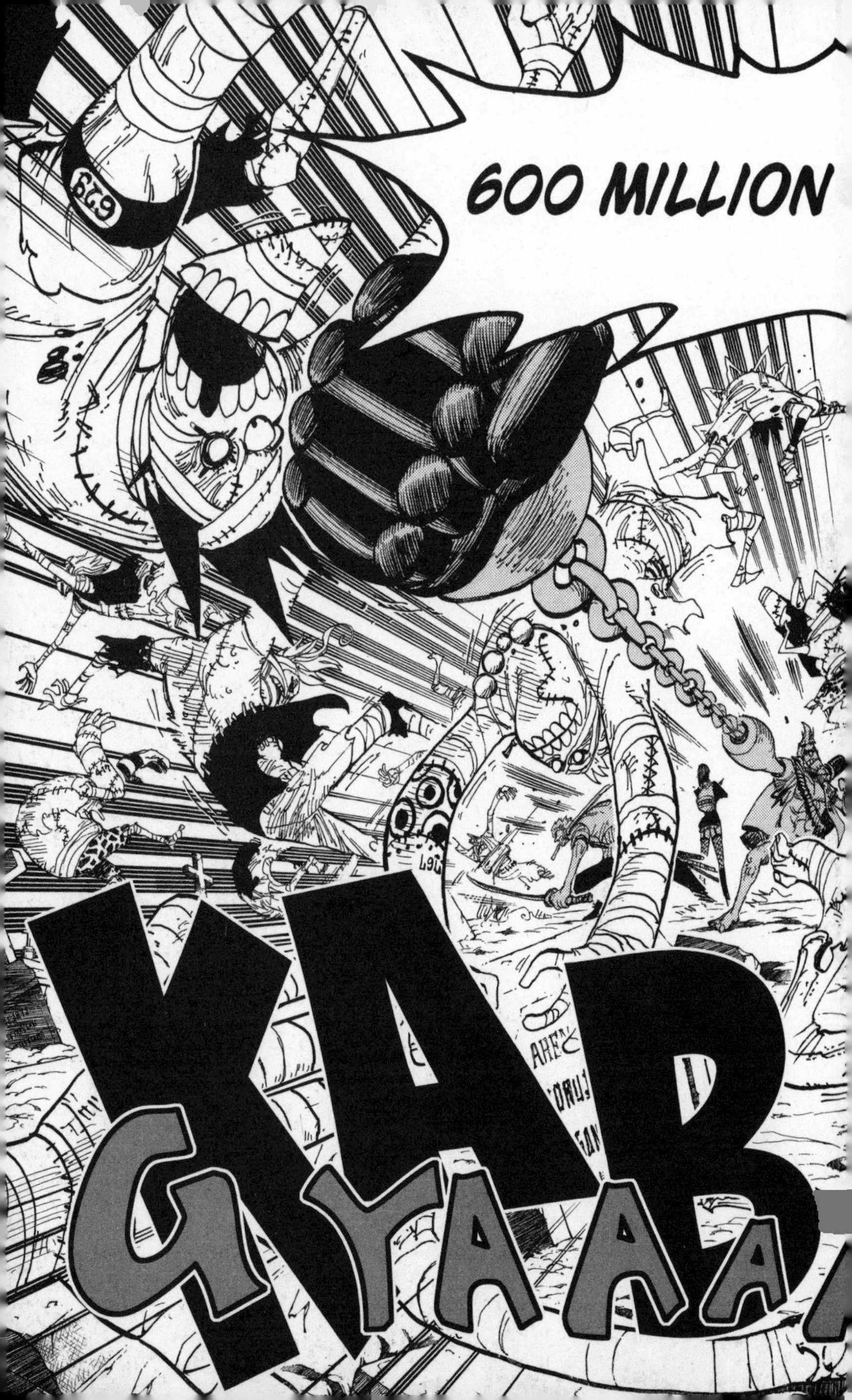
600 MILLION
KAB
GYAAA

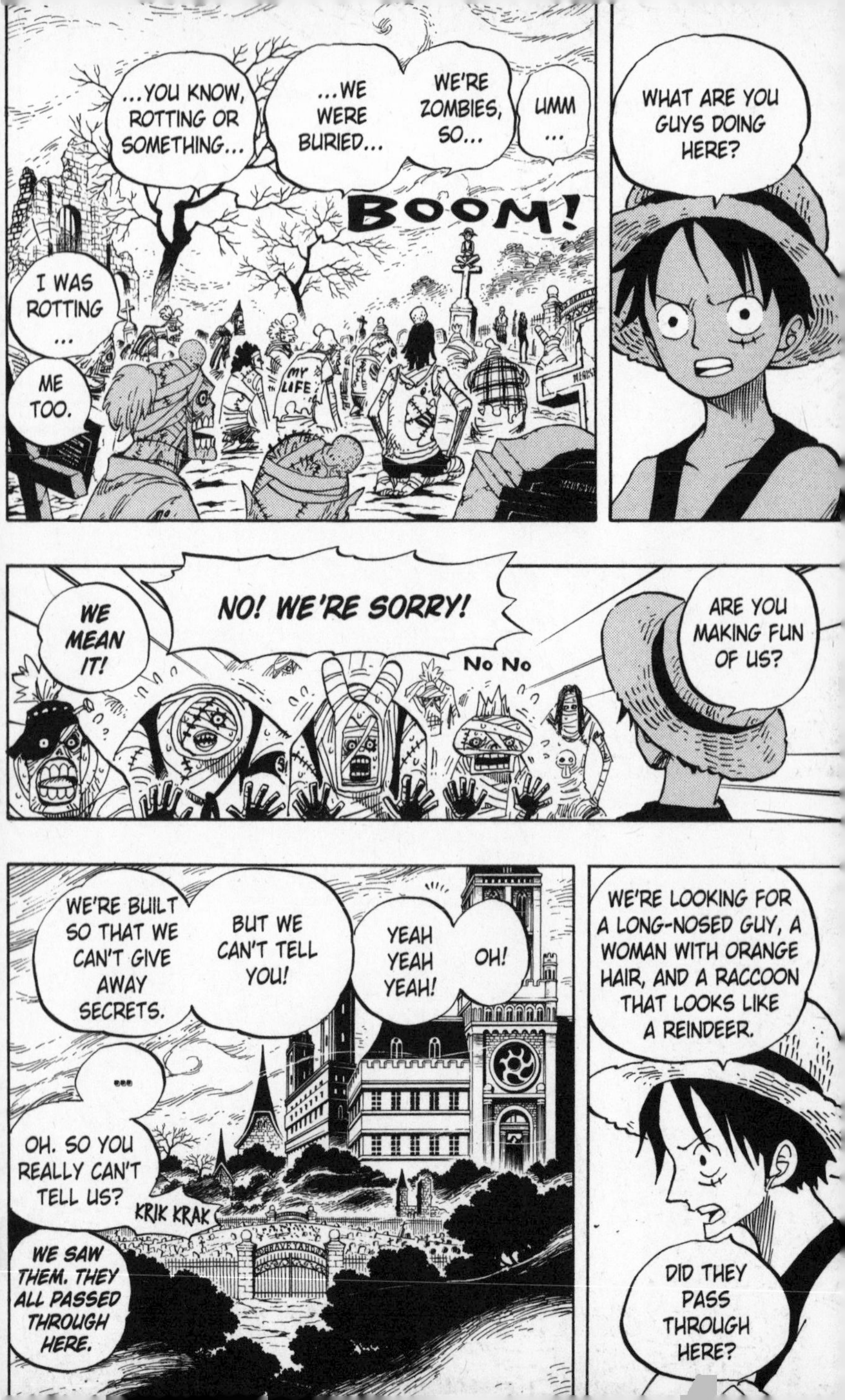
WHAT ARE YOU GUYS DOING HERE?
UMM ...
WE'RE ZOMBIES, SO...
...WE WERE BURIED...
...YOU KNOW, ROTTING OR SOMETHING...
BOOM!
MY LIFE
I WAS ROTTING ...
ME TOO.
ARE YOU MAKING FUN OF US?
No No
NO! WE'RE SORRY!
WE MEAN IT!
WE'RE LOOKING FOR A LONG-NOSED GUY, A WOMAN WITH ORANGE HAIR, AND A RACCOON THAT LOOKS LIKE A REINDEER.
DID THEY PASS THROUGH HERE?
OH!
YEAH YEAH YEAH!
BUT WE CAN'T TELL YOU!
WE'RE BUILT SO THAT WE CAN'T GIVE AWAY SECRETS.
...
OH. SO YOU REALLY CAN'T TELL US?
KRIK KRAK
WE SAW THEM. THEY ALL PASSED THROUGH HERE.

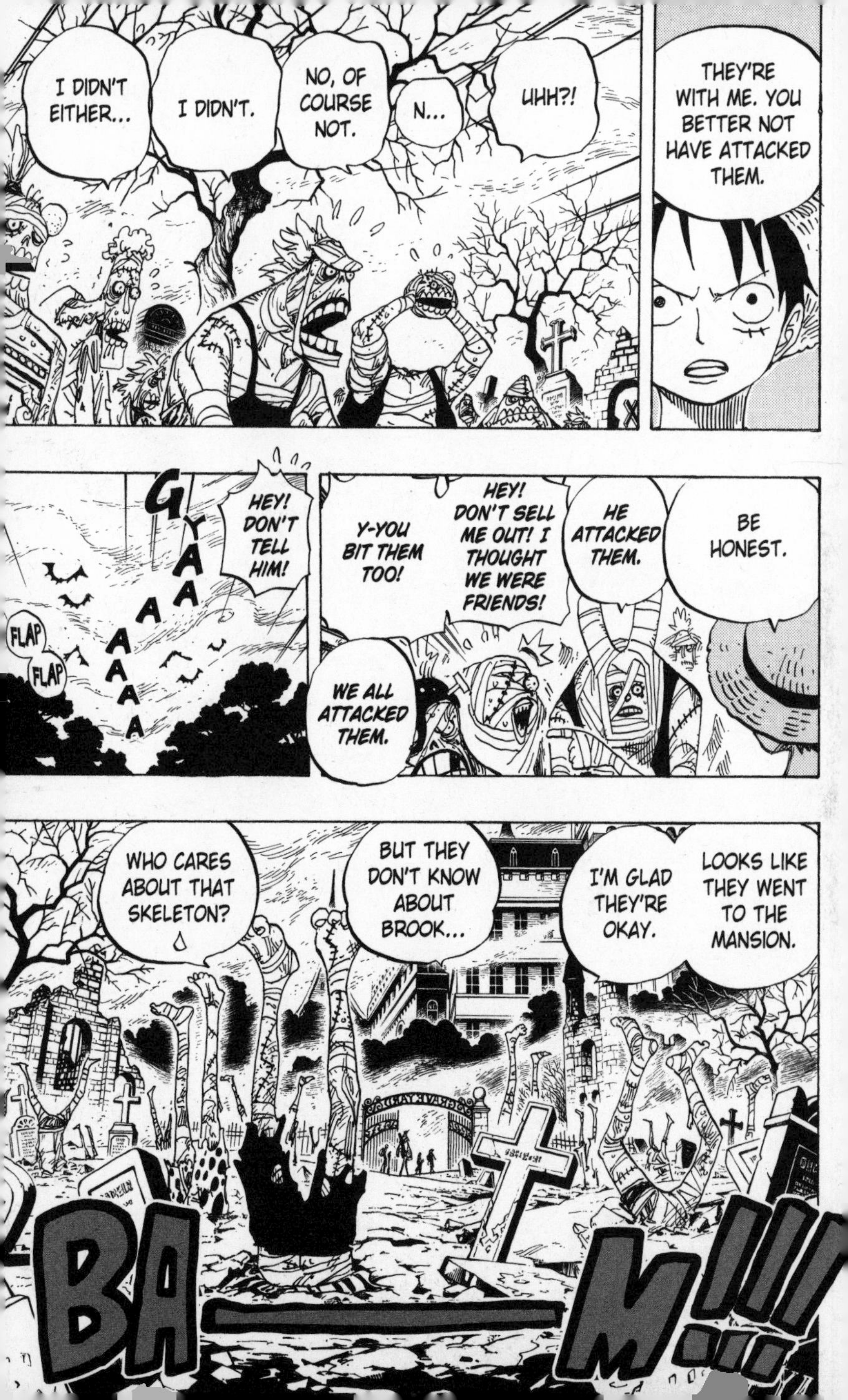
THEY'RE WITH ME. YOU BETTER NOT HAVE ATTACKED THEM.
UHH?!
N...
NO, OF COURSE NOT.
I DIDN'T.
I DIDN'T EITHER...
BE HONEST.
HE ATTACKED THEM.
HEY! DON'T SELL ME OUT! I THOUGHT WE WERE FRIENDS!
Y-YOU BIT THEM TOO!
WE ALL ATTACKED THEM.
HEY! DON'T TELL HIM!
GYAAAAAAAA
FLAP
FLAP
LOOKS LIKE THEY WENT TO THE MANSION.
I'M GLAD THEY'RE OKAY.
BUT THEY DON'T KNOW ABOUT BROOK...
WHO CARES ABOUT THAT SKELETON?
BA—M!!!

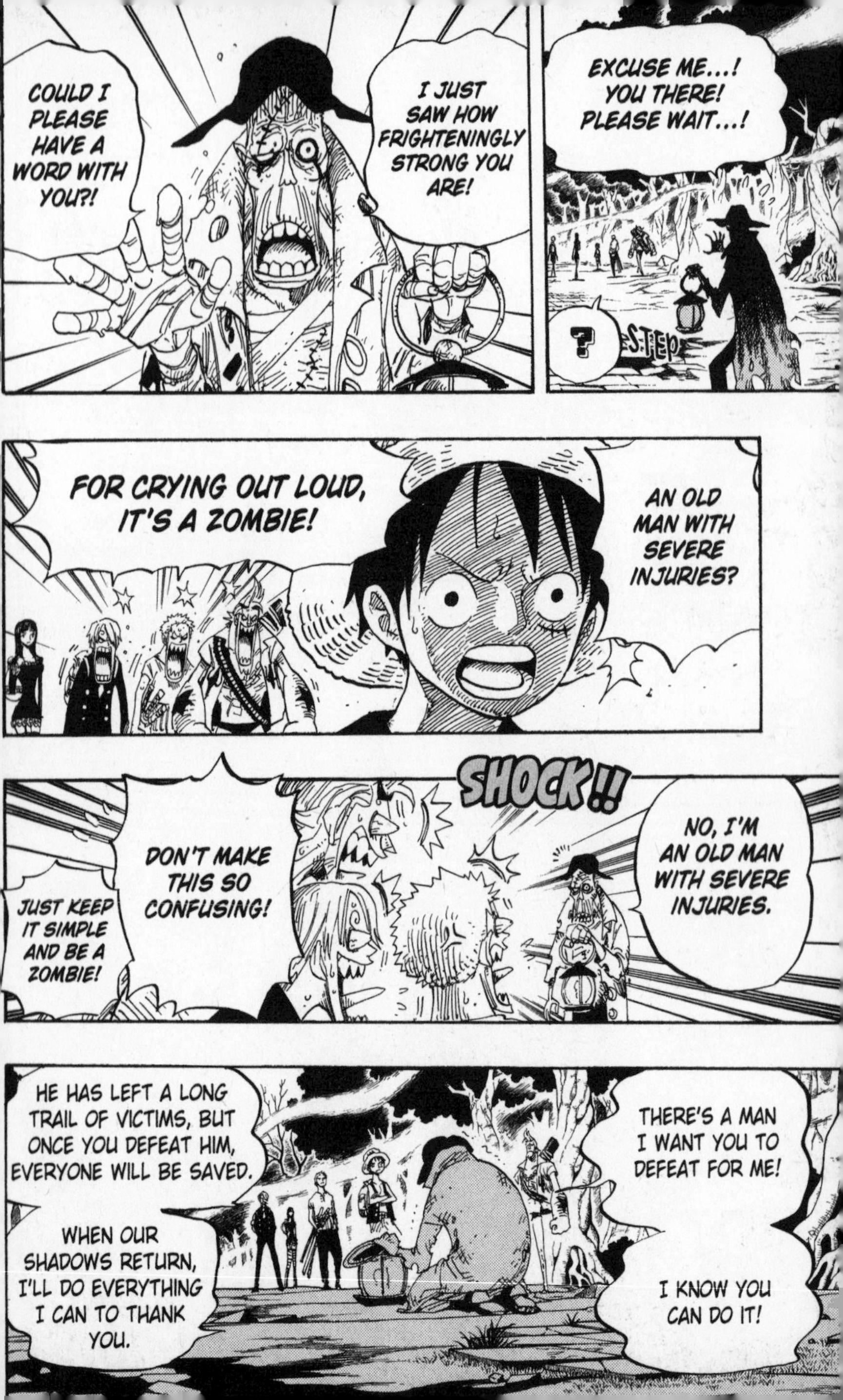
EXCUSE ME...! YOU THERE! PLEASE WAIT...!
?
STEP
I JUST SAW HOW FRIGHTENINGLY STRONG YOU ARE!
COULD I PLEASE HAVE A WORD WITH YOU?!
AN OLD MAN WITH SEVERE INJURIES?
FOR CRYING OUT LOUD, IT'S A ZOMBIE!
NO, I'M AN OLD MAN WITH SEVERE INJURIES.
SHOCK!!
DON'T MAKE THIS SO CONFUSING!
JUST KEEP IT SIMPLE AND BE A ZOMBIE!
THERE'S A MAN I WANT YOU TO DEFEAT FOR ME!
HE HAS LEFT A LONG TRAIL OF VICTIMS, BUT ONCE YOU DEFEAT HIM, EVERYONE WILL BE SAVED.
WHEN OUR SHADOWS RETURN, I'LL DO EVERYTHING I CAN TO THANK YOU.
I KNOW YOU CAN DO IT!

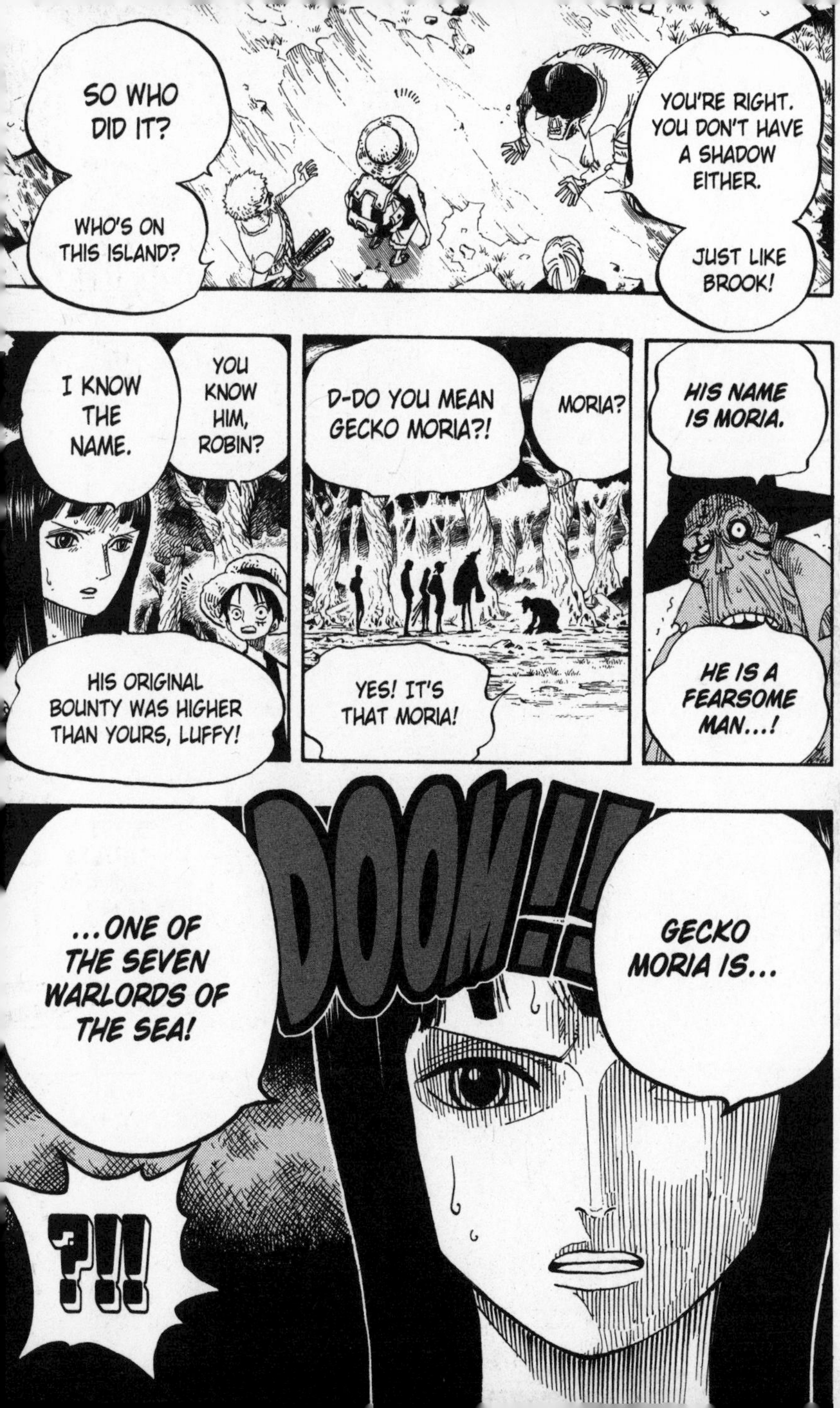

YOU'RE RIGHT. YOU DON'T HAVE A SHADOW EITHER.
JUST LIKE BROOK!
SO WHO DID IT?
WHO'S ON THIS ISLAND?
HIS NAME IS MORIA.
HE IS A FEARSOME MAN...!
MORIA?
D-DO YOU MEAN GECKO MORIA?!
YES! IT'S THAT MORIA!
YOU KNOW HIM, ROBIN?
I KNOW THE NAME.
HIS ORIGINAL BOUNTY WAS HIGHER THAN YOURS, LUFFY!
GECKO MORIA IS...
DOOM!!
...ONE OF THE SEVEN WARLORDS OF THE SEA!
?!!

MONSTERS OF THRILLER BARK

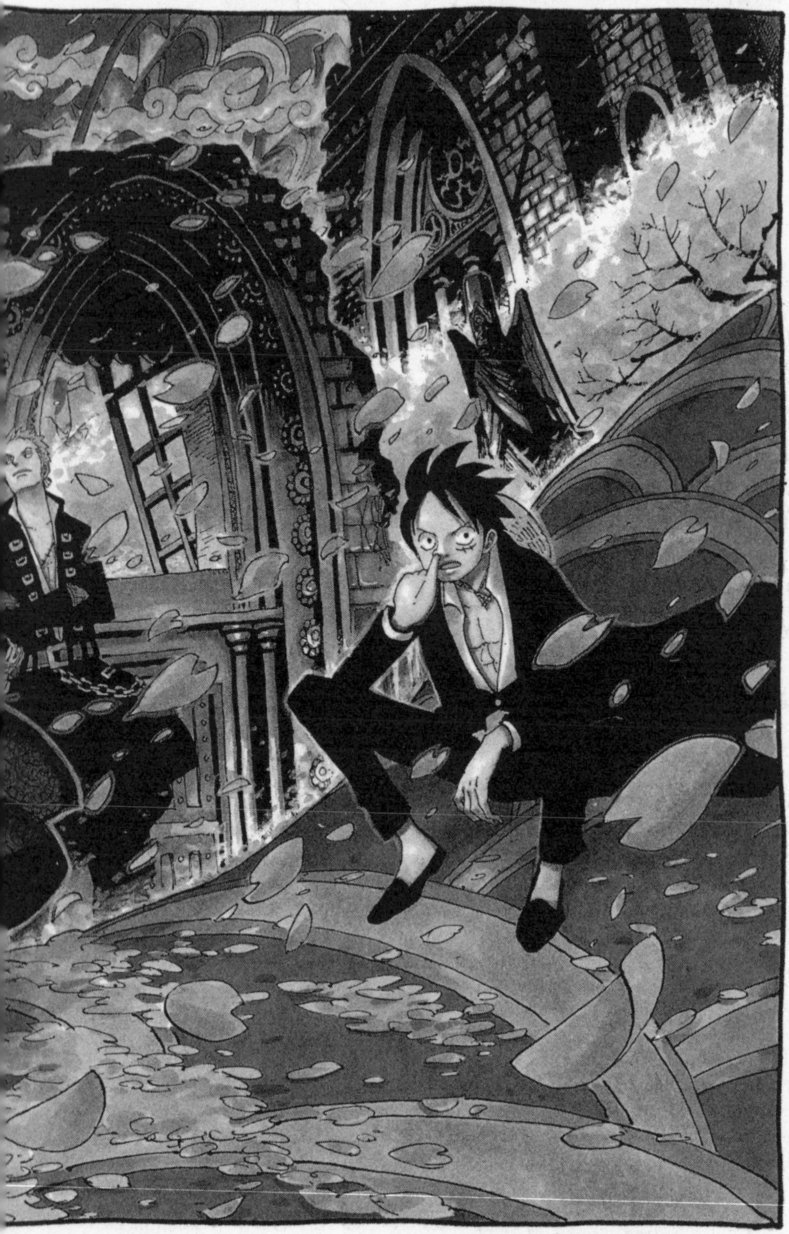

Chapter 449: THE FOUR

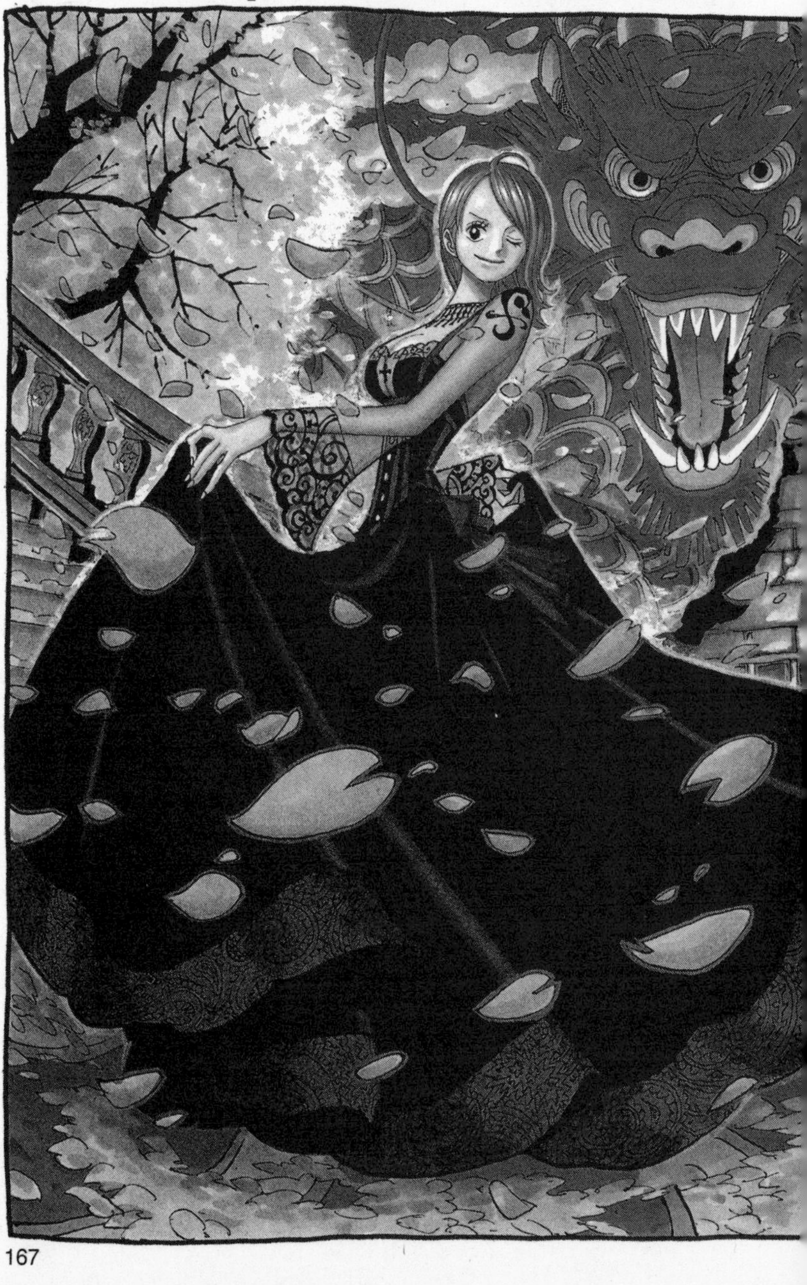

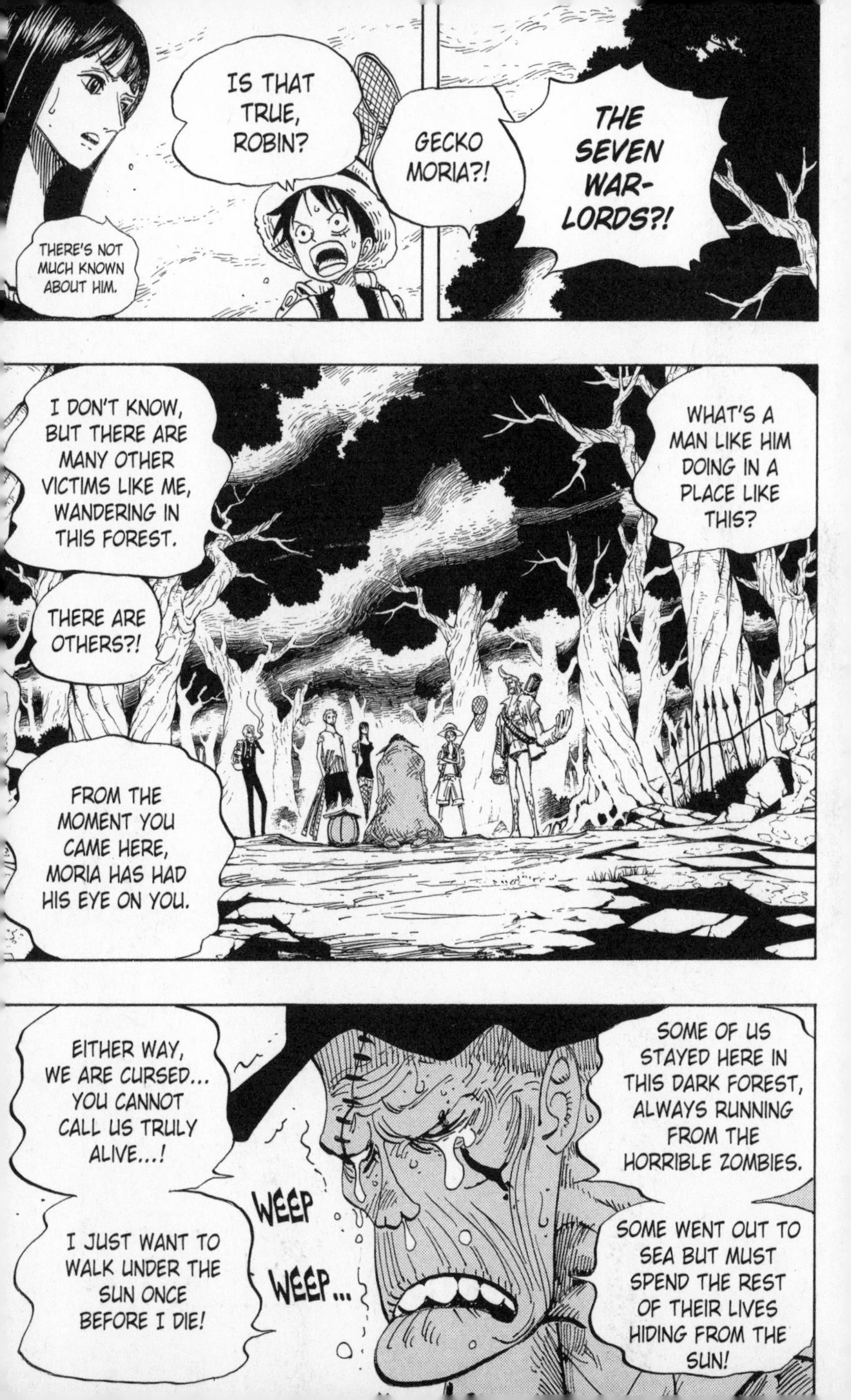
THE SEVEN WAR-LORDS?!
GECKO MORIA?!
IS THAT TRUE, ROBIN?
THERE'S NOT MUCH KNOWN ABOUT HIM.
WHAT'S A MAN LIKE HIM DOING IN A PLACE LIKE THIS?
I DON'T KNOW, BUT THERE ARE MANY OTHER VICTIMS LIKE ME, WANDERING IN THIS FOREST.
THERE ARE OTHERS?!
FROM THE MOMENT YOU CAME HERE, MORIA HAS HAD HIS EYE ON YOU.
SOME OF US STAYED HERE IN THIS DARK FOREST, ALWAYS RUNNING FROM THE HORRIBLE ZOMBIES.
EITHER WAY, WE ARE CURSED... YOU CANNOT CALL US TRULY ALIVE...!
SOME WENT OUT TO SEA BUT MUST SPEND THE REST OF THEIR LIVES HIDING FROM THE SUN!
WEEP
WEEP...
I JUST WANT TO WALK UNDER THE SUN ONCE BEFORE I DIE!

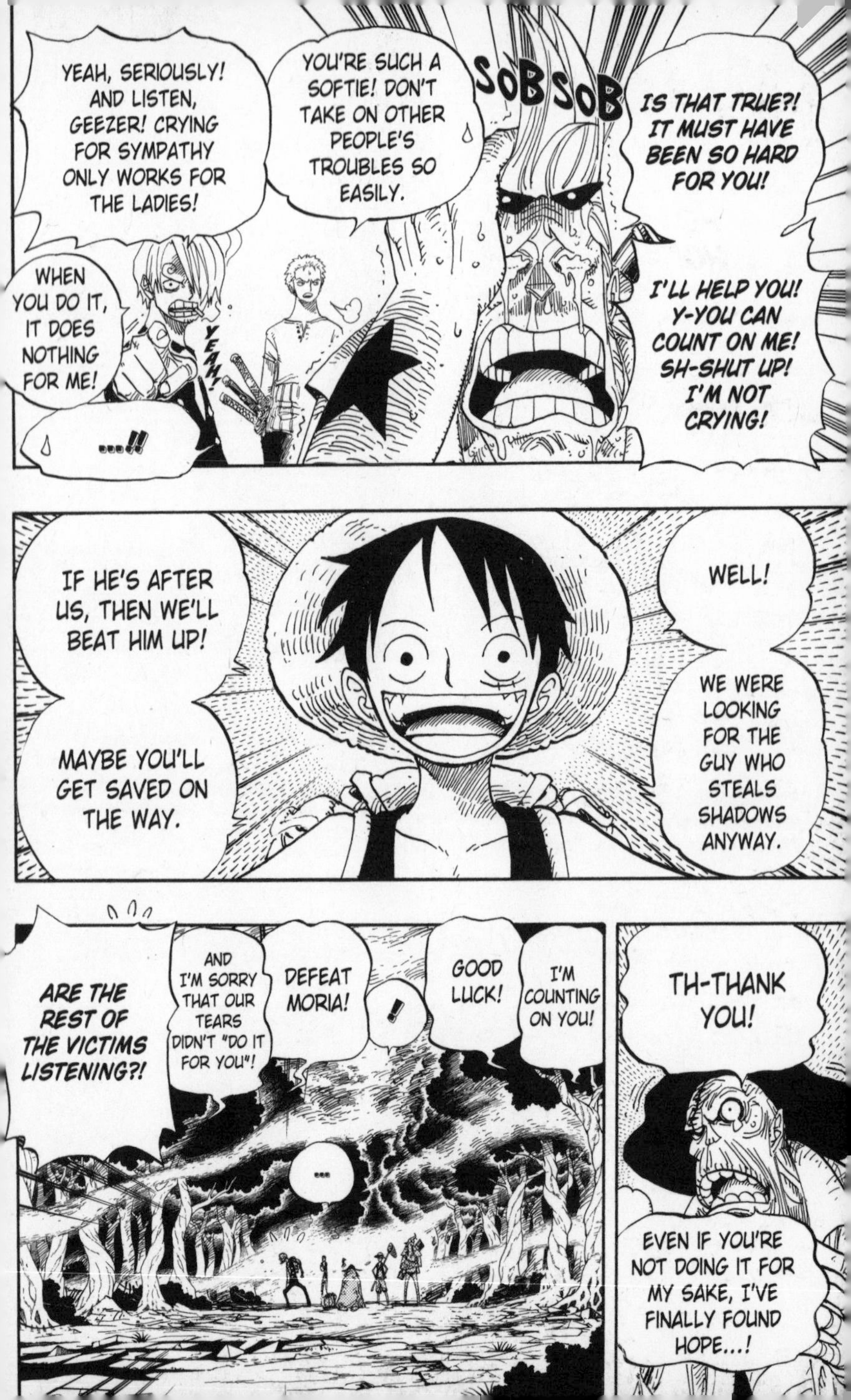
SOB SOB
IS THAT TRUE?! IT MUST HAVE BEEN SO HARD FOR YOU!
I'LL HELP YOU! Y-YOU CAN COUNT ON ME! SH-SHUT UP! I'M NOT CRYING!
YOU'RE SUCH A SOFTIE! DON'T TAKE ON OTHER PEOPLE'S TROUBLES SO EASILY.
YEAH, SERIOUSLY! AND LISTEN, GEEZER! CRYING FOR SYMPATHY ONLY WORKS FOR THE LADIES!
YEAH!
WHEN YOU DO IT, IT DOES NOTHING FOR ME!
...!!
WELL!
WE WERE LOOKING FOR THE GUY WHO STEALS SHADOWS ANYWAY.
IF HE'S AFTER US, THEN WE'LL BEAT HIM UP!
MAYBE YOU'LL GET SAVED ON THE WAY.
TH-THANK YOU!
EVEN IF YOU'RE NOT DOING IT FOR MY SAKE, I'VE FINALLY FOUND HOPE...!
I'M COUNTING ON YOU!
GOOD LUCK!
!
DEFEAT MORIA!
AND I'M SORRY THAT OUR TEARS DIDN'T "DO IT FOR YOU"!
ARE THE REST OF THE VICTIMS LISTENING?!
...

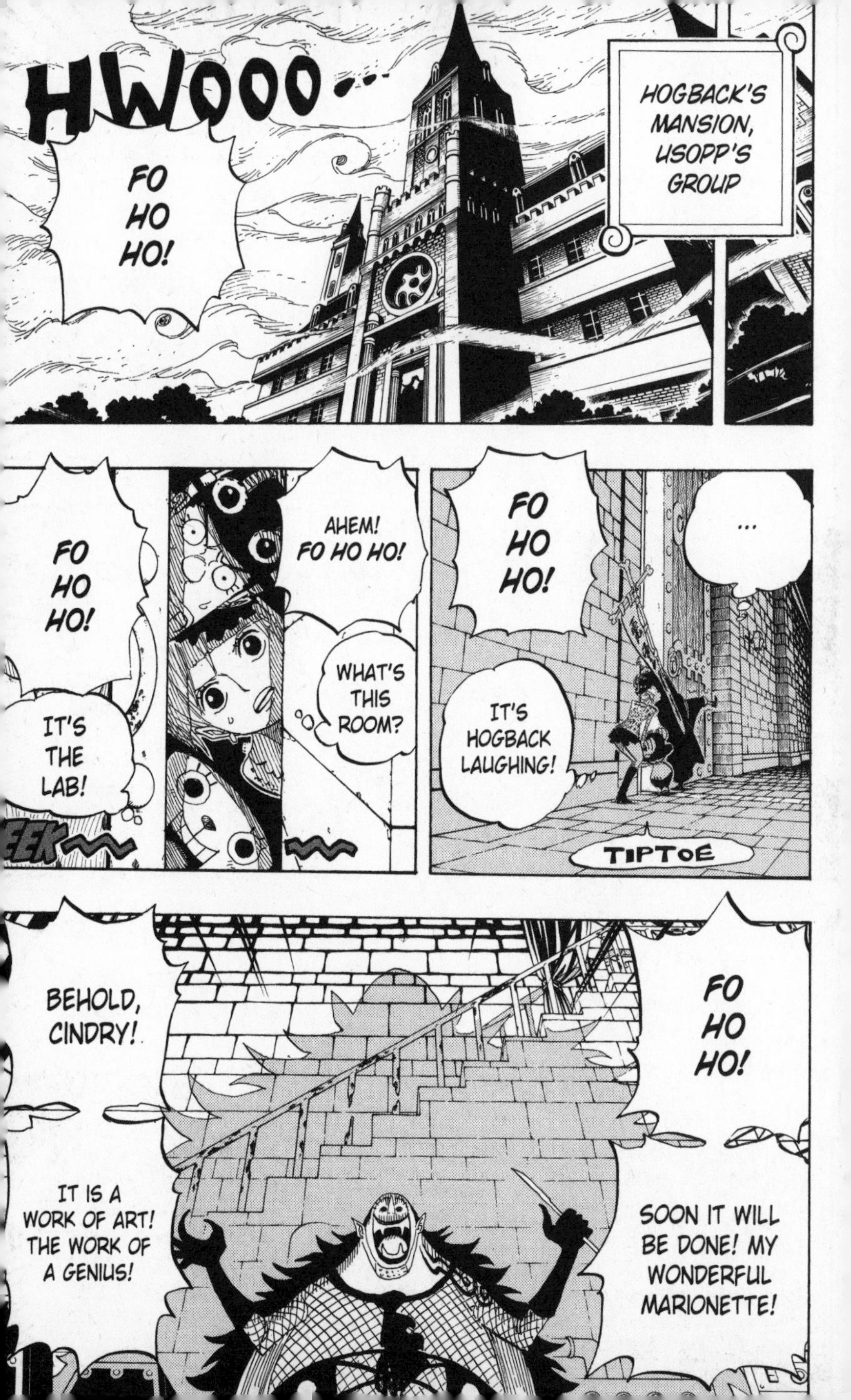
HOGBACK'S MANSION, USOPP'S GROUP
HWOOO...
FO HO HO!
...
FO HO HO!
IT'S HOGBACK LAUGHING!
TIPTOE
AHEM! FO HO HO!
WHAT'S THIS ROOM?
FO HO HO!
IT'S THE LAB!
FO HO HO!
BEHOLD, CINDRY!
SOON IT WILL BE DONE! MY WONDERFUL MARIONETTE!
IT IS A WORK OF ART! THE WORK OF A GENIUS!

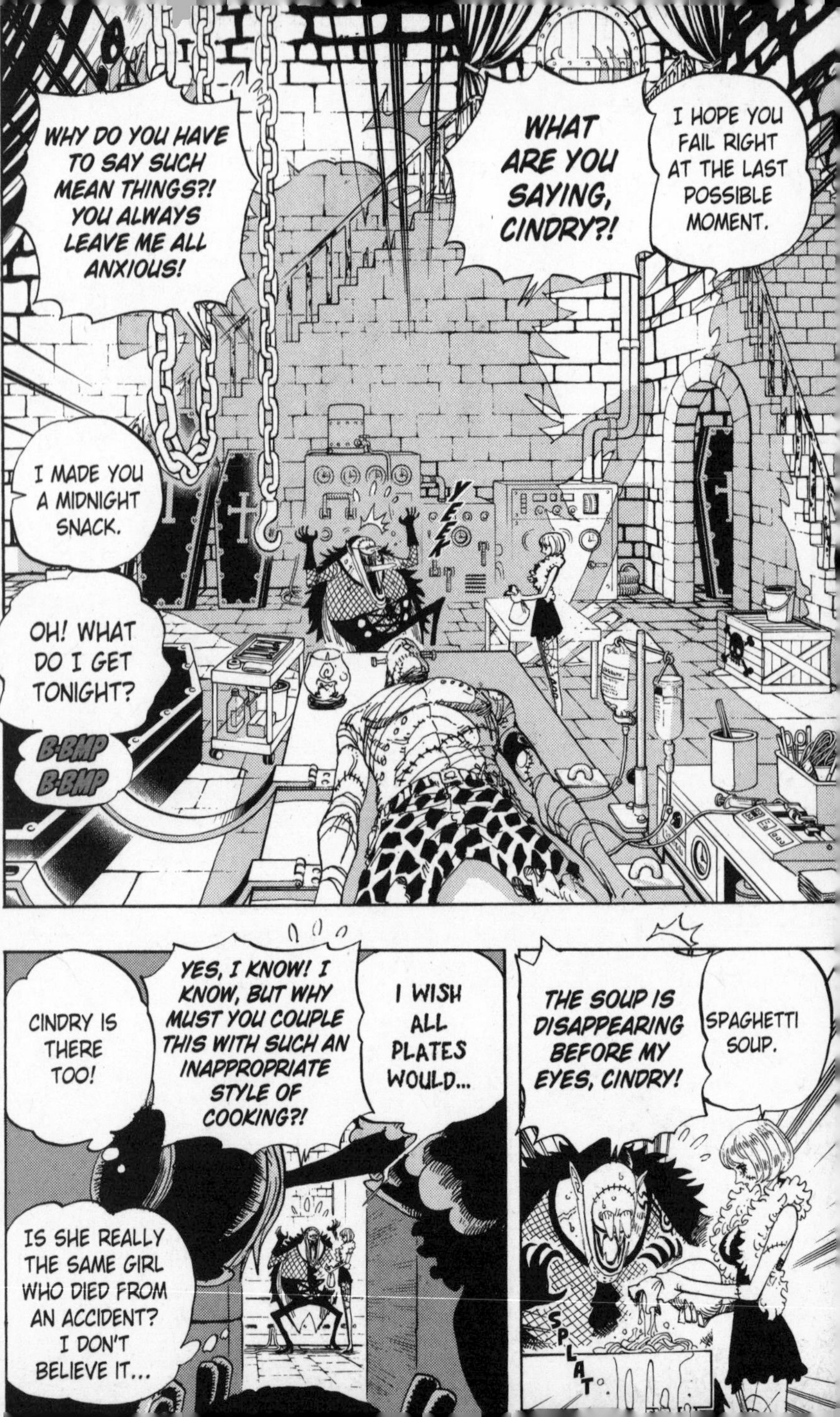
I HOPE YOU FAIL RIGHT AT THE LAST POSSIBLE MOMENT.
WHAT ARE YOU SAYING, CINDRY?!
WHY DO YOU HAVE TO SAY SUCH MEAN THINGS?! YOU ALWAYS LEAVE ME ALL ANXIOUS!
YEEK
I MADE YOU A MIDNIGHT SNACK.
OH! WHAT DO I GET TONIGHT?
B-BMP B-BMP
SPAGHETTI SOUP.
THE SOUP IS DISAPPEARING BEFORE MY EYES, CINDRY!
SPLAT
I WISH ALL PLATES WOULD...
YES, I KNOW! I KNOW, BUT WHY MUST YOU COUPLE THIS WITH SUCH AN INAPPROPRIATE STYLE OF COOKING?!
CINDRY IS THERE TOO!
IS SHE REALLY THE SAME GIRL WHO DIED FROM AN ACCIDENT? I DON'T BELIEVE IT...

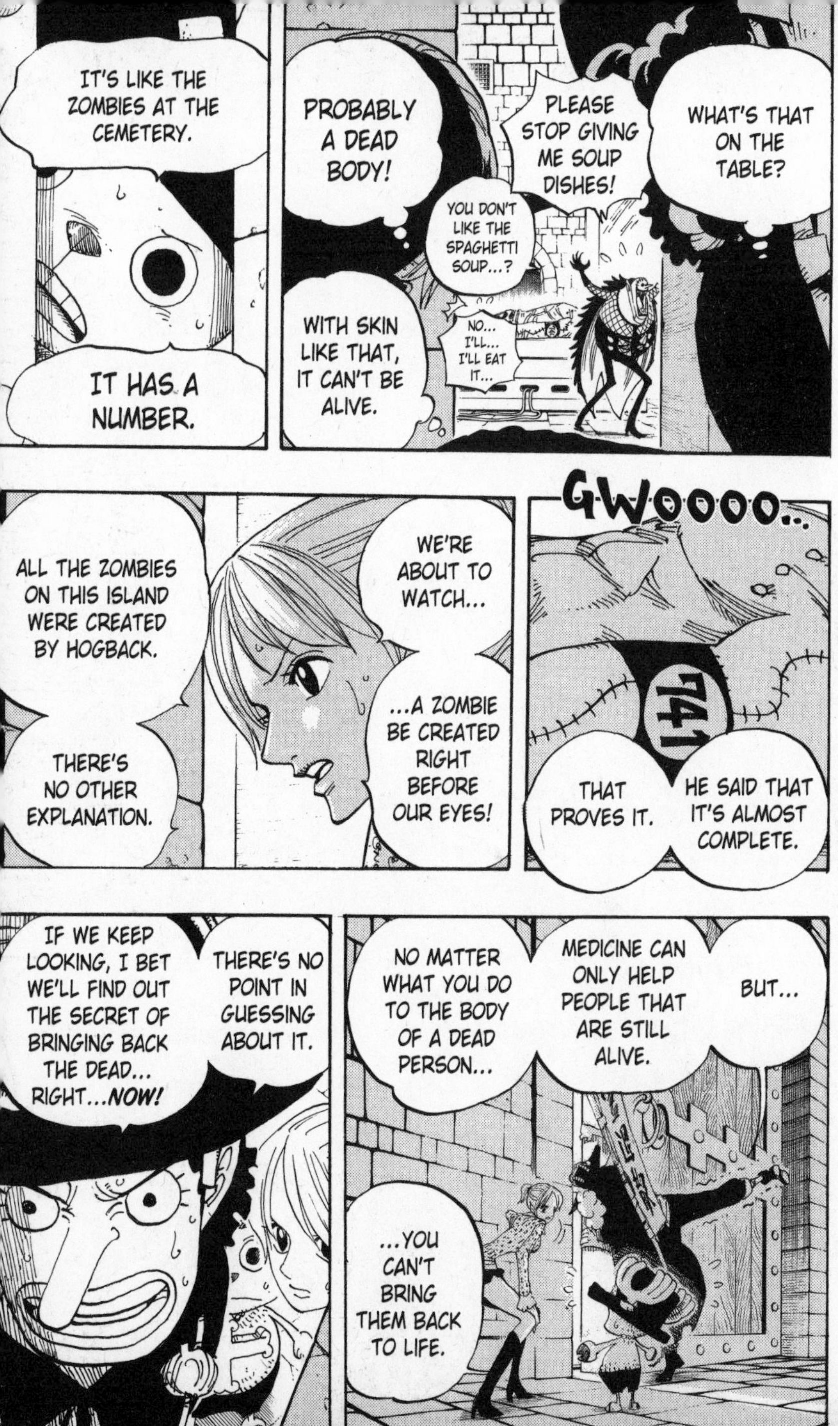
WHAT'S THAT ON THE TABLE?
PLEASE STOP GIVING ME SOUP DISHES!
YOU DON'T LIKE THE SPAGHETTI SOUP...?
NO... I'LL... I'LL EAT IT...
PROBABLY A DEAD BODY!
WITH SKIN LIKE THAT, IT CAN'T BE ALIVE.
IT'S LIKE THE ZOMBIES AT THE CEMETERY.
IT HAS A NUMBER.
GWOOOO...
741
HE SAID THAT IT'S ALMOST COMPLETE.
THAT PROVES IT.
WE'RE ABOUT TO WATCH...
...A ZOMBIE BE CREATED RIGHT BEFORE OUR EYES!
ALL THE ZOMBIES ON THIS ISLAND WERE CREATED BY HOGBACK.
THERE'S NO OTHER EXPLANATION.
BUT...
MEDICINE CAN ONLY HELP PEOPLE THAT ARE STILL ALIVE.
NO MATTER WHAT YOU DO TO THE BODY OF A DEAD PERSON...
...YOU CAN'T BRING THEM BACK TO LIFE.
THERE'S NO POINT IN GUESSING ABOUT IT.
IF WE KEEP LOOKING, I BET WE'LL FIND OUT THE SECRET OF BRINGING BACK THE DEAD... RIGHT...NOW!

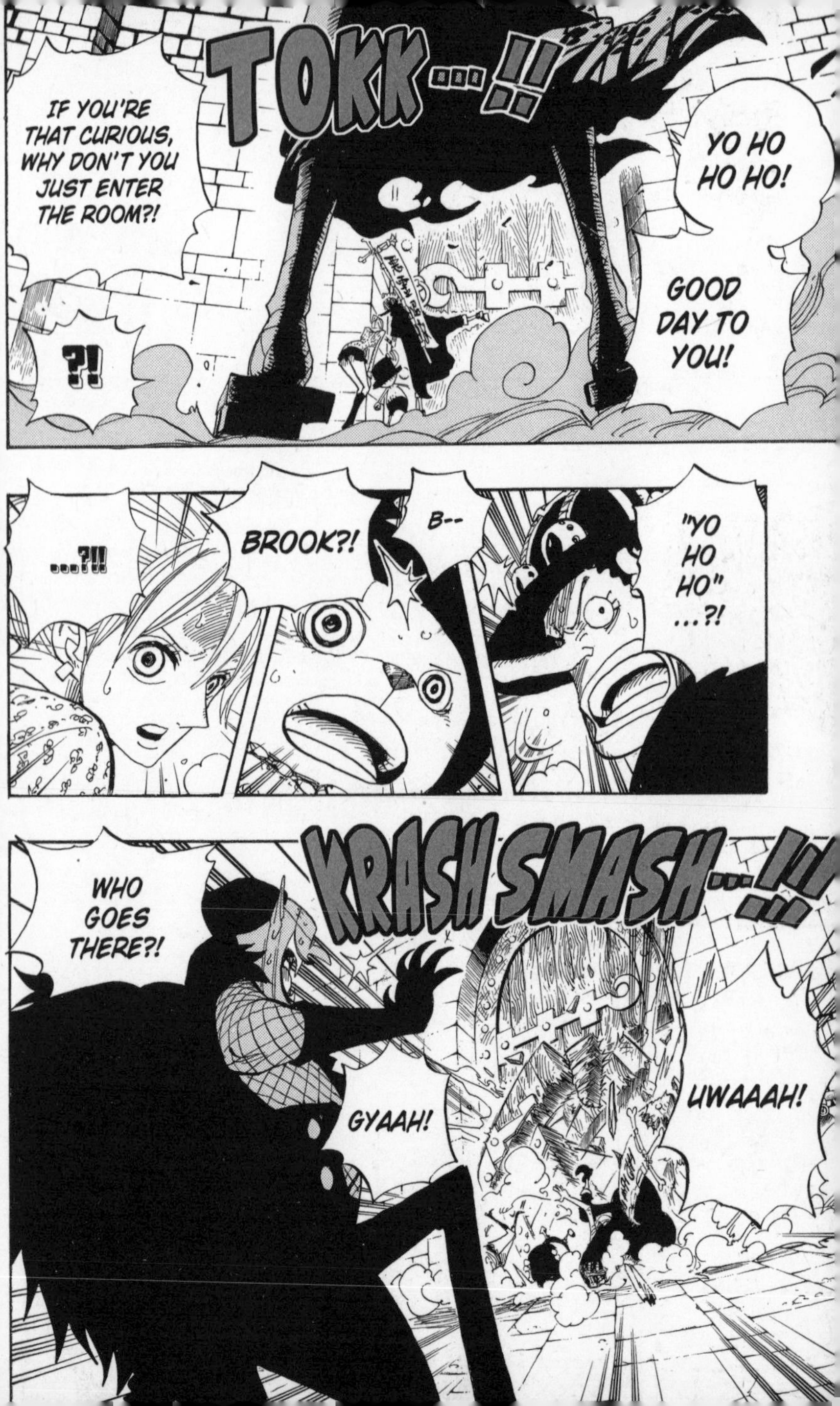
YO HO HO HO!
TOKK...!!
GOOD DAY TO YOU!
IF YOU'RE THAT CURIOUS, WHY DON'T YOU JUST ENTER THE ROOM?!
?!
"YO HO HO"...?!
B--
BROOK?!
...?!!
KRASH SMASH...!!
UWAAAH!
WHO GOES THERE?!
GYAAH!

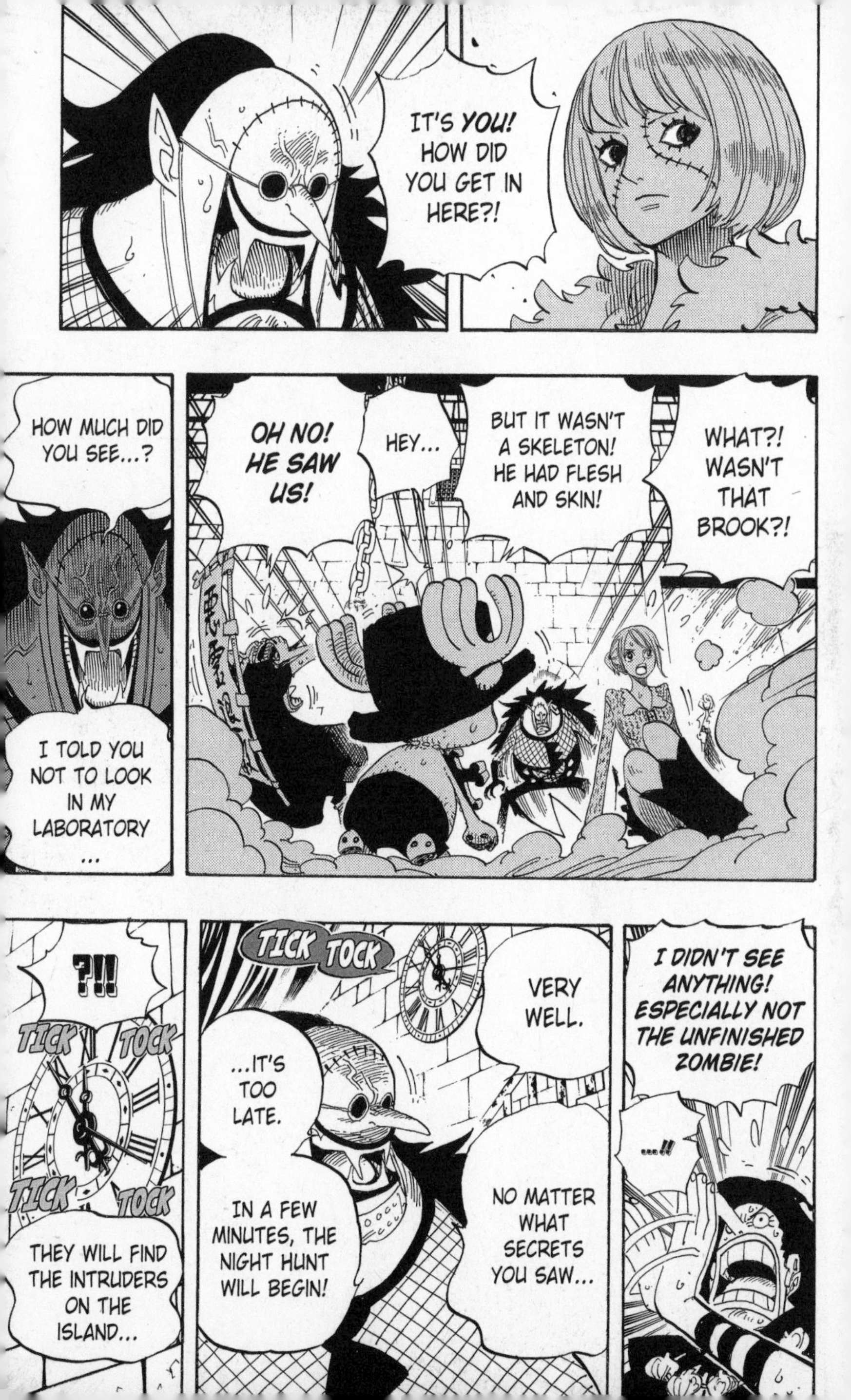
IT'S YOU! HOW DID YOU GET IN HERE?!
WHAT?! WASN'T THAT BROOK?!
BUT IT WASN'T A SKELETON! HE HAD FLESH AND SKIN!
HEY...
OH NO! HE SAW US!
HOW MUCH DID YOU SEE...?
I TOLD YOU NOT TO LOOK IN MY LABORATORY ...
I DIDN'T SEE ANYTHING! ESPECIALLY NOT THE UNFINISHED ZOMBIE!
...!!
TICK TOCK
VERY WELL.
...IT'S TOO LATE.
NO MATTER WHAT SECRETS YOU SAW...
IN A FEW MINUTES, THE NIGHT HUNT WILL BEGIN!
?!!
TICK TOCK
TICK TOCK
THEY WILL FIND THE INTRUDERS ON THE ISLAND...

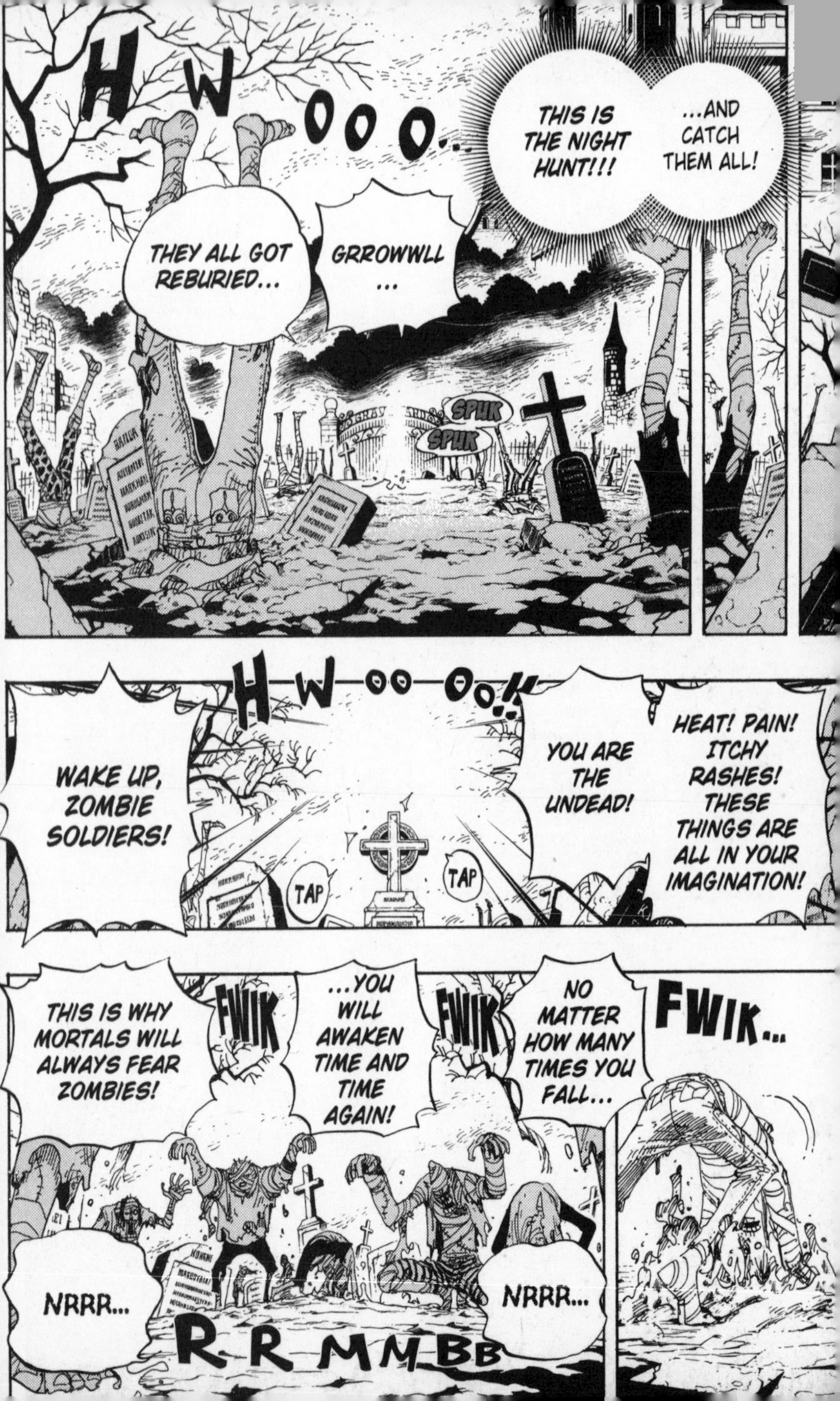
...AND CATCH THEM ALL!
THIS IS THE NIGHT HUNT!!!
HWOOO...
GRROWWLL ...
THEY ALL GOT REBURIED...
SPUK
SPUK
HEAT! PAIN! ITCHY RASHES! THESE THINGS ARE ALL IN YOUR IMAGINATION!
YOU ARE THE UNDEAD!
HWOO OOK
TAP
TAP
WAKE UP, ZOMBIE SOLDIERS!
FWIK...
NO MATTER HOW MANY TIMES YOU FALL...
FWIK
...YOU WILL AWAKEN TIME AND TIME AGAIN!
FWIK
THIS IS WHY MORTALS WILL ALWAYS FEAR ZOMBIES!
NRRR...
NRRR...
RRMMBB

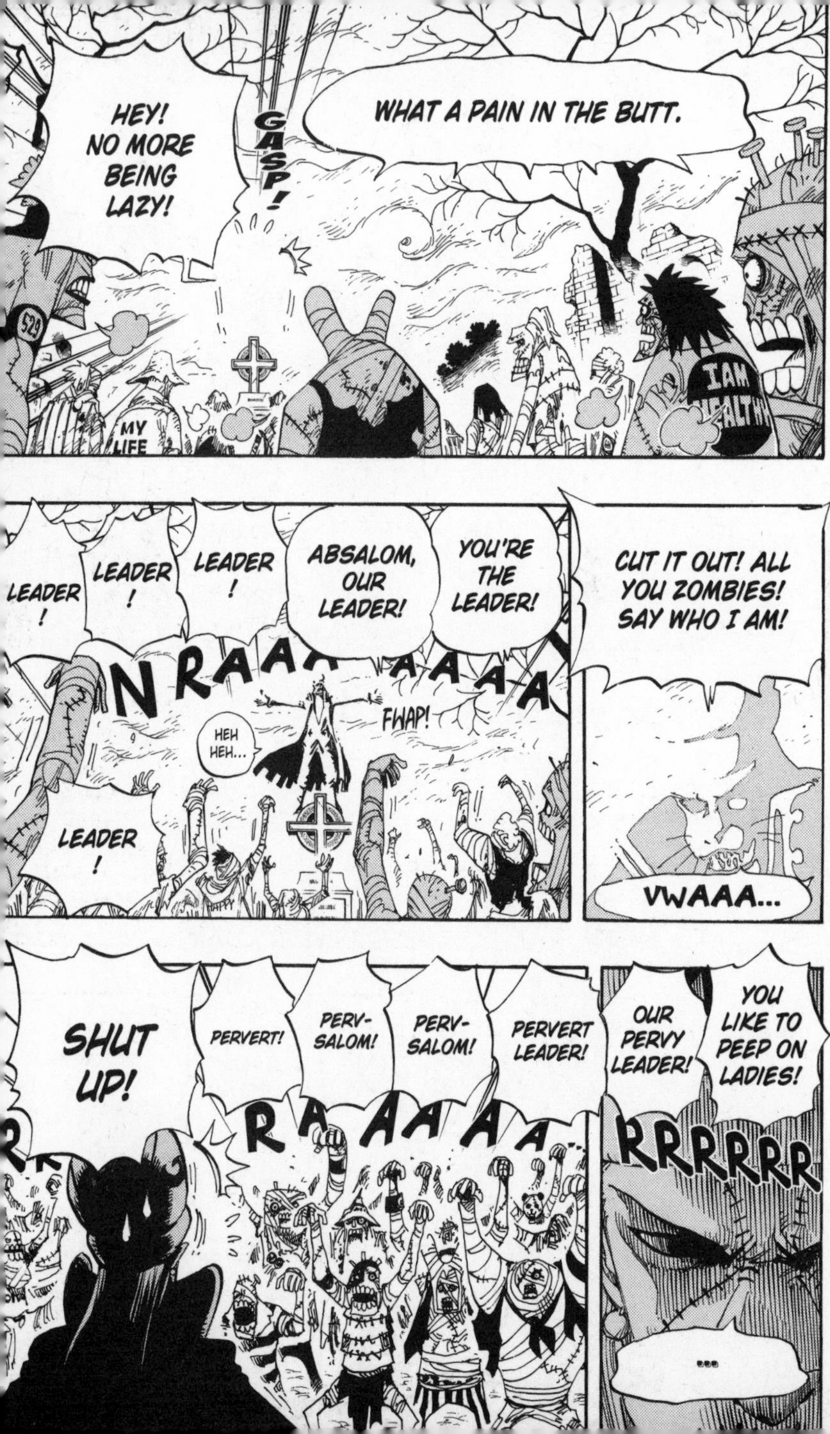
WHAT A PAIN IN THE BUTT.
GASP!
HEY! NO MORE BEING LAZY!
529
MY LIFE
CUT IT OUT! ALL YOU ZOMBIES! SAY WHO I AM!
VWAAA...
YOU'RE THE LEADER!
ABSALOM, OUR LEADER!
LEADER!
LEADER!
LEADER!
NRAAAAAAA
FWAP!
HEH HEH...
LEADER!
YOU LIKE TO PEEP ON LADIES!
OUR PERVY LEADER!
RRRRRR
...
PERVERT LEADER!
PERV-SALOM!
PERV-SALOM!
PERVERT!
RAAAAA
SHUT UP!

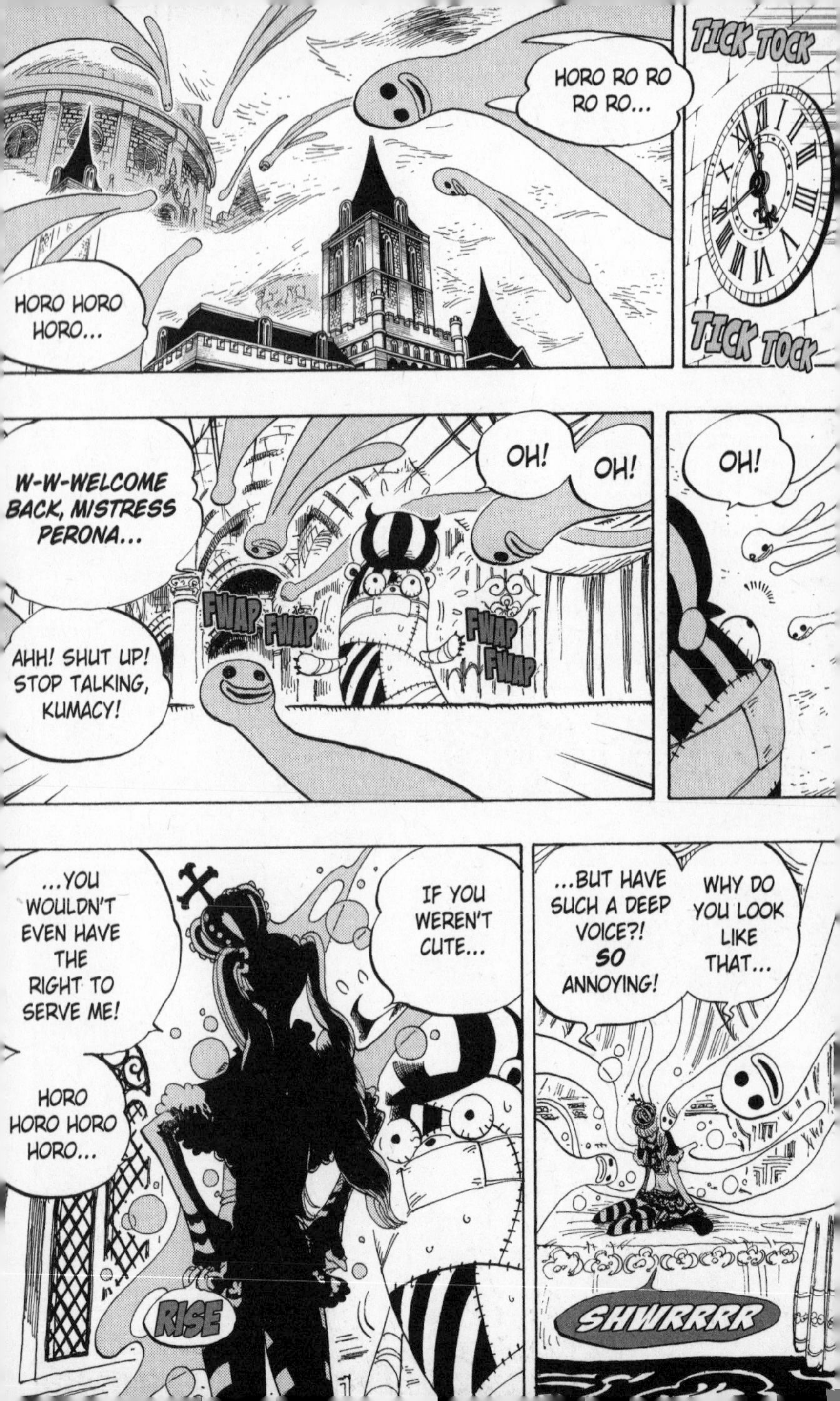
TICK TOCK
TICK TOCK
HORO RO RO RO RO...
HORO HORO HORO...
OH!
OH!
OH!
W-W-WELCOME BACK, MISTRESS PERONA...
FWAP FWAP
FWAP FWAP
AHH! SHUT UP! STOP TALKING, KUMACY!
WHY DO YOU LOOK LIKE THAT...
...BUT HAVE SUCH A DEEP VOICE?! SO ANNOYING!
SHWRRRR
IF YOU WEREN'T CUTE...
...YOU WOULDN'T EVEN HAVE THE RIGHT TO SERVE ME!
HORO HORO HORO HORO...
RISE

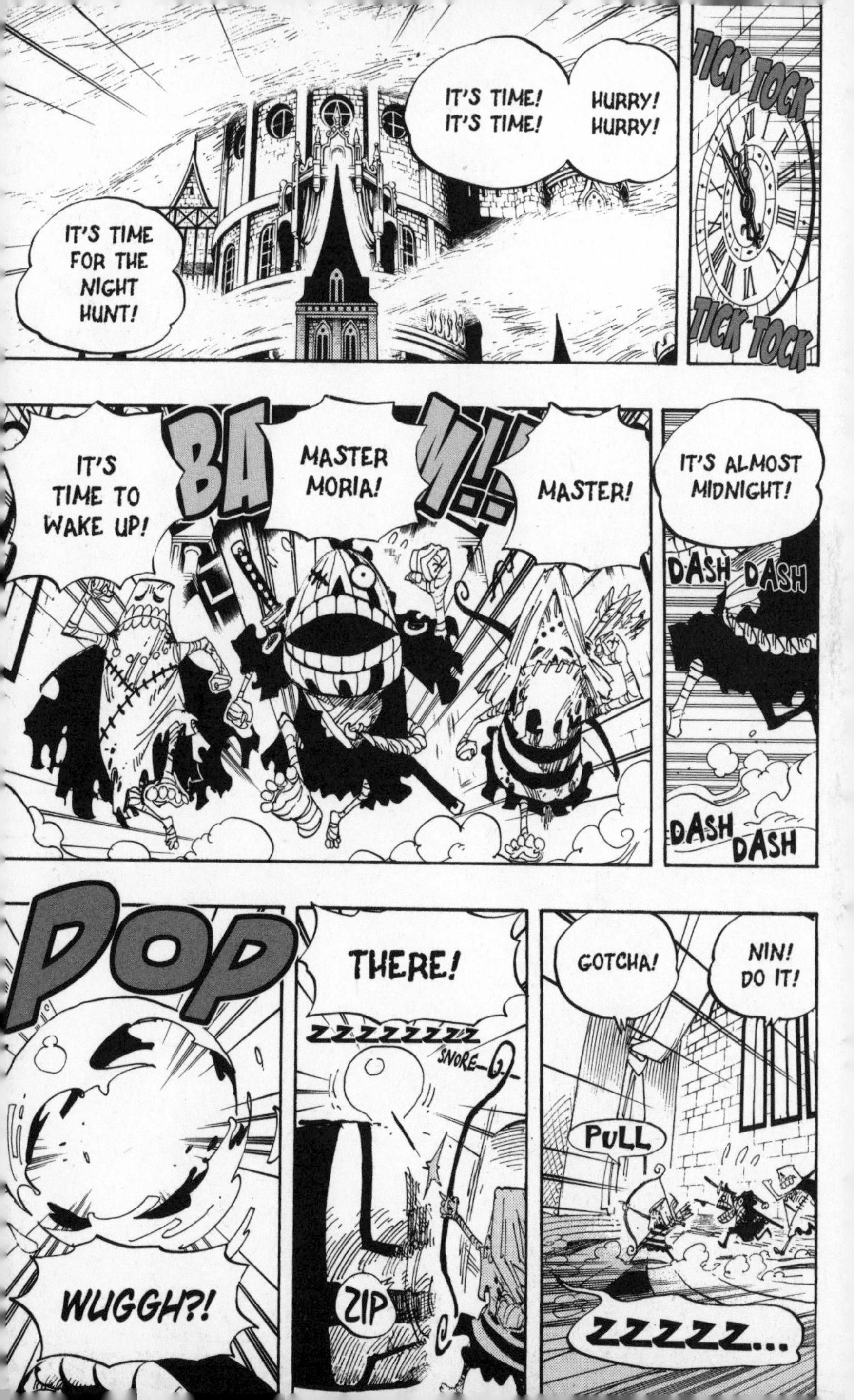
TICK TOCK
TICK TOCK
HURRY! HURRY!
IT'S TIME! IT'S TIME!
IT'S TIME FOR THE NIGHT HUNT!
IT'S ALMOST MIDNIGHT!
DASH DASH
DASH DASH
MASTER!
BA
M!!
MASTER MORIA!
IT'S TIME TO WAKE UP!
NIN! DO IT!
GOTCHA!
PULL
ZZZZZ...
THERE!
ZZZZZZZZZ
SNORE
ZIP
POP
WUGGH?!

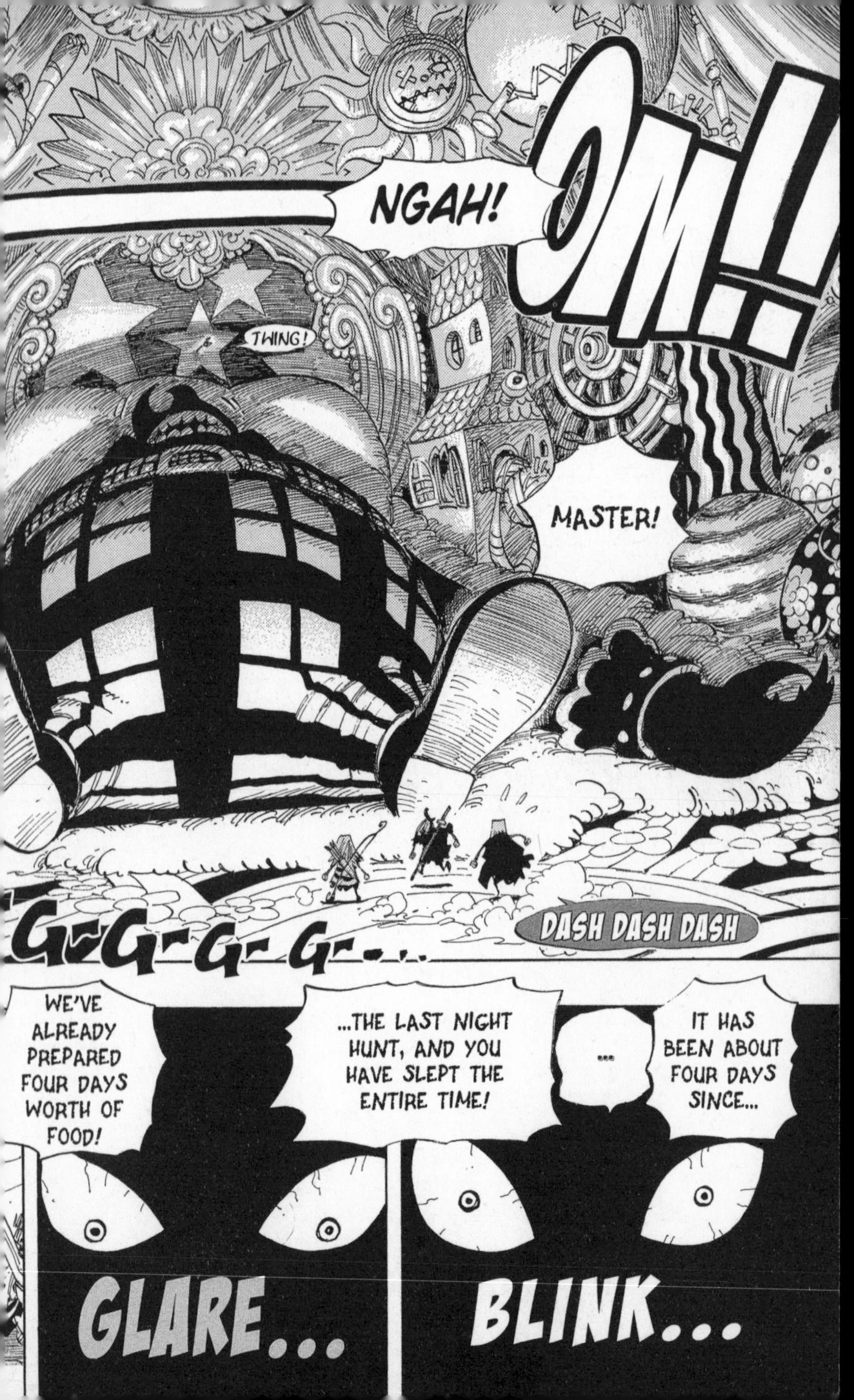
OM!!
NGAH!
MASTER!
TWING!
DASH DASH DASH
G-G-G-G-...
IT HAS BEEN ABOUT FOUR DAYS SINCE...
...
...THE LAST NIGHT HUNT, AND YOU HAVE SLEPT THE ENTIRE TIME!
WE'VE ALREADY PREPARED FOUR DAYS WORTH OF FOOD!
BLINK...
GLARE...

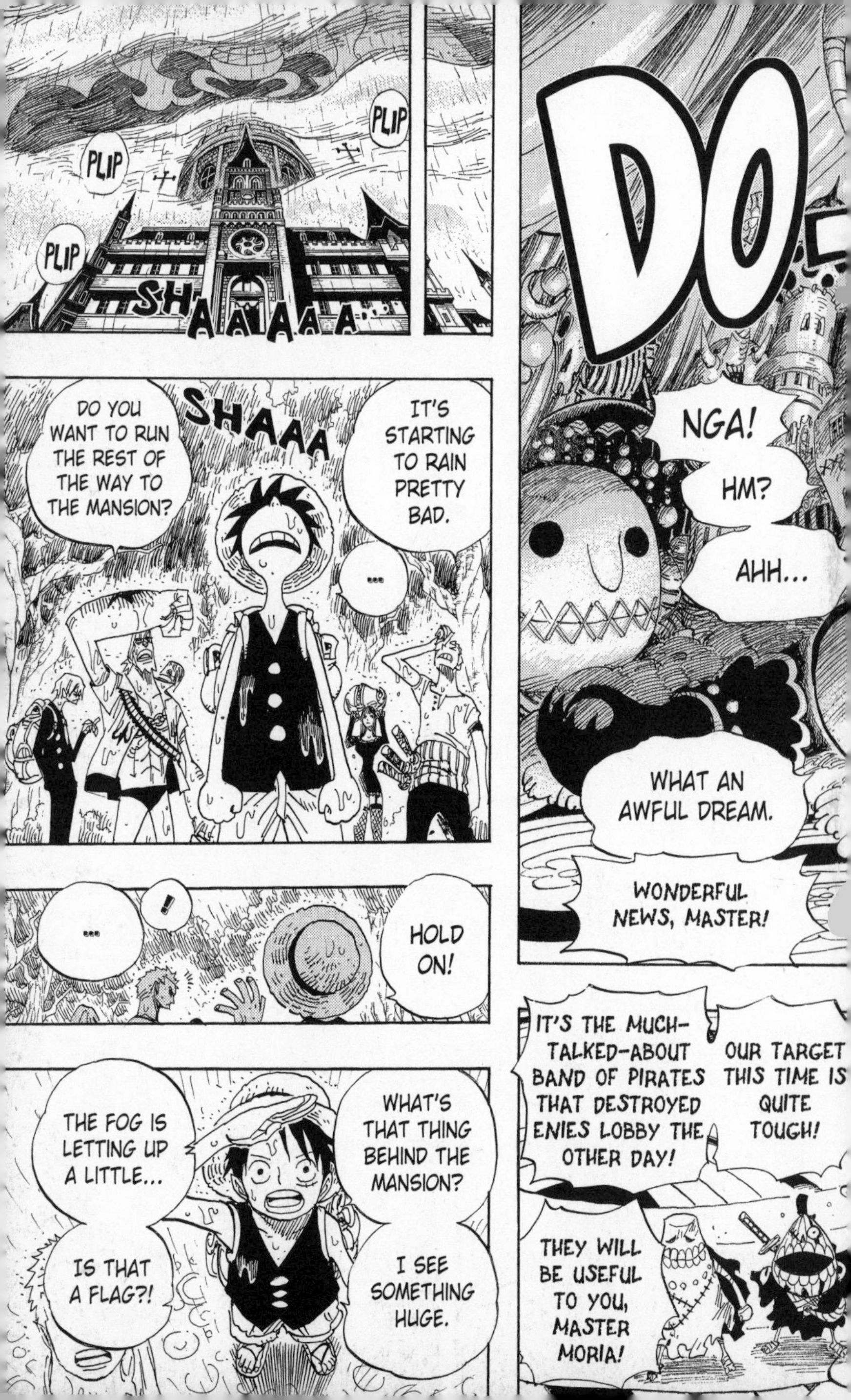
DO
NGA!
HM?
AHH...
WHAT AN AWFUL DREAM.
WONDERFUL NEWS, MASTER!
OUR TARGET THIS TIME IS QUITE TOUGH!
IT'S THE MUCH-TALKED-ABOUT BAND OF PIRATES THAT DESTROYED ENIES LOBBY THE OTHER DAY!
THEY WILL BE USEFUL TO YOU, MASTER MORIA!
PLIP
PLIP
PLIP
SHAAAAAA
IT'S STARTING TO RAIN PRETTY BAD.
SHAAA
DO YOU WANT TO RUN THE REST OF THE WAY TO THE MANSION?
...
HOLD ON!
!
...
WHAT'S THAT THING BEHIND THE MANSION?
I SEE SOMETHING HUGE.
THE FOG IS LETTING UP A LITTLE...
IS THAT A FLAG?!

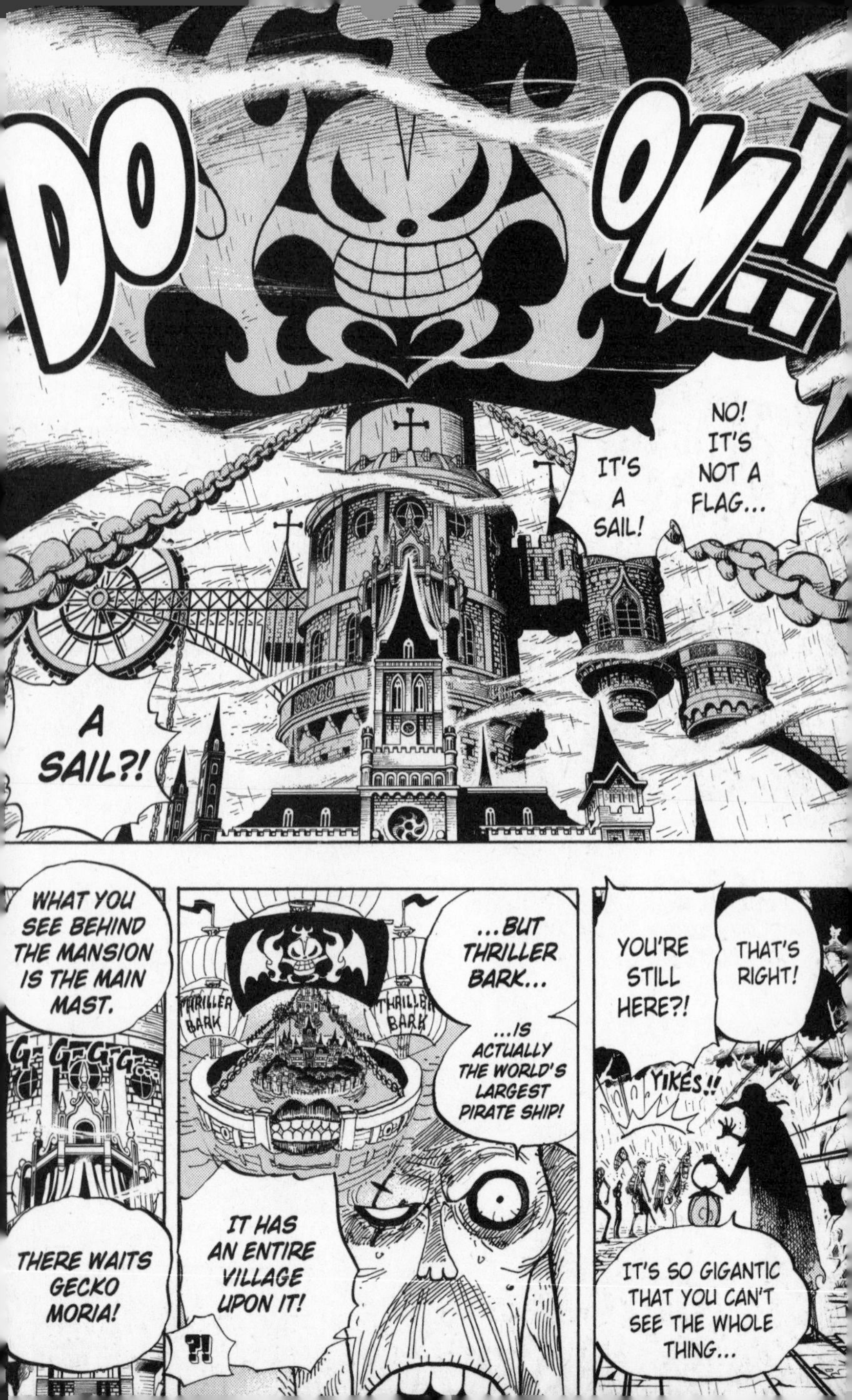
DOOM!!
NO! IT'S NOT A FLAG...
IT'S A SAIL!
A SAIL?!
THAT'S RIGHT!
YOU'RE STILL HERE?!
YIKES!!
IT'S SO GIGANTIC THAT YOU CAN'T SEE THE WHOLE THING...
...BUT THRILLER BARK...
THRILLER BARK
THRILLER BARK
...IS ACTUALLY THE WORLD'S LARGEST PIRATE SHIP!
IT HAS AN ENTIRE VILLAGE UPON IT!
?!
WHAT YOU SEE BEHIND THE MANSION IS THE MAIN MAST.
THERE WAITS GECKO MORIA!

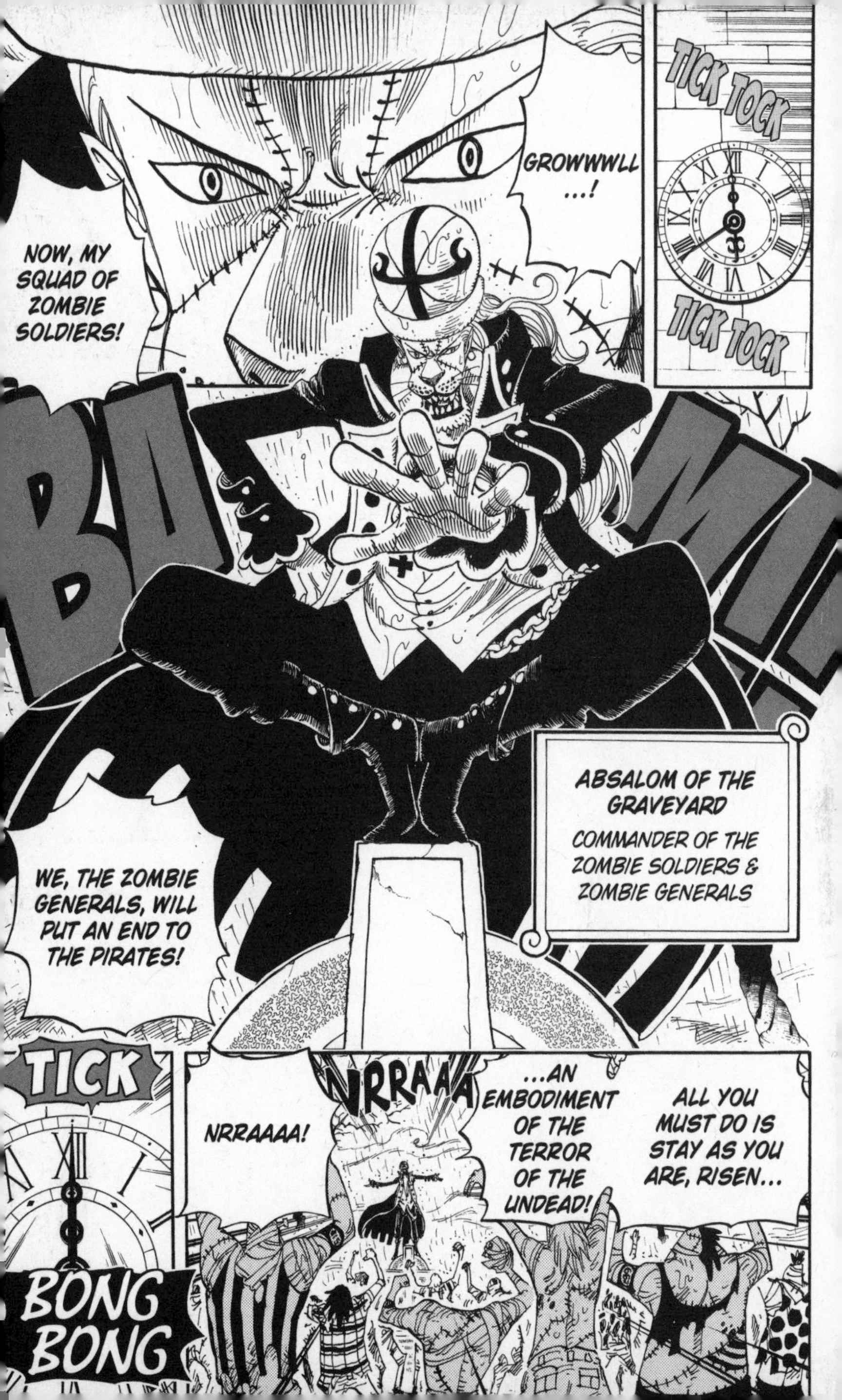
TICK TOCK
TICK TOCK
GROWWWLL ...!
NOW, MY SQUAD OF ZOMBIE SOLDIERS!
BA
MU
ABSALOM OF THE GRAVEYARD
COMMANDER OF THE ZOMBIE SOLDIERS & ZOMBIE GENERALS
WE, THE ZOMBIE GENERALS, WILL PUT AN END TO THE PIRATES!
ALL YOU MUST DO IS STAY AS YOU ARE, RISEN...
...AN EMBODIMENT OF THE TERROR OF THE UNDEAD!
NRRAAA
NRRAAAA!
TICK
BONG BONG

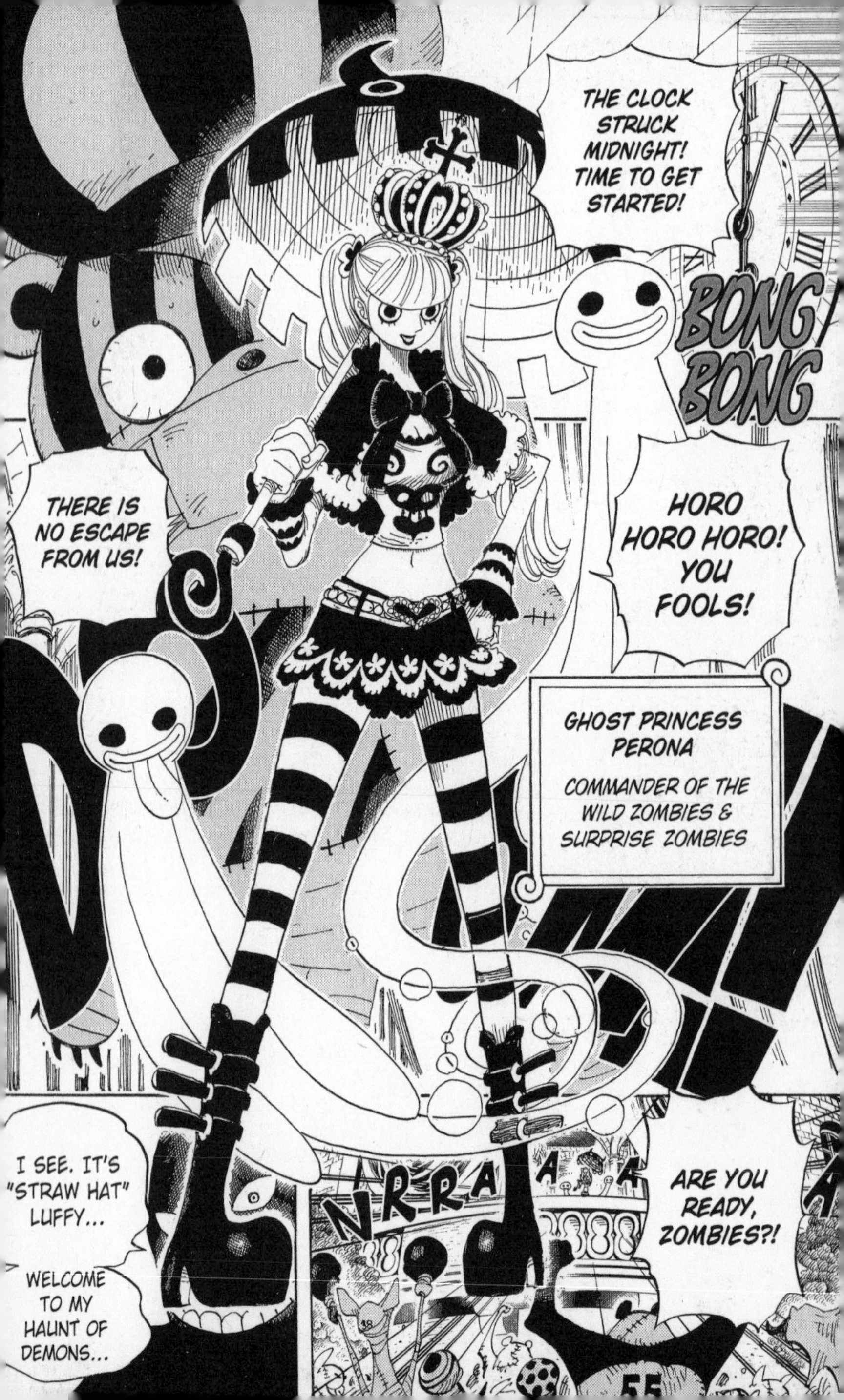
THE CLOCK STRUCK MIDNIGHT! TIME TO GET STARTED!
BONG BONG
HORO HORO HORO! YOU FOOLS!
THERE IS NO ESCAPE FROM US!
GHOST PRINCESS PERONA
COMMANDER OF THE WILD ZOMBIES & SURPRISE ZOMBIES
ARE YOU READY, ZOMBIES?!
NRRAAAA
I SEE. IT'S "STRAW HAT" LUFFY...
WELCOME TO MY HAUNT OF DEMONS...

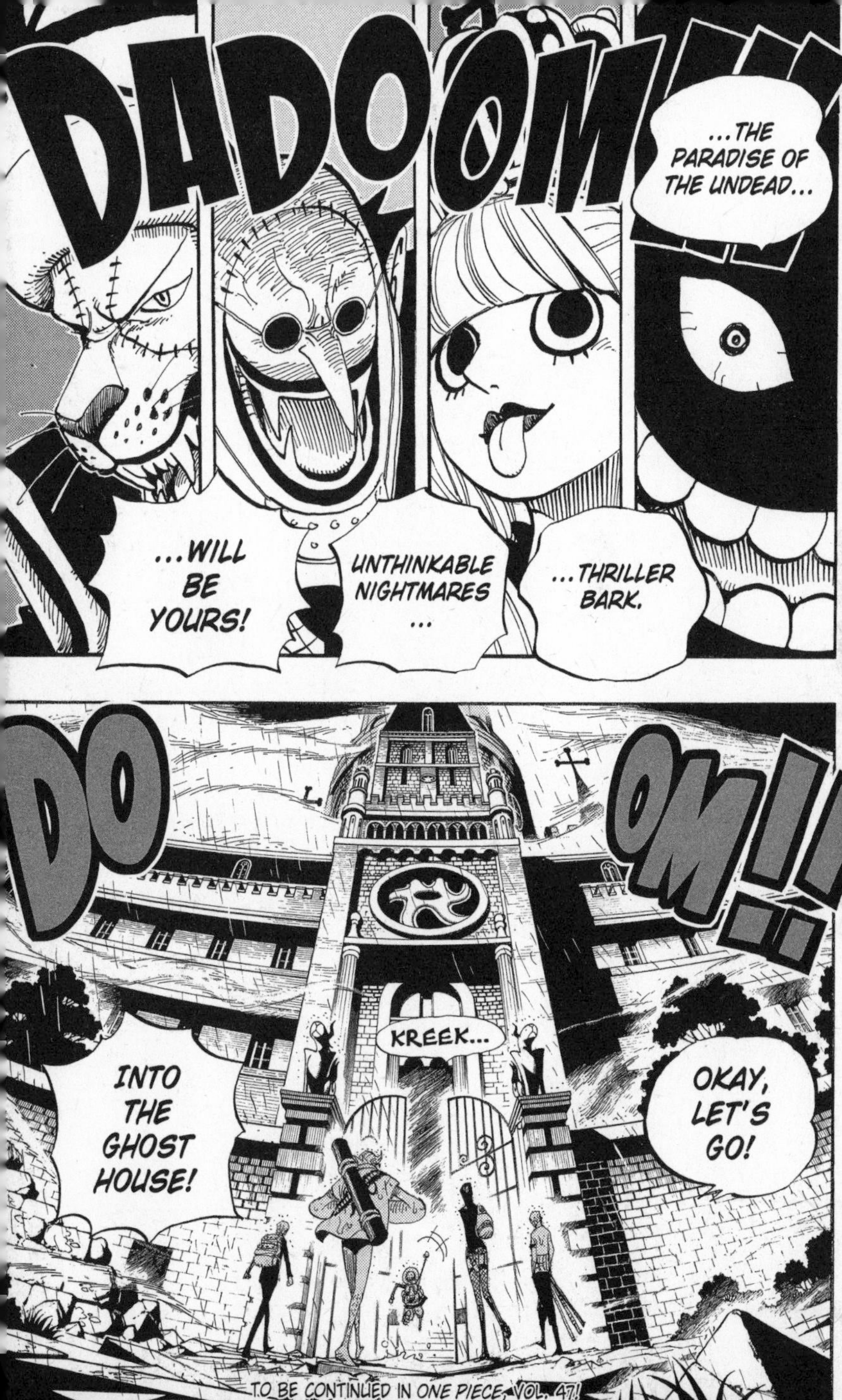
DADOOM!!!
...THE PARADISE OF THE UNDEAD...
...THRILLER BARK.
UNTHINKABLE NIGHTMARES ...
...WILL BE YOURS!
DOOM!!
KREEK...
OKAY, LET'S GO!
INTO THE GHOST HOUSE!
TO BE CONTINUED IN ONE PIECE, VOL. 47!

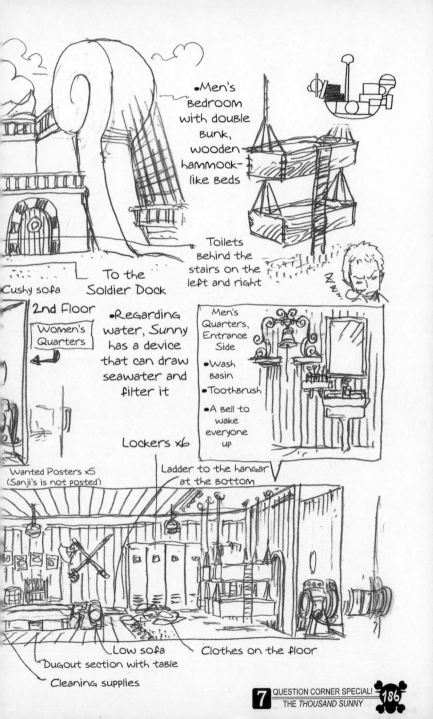

• Men's Bedroom with double Bunk, wooden hammock-like Beds

Toilets Behind the stairs on the left and right

Cushy sofa

To the Soldier Dock

2nd Floor

Women's Quarters

• Regarding water, Sunny has a device that can draw seawater and filter it

Lockers x6

Men's Quarters, Entrance Side

• Wash Basin
• Toothbrush
• A Bell to wake everyone up

Wanted Posters x5 (Sanji's is not posted)

Ladder to the hangar at the Bottom

Low sofa

Clothes on the floor

Dugout section with table

Cleaning supplies

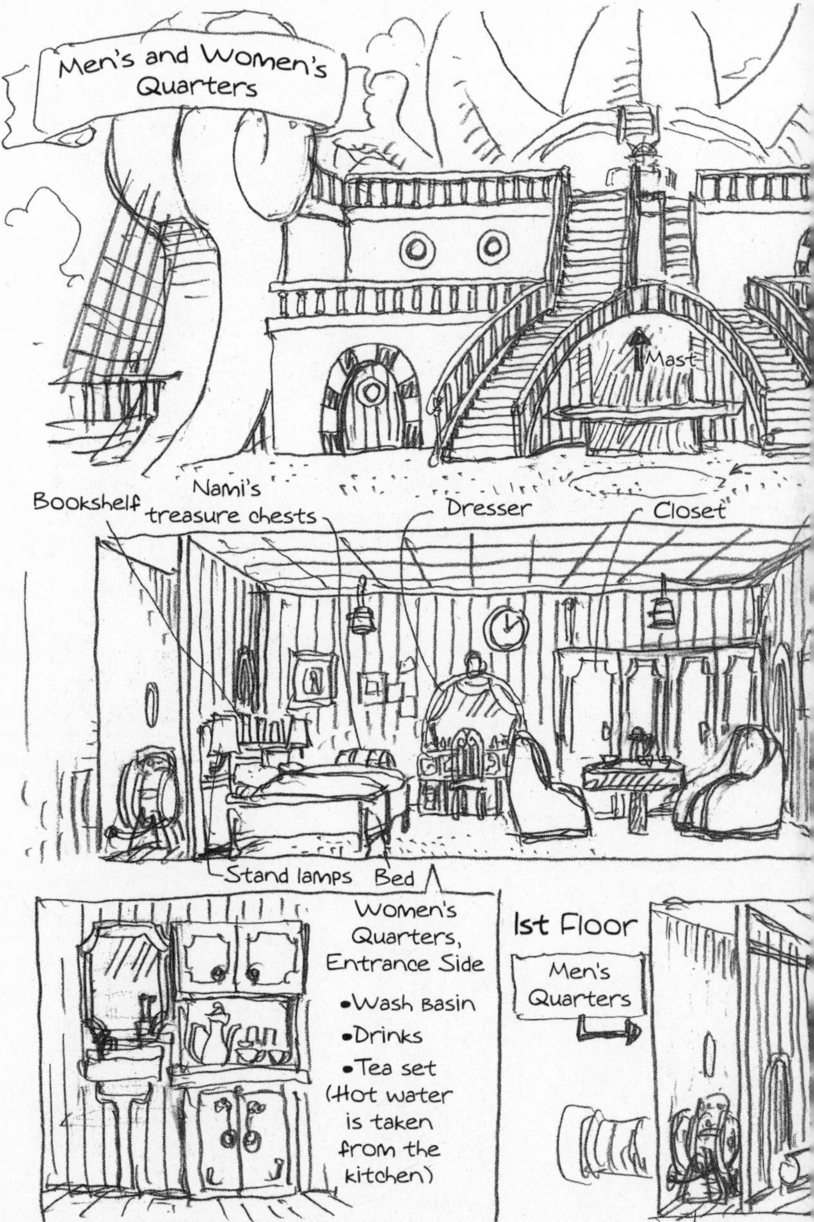
Men's and Women's Quarters
Mast
Bookshelf
Nami's treasure chests
Dresser
Closet
Stand lamps
Bed
Women's Quarters, Entrance Side
•Wash basin
•Drinks
•Tea set
(Hot water is taken from the kitchen)
1st Floor
Men's Quarters
Cannon

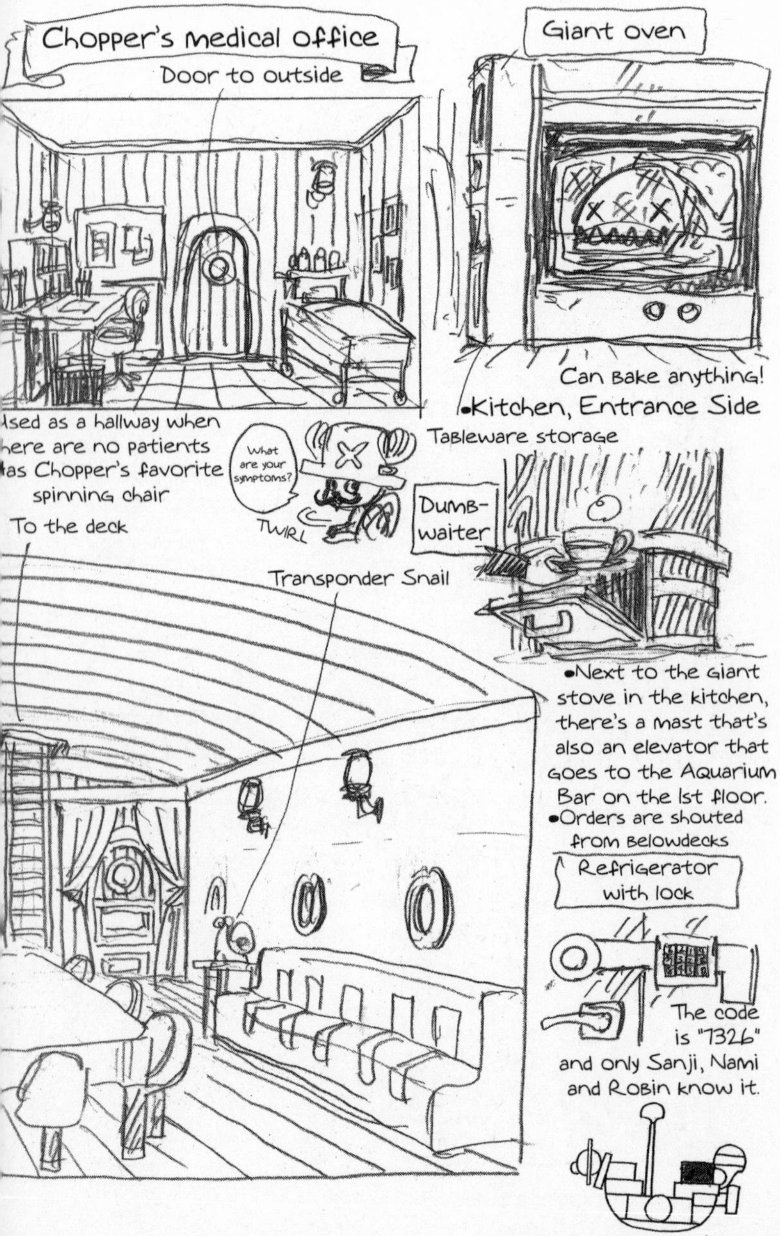
Giant oven
Can bake anything!
•Kitchen, Entrance Side
Chopper's medical office
Door to outside
sed as a hallway when
here are no patients
as Chopper's favorite
spinning chair
Tableware storage
Dumb-waiter
What are your symptoms?
TWIRL
To the deck
Transponder Snail
•Next to the giant stove in the kitchen, there's a mast that's also an elevator that goes to the Aquarium Bar on the 1st floor.
•Orders are shouted from belowdecks
Refrigerator with lock
The code is "7326" and only Sanji, Nami and Robin know it.

Kitchen and Dining

Food storage
(Raw Ingredients, so even Luffy won't touch them)

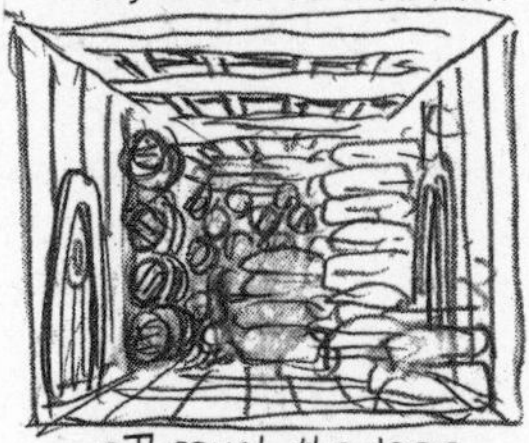

• Through the door behind the mast

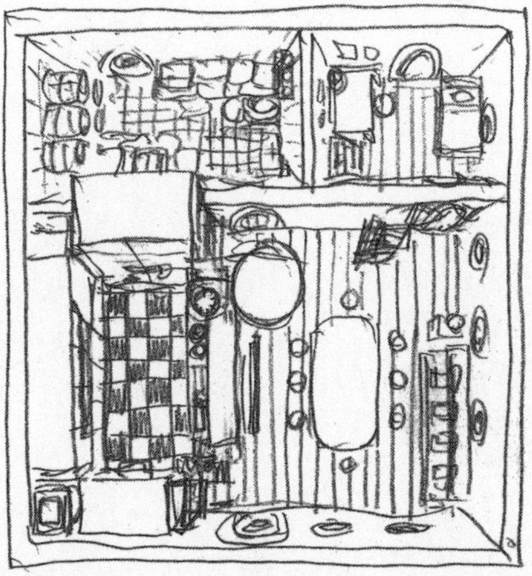

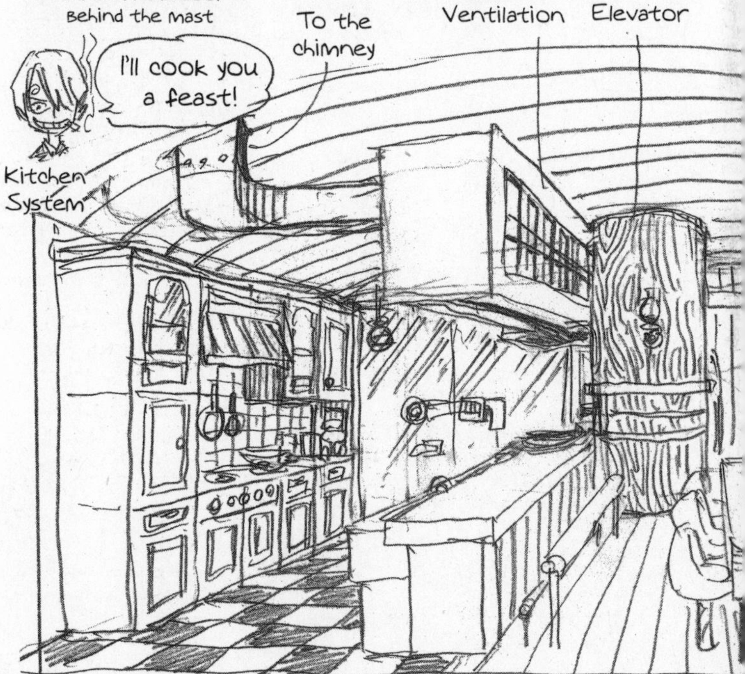
To the chimney
Ventilation
Elevator
I'll cook you a feast!
Kitchen System

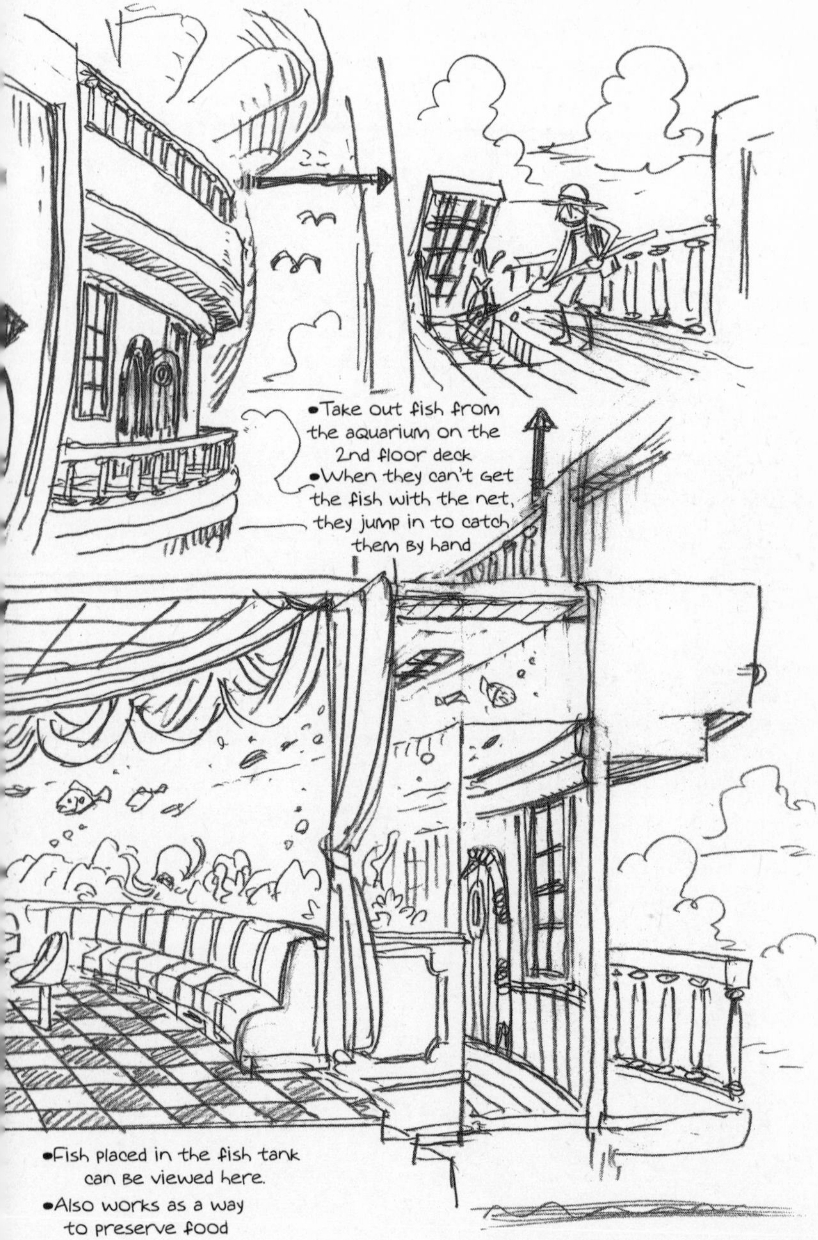
•Take out fish from the aquarium on the 2nd floor deck
•When they can't get the fish with the net, they jump in to catch them by hand
•Fish placed in the fish tank can be viewed here.
•Also works as a way to preserve food

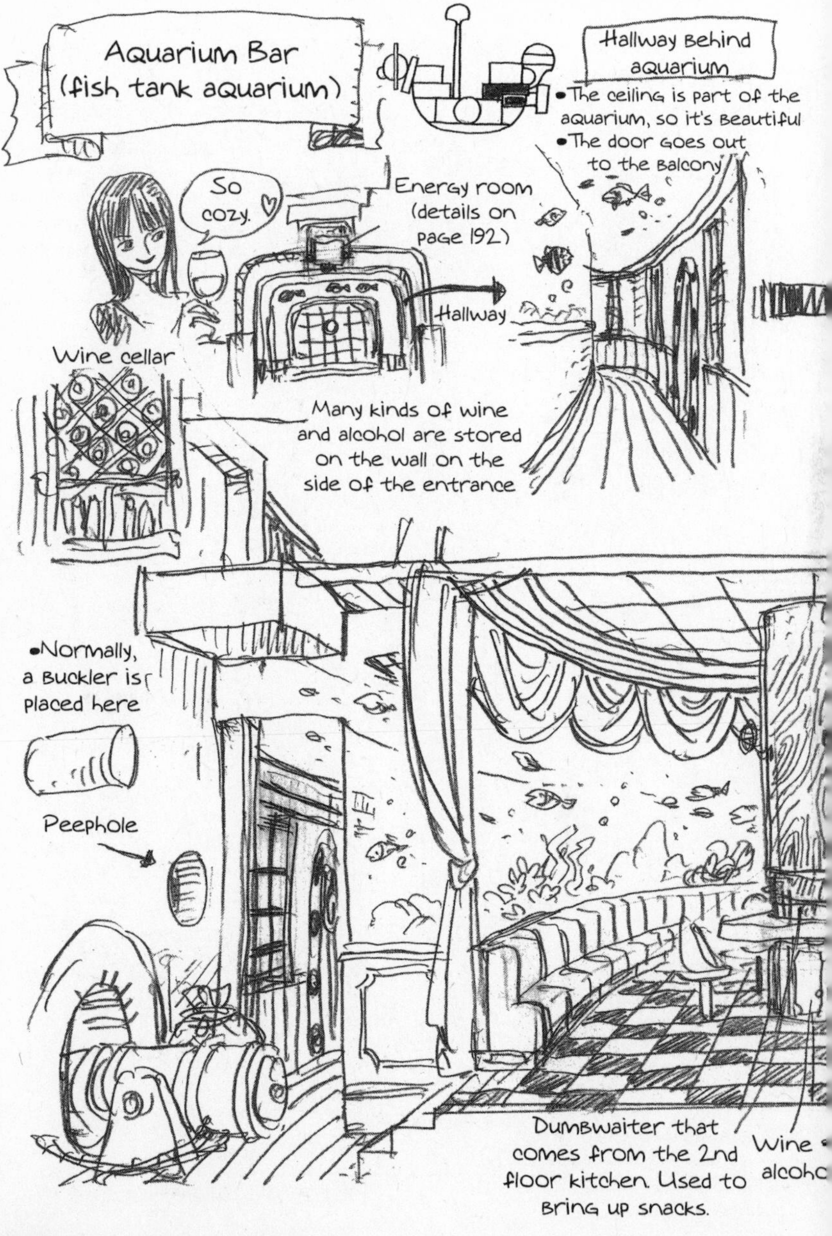
Aquarium Bar (fish tank aquarium)
Hallway behind aquarium
•The ceiling is part of the aquarium, so it's beautiful
•The door goes out to the balcony
So cozy.
Energy room (details on page 192)
Hallway
Wine cellar
Many kinds of wine and alcohol are stored on the wall on the side of the entrance
•Normally, a buckler is placed here
Peephole
Dumbwaiter that comes from the 2nd floor kitchen. Used to bring up snacks.
Wine

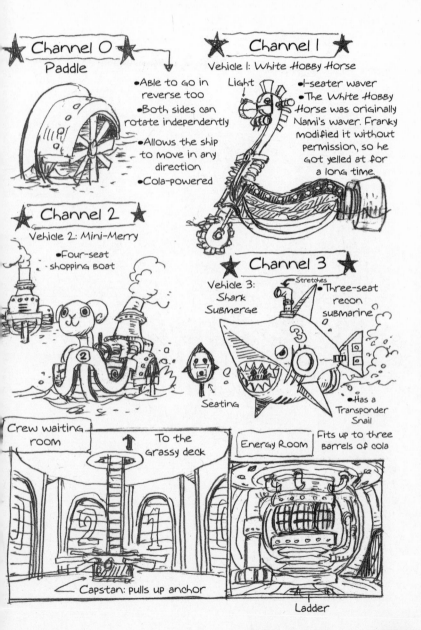

⭐ Channel 0 ⭐
Paddle

- Able to go in reverse too
- Both sides can rotate independently
- Allows the ship to move in any direction
- Cola-powered

⭐ Channel 1 ⭐
Vehicle 1: White Hobby Horse

Light

- 1-seater waver
- The White Hobby Horse was originally Nami's waver. Franky modified it without permission, so he got yelled at for a long time.

⭐ Channel 2 ⭐
Vehicle 2: Mini-Merry

- Four-seat shopping boat

⭐ Channel 3 ⭐
Vehicle 3: Shark Submerge

Stretches

- Three-seat recon submarine
- Has a Transponder Snail

Seating

Crew waiting room

To the grassy deck

Capstan: pulls up anchor

Energy Room — Fits up to three barrels of cola

Ladder

Soldier Dock System
Lumber storage
Hallway
This is my masterpiece!
★On how to change the channel (Page 146)
Hallway, to Usopp's Factory
•Turning
VWEEEN
Inside Dock
Filled with water
0
1
2
KLANG
Rolling shutter
0
1
2

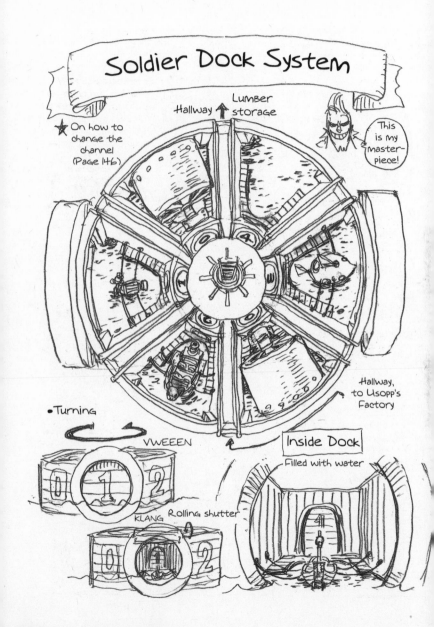

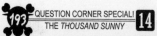

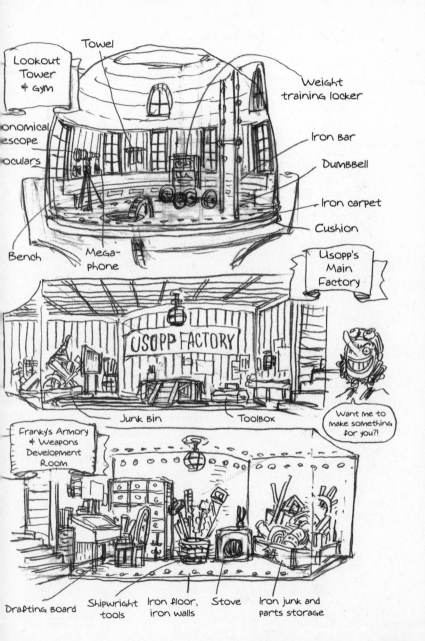

Lookout Tower & Gym

Towel

Weight training locker

Iron Bar

Dumbbell

Iron carpet

Cushion

onomical escope

oculars

Bench

Mega-phone

Usopp's Main Factory

USOPP FACTORY

Junk Bin

Toolbox

Want me to make something for you?!

Franky's Armory & Weapons Development Room

Drafting Board

Shipwright tools

Iron floor, iron walls

Stove

Iron junk and parts storage

Library, Surveying Room, Bath

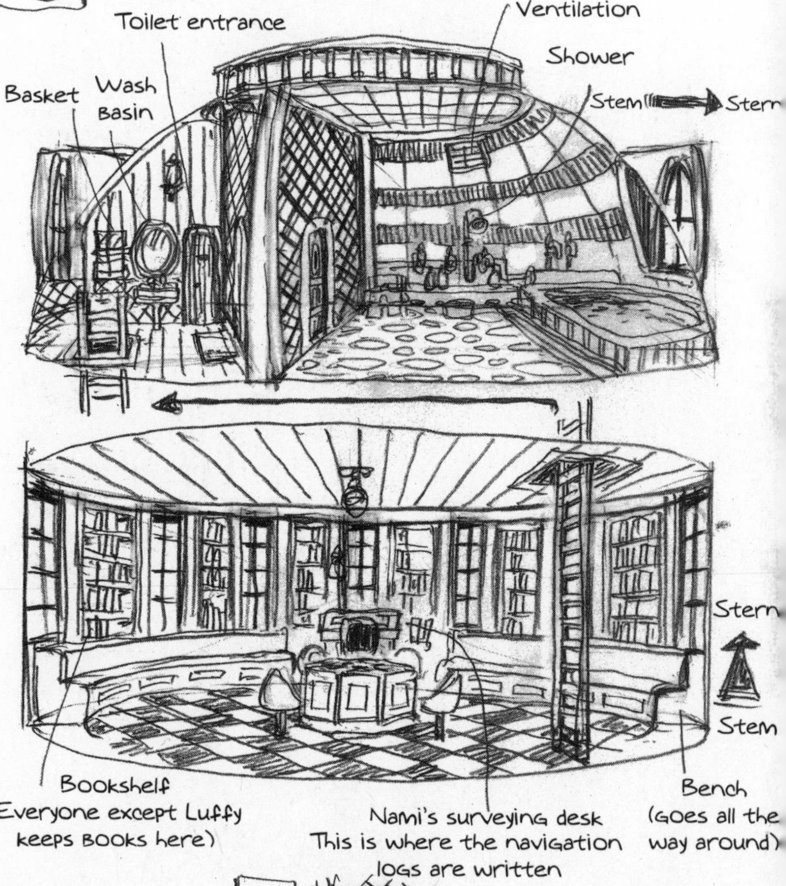
Toilet entrance
Ventilation
Shower
Basket
Wash Basin
Stem → Stern
Stern
Stem
Bookshelf
(Everyone except Luffy keeps books here)
Nami's surveying desk
This is where the navigation logs are written
Bench
(Goes all the way around)

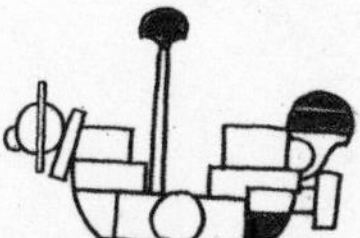

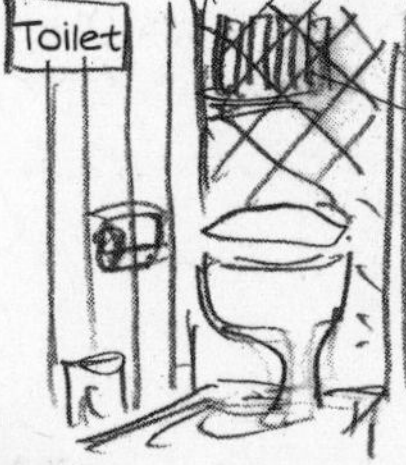
Toilet
Books

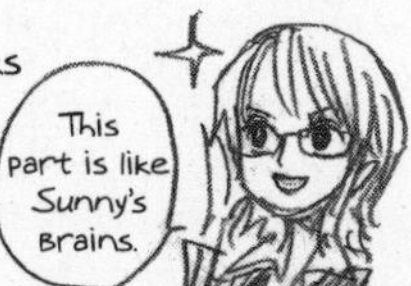
This part is like Sunny's Brains.

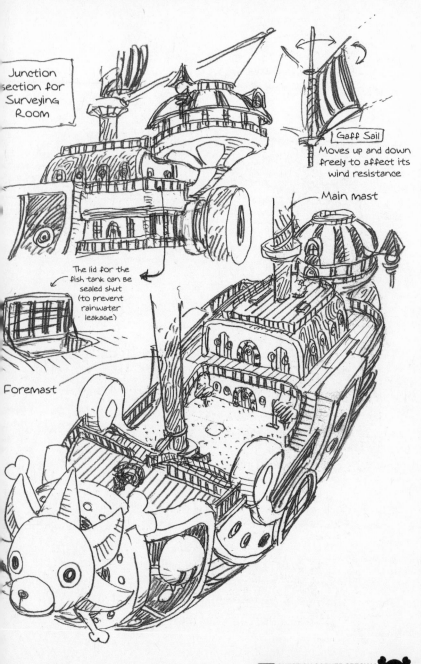

Junction section for Surveying Room

Gaff Sail
Moves up and down freely to affect its wind resistance

Main mast

The lid for the fish tank can be sealed shut (to prevent rainwater leakage)

Foremast

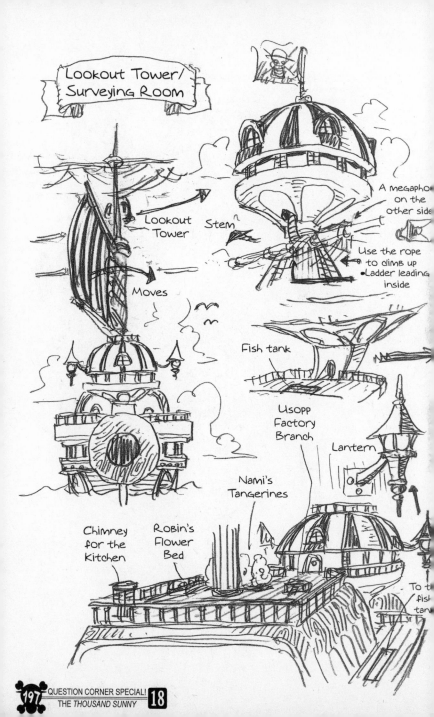

Lookout Tower/ Surveying Room

Lookout Tower

Stem

Moves

A megaphone on the other side

Use the rope to climb up
•Ladder leading inside

Fish tank

Usopp Factory Branch

Lantern

Nami's Tangerines

Chimney for the Kitchen

Robin's Flower Bed

To the fish tank

COMING NEXT VOLUME:

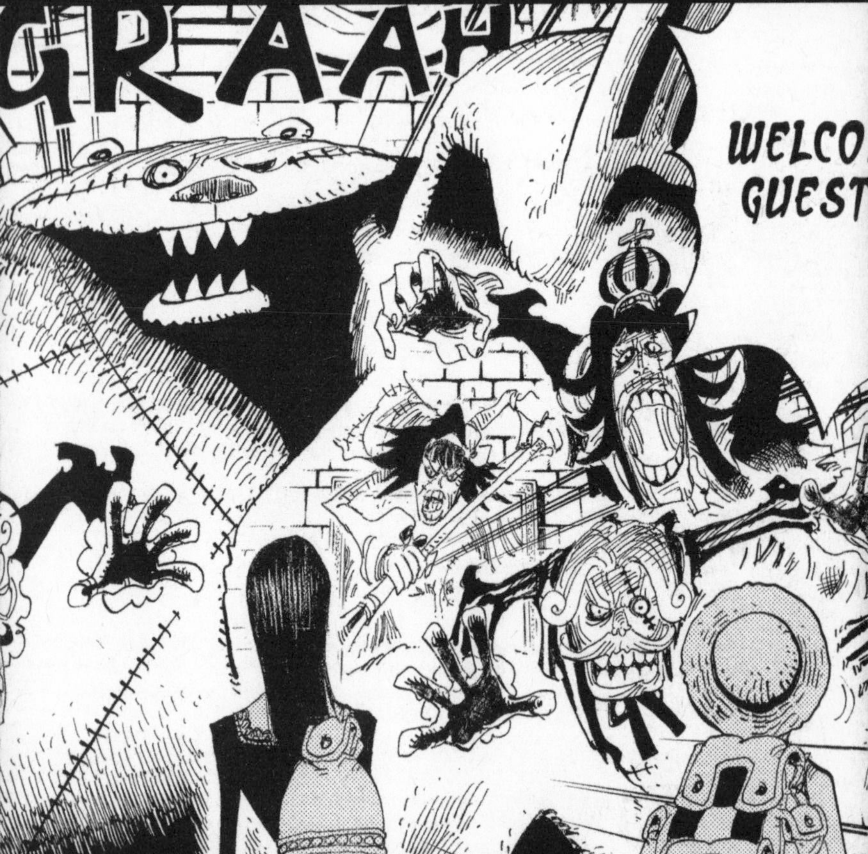
GREAAH
WELCO
GUEST

The Straw Hats find themselves caught in the Florian Triangle when the mysterious island Thriller Bark suddenly appears. They soon find out Gecko Moria, one of the Seven Warlords of the Sea, and his zombie army are also on the island. With the Night Hunt about to begin, can the crew survive this fearsome evening?

ON SALE NOW!

Set Sail with

Read all about **MONKEY D. LUFFY**'s adventures as he sails around the world assembling a motley crew to join him on his search for the legendary treasure "**ONE PIECE.**" For more information, check out **onepiece.viz.com**.

EAST BLUE
(Vols. 1-12)
Available now!

See where it all began! One man, a dinghy and a dream. Or rather… a rubber man who can't swim, setting out in a tiny boat on the vast seas without any navigational skills. What are the odds that his dream of becoming King of the Pirates will ever come true?

BAROQUE WORKS
(Vols. 12-24)
Available now!

Friend or foe? Ms. Wednesday is part of a group of bounty hunters—or isn't she? The Straw Hats get caught up in a civil war when they find a princess in their midst. But can they help her stop the revolution in her home country before the evil Crocodile gets his way?!

SKYPIEA
(Vols. 24-32)
Available now!

Luffy's quest to become King of the Pirates and find the elusive treasure known as "One Piece" continues…in the sky! The Straw Hats sail to Skypiea, an airborne island in the midst of a territorial war and ruled by a short-fused megalomaniac!

WATER SEVEN
(Vols. 32-46)
Available now!

The *Merry Go* has been a stalwart for the Straw Hats since the beginning, but countless battles have taken their toll on the ship. Luckily, their next stop is Water Seven, where a rough-and-tumble crew of shipwrights awaits their arrival!

THRILLER BARK
(Vols. 46-50)
Available now!

Luffy and crew get more than they bargained for when their ship is drawn toward haunted Thriller Bark. When Gecko Moria, one of the Warlords of the Sea, steals the crew's shadows, they'll have to get them back before the sun rises or else they'll all turn into zombies!

SABAODY
(Vols. 50-54)
Available now!

On the way to Fish-Man Island, the Straw Hats disembark on the Sabaody archipelago to get soaped up for their undersea adventure! But it's not too long before they get caught up in trouble! Luffy's made an enemy of an exalted World Noble when he saves Camie the mermaid from being sold on the slave market, and now he's got the Navy after him too!

IMPEL DOWN
(Vols. 54-56)
Available now!

Luffy's brother Ace is about to be executed! Held in the Navy's maximum security prison Impel Down, Luffy needs to find a way to break in to help Ace escape. But with murderous fiends for guards inside, the notorious prisoners start to seem not so bad. Some are even friendly enough to give Luffy a helping hand!

You're Reading in the Wrong Direction!!

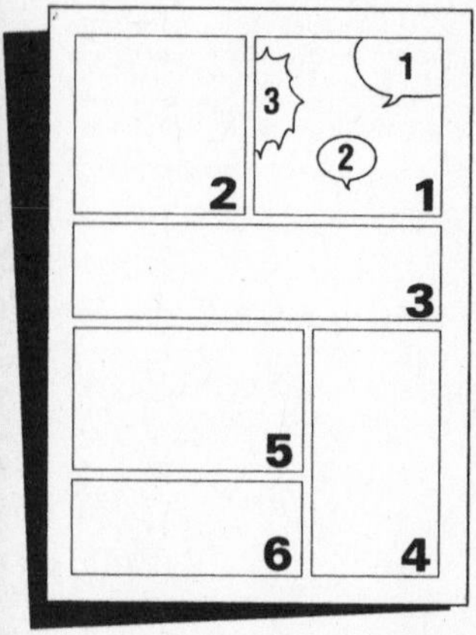
1
2
3
1
2
3
4
5
6

Whoops! Guess what? You're starting at the wrong end of the comic!

...It's true! In keeping with the original Japanese format, **One Piece** is meant to be read from right to left, starting in the upper-right corner.

Unlike English, which is read from left to right, Japanese is read from right to left, meaning that action, sound effects and word-balloon order are completely reversed...something which can make readers unfamiliar with Japanese feel pretty backwards themselves. For this reason, manga or Japanese comics published in the U.S. in English have sometimes been published "flopped"– that is, printed in exact reverse order, as though seen from the other side of a mirror.

By flopping pages, U.S. publishers can avoid confusing readers, but the compromise is not without its downside. For one thing, a character in a flopped manga series who once wore in the original Japanese version a T-shirt emblazoned with "M A Y" (as in "the merry month of") now wears one which reads "Y A M"! Additionally, many manga creators in Japan are themselves unhappy with the process, as some feel the mirror-imaging of their art skews their original intentions.

We are proud to bring you Eiichiro Oda's **One Piece** in the original unflopped format. For now, though, turn to the other side of the book and let the journey begin...!

–Editor

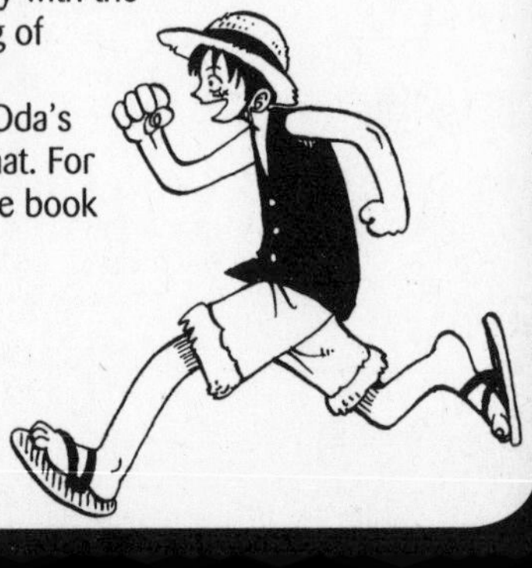